P9-BBP-044

UNIVERSITY OF CINCINNATI

CLASSICAL STUDIES

II

LECTURES IN MEMORY OF
LOUISE TAFT SEMPLE

II

EDITED BY

C. G. Boulter, D. W. Bradeen, A. Cameron,
J. L. Caskey, A. J. Christopherson, G. M. Cohen, P. Topping

LECTURES
IN MEMORY OF
LOUISE TAFT
SEMPLE

Second Series, 1966–1970

Erik Sjöqvist
Malcolm F. McGregor
G. M. A. Grube
Glanville Downey

Fordyce W. Mitchel
Eugene Vanderpool
E. Badian
Eric A. Havelock

UNIVERSITY OF OKLAHOMA PRESS

FOR THE UNIVERSITY OF CINCINNATI

1973

Library of Congress Cataloging in Publication Data
Main entry under title:

Lectures in memory of Louise Taft Semple.

(University of Cincinnati. Classical studies, v. 2)
CONTENTS: Sjöqvist, E. Lysippus: I. Lysippus' career reconsidered.
II. Some aspects of Lysippus' art.—McGregor, M. F. Athenian policy, at
home and abroad: I. Citizens and citizenship. II. Ships and cash: Thucy-
dides, I, 96.—Grube, G. M. A. How did the Greeks look at literature?
I. General attitudes. II. Specific questions. [etc.]
    1. Classical philology—Addresses, essays, lectures. I. Semple, Louise
Taft. II. Sjöqvist, Erik, 1903–III. Boulter, Cedric G., 1912–   ed. IV.
Series: Cincinnati. University. Classical studies, v. 2.
PA26.S45L42 1973   913.38'03   72–9256
ISBN 0–8061–1062–7

Preface

THIS VOLUME contains the second series of lectures in honor of Louise Taft Semple, delivered at the University of Cincinnati from April, 1966, to November, 1970. Like their predecessors in the first series, published in 1967 as Volume I of the University of Cincinnati Classical Studies, these lectures have appeared previously in a preliminary printing which was distributed to a limited number of colleagues.

Once again we should like to acknowledge our debt of gratitude to Mrs. Semple for her benefactions to this department, and to thank the lecturers for the contributions they have made to honor her memory.

THE EDITORS

Contents

I

Lysippus

BY ERIK SJÖQVIST

Delivered April 11 and 12, 1966

LYSIPPUS

BY ERIK SJÖQVIST

I. LYSIPPUS' CAREER RECONSIDERED

THE topic I have chosen is a complicated and controversial one: Lysippus, his career and art.

The fundamental difference between an art historian working in the field of Renaissance and later art, and his colleague who tries to shed some light on the history of ancient art, lies in his relationship to his sources. The former has access to external source material which flows ever more abundantly, the closer he comes to contemporary periods. Treatises, letters, autobiographies and biographies, sketch books, drawings, accounts and inventories provide him with a solid framework for his research. One of his tasks is to sift this material, to separate the chaff from the grain, and to make use of what he considers to be valuable and reliable. It is not an easy task and can sometimes be likened to that of a man who cuts his way through a jungle.

In comparison to him the historian of ancient art is a wanderer through a desert. His external sources flow very meagerly and leave him with regrettably scanty information. He may gather the bare facts of an approximate chronology of the life of an artist, but he knows next to nothing of the essential events and the crucial turning points in his life. He has few possibilities of gathering any information on the development of the artist's personality, of his relationships with his fellow artists and the leading intellectuals of his time, and, hence, of the development of his style.

The external source material becomes therefore extremely precious to him, and tempts him to squeeze out of it every possible bit of information. Here lies a danger of which he should always be conscious, but the danger cannot prevent him from using his external sources with a mixture of confidence and criticism. He takes his calculated risk and tries to protect himself against over-evaluation, on one side, and nihilistic hypercriticism on the other.

This is particularly the case when he is confronted with a writer to whom he is constantly referred: Pliny the Elder. This solid Roman citizen of equestrian rank, with a flawless career in civil and military service, has been very differently judged by historians and by philologists. He was a prolific writer during the better part of his life which spanned the years A.D. 23-79. His only surviving work, the Natural History, has come down to us practically complete in thirty-seven volumes. It is an encyclopaedic summary of all the useful knowledge of the time relating to his subject. This circumstance makes it immediately clear that Pliny who ended his life as commander of the naval forces in the Gulf of Naples in A.D. 79 had no ambition to be considered an art historian or an art critic. His heroic death while on a rescue expedition to the city of Stabiae is immortalized by his nephew Pliny the Younger in two letters written to the historian Tacitus (VI, 16 and 20). These letters, incidentally, are the only eyewitness report of the catastrophic eruption of Vesuvius which buried not only Stabiae but also the towns of Pompeii and Herculaneum. For our purposes they are valuable for the insight they give us into the indefatigable writer's personality, and may have some bearings on our evaluation of his writings. The account of this episode from the end of his life reveals his inquisitive mind, his cold reasoning power, and his absorbing interest in registering phenomena and facts.

His style is pedestrian and without rhetorical embellishment. He is sometimes repetitive, but rarely without reference to his earlier mention of the same topic. He is not free from obvious confusion of data, and he seems uninterested in the historical sequence of events, but his statements are mostly direct and to the point. One must admire his ambition to master so wide a range of subject matter from cosmology, geography, and ethnology to botany, pharmacology, zoology and metallurgy.

Art comes into his Natural History only incidentally in the books on mineralogy and metallurgy (33-37). Book 34 deals with copper and bronze and branches out into a treatise on sculpture, while Book 35 which records various pigments becomes a brief handbook in the history of painting with short flashbacks into sculpture. The two remaining books deal with petrography and return tangentially to sculpture and glyptic art.

A question of primary importance immediately presents itself: how reliably useful can these Plinian notes be to a historian of ancient art? The answer depends on two different issues: on the dependability of his sources, and on his own working methods.

His relationship to his Greek and Latin sources almost exclusively occupied the interests of scholars who worked with Plinian criticism in the nineteenth century. From O. Jahn in 1850[1] to K. Jex-Blake and E. Sellers in 1896[2] Plinian criticism remained mainly analytical and "stratigraphic" as Silvio Ferri happily characterizes it.[3] The many scholars' main interest lay in their attempts to ferret out of Pliny's text the Hellenistic sources on which he built his compilation. Out of their analysis crystallized the lost Greek forerunners of a history of ancient art. Their relative importance to Pliny was differently judged and the names of Menaichmos, Xenocrates, Douris from Samos, Antigonos from Carystos and Pasiteles received varied emphasis. It was also generally admitted that much of this Greek material had been filtered through the Roman scholar Varro's works before it was cast in its final Plinian form.

Valuable as this work is, particularly in the form in which we meet it in B. Schweitzer's work *Xenokrates von Athen* (1932), it neglects the other approach to Pliny criticism which I just mentioned: the evaluation of our author's character, learning, and working methods. Such an approach may turn into a more exegetic and constructive form of criticism which may in a salutary way modify and supplement the older form.

Reading his own preface to his work which is dedicated to the Emperor Titus, we meet an interesting mixture of self-confidence and modesty. He calls his subject a *sterilis materia*: the nature of things and life itself. He admits that his work does not require

---

[1] O. Jahn, "Ueber die Kunsturteile des Plinius," *Berichte d. sächs. Akad.*, 1850, pp. 105-142.

[2] K. Jex-Blake and E. Sellers, *The Elder Pliny's Chapters on the History of Art*, 1896.

[3] *Plinio il Vecchio, Storia delle Arti Antiche*. Teste, trad. e note a cura di S. Ferri, 1946.

great talent (*ingenium*) of which he confesses that he possesses only a quite moderate amount. At the same time he asserts that no Latin author (*apud nos*) has ever tried a similar task and that even among the Greeks no one had tried it single-handed. These statements are correct with regard both to his lack of literary talent and to the formidable magnitude and uniqueness of his work.

His intellectual honesty and his orderly and systematic procedure is clearly reflected in his first volume which is nothing but a detailed table of content of the entire work, and an enumeration of his bibliographical sources, arranged volume by volume. Within each volume he separates Latin and Greek authors, and we find that he used more Greek material for his compilation than Latin. He relies on one hundred authors of two thousand books, in round figures, which constitutes a very respectable bibliography. He was certainly a book-minded man and a man of great and encyclopaedic learning. But how well organized was he and how did the intensely busy administrator of civil and military affairs find time to do all this reading and condense it in his own writings?

Parts of the answers to these questions can be found in a third letter of his nephew Pliny the Younger (3.5) addressed to Baebius Macer. It is worth quoting at some length because of its revealing character:

> You may wonder how a man as busy as he was could find time to compose so many books, and some of them too involving such care and labor. . . . But he had a keen intelligence, incredible devotion to study, and a remarkable capacity for dispensing with sleep. His method was to start during the last week of August rising by candlelight and long before daybreak, not in order to take auspices, but to study. And in winter he got to work at one or at latest two a.m. and frequently at midnight. He was indeed a very ready sleeper, sometimes dropping off in the middle of his studies and then waking up again. . . . After returning home [from morning duties] he gave all the time that was left to study. Very often after lunch . . . in the summer, if he had no engagements, he used to lie in the sun and have a

book read to him, from which he made notes and extracts; he read nothing without making extracts from it—indeed he used to say that no book is so bad but that some part of it has value. After this rest in the sun he usually took a cold bath and then a snack of food and a very short siesta, and then he put in what was virtually a second day's work, going on with his studies till dinner time. Over his dinner a book was read aloud to him and notes were made, and that at a rapid pace. I remember that one of his friends, when the reader had rendered a passage badly, called him back and had it repeated; but my uncle said to him: "Surely, you got the sense?" and on his nodding assent continued: "Then what did you call him back for? This interruption of yours has cost us ten more lines!" Such was his economy of time. . . . In vacation, only the time of the bath was exempted from study; and when I say the bath I mean the more central portion of that ritual, for while he was being shampooed and rubbed down he used to have someone read to him or to dictate. On a journey he seemed to throw aside all other interests and used the opportunity for study only; he had a secretary at his elbow with book and tablets, his hands in winter protected by mittens so that even the inclemency of the weather might not steal any time from his studies; and with this object he used to go about in a sedan chair even in Rome. . . . This resolute application enabled him to go through all those volumes, and he bequeathed to me 160 sets of notes, written on both sides of the paper in an extremely small hand, a method that multiplies this number of volumes. . . . (translated by H. Rackham)

So far, his nephew's description of Pliny the Elder's work day. It gives us not only a very engaging portrait of an indefatigable intellectual worker, but also a revealing insight into his methods which may serve as a foundation for a more exegetic and constructive Plinian criticism. From such a viewpoint certain salient points stand out:

1) He never read without taking notes or having a secretary do so.
2) When using a reader he took notes himself.

3) His notes aimed at getting the sense, not the wording of his sources.

These are all positive assets which inspire us with confidence. When it comes to grasping the sense of a quoted author Pliny's own apprehension and judgement are particularly involved. The same was true, to a still higher degree, when he had to decide which of his sources were reliable and which should be distrusted. In these cases his subjective judgement governed his decisions as he himself asserts: "I never follow one single author, but from case to case the one I consider most truthful" (*Nat. Hist.* 3.1). Ultimately we thus depend on the power and precision of his judgement.

Less confidence inspiring are other features of his methods which can be read out of his nephew's letter:

1) He now and then fell asleep while working
2) His readers kept a high pace
3) He gathered his excerpts in 160 sets of notes written in a very small hand on both sides of the paper.

The first of these two human factors may account for some of the provable mistakes in his monumental treatise, while the third is of a special interest to us. To write an encyclopaedia single-handed before the invention of such practical bibliographical tools as the card index and the cross reference index, seems to us an impossible project. To have raw material gathered in the Plinian way, in what must have been small notebooks or scrolls, makes it practically impossible to obtain an orderly sequence of facts and events in the final version of the manuscript. The situation was worsened by the crowded pages. The facts and events may in themselves be true, but the order of narration does not necessarily follow a chronological sequence, nor do they reflect a gradual development. Being deprived of the facility of a card index, Pliny had to rely heavily on the order in which his notes from the two thousand books were read and excerpted. Such an order necessarily becomes arbitrary, and should be evaluated accordingly.

This circumstance is of particular interest for Plinian criticism in the art historical field. We may keep Pliny's factual information and depend upon it, but we are entitled, I submit, to consider it as so many cards in an index, the order of which is subject to rearrangement. This is a delicate task, but if carried out in a critical and conscientious way, it may open a new avenue to our understanding and appreciation of Pliny as a source for the history of ancient art. If his statements are put in an organic order many of the apparent contradictions may be eliminated, and instead be understood as referring to different stages in the lives and works of the artists he writes on. Such a procedure would give us a higher degree of "exegetic and constructive" Plinian criticism than even Silvio Ferri envisaged when he first used these terms.

When applied to the history of the most renowned and productive Greek sculptor of the fourth century B.C., Lysippus, I believe it can produce some interesting and enlightening results. But the information obtained from Pliny, important and central as it is, must be read and interpreted in conjunction with all other accounts of his life and work which can be gathered from other authors, or from epigraphical sources. All this material, as it was available in 1927, was collected by Franklin P. Johnson, in his monograph on Lysippus published in that year, a work to which every student of Lysippus is inevitably referred.

In piecing together the story of Lysippus' life and career from the scattered and fragmentary notes we have, it is wise to begin with Pliny's brief statement (34.51): "Lysippus lived in the 113th Olympiad in the days of Alexander the Great." In our time reckoning system that means the years 328-325 B.C. It does not mean, however, that he was of the same age as Alexander who was born in 356 B.C., only that their lives overlapped. This becomes immediately clear from another piece of information obtained from the same source (34.63): "He also made a number of portraits of Alexander, beginning from his boyhood"; *a pueritia eius ortus*. As a technical term *pueritia* in Latin normally applies to a boy before he enters into his *adulescentia* and signifies that he is less than seventeen years old. If we calculate conservatively that Lysippus' first portrait of Alexander was made when the sitter was fourteen years old we arrive at the year 342 B.C. To obtain such an honorable commission our sculptor must certainly have proved himself in a convincing way, and must thus have had a considerable part of his career behind himself at so early a date. Supposing, hypothetically, that on this occasion he was at least thirty years old, we must conclude that he was born not later than 372 B.C. That makes him come closer to the generation of Aristotle who was born in 385 B.C., than to that of Alexander. I mention Aristotle, because in 343-342 B.C. he was called by Alexander's father, king Philip of Macedon, to his capital Pella to serve as tutor to the young crown prince. These years coincided with the period when we believe that Lysippus also dwelt at the Macedonian court. The two intellectuals in the circle around the young Alexander might have seen a great deal of one another during these years, and exchanged thoughts and ideas. It is reasonable to believe that in this exchange Lysippus was mainly on the receiving end.

Can this early date of Lysippus be vindicated from other independent evidence? Leaving aside a debatable dedicatory inscription from Olympia connected with Lysippus and read by Pausanias in the 2nd century A.D. (Paus. 6.1, 4-5), we can answer the question in the affirmative. In June 1939 there came to light in the French excavations at Delphi considerable fragments of an inscription on a statue base (fig. 1). They are in a remarkably crisp and fresh state of preservation which means that the inscription had not long been exposed to weathering before it was taken down and broken up. It is a distich epigram in four lines followed by the names of the person honored, the dedicators, and the sculptor. The latter is Lysippus, the dedicators are the Thessalians and the statue represented the Theban general Pelopidas, on whose career in Thessaly we are rather well informed. The epigram is preserved only in the beginnings of the four lines which read: Σπάρτημ με . . . εὐλογίαι πίσ[τει] . . . [πλε]ιστάκι δὴ . . . [στῆ]σαι Βοιω[τῶν] . . . which in translation gives an equally fragmentary sense: "Sparta . . . Blessings and trust . . . Often indeed . . . Erect of the Boeotians . . ." This leaves a wide margin for imaginative supplementation of the elegiac distich. The old epigraphic master Adolf Wilhelm in Vienna composed one (*Oesterreichische Jahreshefte*, Vol. 33, 1941) of admirable metric perfection. It would be going too far to discuss the reconstruction here and it will suffice to say that Wilhelm believed that the statue was erected during Pelopidas' lifetime. His crucial argument is that the line beginning with "Often, indeed . . ." should continue in form of a vow ". . . may other statues be erected to you." This seems to me more persuasive than convincing, and the line could obviously have continued in innumerable other ways. The finder and original editor of the base, J. Bousquet (*Rev. Arch.* Vol. 14, 1939, pp. 125-132) refrained wisely from any conjectural supplementation, and connected the inscription with a passage in Cornelius Nepos' Life of Pelopidas (5.5), in which the Roman author tells us that after the death of Pelopidas all Thessalian city states honored his memory with golden crowns and statues. This seems to me to be a sounder method, particularly after the finding in 1963 of another small fragment of the same inscription (fig. 1) which proves that in any case the first line of Wilhelm's reconstruction is wrong. (*B.C.H.*, 87, 1963, 206-208).

All of this would be of small interest to us, were it not for the fact that, if we follow Wilhelm, the statue must have been erected in 369 B.C., and if we follow Bousquet the event can have taken place only in 364 or 363 B.C. It means a difference of five or six years in the date of the earliest indisputable document we have of the artistic career of Lysippus.

To obtain the commission from the city states of Thessaly for a statue of their hero and liberator to be erected in the important Panhellenic sanctuary of Delphi was an honor comparable to that which Lysippus received from King Philip of Macedon in 342 B.C. Whether this happened in 369 or, as I believe, in 363 B.C. it projects Lysippus' career backwards in time a considerable number of years. The year of his birth can no longer be placed in the 370's, but must be pushed back at least into the 380's B.C. This is important for our understanding of his art, and becomes more so, if we can through independent evidence obtain an estimate of how long he lived.

Through a passage in Athenaeus (*Deipnosophistae* 11. 784) we learn that King Cassander of Macedon engaged the great Lysippus for a humble job when he founded his new capital of Cassandria. He had him design the jars in which the famous Mendaean wine was exported. This brings us down at least to the

year 316 B.C. when Cassandria was founded. But we can follow
Lysippus still further down in time. The learned and reliable
Renaissance humanist Pietro Sabino saw in Rome, and copied, an
inscription which bore the signature of Lysippus on the base of a
statue of Seleucus I with the title of βασιλεύς, King. Seleucus
adopted the official royal title only in 306 B.C., so at that time
Lysippus was still alive and at work. He was then over eighty years
old, and his life spanned almost the entire fourth century B.C.

This conforms well with the anecdotal material that has come
down to us from various ancient sources relating to his old age and
proverbial productivity.

From these simple biographical data we may now turn to his art.
A great and creative artist, the leading sculptor of his long generation, Lysippus had lived through one of the most turbulent periods
in the history of Greece. As a young man he had witnessed the
rise of Thebes under Epaminondas; as a mature man he had lived
through the revolutionary years when Philip of Macedon crushed
the freedom of the Greek city-states, and forced Greece against
her will into something that resembled a national unit. Then followed Alexander's conquest of the East, which Lysippus as his
court sculptor must have sporadically followed in the center of
events. In his old age the heritage of Alexander dissolved in the
rival Hellenistic kingdoms of the Diadochs, at least one of whom—
Seleucus—Lysippus served. It was, indeed, a life full of dramatic
and shifting outer events. Not less dramatic was the intellectual
life of the period. In Lysippus' youth Antisthenes, the founder of
the individualistic philosophy dominated, together with Plato, the
intellectual stage. Aristotle, the rationalist, was his contemporary
and, probably, his friend since their common stay in Pellá.
Epicurus and Zenon were the leading philosophers at the time
when Lysippus was growing old. His lifetime covered highly
dynamic events not only in the realm of history and politics, but
also in the field of speculative philosophy and the intellectual life
of mankind.

We know that he was the leading sculptor of his long generation and the influential head of a school of talented pupils. Could
he have remained so if he had expressed the same ideas in the

same form through all the sixty years of his creative life? It might perhaps have been possible, had he lived in a quieter and ideologically more homogeneous period, but the proposition becomes highly improbable in his own troubled fourth century. We have to reckon with a more or less continuous development of style in Lysippus' work, a development that made the works of his youth look very different from those of his mature years, or of his old age. Within the frame of such a development certain indelible personal features and characteristics may remain like a permanent signature covering his entire oeuvre, but both form and content are apt to shift and change. To a historian of later art this may seem self-evident, but strangely enough it generally remains a neglected issue in the field of ancient art. When applying this idea to the study of the art of Lysippus, it is wise to look into our written sources again, and search in them for any indication of such a development. This will inevitably bring us back to Pliny the Elder.

He tells us that Lysippus was born in Sicyon, that he had no teacher and that in his youth he worked in a foundry (34.61). Sicyon was the home town of that great sculptor of the fifth century, Polycleitus, and the traditions of the old master were certainly strong, particularly in such conservative environs as in a bronze foundry. We should therefore not be surprised when Cicero tells us (*Brutus*, 86) that Lysippus used to say that the Lancebearer of Polycleitus (fig. 2) was his teacher. This sturdy figure which embodies the structural and formal ideals of the last half of the fifth century was in the fourth century the incarnation of idealistic conservatism. As a starting point for a new style it hardly looks promising. And yet, the young apprentice must have felt strongly the influence of Polycleitan style and principles in the beginning of his career, particularly as he grew up in the town of the venerated master of the past generation.

Our literary sources thus give us good reason to believe that we have to reckon with an early style of Lysippus which in its main principles was conservative and a continuation of the classical traditions of the preceding generation. A visual documentation of this style is at present very difficult to obtain. I have myself, several years ago, tried to do so with somewhat uncertain results,[4] and Schuchhardt made another attempt one year later without much success.[5] If the Pelopidas statue of the 360's had survived, and not its dedicatory inscription alone, our task would be much easier. As things now stand, we have to be content with the reasonable surmise that such a phase existed in the development of Lysippan sculptural style.

Pliny's next statement, which is a direct continuation of his first sentence, is in clear contradiction to the existence of any traditional trend in Lysippus' work. He tells us that Lysippus adopted a principle expressed by the Sicyonian painter Eupompus, that no artist should be imitated, but only nature itself: "*Natura ipsa imitanda est.*" Nothing could be more clearly opposed to the Polycleitan ideal which transcended nature, and constructed the human figure in accordance with unchangeable mathematical principles, in order to give it a higher degree of permanence, elevated above the transient phenomena of physical appearance. To a traditionalist such a dictum must have seemed very revolutionary. It can only be reconciled with our hypothesis of an early Polycleitan style of Lysippus, if we apply our principle of constructive and exegetic criticism of Pliny. The pronouncement has to be accepted, but it belongs, as it were, to another card in Pliny's nonexistent card index. In other words, it does not belong to the early stage of Lysippus' career, where it comes in Pliny's narrative, but must refer to a later stage of his artistic development. The facts are not incompatible; they have only to be considered consecutively and not simultaneously. Of Eupompus' life and work we know next to nothing, but he seems in any case to have been an older contemporary of Lysippus, if not an altogether earlier Sicyonian artist. I do not exclude that a painter was the first artist to embrace a naturalistic ideal, because painters generally led the artistic avant-garde development in Antiquity, as they seem to do still today. What is of greater interest to us is to attempt to fix in time when this decisive change took place in Lysippus' own work.

[4] *Opusc. Atheniensia*, Vol. I, 1953, pp. 87 ff.
[5] *Beiträge z. Klass. Altertumswiss. Festschrift Bernhard Schweitzer*, 1954, pp. 222-226.

Art as an imitation of nature is an Aristotelian principle: ἡ τέχνη μιμεῖται τὴν φύσιν. This is one of the reasons why Aristotle gives a generally low grade to the artists who, after all, are only unaccomplished imitators. I would like to believe that these problems were discussed by the philosopher and the sculptor up in Pella during their common years at the Macedonian court in 343-342 B.C., and suggest that these discussions left their mark on Lysippus' mind. The challenge was great, and may conceivably have spelled a decisive turning point in Lysippus' concept of art. If this is true, it was in the late 340's that he broke with his earlier style.

To these very years we can date the bronze original of the statue of Agias, erected in Pharsalus in Thessaly on commission of the local dynast Daochus and signed by Lysippus. The bronze has perished, but a practically contemporary marble replica has survived in the famous dedicatory group in Delphi (fig. 3). This marble replica was made not later than 332 B.C. to judge from general historical arguments and circumstances. It gives us the first and only reliable insight into what I would call Lysippus' second style. A confrontation with the Polycleitan figure is most revealing. Instead of the solid, self-contained early figure, we have here an individual who seems to shiver in a restless idleness (fig. 4). There is an inner tension in the seemingly quiet pose which points into the third dimension, in contrast to the calm frontality of the Lancebearer. There is an intentional restriction in the use of sculptural means in comparison with the heavy muscular articulation of Polycleitus' work. What comes to mind is another word of Pliny's, telling us that among Lysippus' achievements was his way of making "the bodies slimmer and drier" than the old masters had done (*corpora graciliora siccioraque*) and the heads smaller, thus increasing the apparent height of his figures (34.65). This detached piece of information seems at least partly applicable to the figure of Agias, and may therefore refer to this second stage in the artist's stylistic development. Most remarkable is perhaps a profile view of Agias' head (fig. 5). Let us remember that it represents a victorious athlete, and study his expression from that point of view. He is a dissatisfied victor full of explosive nervousness and restrained emotion, far removed from the inner harmony and serene calm which characterize his many forerunners in Greek art. He is an individual, not an idealized type, and can thus be said to represent the first portrait rendered in a Greek victory dedication. "Natura ipsa imitanda est," whether we understand "nature" as a physical reality or the inner nature of things, the character of an individual.

Agias is a great work of art characterized by high quality and masterly execution, even if he has not gained the praise of all modern critics. Around him can be grouped a considerable number of related figures, first of all another of the statues on the same dedication base in Delphi, his brother Agelaus (fig. 6). The figure obviously is exactly contemporary with that of Agias, but its stance is still more pronouncedly three-dimensional, and may thus point forward toward a further stylistic development and experimentation in Lysippus' art. Such a trend can be traced with some clarity, particularly when using the athletic figure as a criterion of style,[6] but such a study lies outside the framework of this sketch.

Let us return to Pliny for some guidance and further information on our sculptor. Immediately after the passage just quoted on Lysippus' principle of making the bodies of his statues "slimmer and drier" there follows this sentence: "He scrupulously preserved the quality of *symmetria*, for which there is no word in Latin, by the new and hitherto untried method of modifying the squareness of the figure of the old sculptors, and he used commonly to say that whereas his predecessors had made men as they really are, he made them as they appeared to be." (Transl. by H. Rackham) *Quales esse viderentur*. There can be no doubt that Pliny's excerpt here comes directly from a Greek source. His inability to translate the Greek word σνμμετρία into Latin is sufficient proof of that. It is a difficult task, and our word symmetry in no way covers the full Greek meaning. The French scholar Charbonneaux makes the happy suggestion that we should understand it as the harmonious equilibrium of surface, volume and void in a sculpture. That was something that Lysippus scrupulously studied, and maintained in the new set of proportions he gave to his figures. So far we may be able to interpret the essential meaning of the first part of the passage. The latter part is more difficult. The confrontation of

[6] See my article, s.v. Lysippos in *Encyclopedia of World Art*.

"what men really are" and "what they appear to be" seems to indicate a decisive step away from his earlier idea of "imitating nature," and open up an avenue leading away from his limited naturalism toward a new field of aesthetic thinking and theory. Part of the true meaning may be sought in his transcendence of the Aristotelian principle and his embracing of a new more illusionistic idea. I suggest that such an idea may be applicable to his later portraits of Alexander the Great, which are so vividly described by Plutarch, Apuleius and other authors. The heaven-gazing Alexander (fig. 7) with "the melting glance in his eyes," "the lion-like fierceness of his countenance" was created by Lysippus, and became the archetype for later rulers who, like Alexander, claimed superhuman and divine qualities. This has been convincingly shown by H. P. L'Orange in his book *Apotheosis in Ancient Portraiture*, Oslo, 1947. Alexander's claim to full divinity came only toward the end of his life in the 320's B.C., and was met by Lysippus, his favorite sculptor, with the creation of a portrait that transcended reality and made him look like a superhuman hero.[7] In the imagination of his contemporaries he seemed to be divine, though born a human. Here we have at least one example of the contrast between *esse* and *videri esse* that is the core of the passage in Pliny. It meant in Lysippus' theory of art the application of an illusionistic principle, superseding his earlier naturalism.

We could observe its forerunners as early as in the modified proportions of the Agias figure of the 340's, but it came into full bloom on another level only in the late portraits of Alexander the Great in the early 320's B.C. The portraits he made of the boy Alexander in Pella, where he stayed together with Aristotle, may have looked quite different.

Applying these results to the wider question of the continuous development of Lysippus' style, we would suggest that the Plinian passage just discussed is not in itself incompatible with his earlier statements on Lysippus' style and career. It is again one of the many excerpts in one of the 160 booklets where he jotted down his notes, and it falls into its proper place as a documentation for a third and late style in Lysippus' art.

---

[7] See my article on Alexander-Heracles in *Bull. Mus. Fine Arts, Boston*, Vol. 51 (1953), pp. 30 ff.

From an early traditionalistic phase in the 360's our sculptor moved on in his mature years to a new naturalism, modified by experimental attempts at creating a new "symmetria." These experiments carried him beyond his old principle of art as an imitation of nature, and brought him in his later years to that form of illusionism which transcribes nature into an imaginative, new, and different reality.

II. SOME ASPECTS OF LYSIPPUS' ART

We know from our ancient sources that in Lysippus' long and productive life he tried his art on many different subjects: on the Olympian gods, such as Zeus, Poseidon, Dionysus and Eros, on allegorical figures such as Kairos, the fleeting moment, on Heracles the hero, at rest and in his labors, on portraits of Alexander and his companions in arms and of Socrates, on animal sculpture and on a large group of athletic victory statues. Of all this not one single indisputable original has survived the ravages of time and come down to us. With the exception of the figure of Agias, which is a contemporary marble replica, we have to reconstruct his oeuvre from the often dim mirrors of Roman copies. The reason for this sad state of affairs lies partly in the fact that his medium was almost exclusively bronze. Metal is apt to be melted down in emergency situations, either to be recast in new statuary, or used in a more utilitarian way in war or in peace.

Under these circumstances it may seem a preposterously daring and hopeless task to try to discuss and interpret some salient features of his art. Our conclusions are bound to remain hypothetical because the premises on which we build them are not original and solid. But still we have to take courage, and we can do so, because the Roman copies were generally at least iconographically exact. The mechanical copying of a statue is based on the so-called pointing process still in use today when a marble cutter translates into his noble material the plaster cast of the sculptor's clay original. Gisela Richter has shown that this method of mechanical reproduction has a long lineage and that it was in use at least as early as the first century B.C.[8] The formal precision of the good Roman copyist was remarkable, as can be seen by a comparison of two or more copies of one and the same lost original.

Whatever consolation can be obtained from these considerations, it remains of course sadly true that no copy, be it ever so faithful, can render full justice to the art of the original master. The marks of the master's chisel strokes and the subtle finish he gave the bending and bulging surfaces of his statue are lost forever,

---

[8] G. M. A. Richter, *Three Critical Periods in Greek Sculpture*, 1951, pp. 42-44.

and what we find instead belongs to the copyist. An ever so faithful
and meticulous copyist cannot catch the quintessence of the original.
He can only guide us toward a fuller appreciation of what we
have lost.

One other negative consideration has to be registered. What is
required of a good and faithful copyist is the capacity to eliminate
as much as possible of his own artistic personality and humbly
follow the master's form. This comes more easily to a sculptor
whose individuality is not pronounced and whose personal ambitions are weak or non-existent, which generally means that he is
a second-rate artist. Faithfulness and quality are therefore rarely
present in the same copy. The good sculptor engaged in copying
a renowned work is subject to the continuous temptation to inject
something of his own personality into the finished product, thereby
"bettering" it, as he would probably say himself. Being a creative
and competent artist he would produce a copy of good sculptural
quality, but the product which leaves his studio may very well
be less faithful to the original than that which was made by an
inferior sculptor. These are the horns of the dilemma which have
to be kept in mind by historians of Greek sculpture who venture
into criticism of Roman copies.

The way out of the dilemma lies in the comparative study of
a sufficient number of copies, when and if they exist. From that
material one may draw one's conclusions and build up a personal
judgement, which may be a guide in less clear cases. It must, as
all criticism, necessarily remain personal and subjective, but that
does not mean that it is arbitrary, nor that it lacks the backing of
objective arguments. As long as these methodological principles
are kept in mind, our task can be undertaken with some confidence.
The path may lead a step or two closer to what we, in elated
moments, call the truth.

The only Lysippan figure which we so far have ventured to
analyze and interpret is Agias, the athletic victory statue in Delphi.
The only reason why the singular honor was bestowed upon Agias
of having his statue sculpted by Lysippus and erected in Delphi
was that he was an ancestor of the Thessalian dynast Daochus, and
that he was a successful athlete and a multiple victor in the roughest
of all Greek sports, the pancration. He had long been dead when

Lysippus made the statue which therefore has nothing to do with a presumed personal likeness. The pungent individuality which characterizes this remarkable work of art is not Agias' own, but springs out of Lysippus' creative imagination. If a Thessalian athlete could inspire Lysippus to such a superb creation, how much more could we not expect from him if his imaginary sitter had been an interesting and truly great man? This question leads us to consider the evidence for Lysippus' portrait of Socrates.

Our literary evidence comes from Diogenes Laertius, the third century writer on the ancient philosophers. After having described Socrates' death he continues (II:43): "So he was taken from among men; and soon afterwards (εὐθύς) the Athenians felt such remorse that they closed the palaestras and the gymnasiums . . . They honored Socrates with a bronze statue, the work of Lysippus, which they placed in the assembly hall of the Panathenaic processions (ἐν τῷ πομπείῳ) . . ." This valuable notice contains a somewhat disturbing chronological difficulty. Socrates died in 399 B.C., when Lysippus was not yet born. When Diogenes uses the adverb, εὐθύς, soon, we must make some allowance for the relativity of such a time indication. F. Poulsen has discussed this question in his papers on the Socrates Statue (*From the Collections of the Ny Carlsberg Glyptothek*, Vols. 1, pp. 40-41, and 2, pp. 169-182) and I consider his interpretation sound.

The Athenians repented, but not very soon, at least if we use that word in a less elastic way than Greeks do today and probably always did. Athenian political rhetors of the first half of the fourth century all seem to approve of the condemnation, and they reflect the public opinion of their times better than anybody else. As late as 350 B.C. Hypereides (Fragm. 55, ed. Kenyon) positively asserts in one of his public speeches: "Our forefathers were right in punishing Socrates." Plato's voice was hardly heard outside the garden walls of his Academy and Xenophon had at this time just published his re-evaluating treatise, the Memorabilia. Diogenes' statement should be considered an exaggerated euphemism created in the perspective of more than five centuries of growing Socratic fame. To these arguments which are mainly Poulsen's, I would add a controllable example of similar kind. Plutarch tells us (*Demosthenes*, 30.5) that "a little later (ὀλίγον ὕστερον) after

Demosthenes' death in 322 B.C. the Athenians honored him with an official statue in the Agora. Through independent evidence we know, however, that the statue was erected 42 years after his death, in 280 B.C. If "a little later" can mean 42 years, "soon afterwards" need not bind us to an early date.

When could a general regret of an old mistake have crystallized into such a gesture of singular honor as erecting a statue of Socrates at public expense and placing it in such a conspicuous place? I believe with Poulsen that Lycurgus was the man behind the achievement. He was the leading man in Athenian politics from 338 to 326 B.C. and a most interesting personality. A pupil of Plato's and a friend of Xenocrates, Plato's successor as the leader of the Academy, he was naturally tied to the memory of Socrates. He was a humanist with a lively interest in philosophy and scenic art, and at the same time an able administrator of Athenian public finances. He was a man of many commemorations, and fond of erecting statues of great men from Athens' past days of glory. Aeschylus, Sophocles and Euripides were thus honored by him when he restored and rebuilt the Theater of Dionysus in Athens. This man with his direct Socratic descent was most probably the moving force behind the project of honoring the greatest son of Athens with a statue by the greatest sculptor of his time. We cannot be far wrong when tentatively dating this event to the years around 330 B.C.[9]

The portrait of Socrates has come down in a great number of Roman copies, all of them heads or busts, which was the fashion commonly followed by the Romans when they desired to decorate their homes with portraits of Greek philosophers, poets and writers. But to the Greeks of the fourth century the human form was an inviolable and indivisible unit, and every portrait sculpture made was therefore a statue of the full figure.

To reconstruct the lost Lysippan work we have, however, to start with the head as it appears in the Roman copies. Thirty-nine such copies exist today. They can be divided into two types of which the second, represented by twenty-eight pieces, obviously

[9] A summary of the argument, with full bibliography, is given by G. M. A. Richter, *The Portraits of the Greeks*, Vol. I, 1965, pp. 109-110, 116.

reflects the famous Socrates portrait and therefore is the type which is of interest to us.[10]

As a representative of this group we may take the head in the Museo delle Terme in Rome (fig. 8). What sort of a likeness can it be? We know from many sources what Socrates looked like: stocky and broad-shouldered, broad nose, Silenus-like face, protruding eyes and bald. Physically he was an ugly man, and some of this external ugliness lingers on in the portrait. If we are right in our assumption, it was made some seventy years after his death and can thus be considered a posthumous reconstruction which left the artist a wide margin of imaginative interpretation within the framework of traditional iconography. Herein resides some of the greatness of this work of art. This is how the artist imagined his Socrates. He is indomitably individualistic with unforgettably personalized features: the high forehead tapering upwards, the vertical wrinkles dividing it into three zones, the broad cheeks with the underlying bone-structure clearly marked, the broad flat nose and a stormy sea of seemingly untidy hair and beard. A pair of tired, near-sighted eyes penetrate the onlooker with deep insight and immeasurable wisdom. There is nothing repulsive in this physically ugly face. It is as indomitable as Socrates' thoughts and his soul, and it catches the tragic fate of greatness not understood, leading to punishment and death. I cannot help thinking of what Euripides says in his *Electra* (295-296): "We pay a high price for having insight. Wisdom hurts." What we have in front of us is the mortal frame of immortal genius. Therefore it is sad, and still triumphant.

From a formal point of view the sculptural means applied to the head seem intentionally restricted. We are reminded of Pliny's words about the "drying out" of the surfaces which characterized Lysippus' style during his mature years. The skeletal frame of the face disciplines the modeling, and the general structure of the head is almost symmetrical. This can be particularly seen in the wavy masses of hair and beard. The mustaches maintain a complete equilibrium on both sides of the mouth, and the curls of the hair

[10] All the material is admirably collected, described and provided with full bibliographies by Richter, *op.cit.*, Vol. I, pp. 109-119.

and beard form an almost symmetrical pattern without decreasing
the effect of dynamic movement. It is indeed a remarkable head,
a great master's vision of a great man.

Can we complete our view of the original, and find some leads
to reconstructing the entire figure? Following the lead of G. Lippold and F. Poulsen, I believe that the question can be answered
in the affirmative.

This badly battered statue (fig. 9) of a seated philosopher
dressed in the typical Greek *pallium* once stood in the open air
in the Villa Ludovisi in Rome. It is now in the Ny Carlsberg
Glyptothek in Copenhagen. Lippold was the first to draw our
attention to the German eighteenth century engraver J. J. Preisler's
album of fifty engravings of ancient statuary (*Statuae antiquae*,
1732) made after drawings by the French sculptor Bouchardon.
Plate 31 (fig. 10) in this album renders our statue when it not
only still retained its head, but was in much better general shape
than it now is. The caption reads: *Socrates philosophus*, and the
head clearly renders the philosopher's head as conceived in the
copies after Lysippus' Socrates portrait. We thus have a very
precious clue to the solution of the problem of reconstituting
Lysippus' work in its entirety. Inspired by this thought Poulsen
had a Danish sculptor, with the engraving as a guide, supplement
in plaster the parts of the body which had been lost since the
eighteenth century, and add to the reconstruction a cast of the
head in Museo delle Terme in Rome. The result (fig. 11) is very
convincing. The only major discrepancy between drawing and
reconstruction is that in the latter the head lacks the twist it has in
the former. This means that the Roman copyist who made the
head as a portrait bust or a herm adapted the neck to a more
frontal view, appropriate in such a case. With this sole reservation,
we can use the Copenhagen reconstruction as a means of understanding and evaluating Lysippus' original work.

The composition is intensely dynamic and three-dimensional.
The old man sits on a simple stool and leans forward as if he were
engaged in presenting an argument or leading a Socratic discussion
as we know them from Plato's dialogues. The left foot is stretched
forward and the right leg is bent sharply at the knee, so that the
right foot is under the stool. This instantaneous and springy pos-

ture lends a great elasticity to the figure, and makes us believe that at any moment he could rise to his feet to drive home his point or emphasize an argument. There is a time element involved in the pose itself which to some extent was present also in the two athletic figures of Agias and Agelaus, but which here, presumably ten years later in Lysippus' career, is driven much further and made more meaningful.

The figure is swathed in the heavy woollen pallium which leaves the torso bare, but falls in simple and clearly defined folds from the left shoulder down over the lower part of the body and around the legs. The treatment of the drapery is honest and basically naturalistic. The sculptor has dispensed with any overly sophisticated trends, which toward the end of the preceding century tended to make the drapery form a pattern of its own, independent of the body around which it was draped. The character of the material is convincingly rendered and the law of gravity rules unchallenged. To characterize the drapery in a few words: it is organic and explanatory in the sense that it enhances the posture and motion of the figure itself, and is indivisibly united to it.

The torso pitilessly reveals the age of the sitter. The flesh over the chest is rendered in fat and flabby masses and the wrinkles over the protruding abdomen are emphasized in an unmistakable way. This is an aging body housing an indomitably young and energetic soul. It is this contrast which seems to have interested the sculptor more than anything else and which we have already seen in the head with its curious mixture of tiredness and energy. The artist is moving on the borderline between the transient and the eternal, and gives us a new and deeply personal interpretation of the truly exceptional man, the genius. Here, even through the mirror of Roman copies and composite reconstructions, we can fathom the depth of our artist's revolutionary innovations. His interest in a human being governed by his divine *daimon* and the capability of rendering him in sculptural form, are clearly documented. In another and very different sphere the same problem had to be faced when portraying the young miracle man Alexander the Great who during his own lifetime rose from the human to the divine status. In both cases Lysippus arrived at a

new and convincing solution. No wonder that Alexander made
him his favorite court sculptor. These intensely intricate and difficult problems seem to have dominated the creative imagination
of our artist during his mature and later years.

F. Poulsen has drawn our attention to the striking and discon-
certing likeness between the Socrates head and the head of a
satyr (fig. 12), the so-called Marsyas Borghese in the Borghese
Gallery in Rome, belonging to a somewhat over lifesize statue
found in a noble Roman villa at Monte Calvo outside Rome in
1824. The morphological and stylistic comparison is compelling.
The architectural structure of the head and the features of the
face are very much alike. The hair and beards of the two heads are
similarly organized, although those of the satyr are somewhat
more ruffled. The reason for this will become clear when we consider the different activities of the two figures. Otherwise we can
follow the physiognomies of the two faces almost feature by
feature.

In the fifth century the satyrs in Greek art were the uncompli-
cated, frolicking, ithyphallic companions of Dionysus and the
maenads. In the Borghese figure it is a basically tragic problem
child who stares at us. Not divine, not human, nor animal, he is
another example of the complicated border figures, who, on a
different level, were exemplified by Alexander the Great and
Socrates. The tension and the insoluble problem involved in being
both superhuman and subhuman, of combining an elevated and a
base nature in one and the same personality, results in a tragic
conflict expressed in the tense features of the Borghese head. The
penetration of this psychological problem and the rendering of it
in convincing sculptural form are comparable to the two previous
examples we have quoted from Lysippus' oeuvre, Socrates and
Alexander. This is the reason why I concur with F. Poulsen in
attributing the Marsyas Borghese to Lysippus.

The entire figure (fig. 13) does not contradict such an attribution. Caught in the spinning movement of a whirling dance on
tiptoe, the ecstatic body seems to contradict the tragic expression
of the face. The composition renders a fleeting moment in the
hectic spiral movement of the figure. The time element as well
as the three-dimensionality are both present in the dancing satyr.

The arms are perhaps somewhat extravagantly restored by Thor-waldsen in the early nineteenth century, but fundamentally the figure as we see him now, can be considered a fair reconstruction of the original. The "dry" modeling of the anatomy and the elongated proportions conform with Pliny's information on Lysip-pus' style, and particularly with that phase in his style develop-ment which leads from what we have called his second to his third style. We therefore suggest that the satyr be chronologically placed some ten years later than the Socrates statue or approxi-mately in the 320's B.C.

If in the Socrates portrait we could discover the dichotomy between an aging body and a young and vigorous mind, we meet in the Borghese figure exactly the opposite: unabated youthfulness in the athletic body and timeless age in the tragic face. In the first case the conflict is solved by the superiority of a brilliant mind over its mortal frame, in the second it remains unsolved and only alleviated by temporary ecstasy. The width and depth of this vital problem must have been vividly present in Lysippus' mind when he approached his old age.

It has already been said that Heracles figured quite often in the works of Lysippus. He produced the whole cycle of the twelve labors for the city of Alyzia in Acarnania, whence it was taken to Rome by a Roman official (Strabo X, 459). A colossal seated statue of the hero was erected in Tarentum, a sculpture which likewise made its way to Rome in later times. Alexander the Great is said to have carried with him on his campaigns a miniature bronze of a seated Heracles by Lysippus known as the Heracles Epitrapezios. Our sculptor also made a "Heracles deprived of his weapons by Love," and finally a bronze statue for the agora of his home town Sicyon also portraying the same popular hero. This is a summary of what our literary sources record on the subject. It is by no means excluded that Lysippus used the same motif even more frequently, because what has trickled down to us from the enormous reservoir of ancient literature are only scattered fragments of an immensely rich material. Counting the labors as twelve separate groups we arrive at the considerable number of sixteen studies of Heracles by our master. This far outnumbers any other recorded subject matter in his oeuvre as far as our literary information goes, and it seems therefore admissible to assume that the figure of Heracles interested Lysippus in a very particular way.

In view of what has already been said such an interest seems readily explicable. The Greek heroes were exceptional men, who in legendary mythology had reached their status by exceptional qualities. They appear in the Homeric epos, in the Attic drama and in later mythological literature as the great men of the past. They were all known as dominant leaders in war and peace, as wise rulers over their fellow countrymen, as founders of cities and dynasties, and as the special favorites of the gods. As such they were venerated and sometimes even worshipped by later generations. The cult places of the heroes were their tombs, because in spite of all their greatness they had one fatal quality in common: they were mortal. Their ancestry may have been traced back to the Olympians, but their heritage did not include the exclusively divine prerogative of immortality. There is only one important exception to this rule: Heracles, the son of Zeus and Alcmene. He gained immortality not only in the memory of men, but in the truly divine, Olympian sense of eternal life. Consequently he had no tomb, like the other heroes, and his worship spread over the entire Greek world, something that was impossible for the normal hero whose cult was bound to a given locality, the spot where he was buried. Heracles, through all his labors and the decision of the gods, gained a seat in the Olympian pantheon. This exceptional status adds interest to his figure from a religious point of view. He was truly a man by birth and in life, but he was equally truly a god. All his earthly life was lived under this double perspective, and gave it a deep transcendental meaning which no other Greek figure can match.

In the visual arts and in the thoughts of the archaic and classical periods these transcendental values of Heracles hardly appear. The invincible hero whom the Dorians took over from the Mycenean past and moulded into the incarnation of their indomitable spirit is a robust superman of little sophistication. He fulfilled his great deeds in a miraculous and effortless way, and we meet him in archaic and classical art fighting monsters and men and conquering them more by his muscles than by his brain.

This is not the place to trace the development of the Greek concept of Heracles. Suffice it to say that at the end of the fifth century the Heracles figure begins to change. The sophist Prodicus is the originator of the moralizing Heracles at the crossroads, where he makes a motivated choice between the broad road of easy success and glory on one side, and the narrow path of self-discipline and toil on the other. Euripides' remarkable play *Heracles' Madness* introduces us to the tragic hero who conquers himself, and submits to the will of his father Zeus that he undertake his labors in the service of an inferior distant relative, King Eurystheus of Mycenae. He does so in expiation of sins unwittingly committed. This moral reevaluation of Heracles became even more pronounced in the speculative philosophy of the fourth century as we meet it in the thinking of Antisthenes, and later in the Stoic school. Heracles became a great moral example of the man who followed the call of duty in unselfish work for others.

His early heroic deeds sink into the background and his two last labors come into focus. These labors were to bring up from the underworld the terrible watchdog Cerberus and to bring back the apples of the Hesperides. To overcome death itself and to secure the fruits of eternal youth and, thereby, eternal life were his two last achievements. They lent themselves readily to philosophical and transcendental interpretation. It is significant that between these labors is usually placed his liberation of Prometheus, the benefactor of mankind, described by Diodorus Siculus (IV, 15, 2): "When Heracles saw Prometheus suffering such punishment because of the benefit he had conferred upon men, he killed the eagle with an arrow, and then persuading Zeus to cease from his anger, he rescued Prometheus who had been the benefactor of all." (Translated by W. A. Oldfather.) At the end of his life he not only conquers death and gains immortality, but pleads with his father Zeus for the salvation of mortals also. Through this act he becomes the symbol of hope for mankind in distress.

The end of his earthly life comes through his voluntary death on the pyre at Oeta. He asked his friends to light the fire. "And immediately" says Diodorus (IV, 38, 4-5), "lightning also fell from the heavens and the pyre was wholly consumed. After this when the companions . . . came to gather up the bones of Heracles and found not a single bone anywhere, they assumed that, in accordance with the oracle, he had passed from among men into the company of the gods." We meet the motif of martyrdom, death and resurrection.

This type of Heracles as the suffering saviour is, as we might expect, totally absent in the visual arts of archaic and classical times. He seems to make his first appearance in the unsettled fourth century, and there we meet him as a type which is generally called the "Weary Heracles."

Roman copies and variations on the theme are many. Johnson in his book *Lysippos* collects forty-four complete figures, and five more heads (*op.cit.* pp. 197-200). This testifies to the great popularity of the type in Roman times and leads us to assume that the original was the work of a famous master. In studying the Roman recensions of the type it is appropriate to begin with an over life-size statue in Palazzo Pitti in Florence (fig. 14), found long ago on the Palatine hill in Rome. It renders the general iconography in a satisfactory way, and shows us the old and tired hero leaning heavily on his club over which is draped the trophy of his youth, the skin of the Nemean lion. In the right hand which he holds behind his back lie the apples of the Hesperides. His earthly toil is close to its end. The position of the right arm and the crossed legs give him a pronounced three-dimensionality. The head leans over to the left and the facial expression is one of sadness and exhaustion. All the bravado of the past is gone. Iconographically the head deviates from the main style but is a typical Roman adaptation. As a matter of fact it is as near to a portrait of the emperor Commodus as a Heracles head can come, and thereby the copy is dated to the end of the second century A.D.

On the side of the base it carries an inscription which is of great interest for our investigation. It reads Ἔργον Λυσίππου, a work of Lysippus. This is not the artist's signature, but only an antique museum label, which however ties the figure to our master in ancient tradition. The type has also generally been connected with a lost bronze original by Lysippus.

What strikes us as un-Lysippan in its style is the heavily articulated muscularity of the old hero. It seems far removed from what we can read about, and have seen, of the "dry" and restricted modeling which belonged to Lysippus' mature years. The elongated proportions and the relatively small head, which are in accordance with Lysippan iconography, do not seem sufficient to overcome the discrepancy in style. But the inscription is there, and the psychological content of the figure seems to tally with the tragic Heracles of the fourth century.

The stylistic difficulties seem rather to increase when we are confronted with the most commonly quoted example of the Lysippan Heracles, the so-called Heracles Farnese in the National Museum in Naples (fig. 15). The statue is of colossal proportions and was found in the sixteenth century in the Baths of Caracalla in Rome, for which place it was originally made. It is thereby dated to the early third century of our era. It was found without legs; these were added by Guglielmo Della Porta after a model made by Michelangelo. In 1560 the original legs were found but were fitted to the statue only in 1796. But for the left hand, which is an eighteenth century addition, we have the ancient work practically complete. The posture and iconography can be compared in detail with the statue in the Palazzo Pitti. They coincide perfectly. When it comes to the style, the non-Lysippan muscularity of the Pitti figure is still more pronounced in the Heracles Farnese. Quite apart from the fact that the latter is of a higher sculptural quality in general, his anatomy displays a still heavier articulation of the musculature. Rolls of flesh mark the volumes of the body which is even more heavily built than its counterpart in Florence.

Of great interest is the head which remains quite uncontaminated by imperial iconography. He looks still sadder and more despondent and his expression is loaded with the emotion of suffering and pain. In that sense it seems to correspond better with the psychological content we might expect from Heracles the sufferer.

This statue also carries an inscription, which is not only a label, but a real artist's signature: Γλύκων Ἀθηναῖος ἐποίησε, Glykon from Athens made it. He must have been a very talented Greek artist in the times of Caracalla who had received the commission to reproduce the famous statue on a colossal scale for the main hall of the imperial baths. In legitimate pride over his work he signed it with his own name. The scale alone makes it quite clear that it cannot have been the product of a faithful copying process

based upon the pointing system. It is a variation on the presumed
Lysippan theme and reflects very much of Glykon's artistic intentions and personality.

We would have remained very much in doubt what the original
figure looked like, were it not for a recent find in the gymnasium
of the city of Salamis in Cyprus (fig. 16). The statue is a fragment in three quarter lifesize, and renders the head and torso of
our hero. It is carved in Pentelic marble and therefore presumably
of Athenian workmanship. Its date is most probably the first half
of the second century, in the time of Hadrian, when the Salamis
gymnasium received some fresh additions to its sculptural decoration. That is a propitious time for faithful copies of renowned
works of the Greek past.

Here we have Heracles Farnese reduced to a more human scale
and stripped of all his overabundant muscular masses. The sensitive modeling works with intentionally restricted means and the
skeletal framework of the body is present everywhere and particularly in the shoulders and collarbones. In that sense he is even
directly comparable to the Agias statue in Delphi (fig. 3).

The head (fig. 17) is permeated by the same mood and spirit as
that of the Heracles Farnese (fig. 15) but the effect is gained by
much more disciplined sculptural means. Instead of the overly
fleshy eyebrows and the deep wrinkles of the forehead, we meet
a drier surface and a noble simplicity which do not decrease the
psychological intensity. We are back in the sphere of true Lysippan
style as we know it from his works previously discussed.

Numismatics provide us with a welcome proof that the "Weary
Heracles" leaning on his club existed as a type in the 320's B.C.
The obverse of a silver tetradrachm of Alexander the Great (fig.
18) struck during that decade shows the enthroned Zeus leaning
on his scepter, with his eagle perched on his outstretched right
hand. Alexander's name frames the composition to the right and
below the eagle we see as a mint symbol the miniature figure of
our Heracles. He is one of several symbols used and they shifted
from issue to issue. The figure is not bigger than a quarter of an
inch, but when enlarged (fig. 19) its iconography is readily
recognizable.

Of special interest is that the minting place of this very type of Alexander coin was Sicyon, Lysippus' home town. As has already been said, Pausanias (II, 9, 8) saw in the agora of Sicyon a bronze statue of Heracles by Lysippus. When for one coin issue of Sicyon the "Weary Heracles" was chosen as a symbol, it is tempting to tie the appearance of the coin and the erection of the statue to the same period. Our scattered evidence seems to fall into place. The suffering and exhausted Heracles, which in the copy in the Palazzo Pitti was called a work of Lysippus, was originally dedicated in the sculptor's own home town in the 320's B.C. The copy from Salamis gives us the essentials of its style which is clearly Lysippan. The ultimate results emerge as renewed confidence in an old attribution, a better understanding of the appearance of the Lysippan original, and an approximate date for its creation.

If we are right in our conclusions, Heracles the sufferer and the saviour truly divine and truly human at the same time, who made his way into Greek thought in the fourth century, found his expression in visual art through the genius of Lysippus. It came late in the artist's career, but from the point of view of content it is comparable to those somewhat earlier works on which we have concentrated our attention today. The profundity of the concept seems to require the full maturation of the sculptor's own philosophical thinking. The image may not correspond to what Heracles was (*qualis erat*) but what he seemed to be (*qualis esse videbatur*) in Lysippus' own speculative imagination. Not only the bodily proportions of his figures were changed in his late style, but also their spiritual proportions, so that they better answered the inner convictions of the artist and the needs of his contemporaries.

[11] V. Karageorghis and C. Vermeule, *Sculpture from Salamis*, I, Nicosia, 1964, pp. 17-18 and pl. 15.

LIST OF ILLUSTRATIONS

1. The Pelopidas inscription in Delphi, with the additional fragment found in 1963

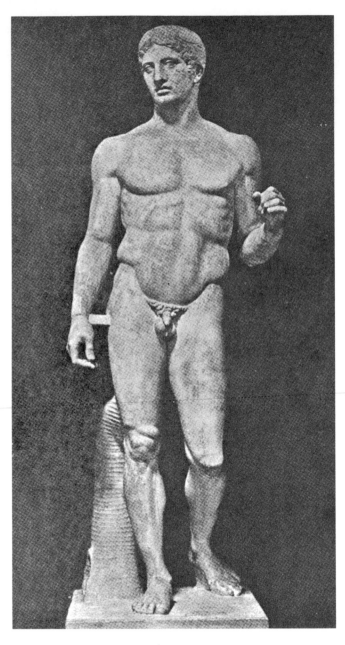

2. The Lancebearer of Polycleitus in
Naples

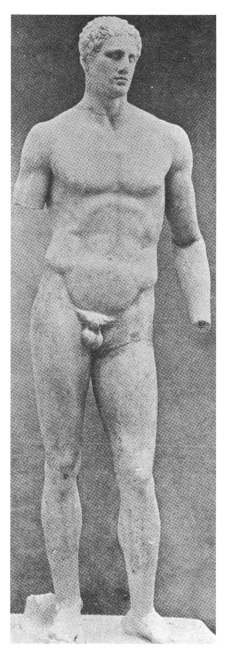 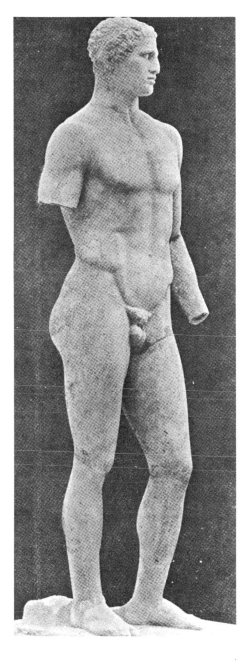

3. The Agias statue in
   Delphi, front view

4. The Agias statue in
   Delphi, side view

5. Head of Agias, profile

6. The Agelaus statue in Delphi

7. Head of Alexander in Ny Carlsberg Glyptotek, Copenhagen

8. Head of Socrates in Museo Nazionale delle Terme
in Rome

9. Socrates statue in Ny Carlsberg
   Glyptotek, Copenhagen

10. Preisler's engraving of statue in Villa Ludovisi

11. Reconstruction of the Socrates statue

12. Head of the so-called Marsyas Borghese

13. The so-called Marsyas Borghese in the Borghese Gallery in Rome

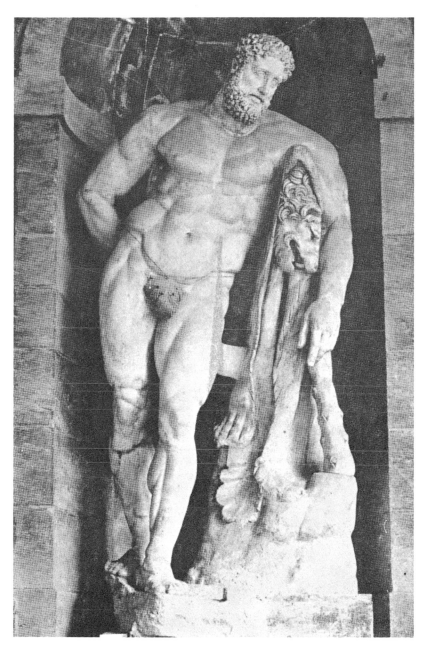

14. Heracles statue in Palazzo Pitti in Florence

15. Heracles Farnese in Museo Nazionale in Naples

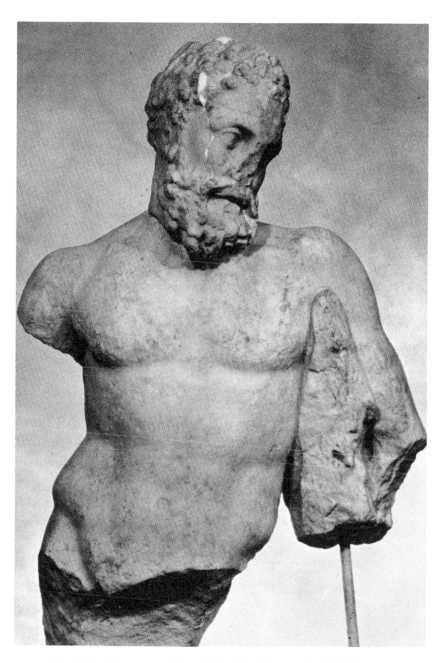

16. Heracles statue from Salamis, Cyprus, in the Museum of Nicosia

17. Head of Heracles statue from Salamis

18. Alexander tetradrachm from Sicyon

19. Detail of Alexander tetradrachm from Sicyon

2

Athenian Policy, at Home and Abroad

BY MALCOLM F. McGREGOR

Delivered November 14 and 15, 1966

ATHENIAN POLICY AT HOME
AND ABROAD

I. CITIZENS AND CITIZENSHIP

THERE is current today, in the books and therefore among students and interested laymen, a fundamental misunderstanding of what citizenship meant to the Athenians. Under the seductive influence of modern liberalism it has become confused with the idea of the brotherhood of man, democratic government, and universal citizenship. So the Athenians of the fifth century are criticised for not having extended their citizenship to the Empire; the democracy draws fire for restricting citizenship, which is somehow interpreted as an undemocratic measure; citizenship is equated with the franchise and so it is denied that women were citizens. I have met other follies, but obviously I cannot deal with all of them in these pages. I therefore propose to concentrate upon the work of Solon, Kleisthenes, and Perikles in connexion with citizenship, in the expectation that a continuous story will emerge and in the hope that the results may clarify the issue as a whole.

First, I join A. W. Gomme in stating dogmatically that "The idea of kinship as the basis of membership of the state was fundamental throughout Greece, and in this respect the nationality of the mother was as important as that of the father; it was not confined to Athens or democracies."[1] In the *polis* of Athens there was never a racial or semi-racial problem; hence this belief in kinship remained peculiarly strong and was perhaps more difficult to overlook than it might have been elsewhere. This is the spirit that pervades Perikles' address to his fellow-citizens in 431 B.C. He has much to say about "our forefathers" but the words that I ask you to keep in mind as an ingrained Athenian conviction and principle are these: "The same people, generation after generation, have always inhabited our land" (τὴν γὰρ χώραν οἱ αὐτοὶ αἰεὶ οἰκοῦντες . . . ἐλευθέραν . . . παρέδοσαν).[2]

---

[1] *Essays in Greek History and Literature* (Oxford, 1937), p. 86.
[2] Thucydides, II, 36, 1.

Before Solon, all citizens belonged to the phratries (brother-hoods) and the tribes and at least professed a kinship based on blood. This early fiction persisted; it was certainly what the Athenians of a later age wanted to believe. Thus citizens could not be manufactured artificially, in courts of law, for example, as they are in our countries today. Athens knew no Department of Immigration and Naturalisation. One can well imagine, then, how shocking to Athenian sensibilities was Solon's law that offered citizenship to aliens on a large scale. The unprecedentedly radical character of this act should not induce us to distrust Plutarch's account, which is in fact confirmed by the history of the next ninety years as well as by Plutarch's own misgivings. This is what Plutarch writes:[3] "he granted the status of citizenship to none but those who were in permanent exile from their own countries or who were moving their households to Athens to ply trades. He did this, they say, not so much to drive away the other foreigners as to entice these immigrants to Athens with a guarantee of citizenship; and at the same time he believed that reliance could be placed on those who had been compelled to renounce their native lands as well as those who had voluntarily abandoned their homes with intent."

Plutarch lived nearly seven centuries later than Solon. Yet, with his perspective and his knowledge of intervening history, he is troubled. "The law causes perplexity" ($\pi\alpha\rho\acute{\epsilon}\chi\epsilon\iota\ \dot{\alpha}\pi o\rho\acute{\iota}\alpha\nu$), he says. It perplexed him because it was contrary to Athenian tradition and his comment, I think, confirms the authenticity of a measure that he would gladly disbelieve. He was a Hellene. Our responsibility is to discover in what extraordinary circumstances Solon could persuade the Athenians to accept his proposal, if only temporarily. It must have been abhorrent to many of them. Of course, he had special powers and thus was probably able to work by decree. I do not believe that an organised assembly ($\dot{\epsilon}\kappa\kappa\lambda\eta\sigma\acute{\iota}\alpha$) existed before Solon, who therefore was not dependent upon the votes of a body of citizens. This, I recognise, is a separate argument. Fortunately, it is irrelevant to our immediate purposes, for Solon's decision became law. Yet

[3] *Solon*, 24, 2 (B. Perrin's text, New York and London, 1928).

he must have been strong enough to meet the anticipated criticism of his fellow-citizens.

First I must ask you to recall the service that Solon rendered to the state, the service that gained him his reputation. Faced with a desperate economic crisis, the result of a poor soil that refused to support the population, he eased the condition of the impoverished farmers and, in the interests of those to whom the land could not afford a livelihood, he injected new energy into the arts and crafts, manufacture and industry (Plutarch's word is τέχναι). It is generally assumed, rightly, I think, that Solon's chief concern was the ceramic industry, the making of pots and their export along with the oil that they contained. Plutarch's chapter 22 in his biography of Solon is significant in that within a single sentence he links three items: (1) the city was steadily becoming filled with people who poured into Attica from all quarters (these were the "other foreigners"); (2) the state had nothing to export; (3) he therefore directed the citizens into craftsmanship (τέχναι).

Solon, then, rebuilt the ceramic industry, partly to provide occupation for Athenians who had abandoned the land and who might otherwise find themselves idle in the city, partly to create goods for export. His success was instantaneous and spectacular. He diverted the urban idle into ceramics and yet a lack of skilled artisans at once became evident; hence his astonishing invitation to aliens. We cannot assume that he was enticing master-craftsmen as teachers; there had always been a ceramic industry at Athens and Solon was not instituting something new. Rather, he was thinking in broad terms; idle Athenians were absorbed and there was room for more hands. Even so, he acted cautiously. Citizenship was not offered to mere drifters, the "other foreigners" (τοὺς ἄλλους) whom according to Plutarch he was not trying to expel; these were the people who had poured aimlessly into Attica. On the contrary, he sought men of some substance and skill, who were potentially what we sometimes call good citizens ("these immigrants," in my translation). The desperate solution to his problem is assurance that the emergency itself was desperate.

There were powerful Athenians who had submitted only temporarily to Solon's flaunting of tradition. That they cherished their resentment is shown by Aristotle's report[4] of the civil strife that broke out soon after Solon's retirement from office and withdrawal from Athens. Three groups appeared in the contest for political domination that lasted for a generation. Two of these were the men of the plain (πεδιακοί) and the men of the shore (παράλιοι), whom we may loosely style Conservatives and Liberals; to these we scarcely need introduction. But now a third element entered Athenian politics, the men of the hills (διάκριοι). There had, we may guess, been radical Athenians before this, many of them oppressed and aggrieved; after Solon, for the first time we find them as a considerable political force with able and respected leadership. Peisistratos seems to have inspired confidence among the poor and discontented; in addition, says Aristotle, Peisistratos was joined by those whose descent was impure and their motive was fear (προσεκεκόσμηντο δὲ τούτοις . . . οἱ τῷ γένει μὴ καθαροὶ διὰ τὸν φόβον). Only one element in Athens could effectively be called impure in descent: the aliens invited to Athens and given citizenship by Solon. Their fear can be readily identified: that they would be deprived of their still precarious citizenship by the other parties or by one of those parties; we may be sure that this had been threatened. Thus we may perceive clearly where the ambitious Peisistratos looked for support and we can hear distinctly the promises he made: a New Deal for the "have-nots"; security for the new citizens. In a sense Solon guaranteed the rise of Peisistratos.

We hear no more of citizens, legitimate or illegitimate, until after the eviction from Athens of Hippias and his kinsmen in 511/0. The *silentium* invigorates the argument. Peisistratos and his son kept their promises. The new citizens and their descendants lived in peace. There is no doubt that the tyrants followed Solon in guarding the interests of the urban population. Probably more aliens came to the city. There is no evidence, however, that there were further grants of citizenship and it is unnecessary to invent such grants.

[4] 'Αθ. Πολ., 13, 4-5.

It is sometimes carelessly said that tyranny at Athens was succeeded by democracy. What really happened, as conscientious historians know, is that Athens experienced a significant interlude of oligarchy accompanied by political unrest. In the struggle that followed the departure of Hippias, two prominent Athenians emerged as leaders: Kleisthenes the Alkmaionid, whose versatile father had once led the men of the shore whom I have called Liberals, and Isagoras, the new champion of the Conservatives, or, to be up to date in my nomenclature, oligarchs. Kleisthenes was worsted and Isagoras found himself free to implement a programme.[5]

I have already quoted and explained Aristotle's statement that Peisistratos was supported by those of impure descent because they were afraid. Aristotle also believes that this fear requires exegesis. Whereas I glanced back Aristotle looks forward; anticipating history by about sixty years, he adds: "that they were afraid is proved by the fact that after the downfall of the tyrants the Athenians conducted a census, since many were participating in the citizenship inappropriately."[6]

I have identified the supporters of Peisistratos with Solon's beneficiaries; Aristotle astutely connects them directly with the census completed later in the century, when it must have been their lineal descendants who were in danger. Naturally, it was the oligarchic Conservatives who especially wished to defend the integrity of Athenian citizenship and who had not ceased to detest Solon's heterodoxy of long long ago. We are not informed in specific terms of Isagoras' policies. But we can reconstruct one: the census was his and he lost no time in putting it into effect. It was a fundamental plank in his platform; ultimately, it failed to support him.

The census deprived many of their citizenship and simultaneously proffered to the lagging Kleisthenes a second chance. Once again an ambitious politician accepted help where he found it. Very much as Peisistratos had done before him, Kleisthenes appealed to those who had been struck from the rolls,

<hr />

[5] Ἀθ. Πολ., 20, 1: ἡττώμενος δὲ ταῖς ἑταιρείαις ὁ Κλεισθένης.

[6] Ἀθ. Πολ., 13, 5: σημεῖον δ', ὅτι μετὰ τὴν τῶν τυράννων κατάλυσιν ἐποίησαν διαψηφισμόν, ὡς πολλῶν κοινωνούντων τῆς πολιτείας οὐ προσῆκον.

probably a substantial number, and promised them restoration and freedom from fear in the future. This is how Aristotle's words, "he wooed the *demos*,"[7] should be understood. Granted, his particular clients had lost their citizenship and so, technically, were not part of the *demos*. It mattered little in those turbulent months; they were many and perhaps dangerous. And probably they had the sympathy of their friends in the *demos*, which in this context must be understood not as the citizen-body but as the popular element in the citizen-body. Besides, Kleisthenes undoubtedly offered attractive prospects to the *demos* itself. Eventually, Kleisthenes was the victor. But Isagoras held the upper hand for some time, perhaps more than two years, at least until the beginning of the year 508/7, when he began the archonship to which he had been elected. He did not finish it. The ill-omened intervention of the Spartan king Kleomenes caused revulsion in Athens: Isagoras was exiled and Kleisthenes returned to work on his own programme without harassment.

Athenian politicians seem to have paid their debts and Kleisthenes was no exception. The repayment took the form of a comprehensive reorganisation of the political structure of Athens. This time the treatment would bring permanent cure. The complexities of the reconstitution of the tribes and therefore of political life will not here detain us. Kleisthenes' motives for so sweeping a reform, however, are part of our investigation. The new composition of the citizen-body in ten tribes rather than in the old four broke up existing blocs; political issues in the sixth and fifth centuries are not the same. The innovations allowed him to remove the emphasis from membership in the phratry as an indication of citizenship. Henceforth, the basic unit would be the deme, a local division of Attica that had no implication of kinship. The deme rather than the patronymic, which might suggest foreign antecedents, would suffice as an official designation of citizenship; enrolment in the deme became a legal criterion of citizenship.

In his study of Kleisthenes, Aristotle missed the point. He did not understand what Kleisthenes did or why he did it. His

---

[7] Ἀθ. Πολ., 20, 1: προσηγάγετο τὸν δῆμον. See also Herodotos, V, 66, 2.

failure has led many students from the truth. In a passage that is blatantly corrupt he says that Kleisthenes enrolled many aliens as citizens.[8] This paraphrase evades the corruption and does no violence to what Aristotle in fact wrote; his blunder may indeed have been more serious, for slaves are also present in the sentence. He has been interpreted, reasonably enough, as asserting that Kleisthenes converted non-citizens into citizens on a large scale. Now Aristotle was a Hellene and sufficiently familiar with Athenian concepts to be disconcerted, just as Plutarch was to be later, and for the same reason. So he takes the trouble to add that men may become citizens unjustly, in which case they are not really citizens at all.[9] The age-old feeling never quite attained oblivion.

The solution is simple and does not require discussion of the textual corruption. Kleisthenes' enrolment of citizens must be read in conjunction with the census promulgated by Isagoras. Kleisthenes did not admit new citizens; he restored to their citizenship those whose names had been deleted by Isagoras, that is, the descendants of the aliens invited by Solon, who to an Athenian conservative were still of impure descent ($\mu\dot{\eta}$ $\tau\hat{\omega}$ $\gamma\acute{\epsilon}\nu\epsilon\iota$ $\kappa\alpha\theta\alpha\rho o\acute{\iota}$).

E. M. Walker, to an extent following Grote, comes close to perceiving what happened and the connexion between Kleisthenes and Solon. He apparently believes, however, that resident aliens multiplied under the Peisistratids and later, and that these benefited from Kleisthenes' reform. "The object," he remarks, "of Cleisthenes in dissociating citizenship from the clan, and connecting it with the deme, was to facilitate the admission to citizenship of those who could not prove pure Athenian descent, and to render their position unassailable for the future." Restricted to those whose residence and citizenship went back to Solon, this is an accurate observation. What Walker appends shows that he has missed the vital and specific motivation of Kleisthenes' reform: "For half a century or more Athens remained faithful to the liberal policy of her great reformer, and her citizenship was open to those who had no claim to pure

---

[8] *Politics*, III, 1275b: πολλοὺς γὰρ ἐφυλέτευσε ξένους καὶ δούλους μετοίκους.
[9] *Politics*, III, 1276a: εἰ μὴ δικαίως πολίτης, οὐ πολίτης.

Athenian blood. It was left to the most famous democratic statesman of the ancient world—Pericles himself—to reverse the enlightened policy of his predecessor, and once more to impose the test of pure Athenian descent on both sides."[10] The second half of this assertion is contradicted by the evidence (to which I shall return), for the first half, with all its glamour, there is no evidence whatever.

The success of Kleisthenes' legislation may be judged by the final disappearance of the clients of Solon, Peisistratos, and Kleisthenes as a subject of political controversy. Perikles' law of 451/0 was unrelated to them.

Aristotle's report of the law is straightforward: "because of the number of citizens they voted on motion by Perikles that citizenship should be confined to those with citizen-fathers and citizen-mothers."[11] The discerning reader will note that women are citizens. That the number of citizens was growing by mid-century is demonstrable. There is a size beyond which a direct democracy cannot function efficiently; in fact, I have sometimes been awed by the accomplishments of a body, the *ekklesia*, in which the quorum was normally, I believe, 6,000. Perikles and other Athenians might well have been worried by the growth of the *demos*, the body of adult males eligible to attend the assembly. Yet, we ask, what effect could the law have upon this? And the answer is, no effect at all. The birth-rate was increasing and this could not be controlled by Perikles' law. We are entitled to conclude, then, that many aliens had surreptitiously inserted their names into the rolls of citizens. Such misdemeanours could always have been stopped and the perpetrators punished. Probably the state had been lax; illegal growth could no longer be tolerated and the law gave notice that in the future enforcement would be more rigorous. And so it was, as we shall see. But the law could not artificially limit citizenship, nor was it intended to do so. The citizens, in the prosperity of the times, continued to multiply.

One might, so far, argue that the law was futile. Still, there

---

[10] *The Cambridge Ancient History*, IV (Cambridge, 1930), pp. 145-146.

[11] Ἀθ. Πολ., 26, 4: ἐπὶ Ἀντιδότου διὰ τὸ πλῆθος τῶν πολιτῶν Περικλέους εἰπόντος ἔγνωσαν μὴ μετέχειν τῆς πόλεως ὃς ἂν μὴ ἐξ ἀμφοῖν ἀστοῖν ᾖ γεγονώς.

was more to it than a reaffirmation of existing law: from this time on an Athenian must prove that both father and mother were citizens. Here was a break with earlier practice. Now it is a curious fact that, while the aristocratic families had bitterly opposed the granting of citizenship to out and out aliens and its retention by their descendants, they had allowed their own young men to bring home foreign brides to be the mothers of citizens; so far as we hear, no protest had ever been uttered. Both Megakles and Hippokleides, of rival aristocratic families, had, about 575 B.C., sought the hand of Agariste, daughter of the tyrant of Sikyon. The date is worth consideration, for this was just the period in which Solon's new citizens foresaw danger to their tenure in Athens. Megakles had won the princess and the first-born son was that very Kleisthenes who had protected those of impure descent and built the democratic constitution in the last decade of the sixth century. No one will deny that Kleisthenes, son of a Sikyonian mother and one-time archon, was an Athenian citizen. How can we avoid the conclusion that, down to the time of Perikles' law, citizenship was inherited from the father alone, and that the state never did "impose the test of pure Athenian descent on both sides"? I remind you of Gomme's dictum, which, you may feel, I endorsed too hastily: "the nationality of the mother was as important as that of the father." The principle remains sound; this was the Athenian conviction, although it was not enacted as law until 451/0. The practice requires that Gomme's words be taken with some reservations, thanks to the aristocracy's habit of issuing its own dispensations while at the same time expressing indignation at the conduct of others. There is, after all, a difference between a man with an Athenian father and one with no acceptable parent at all. And in sixth-century Athens there was a difference between an aristocrat and a commoner.

We can identify other examples of foreign blood among the notable families; one thinks of Kimon, son of Miltiades' Thracian bride, and Thucydides the historian, son of Oloros, of the same family; his patronymic betrays his ancestry. Historians should be embarrassed to admit that there has been debate whether Perikles' law was retroactive. Obviously, it was not, for Kimon served as general after passage of the law. It did not affect those with unimpeachable claims to citizenship or those guaranteed security by Kleisthenes; nor did it "reverse the enlightened policy" of Kleisthenes, to which it had no reference.

Strictly, the mixed marriage defied Athenian principles. The precedent had been set by the Few in the sixth century. To what extent the Many followed this precedent in the fifth century we can only guess. I am prepared to believe that in the generation after the Persian invasions substantial numbers of young Athenians saw the world and liked what they saw—or whom they saw. The result was something like our own experience on this continent after the Second World War. Reaction to the imported bride in North America has sometimes been strongly hostile. Borrowing a hint from Gomme, I suspect that there developed in Athens a growing fear that many Athenian girls would be left without husbands. One needs little imagination to believe that Athenian mothers with marriageable daughters became increasingly vocal; and they would have been joined, of course, by fathers and brothers. The consequent domestic pressure would not have been trivial and would have helped to force passage of the law of 451/0, moved by Perikles himself. There might also have been a little malice. In earlier generations the foreign bride had been acceptable to the Few; the Many, perhaps, though they themselves had become involved, relished the law as a rebuke to the Few. Or possibly the Many had adopted the practice of the Few without discretion, had spoiled a good thing, so to speak, and forced action by the state. In any case, this aspect of the law was pertinent and no doubt effective, as Perikles himself was to discover. More, it may betray a hint of another motive: if the *demos* was to grow, which could scarcely be avoided, it became imperative that it be kept racially pure.

Discouragement of marriage with foreigners has been seen as a means of limiting the citizen-body. A moment's reflexion shows that this will not do. Apart from the fact that the law was not retroactive, obedience to the law would not increase bachelors or serve as a contraceptive. Young Athenians, concerned about the status of their future children, would simply

marry Athenian girls, who, we may presume, were no less fer-
tile than women from abroad, Hellenes or barbarians.

Perikles' law is dated firmly by Aristotle to the archonship
of Antidotos, 451/0 B.C. Six years later the Egyptian Psammetichos sent a generous gift of corn to Athens for distribution
among the citizens.[12] It has been claimed that the law should be
connected with the gift: an avaricious *demos*, with an eye on
their share of the distribution, voted to restrict citizenship. But
the interval of six years makes this view improbable. Men are
persistent, however, and, to avoid the dilemma, the proposal
has been made that the law should be re-dated to 445. On the
contrary, the two events were quite separate, that is, the law
had nothing to do with the gift.

Nevertheless, the gift did cause upheaval. The Athenians
held a διαψηφισμός, a scrutiny of the rolls of citizens, and, according to Philochoros, 4,760 names illegally present were
stricken.[13] Plutarch sees that the gift led to the scrutiny. Again,
the Athenians are accused of greed. The charge is ill-based. The
gift was for the citizens and it was reasonable to examine the
records. If Philochoros' figure is accurate (it has been questioned), we must surely assume that this was the first rigorous
examination since passage of Perikles' law. That no scrutiny had
been held after approval of the law is perhaps surprising. The
gift put an end to delay and the result, the discovery of 4,760
pseudo-citizens, supplies the principal motivation for the law;
indeed, it justifies the law. There *were* many enrolled who had
no right to citizenship. Those whose liberal feelings are pained
by the scrutiny should be reminded that in our society an election is normally preceded by a revision of the voters' list. There
are certain privileges that belong to citizens alone. This is not
to deny that unworthy motives may have excited some of the
prosecutions that occurred in Athens.

The law was embodied in the Athenian code and the scrutiny
provoked no violent objections. In the last year of his life
Perikles, having lost both his legitimate sons, pleaded that his

---

[12] Philochoros, frag. 119 Jacoby (schol. Aristophanes, *Wasps*, 718); Plutarch,
Pericles, 37, 3.
[13] Philochoros, frag. 119; Plutarch, *Pericles*, 37, 4.

son by Aspasia be enrolled as a citizen in contravention of his own law. The *demos* granted his plea.[14] There were no protests; every Athenian understood the principle: a citizen was one who had always inhabited the land. No one else had a right to citizenship, which might occasionally be voted as a special privilege.

The law of Perikles and the Athenian ideas of citizenship have caused great distress among historians, from whom I select a few sentences. The Athenians' "conception of political democracy was a partial one, not extending to women, aliens or slaves within the state or relations with other states, hence huge resources of co-operative energy, devotion to the common good, and potential leadership were left untapped."[15] The law "is just as likely to reflect a desire on the part of the privileged to limit their own numbers in response to an increase in the value of their privileges."[16] ". . . it may seem a paradox that the name of the most famous champion of the popular cause in the ancient world should be associated with a measure which seems to the modern mind so essentially undemocratic . . . few measures of constitutional reform at Athens have a better right to be called reactionary. Cleisthenes had broken down the old barriers which excluded, not only the resident alien, but the offspring of mixed marriages" (we have already seen that this is not true). The law "meant the assertion of the principle of privilege in its most offensive form. It proclaimed that the Empire existed for the benefit of Athens."[17]

We had better look cold-bloodedly at political democracy. What is it? To a Hellene—and why not to a modern?—it is government by the *demos*, the citizen-body; it is government in which all the citizens (adult males in Athens) have equal privilege. It goes without saying that in a democracy citizenship may not be restricted arbitrarily. I contend that there is nothing arbitrary about an age-old tradition that defines citizenship as a privilege and responsibility to be enjoyed by those who be-

[14] Plutarch, *Pericles*, 37, 2 and 5.

[15] W. R. Agard, *What Democracy Meant to the Greeks* (Madison, Wis., 1960), p. 256.

[16] A. French, *The Growth of the Athenian Economy* (New York, 1964), p. 148.

[17] Walker, *C.A.H.*, V (1935), pp. 102-103.

long to the *polis*, the state, those who possess "Athenianness," if I may invent a word. We are willing to give our citizenship to an alien after five years of residence, an act of faith that would have seemed unnatural to an Athenian. We on our part are entitled to wonder why generations of residence could not imbue an alien's family with "Athenianness." We may term this over-conservative; what we have no right to do is for this reason to call the Athenian conception of political democracy a partial one. Democracy does not depend on the privileges and responsibilities allotted to outlanders. And let us not forget that our own system, to an Athenian, is oligarchy. It is not necessary in this audience, I hope, to extend the argument in order to demonstrate that the relationship with the Empire has nothing to do with political democracy. Incidentally, it is an indulgence of the imagination to think that citizens of the states of the Empire even wanted Athenian citizenship.

I have no objections to referring to citizens as "the privileged," on the condition that the term carries no unpleasant connotation. The citizen had privilege; he also had responsibility. The privileged, as citizens, could not and did not limit their own numbers; they did agree that infiltration by foreigners should be stopped. Whether they did this in response to an increase in the value of their privileges is debatable. There are chronological problems, to one of which, the interval between the law and the gift by Psammetichos, I have already alluded. The law was passed in 451/0, before the peace with Persia, before the colony to Brea, perhaps before despatch of most of the klerouchies. It is too facile, I think, even in a democracy, always to seek the personal and selfish motive, especially when another explanation, based upon tradition and far more credible, is ready to hand. The simple answer is often the right answer.

Perikles, that famous champion of the popular cause, was an Athenian. He expressed a popular conviction that had never gone out of style. This is proved not only by the fact that the law was passed by the *ekklesia* but also by the absence of reaction later. Kleisthenes had broken down no barriers. He had merely eliminated a specific problem, at the same time furthering his own ambitions. Walker sees an "organic connection" between the introduction of pay (the date of which we do not know) and the restriction of the franchise by Perikles. He writes of Greek democracy as "not the overthrow of privilege, but merely the extension of its area." This interpretation, if it is pertinent at all, seems to me little more than a desperate and superfluous attempt to defend an already innocent democracy. We do not have to consider the Empire, whether it existed for the benefit of Athens, because this has nothing to do with the purpose of the law. The Empire, I concede, may have contributed to the prosperity that attracted so many aliens to Athens. If many of these had their names inserted illegally into the rolls of citizens, the resulting situation could have made an investigation, and in due course the law, inevitable.

Finally, there is nothing undemocratic about a law that restricts citizenship to those who are genuinely citizens by descent. (I do not argue whether the policy is wise or unwise.) It is comforting, however, to have a villain and I am prepared to make a nomination. In a series of incidents that are thoroughly comprehensible in their contexts and motives, we find our villain in Solon, who has no defence against a charge of un-Athenian activities.

II. SHIPS AND CASH:
THUCYDIDES, I, 96

Παραλαβόντες δὲ οἱ Ἀθηναῖοι τὴν ἡγεμονίαν τούτῳ τῷ τρόπῳ
ἑκόντων τῶν ξυμμάχων διὰ τὸ Παυσανίου μῖσος, ἔταξαν ἅς τε ἔδει
παρέχειν τῶν πόλεων χρήματα πρὸς τὸν βάρβαρον καὶ ἃς ναῦς·
πρόσχημα γὰρ ἦν ἀμύνεσθαι ὧν ἔπαθον δῃοῦντας τὴν βασιλέως χώραν. καὶ Ἑλληνοταμίαι τότε πρῶτον Ἀθηναίοις κατέστη
ἀρχή, οἳ ἐδέχοντο τὸν φόρον· οὕτω γὰρ ὠνομάσθη τῶν χρημάτων ἡ φορά. ἦν δ' ὁ πρῶτος φόρος ταχθεὶς τετρακόσια τάλαντα
καὶ ἑξήκοντα. ταμιεῖόν τε Δῆλος ἦν αὐτοῖς, καὶ αἱ ξύνοδοι ἐς τὸ
ἱερὸν ἐγίγνοντο.

Thucydides is our fundamental source for the first congress of
the Athenians and their allies on Delos in the winter of 478/7
B.C. Yet, despite the value of what he tells us in I, 96 and elsewhere in the *pentekontaetia*, there is much that he omits, with
the result that we are forced, in reconstructing the detail, to
summon the aid not only of Aristotle and Plutarch[1] but also of
the non-literary evidence, in particular, the assessment-lists and
quota-lists of the Athenian Empire. In recent years I have enjoyed many discussions with colleagues about the formation of
the Confederacy of Delos and its early history and these have
persuaded me that it is worth while undertaking another examination of Thucydides' crucial chapter and its implications.[2]

The latest published study is by Mortimer Chambers, who,
in a paper entitled "Four Hundred Sixty Talents," concludes
that Thucydides "was wrong when he wrote, as he probably
did, that the first *phoros* of the League was 460 T."[3] In reaching this judgment Chambers makes the following points: (1)
the activities described in I, 96 are set out in chronological order; (2) the figure 460 talents was meant by Thucydides to
exclude the value of contributions in ships; (3) it would have

---

[1] Aristotle, Ἀθ. Πολ., 23, 5; Plutarch, *Aristeides*, 24.

[2] These colleagues include John Crook, Mortimer Chambers, A. H. M. Jones,
A. E. Raubitschek, William Wallace, A. G. Woodhead, C. W. J. Eliot, Benjamin
D. Meritt, and D. W. Bradeen. Some disagreed, all helped me.

[3] *Class. Phil.*, LIII (1958), pp. 26-32; the quotation is from p. 30. See also
Classical World, LVII (1963), p. 10.

been difficult to express in cash the obligation of a contributor of ships; (4) no reference to ships is found in any assessment-list. Chambers is not alone in his opinions, as my conversations with others have shown; he is a convenient target, however, because he has been good enough to put his views into print.

B. D. Meritt, H. T. Wade-Gery, and McGregor, on the other hand, as well as A. W. Gomme, accepting the figure given by Thucydides, have maintained that 460 talents was the total obligation of the allies assessed in the first instance in cash according to each member's resources; that the division into those who were to supply ships and those who were to contribute in cash followed the determination of the assessment.[4]

The lines of combat are sharply drawn and it remains for me to try to enlist you as allies of the right side.

Thucydides does not tell us much about the machinery involved in the financial arrangements in 478/7 or later. He says nothing of any other assessment, nothing of an original assessment of ships. He mentions commutation by the allies from ships to cash in I, 99, his well-known chapter on the causes of revolt; he notes the change as a punitive measure after the revolt of Thasos and we assume the same treatment for Naxos, which revolted rather earlier.[5] But all commutation was not a consequence of revolt; many allies saw that less hardship was incurred by payment of cash than by personal naval service and were allowed, or encouraged, to change their method of support. Thucydides omits the moving of the treasury from Delos to Athens in 454 B.C., which we regard as a significant act in the development of the Athenian Empire; Plutarch includes it[6] in an anecdote about Aristeides and it is guaranteed by the first quota-list, which was inscribed in Athens in the spring of 453. Nor does he describe as such the drawing up of the charter of the Confederacy or the swearing of the oaths; this last we find in Aristotle,[7] although, to be sure, Thucydides implies the

---

[4] *The Athenian Tribute Lists*, III (Princeton, 1950), especially pp. 229-230, 234-237; *A Historical Commentary on Thucydides*, I (Oxford, 1945), p. 284.

[5] I, 101, 3 (Thasos) and 98, 4 (Naxos).

[6] *Aristeides*, 25, 2.

[7] Ἀθ. Πολ., 23, 5.

oaths when he writes that Naxos was subjugated in contravention of the established agreement.[8]

Obviously, Thucydides' omissions do not necessarily signify ignorance on his part. In reference to the first congress on Delos, however, although he may have seen some of the relevant documents (the charter may have been engraved on Delos), we may still ask how much he knew; that is, were there not some details that he did not know? Did he know, for example, the value assigned to a ship (if there was one)? Had he seen a full roster of the original membership? Did he know the order of business at the first congress, had he scrutinised the agenda? Had he examined what we should call the minutes? All this demanded research, of which, indeed, he was capable.

Some knowledge he had, or he could not have written chapter 96. But the answers to my questions are probably negative in all cases. Yet the questions are irrelevant and were so for Thucydides. We are not justified in supposing that I, 96 reflects the order in which the delegates transacted their business or even the historical order of events, which is not the same thing. What we have in this chapter is a selection made by Thucydides of the results of the congress that he deemed appropriate to his purpose. These results he knew, as did a great many other interested persons: the assessed *phoros* amounted, all told, to 460 talents; some paid their obligations in ships, some in cash; Athenian *hellenotamiai*, stewards of the Hellenes' money, were by common consent to watch over the treasury on Delos; the synods met in the precinct on that island. The first congress, having organised itself, passed enabling resolutions and Thucydides incorporates in his *History*, although not comprehensively, what happened in consequence; but the order of composition in this chapter is almost accidental, it has no special historical meaning.

The narrative of the *pentekontaetia* proper, in which Thucydides describes, in scrupulously strict chronological order, the growth of the Athenian Empire, begins in I, 98. In I, 97, which he composed later as an introduction, he assures us that he has avoided the chronological inaccuracies of Hellanikos. The open-

---

[8] I, 98, 4: παρὰ τὸ καθεστηκός.

ing word of I, 98 is πρῶτον, "first of all." Chapter 96 is not part of this narrative; rather, it is descriptive, it comprises the stage-setting, and the author is not committed to any particular chronological pattern. Chapter 99, the excursus on revolt, is similarly descriptive; it is not part of the narrative of events but ranges in its application over a fairly long period of time.

No one will deny that the planning implicit in I, 96 occurred on Delos. Yet Thucydides does not name the island until the last sentence, and it is almost as an after-thought that he links Delos to the synods. One may, I think, reconstruct Thucydides' train of thought and so understand why he made the selection that he did make. Chapter 95 leads to the opening of 96: "This is how the Athenians took over leadership of willing allies" (παραλαβόντες . . . τὴν ἡγεμονίαν τούτῳ τῷ τρόπῳ ἑκόντων τῶν ξυμμάχων). These allies were divided (when is immaterial here) into two classes: "the Athenians decided which should contribute cash and which ships" (ἔταξαν ἅς τε . . . χρήματα . . . καὶ ἃς ναῦς). Money and ships need explanation: "for it was their intention to lay waste the King's land" (πρόσχημα γὰρ ἦν . . . δῃοῦντας τὴν βασιλέως χώραν). The money had to be stewarded: "hellenotamiai were established and they received the phoros" (Ἑλληνοταμίαι . . . κατέστη . . . οἳ ἐδέχοντο τὸν φόρον). Here is a technical word that asks for definition: "this is what the contribution of the money was called" (. . . τῶν χρημάτων ἡ φορά). The reader should know what the assessed total of the phoros was: "the first assessment of phoros came to 460 talents" (ἦν δ' ὁ πρῶτος φόρος ταχθείς). There had to be a depository for the money: "Delos was their treasury" (ταμιεῖόν τε Δῆλος ἦν αὐτοῖς). "Delos, of course, was the site of the meetings" (αἱ ξύνοδοι ἐς τὸ ἱερὸν ἐγίγνοντο; the plural embraces the future).

This, I suggest, is how Thucydides thought; to contend that he deliberately preserves the order of business is unjustified and probably imputes to him knowledge that he lacked. Further, it applies the acknowledged chronological principles of his pentekontaetia to a passage that does not belong to it. What he does include, however, was familiar to many Hellenes and the same is true of some of his omissions: the formal election of Athens (through her representative) as chairman, the entrusting of the assessment to Aristeides, the swearing of the oaths, the compilation of a roster of membership.

I digress for a moment to look a second time at the clause that I have rendered as "it was their intention to lay waste the King's land." The noun for "intention" is πρόσχημα and, according to one proposal,[9] it may mean "that this was only the specious claim of the Athenians." This interpretation charges ulterior imperialistic motives to the Athenians as early as 478, which is difficult to credit. I take the sentence as explanatory of the intentions of the allies; this was why they invited the Athenians to lead them, this was largely the purpose of the new Confederacy. Athens was not alone in having suffered at the hands of the King.

To return to the argument. No classification of allies could have been contemplated until the purpose of the organisation had been established and the necessity for resources agreed upon. How division could have been made before assessment had been carried out is not easy to understand; who knew which states could endure a future assessment in ships? Many vessels had been destroyed in the recent campaigns and Aristeides could not have known the surviving naval strength in each case. Before any assessment could be finally determined Aristeides had work to do and his visits of inspection to various parts of the Confederacy and his computation of equitable levies occupied part of the winter. How much we cannot say. The preparation of a rough draft of assessment on Delos and familiarity with what the Persians had done where the results were available could have eased his labours. He assessed according to each state's resources and capacity: κατ' ἀξίαν ἑκάστῳ καὶ δύναμιν.[10] It is an attractive thesis that Aristeides borrowed the survey of the Ionian states that had been conducted by Artaphrenes the Persian as a basis for taxation after the Ionian revolt. If so, there are two items to be remembered: (1) the survey, according to Herodotos,[11] was of the land; (2) there were many char-

[9] Chambers, *Class. Phil.*, LIII (1958), p. 31, note 5.
[10] Plutarch, *Aristeides*, 24, 1.
[11] VI, 42, 2.

ter-members of the Confederacy of Delos who were not Ionians. Possibly the same enterprise was completed by the Persians in Aiolis, Karia, and the Hellespont; Herodotos does not say so. In any case, there still remained places where Aristeides was compelled to make his own survey, though he may have taken advantage of the base chosen by Artaphrenes. The Persian survey of the land was to yield an assessment expressed in cash (*phoros*); Aristeides surely employed the same system. A member's comparative wealth might be ill represented by the number of warships she had available and assessments in two commodities could have produced inequities, to say nothing of confusion. My version of Plutarch's phrase is deliberately neutral: "according to each state's resources and capacity." Perrin, uninfluenced by controversy, translates: "according to each member's worth and ability to pay." He is probably right. I do not emphasise that ἀξία, in such a context as this, usually connotes value or worth in money. So commitments were first "reckoned in terms of that universal common denominator, cash."[12] Only then could a separation be made between those who were able (and chose) to contribute in ships and those who would contribute in cash because they were unable (or unwilling) to contribute in ships. In 478 there may even have been an element of choice; there could hardly, in that enlightened and enthusiastic atmosphere, have been compulsion.

Finally, if the order of I, 96 reflects the order of business (or action) and if the assessed *phoros* of that chapter excludes the obligations of naval members, there is a glaring omission in what Thucydides recalls. We expect the following developments: (1) the Athenians decided which states should contribute ships and which cash; (2) the assessed cash amounted to x talents; (3) the assessed ships amounted to y. We have (1) and (2); is not the absence of (3) intolerable? Does it not suggest that the assessed contribution (φόρος ταχθείς) is a comprehensive figure? It may be answered that the argument is *e silentio*; possibly so, yet it seems to me a logical question to address to those who insist that the chapter reports the order of events and that the assessed *phoros* excludes naval assessment.

[12] *A. T. L.*, III, p. 236.

My own belief is that the order is irrelevant; probably, the assessment preceded the division.

Although we reconstruct the charter of the Confederacy mostly from Thucydides, we should not forget that I, 96 is an amalgamation of what was decided at the meeting and what happened later. The synod agreed on policy, as Thucydides says ("to take vengeance for what they had suffered"). The synod agreed that there must be an assessment; Thucydides confirms that an assessment (one) was compiled, not that it was implemented. The synod probably agreed that some (unidentified) should contribute ships, some (unidentified) cash; Thucydides reports that the Athenians acted upon this decision and in fact separated the two classes of members. The synod agreed that *hellenotamiai* should be appointed by the Athenians as stewards of the funds to come; Thucydides assures us that the Athenians responded to the request (it is most improbable that the appointments were made on Delos during the conference). The only list assembled (and this is not in Thucydides) must have been a roster of membership, which was indispensable to Aristeides. Again, then, I cannot believe that Thucydides' rather miscellaneous summary reproduces the order either of decisions or of activation.

I pass on to Thucydides' statement about the assessment, in which he transmits information that could have been accumulated only after the meeting: ἦν δ' ὁ πρῶτος φόρος ταχθεὶς τετρακόσια τάλαντα καὶ ἑξήκοντα. Chambers translates: "The first collection of money which was assessed was 460 T." It has been suggested to him "that the words ἦν . . . ταχθείς comprise a periphrastic pluperfect passive, and should be translated, 'The first collection *had been assessed* at 460 T.'" But Thucydides says nothing at all about collection and it is misleading to give the impression, by translation, that he does; neither version is acceptable. In the pertinent sense of the verb, one cannot assess a collection; one may assess the *phoros*, assess a tax, decide the amount due (φόρον τάττειν ταῖς πόλεσιν) and hope for the best. In 478/7, no doubt, hopes were largely realised, although it is a question whether Thucydides knew what was collected.

The weight of the phrase ὁ πρῶτος φόρος ταχθείς lies undoubtedly in the participle: "the first assessment of *phoros* amounted to 460 talents."[13] If Thucydides had reported the assessment of 425/4, the published copy of which he saw on marble, he might have done so in these terms: ἦν δ' ὁ φόρος ταχθεὶς χίλια καὶ τετρακόσια τάλαντα καὶ ἑξήκοντα. The words ὁ φόρος ταχθείς are thus the literary equivalent of the familiar heading of an assessment list (*e.g.*, A9): τάχσις φόρο. In 425/4 the Athenians did not gather the assessed *phoros* of 1460 talents, yet the words I have inserted into Thucydides' manuscript are quite accurate. In 478/7 the *taxis* came to 460 talents; in 425/4 it totalled 1460. In each case the assessment was expressed in cash, in talents.

The connotation of the word φόρος changed during the fifth century. Coming from φέρω, it ought not implicitly to mean money; "contribution" is probably the best English version in the early years of the Confederacy, when it had no unpleasant ring; the *phoros* of the naval allies was ships. It has been proposed to me in conversation that, since operations were to be primarily naval, an assessment in ships is conceivable. That this is not true of 478/7 is proved by tally of the assessment in talents, cash. Thucydides would have had no reason to translate ships into cash, a preposterous thought. Besides, not all the members possessed ships; all, presumably, had money. As time went on, φόρος lost its innocuous connotation and became synonymous, to some at least, with Athenian oppression; it meant cash and we may legitimately (after, say, the Peace of Kallias in 449) render it as "tribute." It is worth noting that the English word is not without ambiguity. The term, however, should be avoided in the context of the Delian Confederacy so long as the latter functioned according to its original principles, with Athens leading autonomous allies who made policy in common synods. So evil did the reputation of the word φόρος become that in the charter of the Second Athenian Confederacy (378/7) σύνταξις replaced it; but there was no essential difference between the φόρος of 478/7 and the σύνταξις of a century later.

---

[13] I was once taught to call the similar and common Latin construction by the label *urbs capta*, a phrase that was used as a model.

The safe course, in the glamour of the early years, is to transliterate φόρος into English.

Thucydides grew to manhood in the heyday of the Empire; he had seen the records of τάξεις φόρου after 454/3. He and Herodotos make no chronological distinction: φόρος in 478/7 was the same as φόρος in 431; it was cash, it was "tribute." Thucydides knew of the first assessment and he surely knew the figure 460. When he uses the term *phoros* of 478/7, he is writing from knowledge; when he equates the word with τῶν χρημάτων ἡ φορά ("the contribution of the money"), he is writing under the influence of his own day, when φόρος meant cash and nothing else. Thucydides realised quite well that many of the allies contributed ships. Nevertheless he considered φόρος appropriate for the first assessment. Consequently he should not be interpreted to mean that the Athenians "assessed their allies to bring in 460 T of cash"; rather, the Athenians constructed an assessment expressed in cash that added up to 460 talents. Thucydides' terminology is accurate; he is reporting a τάξις. This does not preclude the later translation of some of the entries into ships, although there need not have been a literal translation, so to speak, an exact correspondence in value between the assessment in money and the ships of a given member. What the use of the word φόρος by Thucydides here *proves* is that the original assessment was made initially and wholly in cash. But one may wonder whether Thucydides knew how many talents found their way to the treasury in 477.

The assessment that was produced in 478/7 was unique: it was the first of its kind, it was part of the process of organisation, it was probably the only occasion on which *all* the allies were included in a single list, and, whether or not the members borrowed from earlier Persian operations (we think they did), there was no regular method of procedure or of keeping records available as a model. Finally, the assessment established a general pattern for the future. Athenian and allied inexperience in 478/7 is matched by our own ignorance today when we grapple with reconstruction; we have the advantage of knowing at least some of what happened later. Aristeides, we suppose, compiled a roster of the allies; he did some conferring and some travelling in order to assess κατ' ἀξίαν ἑκάστῳ καὶ δύναμιν. The rôle of assessor had been entrusted to the Athenians, that is, to Aristeides, as Aristotle says: τοὺς φόρους οὗτος ἦν ὁ τάξας ταῖς πόλεσιν.[14] So had the responsibility of dividing the assessed allies into categories, information that we owe to Thucydides: ἔταξαν ἅς τε ἔδει παρέχειν τῶν πόλεων χρήματα . . . καὶ ἃς ναῦς. The two sentences nicely illustrate the two meanings of τάττειν and their respective constructions. Perhaps Aristeides had been given power to act by the *demos* or synod (we do not know). In any case, the complete transaction required time, whatever preliminary agreements were voted by the synod.

There is no evidence that any permanent record of these operations was made on Delos. No doubt records of some sort were kept on perishable materials and in the same way the *hellenotamiai*, appointed by the Athenians (in Athens), noted the contributions in cash as they were delivered. We may ask, was a record inscribed of ships prepared for confederate service? Possibly; but in the absence of any evidence after 454 in assessment-lists and quota-lists, we may suppose that no public record was deemed necessary. The information must, of course, have entered the archives, whose existence we should take for granted.

Without doubt several states joined the Confederacy during the winter of 478/7. They too were assessed according to their resources and Aristeides decided whether each should accept responsibility for ships or cash. Thucydides' figure probably includes the assessments of all those recruits who entered before the deadline, the opening of the campaigning season of 477 B.C. Once the confederates went into action, there were bound to be further adherents. Some joined voluntarily; Karystos and others were brought in under compulsion, always to pay cash, for they could not be trusted to supply ships. These too had to be assessed, by an Athenian board, I imagine (assessment was later the function of the τάκται), on the scale of the assessment of Aristeides, who had established a tolerable base.

In the years between 477 and 454 many, perhaps most, naval allies commuted their obligations from ships to cash; there were

[14] Ἀθ. Πολ., 23, 5.

fourteen survivors, we think.[15] Some, encouraged by Kimon, made the change peaceably; others revolted and, after subjection, perforce contributed cash (*e.g.*, Naxos and Thasos). How was the amount determined? Thucydides says:[16] χρήματα ἐτάξαντο ἀντὶ τῶν νεῶν τὸ ἱκνούμενον ἀνάλωμα φέρειν, "they accepted assessments in cash as their appropriate contributions in place of their ships." If cities like Naxos and Thasos had originally been assessed in monetary terms, though in fact they despatched ships, then all that was needed when they changed their status was a glance at the original assessment.

That Naxos, Thasos, and others (who were encouraged) could commute easily to an "appropriate" sum may at first glance suggest that a rough equation was known; but it may have been no more than rough, so long as the original assessment was accessible. Chambers says that, in the cases of those who changed their status, "the money payments were set approximately at what they had been spending on ships." This cannot be so. Working from his initial thesis (that the assessment preserved by Thucydides excluded the responsibilities of naval members), he is led to write, "it is not immediately easy to see how Aristides or the Athenians would have expressed a state's ship obligation in terms of cash"; he perceives, I suspect, that naval costs must have varied from season to season. It would have been impossible to anticipate naval expenses in a given campaign and booty was another unknown quantity. This was also true for later recruits. But, if we posit an original assessment of all members in cash, the difficulties vanish. The assessment was computed κατ' ἀξίαν ἑκάστῳ καὶ δύναμιν. Certain members, because they possessed warships and were eager, were detailed to supply vessels of war. The numbers required from one year to another must have varied. The naval ally, then, might have been asked to supply, on demand, a squadron of a stipulated maximum in size, perhaps according to an approximate equation, perhaps according to its naval resources (not necessarily the same thing); not all ships on call would be mustered each year. Athenian contingents would also have

---

[15] *A. T. L.*, III, pp. 267-268.
[16] I, 99, 3.

varied in strength; the force levied depended upon the nature of the contemplated campaign. When Naxos was compelled to fulfill her obligations in cash, the original figure was a matter of record. When new members joined, they were assessed κατὰ τὴν Ἀριστείδου τάξιν (*i.e.*, κατ᾽ ἀξίαν ἑκάστῳ καὶ δύναμιν). If we wish to be inhumane, we shall acknowledge that, economically, the continuous responsibility of paying a set annual sum was heavier than the varying annual call for ships and men. Human life, however, cannot be given a cash-value and this, I am sure, is why so many allies preferred the annual payment in cash.

That there was an assessment of the allies in 478/7 we learn from Thucydides and Aristotle; that an assessment was conducted in Athens for the first time in 454/3 we know because the first quota-list of a numbered and dated series presupposes it. This was the assessment cited, we believe (not all agree), by Krateros. From now on the Athenians formally reassessed the allies every four years on the average. We are not informed about the procedure in 454/3 and our knowledge of the mechanics of assessment comes from the quota-lists, a later assessment-list along with accompanying and informative decrees (A9 of 425/4), and certain Athenian enactments (*e.g.*, the decree of Kleinias, voted in 448/7) concerning the imperial administration. In 454/3 there must have been extensive reorganisation and innovation: *taktai* (assessors) were appointed (this is a guess), dedication of the quotas (ἀπαρχαί) to Athena was instituted, and the list of these quotas was to be engraved on marble. Procedure would be systematic.

What shall we say of the years between 477 and 454? Were there reassessments? What records were maintained? To these questions and to others we can give no answers subject to proof; we can do no more than conjecture. The *phoros* levied in Aristeides' day (ὁ ἐπ᾽ Ἀριστείδου θόρος) or, for new members, on the scale of Aristeides' assessment (κατὰ τὴν Ἀριστείδου τάξιν) was looked upon later as a model of justice and temperance. It is not unlikely (and I am convinced) that the original assessment was observed without revision until the treasury was moved and the Athenians undertook the confederate administration, which was to become imperial, as a normal function of the state; a mechanism was devised and records were kept as a matter of course, including public, and therefore permanent, audits of the quotas. We have no evidence that documents were brought from Delos, although they might have been and Thucydides might have consulted them. Nothing in his text implies that he did so, except, perhaps, his citation of 460 talents. But this was a notable figure, which must have been familiar to any interested person.

The quota-list of 454/3, the first such record to be engraved (certainly at Athens), publishes an audited account of the ἀπαρχαί, the first-fruits or sixtieths, not the delivered φόροι; the latter were entered in the books (the σανίδες, wooden tablets?) but not entrusted to the mason. Are we to believe that in this year the ἀπαρχαί were set aside for the first time? That is, had ἀπαρχαί been paid to Apollo on Delos? John P. Barron, in an interesting study entitled "Religious Propaganda of the Delian League," appears to look upon the payment of ἀπαρχαί in 454/3 as a novelty. ". . . the proposal to move the treasury from Delos to Athens was made by the Samians themselves. As newly appointed patron of the League, Athena Polias received an *aparche* of the annual tribute immediately from the outset of the new arrangements. The Samian motion in the League synod must therefore have provided for the payments to Athena as well as for the transfer of funds to her keeping."[17] Definitive answers cannot be given but I am attracted by Barron's daring (he may be right) in proposing that the ἀπαρχαί were one of the Athenian innovations in 454/3, pious offerings to Athena, loosely akin to the cow and the panoply that all the allies were (later?) instructed to bring to the Great Panathenaia; an Athenian innovation even though the amounts were registered in the names of the allies.

In the first year of the Confederacy (478/7) some contributed in ships; but, according to my thesis, there was no mention of ships in the assessment-list. When the roster itself was drawn up, the assessors (*i.e.*, Aristeides) could probably not identify precisely which allies would supply ships. To assess

[17] J. H. S., LXXXIV (1964), pp. 35-48, especially 48.

uniformly in cash was the obvious and simple way. In a sense a pattern was set in 478/7 that was to last for nearly a quarter of a century. The year of the charter was the only one in which an arrangement was necessary whereby some assessments in cash veiled obligations that were in the outcome to be fulfilled in ships. It is very doubtful if those who newly joined the Confederacy in the campaigns that followed included any naval allies at all; the tendency after 478/7 was certainly to reduce the existing number. In the extant quota-lists and assessments there is no trace of ships. The *hellenotamiai*, from the beginning, stewarded the *phoros*, in Thucydides' sense of the word ($\dot{\epsilon}\delta\dot{\epsilon}$-χοντο τὸν φόρον). Since, in my judgment, there had been no reassessment since 478/7, the Athenians in 454 found no precedent for any mention of ships in an assessment of *phoros*. Nor, incidentally, is there evidence that a naval ally ever paid the *aparche*.

The assessment of 454/3, which broke new ground in that it was the first to be completed in Athens, did not include the remaining naval allies in any guise and in this respect differed from its only predecessor, that of 478/7. The critic may ask why this was so and what record was kept of naval responsibilities, owed and delivered. I reconstruct and at the same time summarise as follows. The assessment of 478/7 was drawn up in cash because naval allies could not be precisely identified. When campaigning began in the spring, many of the allies manned ships; the maximum number had been agreed upon in each case by the assessing power and the ally. By 454/3 only fourteen were classed as naval. But the τάξις φόρου, according to precedent, dealt in cash only; more than that, it was to realise cash only. Because the naval allies were now identifiable, as were their exact obligations, there was no need to give them a temporary home among their moneyed brethren. Their relationship to the Confederacy, or, more properly perhaps, to Athens, belonged to a separate administrative transaction. They paid no money for Athena to watch over, consequently no *aparche* was dedicated to the goddess, there was no account to be audited. Naval records there *may* have been, entrusted to the archives; nothing, however, was published on marble. I do not overlook the possibility of a very loose pact between Athens and the naval allies, whereby the latter's squadrons joined the fleet only upon call.[18] In 428 the Mytilenaians appealed to the Spartans in suggestive words: "the allies, with the exception of the Chians and ourselves, were subjugated. We, who were indeed autonomous and free in name, joined the expeditions."[19] Those who were still contributing ships in the first assessment-period of the new era (454/3-451/0) have been identified in part by their absence from the corresponding quota-lists. We take one step further: they did not, therefore, appear in the assessment. It is a pity that we possess no fragments of the assessments inscribed before 425/4, although we believe that Krateros quoted from that of 454/3.

I am convinced and I have argued that Thucydides wrote 460 talents and that he understood this as the value in cash of the total assessment of all the allies. My argument has been partly linguistic and in part based upon probability. Some may feel that the case is not conclusively proved. There is, however, other evidence of a different kind: the quota-lists of the first assessment-period, 454/3-451/0. This investigation has been set out in detail in *The Athenian Tribute Lists*, III, and I here summarise rather than repeat all the arguments and figures.[20] What I emphasise is that the study was undertaken independently of Thucydides' 460 talents. Only after conclusions had been reached were comparisons made with his total.

Using the evidence that we possess, chiefly the lists that begin in 454/3, we identified an original membership in the Confederacy of over 140 states. We then assessed these charter-members, taking it for granted that all were assessed in cash and that no significant change had been made in Aristeides'

[18] Between 477 and the siege of Samos Thucydides often mentions allied contingents. He gives numbers only twice: twenty-five ships from Chios and Lesbos at Samos (I, 116, 2), followed by another thirty (I, 117, 2). Routine cruising must have been frequent.

[19] Thucydides, III, 10, 5: οἱ ξύμμαχοι ἐδουλώθησαν πλὴν ἡμῶν καὶ Χίων· ἡμεῖς δὲ αὐτόνομοι δὴ ὄντες καὶ ἐλεύθεροι τῷ ὀνόματι ξυνεστρατεύσαμεν.

[20] A. T. L. III, pp. 19-28 ("The Assessment of 454/3 B.C."), 194-224 ("The Original Membership of the Confederacy"), 234-243 ("The Assessment of 478/7 B.C."), 265-274 ("The Collection of 454/3 B.C.").

scale before 446. Chios, Lesbos, and Samos were charter-members but, since they never paid *phoros* and we therefore have no later figures, we were compelled to estimate their original assessment, which we placed at 30 talents each, on the analogy of Aigina, another large island; no assessment exceeded 30 talents before 425. Our computations yielded an assessment in 478/7 of a little more than 493 talents. If we place this sum alongside Thucydides' 460 talents, the total is high. Yet, in the light of the nature of our evidence, which comes from a quarter of a century later, and the inevitable unknowns, *e.g.*, the assessments of the three large islands, it does not seem to me unreasonably high. More, it is close enough to inspire confidence in our method, in Thucydides' 460, and in our assumption that notations in cash were attached to the names of potential naval allies. Having announced my confidence in the preliminary results, I hope you will not accuse me of manipulation if, for the sake of the more sceptical, I now show how our figure and Thucydides' may be brought closer together. Our roster of membership is a maximum and certain names had already been marked as doubtful. If we now delete them, we find that our figure has been reduced to *ca.* 475 talents, which, as a conjectural total against Thucydides' sure 460, may appear to be a more satisfying result. The evidence, I repeat, is still demonstrably imprecise and, as we have pointed out, "we have only to suppose that a city like, say, Perinthos lagged to bring our computation in cash very close to 460 talents." Perinthos, of course, is cited merely as an example; there may be others whom we mistakenly admitted as charter-members. Or perhaps 90 talents are too much to allow for Chios, Lesbos, and Samos.

For my part, this juggling of names for the sake of more exact agreement between our figure and Thucydides' is without attraction. Because I am impressed by the difficulties inherent in reconstruction, I think the total of 493 talents indicates that we are on the right track. It will be observed that we followed what we believe to have been Aristeides' method: we drew up the roster and we assessed each name in cash. The result was 493 talents (or, adjusted, 475). The excess over 460 is our unavoidable margin of error. Observe that 460 is a round figure, the total of individual amounts, *i.e.*, Aristeides did not select 460 as the desired result and share it among the members.

Our assessment for 478/7 included some 106 talents for states that contributed ships at first but later commuted to cash and 90 talents for the three large islands that never paid money. These 196 talents were thus not realised as such in 477. In *A.T.L.*, III, because in our opinion many more states, now unidentifiable, were supplying ships in the early years, we speculated that the assessment of 460 talents was, in due course, about evenly divided between contributors of cash (about 230 talents) and contributors of ships (in lieu of about 230 talents).

Our computation of the effective assessment of 454/3 realised about 410 talents from 165 names. About 390 talents were actually collected from 139 cities before publication of the record. Of this figure we have some confirmation in the summation of receipts attached to List 1. The gap of 26 names and about 20 talents is not large. Some, no doubt, defaulted; some we should probably not have admitted to our assessment. Our roster was compiled on the assumption that no naval ally merited a place; and there remained seventeen naval allies, including Samos, Chios, and Lesbos, in 454. The results (390 talents collected from a maximum of 410 anticipated), I believe, demonstrate the fundamental soundness of our reconstructed assessment.

The critics who argue that Thucydides' figure of 460 talents ignores the contributions of naval allies face a dilemma of their own making. We know that between 477 and 454 many commuted from ships to cash and that the Confederacy expanded its membership. The money booked at Athens in 453 must have been considerably in excess of the sum entrusted to the *hellenotamiai* in 477. The rather less than 400 talents of 453 do not meet this requirement. So, the critics assert, Thucydides' 460 is wrong; either he blundered or the text is corrupt. Or, adds Chambers, "the first assessment was unusually high, perhaps too high, and was later scaled down."[21] This last remedy is invalidated by the reputation that Aristeides' assessment enjoyed for the next sixty years or so.

---

[21] *Class. World*, LVII (1963), p. 10.

Let us meet the objections to Thucydides' text by assuming that Aristeides and the *hellenotamiai* never expected to see 460 talents, *i.e.*, that naval allies who were on the roster of membership were in the first instance allotted cash-assessments as a matter of convenience and common sense. On this basis I summarise the figures: (1) the assessment of all the allies in 478/7 added up to 460 talents (our own computation is about 475), of which about 230 were duly banked on Delos; (2) over the years membership grew and in addition many naval allies changed their status; (3) the assessment of 454/3, which did not include naval allies at all, came, effectively, to about 410 talents, of which some 390 were collected. So revenue had increased from about 230 to about 390 talents. We can produce an even more impressive figure if we now remodel our assessment of 454/3 and work as Aristeides had worked years earlier. To our 410 we add the late-payers and allies in revolt whom we did not count as "effectively" assessed, the naval allies insofar as we can identify them, and Samos, Chios, and Lesbos. I spare you the arithmetic and expect you to take my word for the answer, 588 talents. Yes, there had been growth; yes, the finances reflect that growth.

These figures present a developing, connected, and credible story; and they confirm Thucydides' 460 talents as a comprehensive sum. To posit textual corruption or to charge Thucydides with error becomes superfluous. It is of course true that Thucydides may make mistakes and that numerals are liable to corruption. Of the latter there is no hint. As for the former, Thucydides decided that he should report the total of the first assessment of *phoros*, which was a notable figure. What he writes fits the other (epigraphic) evidence, it does not quarrel with independent investigation and computation, and it is subject to rational explanation. We have no reason to question his accuracy.

3

How Did the Greeks Look at Literature?

BY G. M. A. GRUBE

Delivered April 4 and 5, 1967

HOW DID THE GREEKS
LOOK
AT LITERATURE?

I. GENERAL ATTITUDES

IN DISCUSSING Greek attitudes to literature—and of course until the middle of the fifth century poetry was the only form of literature—we can do no better than start with Homer, or rather with some aspects of the Homeric inheritance. Modern scholars date the Homeric epic somewhere between the late ninth and early seventh centuries B.C. with, at the present time, a strong current of opinion running towards the later date. That thorny problem we need not deal with here, for on one point we can all agree, namely that for the classical Greek Homer had always been there, so that, while we cannot with any confidence speak of the time of Homer, we can speak confidently of the Homeric inheritance. Few would deny that this inheritance had considerable influence upon many aspects of Greek life, and not least upon literature and the Greek's feelings towards it.

Perhaps we should rather speak of the *epic* inheritance, since it is quite certain that Homer represents the culminating point of a long process of development of epic poetry which had spread over several generations, probably several centuries. Technically, there is nothing primitive about the Homeric epic; the hexameter itself is a highly sophisticated meter as Homer employs it, a clear and definite form, and yet capable of infinite variety. Homer remained "the poet" to the Greeks for over two thousand years, and is still, even in translation, a best seller today, still recognized as the greatest of all epic poets. He held a major place in the education of the classical Greeks. Greek boys were thus introduced to their childhood heroes in splendid poetry, which in itself conditioned them to poetry. One imagines that many a boy must have slept with Homer under his pillow before Alexander the Great did so, and dreamed of being another Achilles. Plato might worry about the moral effect of this, but Achilles and Odysseus are certainly to be preferred to Batman and Superman.

Perhaps the first thing we should notice is that the universal appeal of poetry is completely taken for granted in Homeric society. Eumaeus the swineherd is charmed by it; queen Penelope is deeply affected by it and so is Odysseus; Achilles himself, the greatest hero of them all, consoles himself, when sulking in his tent, by reciting, perhaps even composing, epic lays; even the suitors, that obstreperous gang of toughs, find pleasure in listening to it. Eumaeus takes it for granted that all men are insatiably eager to hear the lovely words which the poet has learned from the Muses, and Aristotle says much the same thing three or four centuries later about *mousikê*, i.e. poetry and music.[1] Evidently, the Greeks retained this belief and acted upon it. Greek dramas, as we know, were performed before audiences of many thousands, and so were the recitations of the rhapsodes and choral performances. Our mental picture of the early epic poets performing in the halls of the nobility is probably false, or at least incomplete. The epic was most probably also recited in the market-place, a popular art from the first. True, Homer describes an aristocratic society and it is the great heroes who do all the fighting that matters, but the ordinary man has never disliked hearing tales of kings and heroes. Greek tragedy was certainly a very popular art when Aristotle said it should concern itself with the actions of the princes of the earth;[2] that Homeric society is aristocratic, even feudal, makes no difference to its popularity. There were poetic as well as athletic contests at most Greek festivals, and authors took the opportunity to read their work to the assembled multitudes. One thinks of Herodotus and Isocrates at Olympia, and there were many others. So far we moderns have only revived the athletic side of the Olympic games.

That poetry, at least great poetry, has a universal appeal was taken for granted throughout the fifth and fourth centuries B.C. Perhaps it is worth reflecting, in this our technological and electronic age, that the undisputedly great contribution which the ancient Greeks made to human life, and to Western civilization in particular, not only in literature and philosophy, but in medicine, mathematics, politics and many other fields, was made by a people whose education consisted almost entirely of poetry, music

[1] *Politics*, VIII, 5 (1340a 4-6).   [2] *Poetics*, ch. 13 (1453a 10).

and athletics, at least in their greatest period. Even Plato's attack upon the poets was due to his very deep conviction that poetry has a powerful influence on the building of character. One also likes to remember that, after the great Athenian military disaster in Sicily in 413 B.C., many of the enslaved Athenian prisoners earned their freedom by reciting from memory from the latest plays of Euripides.[3] This throws light not only upon the Athenians, but also upon the Syracusans.

This universal appeal of poetry was not challenged until the centre of culture had shifted to Alexandria under the Ptolemies in the third century B.C. There, in the more rarefied atmosphere of the Museum's great library, were gathered scholars from all over the expanded Greek world, who had little or no connection with the native population but were in effect a foreign coterie attached to a foreign, Macedonian court. Alexandrine poetry was then written for a much more restricted audience of cognoscenti, and the poet-scholars began to be contemptuous of the mob. Horace's famous *"Odi profanum vulgus et arceo"*[4] is an echo from Alexandria, though it is true that even in Rome poetry never had the universal appeal which it had had in Greece from times immemorial.

It is worth noting here that Greek poetry, popular as it was, was always formal, even formalized. Epics continued to be written through the fifth and fourth centuries, though these have not survived. At Alexandria it became epic of the study rather than of the market-place, as we can see in the *Argonautica* of Apollonius, the only other epic we have in Greek, except for the very late ones of the fourth and fifth centuries A.D. These were still written in Homeric hexameters, five hundred years after Virgil and more than ten centuries after Homer. The spirit of them was very different, but the form changed hardly at all.

The Greeks always had a somewhat rigid theory of genres and their appropriate conventions, yet poetry was a far more important part of the life of the community in the classical centuries than it has ever been since, probably anywhere. I emphasize this— it may seem a paradox—because some of our contemporary poets

---

[3] Plutarch, *Nicias*, ch. 29.   [4] Horace, *Odes*, III, 1.

seem to feel that they should break through all conventions, all laws of the genres and even mix their media in order to get closer to life. I do not know what is meant by life in this connection, but these innovations will not bring them nearer to the life of the people or regain for poetry any strong or widespread influence. On the contrary, the danger is, it seems to me, that their art may become more and more esoteric, and be understood, if understood at all, by fewer and fewer people, until they reach a kind of extreme solipsistic Alexandrianism.

For poetry, and art generally, to be popular and powerful, must be familiar in form. Chaos, by its very nature, can never be understood. It is largely because Greek poets and other artists were satisfied to build upon the work of their predecessors, thus achieving perfection very slowly and gradually, and because they never, in their best period, pursued originality for its own sake, that they were able to attain and retain their great popularity, that they were able to speak to the mass of their fellow-citizens and be understood by them. The spirit of Euripidean tragedy, for example, was different from that of Aeschylus and Sophocles, but he felt as much bound by the conventions of the theatre and the tragic genre as they were.

I am not suggesting that there is any particular virtue in keeping a literary form unchanged for ten centuries, and, in spite of their theories of genres, the Greeks did in fact invent and develop many different types of literature throughout antiquity. Literary forms should of course not become tyrannical; they may well be altered and combined in new ways, and experimentation should go on at all times—though one may feel that the cruder experiments should perhaps take place in private. Self-expression is always valuable for the individual concerned, but it is surely natural for the rest of the community to make sure that the self has something about it which is worth expressing before the general interest can be awakened. At the present time, when we are told in all seriousness that any collocations of sound are music, or that any haphazard collection of words is poetry, that anything is art, and even that art is what you can get away with, we may well proclaim that such theories empty the words music, poetry and art of any meaning whatever. Unformed material is not art, nor material which has not been submitted to the discipline of significant form.

The greatness of any work of art depends, it seems to me, upon the depth of content, appropriateness of form, and the number of people to whom it can ultimately be communicated, though these people need not be contemporaries of the artist, or at least not all of them need be. The Greeks, obviously, were strikingly successful in these respects.

I believe that the history of poetry largely supports the Greek view that great poetry has, or can have, great popularity. And I rather wish that those who manage our great mass media shared that conviction, and acted on it, for it is probably within their power to create the conditions in which such a widespread appeal would again be possible, to the great benefit of our culture and our civilization. Of course, the supply of really great poetry is never plentiful, but here the responsibility lies with the poets themselves.

There is another aspect of the Homeric inheritance which greatly affected later literature, and that is the habit of dramatization. It has often been remarked that three-fifths of the *Iliad* and the *Odyssey* are in direct speech. Many a scene, almost whole books, could be put on the stage with very little change, merely by omitting a few lines between speeches such as: "And in answer swift-footed Achilles spoke." A good deal of the rest, vividly described as it is, could be acted. The Greeks continued to be very fond of this dramatization, i.e. of direct speech. Personal lyric is largely dramatic in this sense; direct speech is frequent in other lyric poetry; dialogue conforms to the same method of presentation and drama entirely so. The immediate parenthood of Greek drama is a matter of controversy, but its more remote ancestor is obviously the epic, and this fondness for dramatization may well be, in part at least, the secret of its success.

The genre in which it is most interesting to follow this fondness for the dramatic is history, and there we can see both its power and its dangers. Herodotus has often been called an epic historian, and the epithet is justified in this respect, as in others. He likes to enliven a situation by speeches, even when he cannot possibly have heard them, as for example the debate on the respective merits of monarchy, aristocracy and democracy among the Persian nobles. It is true that he insists that the debate did take place, but nobody believes him.[5]

By the time Thucydides wrote his History of the Peloponnesian war at the end of the fifth century, dramatization by speeches was a recognized characteristic of the genre, and for all his regard for strict historical truth, he does not even consider abandoning the practice. However, in the justly famous chapters in which he discusses the duties of the historian,[6] he does place two important limitations upon the use of speeches: first, that he made every effort to find out what was actually said and then stayed within the general tenor of what was said; and, secondly, that he put into the mouth of his speakers only such arguments as the situation required (τὰ δέοντα).

This habit of the historians to dramatize by the use of speeches is a Homeric inheritance rather than due to rhetorical influence. In the hands of a genius like Thucydides it is a wonderfully vivid presentation of different points of view or of the factors involved in a situation. Moreover it is a method which is not available to a modern historian who may not include speeches unless he has a verbatim record of them before him, without being accused of writing a historical novel.

The method, however, had its dangers. After Thucydides, or more exactly after Xenophon, who sticks pretty well to the Thucydidean limitations when he is writing history—dialogue, encomium, etc. are other genres to which historical accuracy does not apply—in the Hellenistic historians, the effects of rhetorical training meant that occasions for speeches became opportunities for rhetorical displays only loosely connected with the particular situation or to what was actually said, if anything. Along with this rhetorical self-indulgence went a diminishing respect for historical truth. Particular events, the capture of a city for example, would be written up with the deliberate intention of playing upon the emotions of the reader. It has even been suggested that there evolved a theory of "tragic history" as a sub-genre, which applied to the writing of history some of the theories about arousing pity

---

[5] Herodotus, III, 80-82, and VI, 43,3.
[6] Thucydides, I, 20-22.

and fear which Aristotle had applied to tragedy in the *Poetics*.[7]

We can also see in the historians the dangers involved in too formulaic an approach to literature. Aristotle had devised or endorsed the formula of three kinds of rhetoric (prose writing) and three only: the forensic or courtroom rhetoric, the deliberative or political, and the epideictic. This last, the rhetoric of display, was intended by him to include mainly funeral orations, and sophistic display speeches. The first two kinds, the forensic and the deliberative, were clearly defined, but when the formula became common property in the rhetorical schools, everything which did not fit into them was lumped under the third.

It would be an exaggeration to say that history degenerated *because* it was included under epideictic, but this classification may well have encouraged the Hellenistic historians in their bad habits. At any rate, even the sober and sensible Quintilian, writing at the end of the first century A.D., still shows traces of history as epideictic rhetoric when he writes:[8]

History is akin to poetry and may be considered as a prose poem; it is intended to tell a story, not to prove anything; a historical work is not directed to taking any action; it is composed to ensure that posterity shall remember, or to achieve recognition for the talent of the historian. Hence, to avoid tedium in its narrative, it may resort to more unusual vocabulary and a freer use of figures.

Quite apart from the habit of dramatization by direct speech, ancient literature, both prose and poetry, was also more dramatic than literature is to us because reading always meant reading aloud, so that it was always *heard*, and in this sense remained oral for many centuries after writing was invented and books were in circulation. The habit of silent reading, if not totally unknown, was certainly very rare as late as the fourth century A.D., and this means a much closer involvement on the part of the hearer. Also, the *sound* of his work was always present to the writer's mind when he composed, and he paid a great deal of attention

[7] On this subject see F. W. Walbank in *Historia* 9 (1960), 216-234, and C. O. Brink in *Proc. Cambridge Philological Soc.* 186 (n.s. 6) 1960, 14-19.

[8] X, 1, 31.

to it. This is unfortunately not true of too many writers today, especially writers of prose.

This sound was what Longinus was to call the music of language charged with meaning, which thus simultaneously appealed to the ear, the mind and the emotions. It is not surprising then that the ancient theorists of style paid a great deal of attention to the sound of words, both single words and words in combination. Several factors contributed to this language music: the pitch of the voice (indicated by the accentuation in our Greek texts, and the subtle distinctions of which very few of us can even try to reproduce adequately), the rhythm (based on the length or shortness of syllables, as all Greek scansion was), the stress accent (which they did not indicate but which is the basis of all our English scansion), as well of course as the quality of the voice itself. And to the total effect the Greeks developed a very high degree of sensitivity. The importance of pitch is shown in the story of the actor who mispronounced γαλήν', with a circumflex accent instead of an acute in a line of Euripides, so that, instead of saying "I see a calm arising from the sea," he said "I see a cat arising from the sea." The whole theatre shook with laughter, but the difference was only the pitch on one letter.

The difference of rhythm is rather more subtle, and we have difficulty in feeling the difference when Longinus tells us that at the end of a long sentence of Demosthenes, his ending, ὥσπερ νέφος, is exactly right, whereas one syllable more, ὡσπερεὶ νέφος, or one syllable less, ὡς νέφος, would have spoilt the rhythm of the sentence. The importance of the stress accentuation we understand easily enough, since we rely on it almost exclusively.

Nor do we have difficulty in understanding the importance of the voice, though we are here much less sensitive than the Greeks. Again and again, in Homer, Hesiod and other early poets, we find such phrases as: "and from his lips his voice flowed sweeter than honey," and indeed the voice was an important part of the gift of the Muses, both in poetry and prose. Even today every lecturer knows that if he allows his voice to drone on in monotone his audience goes to sleep, and a monotonously repeated rhythm (in our case it would be stress) is equally soporific. It was Demosthenes who said that delivery is the most important thing in oratory; and it was also the second important thing and the third. The Greek word for delivery also means acting (ὑπόκρισις).

This reminds us that in the Greek theatre, where the actors were masked, wore high buskins and long robes, and acted before many thousands in daylight, facial acting was impossible and violent gesticulation at least difficult; the actors had to rely almost entirely upon the music of language as expressed by the voice. This certainly did not mean, however, that Greek tragedy was monumental, cold or dispassionate, which some people mistakenly call classical. Quite the contrary. You have only to look at almost any Greek play to realize that its appeal to the emotions was violent and intense. This is true not only of Euripides who was known in antiquity for his dramatizations of violent passions, even of madness; it is equally true of Sophocles and Aeschylus. Think of Oedipus and Antigone, of Clytemnestra and the Furies, as well as of Medea and Agave. It was not without reason that Dionysus, the god of passion and ecstasy, was also the god of tragedy. And if we realize that actors had to rely entirely on their voices we shall better understand how Prometheus, chained unmoving to his rock, can be an effective tragic hero.

There is another ancient attitude to poetry which disturbs modern commentators, though perhaps less today than it did a generation or two ago, namely that the Greeks frequently criticized the poets from the moral point of view. This attitude is first formulated explicitly in our extant texts of Aristophanes:[9] "Boys have their teachers at school, we poets are the teachers of men," but, as a feeling if not a theory, it is certainly very much older, and can indeed be traced back to the time when poetry was oral in every sense, before alphabetic writing was in use, when poetry was orally composed and orally transmitted. At that time there were no written records, and the history of the people was enshrined, in so far as they had one, in the epics. Not only that, but poetry also transmitted ethical and religious traditions—the νόμοι καὶ ἤθη of Hesiod who not without reason made the Muses the daughters of Memory.

In his recent book, *Preface to Plato*, Professor Havelock[10] maintains that this older attitude to poetry largely persisted into the

[9] *Frogs*, 1054-1055.
[10] E. A. Havelock, *Preface to Plato* (Oxford, Blackwell 1963), especially Chapters 2-8. Hesiod, *Theogony*, 53-67.

fifth and even the fourth century, so that Plato was attacking
more than what we would call poetry in the *Republic*; indeed he
was attacking a whole way of thought and life. Without following Havelock all the way, I think we should be grateful to him
for pointing this out, and his main point has a good deal of merit.
We know that Homer still occupied a highly honoured place in
the educational system, and this obviously had consequences which
we do not always fully realize.

There was no preaching in the temples of the Olympian gods
who, except for a few primitive ethical imperatives such as the
sanctity of an oath, respect for parents and the duties of hospitality, remained singularly indifferent to the moral conduct of
their worshippers as long as the proper rituals were observed.

Homer, one feels, might well have been disconcerted at the important educational position thus thrust upon him, for there is no
trace in the epic of any other function for poetry than to entertain. Hesiod, however, would obviously have accepted it; indeed
he claimed it. Pindar made similar claims, while Aeschylus was
obviously concerned to establish the gods as defenders of justice.
Aristophanes claims even for comedy the right to enlighten, and
it is probably significant that he makes Euripides agree with
Aeschylus that the duty of the poet is to make men better. This
feeling then, that poets were the teachers of men, was of great
antiquity and never quite died out.

And indeed why should it? It is surely obvious that criticism
of art for its moral effect upon society and upon the individuals
of which it is composed is perfectly legitimate, as long as we know
what we are doing and do not confuse moral and artistic criteria.
In a society like that of ancient Greece, where poetry played such
a vital role in the life of the community, the poet could not
escape his social responsibilities. It is therefore no surprise to find,
as early as 500 B.C., both Xenophanes and Heraclitus attacking
Homer for the immoral conduct of his gods.

Meantime of course men's conception of the gods had changed;
in Homer the gods are natural or psychological powers personi-
fied; their divinity lies in their power; their personal behaviour
has nothing to do with their divinity and is a subject for poetic
fancy. But as anthropomorphism developed and became more

sophisticated, the gods came to be worshipped as divine persons with certain powers, and then their personal behaviour came to be relevant, for men will not continue to worship personal gods who behave worse than they do themselves. The gods must then become the guardians of a moral order in the universe. This Homer's gods were not, and their behaviour, as has often been remarked, was worse than the behaviour of the heroes themselves who at least had a moral code which one can understand and respect. And so the first criticism of poetry was moral criticism. Plato clearly, but also Aristotle, wanted the poets to face their moral responsibilities. The idea that the poets were the teachers of men was not challenged until Alexandrian times, and it was natural that it should be challenged there, since the scholars and writers of the Museum had no roots among the people.

It reasserted itself later. The Romans, as one would expect from so practical a people, were even more convinced than the Greeks that poets should teach as well as entertain. The Greeks always loved poetry for its own sake whatever their critics or philosophers might say, but sheer poetry had much less appeal for the practical Roman. Many of you will remember Horace's advice—it comes strangely from the lips of a poet, especially such a careful craftsman as Horace—"if the subject is well chosen, neither words nor structure will desert you" and again: "that poet will take every prize who mixes the useful with the pleasant, who is both teacher and entertainer."[11] It is hard not to smile when we hear Quintilian saying of Alcaeus that he had great qualities as a poet but unfortunately he turned to playful and erotic verse, though he had talent for better things: *sed et lusit et in amores descendit, maioribus tamen aptior.*[12] It is the same feeling which no doubt accounts for the less than complimentary references to Catullus, now considered one of their greatest poets, in Cicero, Horace and Quintilian. They required the same usefulness from the art of prose, but there we may be more willing to accept the utilitarian view of the art.

I have dealt so far with some very general attitudes to literature which were shared by writers and audiences and were part of

---

[11] Horace, *Ars Poetica*, 40-43 and 343-6.
[12] X, 1,63.

the general Greek point of view. I will now turn to the attitudes of those who, as critics, contributed to literary criticism and literary theory.

As we have seen, literary criticism began as criticism of content, from the moral point of view. We may call this the philosophical approach, and it is probable that it continued throughout the fifth century, and that the lost works of the Socratic circle adopted this approach to literature. Aristophanes, in his comedies, also criticized the poets in this way, particularly Euripides, but in the famous contest between Aeschylus and Euripides for the Chair of Tragedy in Hades, which he stages in the *Frogs*, moral and technical criticisms are much more clearly separated than is usually allowed, and in the end Dionysus, who chairs the contest, refuses to choose between them on the basis of poetic merit. Actually Aristophanes is much more balanced and fair in his criticism than one might expect. Indeed, he has some claim to be considered the first Greek literary critic, and a number of terms which later became technical first appear in his comedies. The contest in the *Frogs* may not be the most profound, but it is certainly the most amusing piece of literary criticism extant from antiquity.

This philosophic approach was continued in the fourth century by both Plato and Aristotle, though they also contributed a great deal to literary theory in the true sense. Both Plato's banishment of the poets from his ideal Republic and Aristotle's theories of tragedy as set forth in the *Poetics* have continued to evoke an almost uninterrupted stream of new interpretations, reinterpretations and misinterpretations, and with some of these theories I intend to deal tomorrow.

It is with the general attitudes of the post-Aristotelian critics that I should like to deal now. They have been very much neglected during the last half century or so, until very recently, especially in the English-speaking world. In the first few years of this century Rhys Roberts published his editions of some of the works of Dionysius of Halicarnassus, as well as of Demetrius *On Style*, and of *On the Sublime*, but even the rest of Dionysius' work, his essays on Thucydides, Demosthenes, Isocrates and other Greek orators were unobtainable either in the original or in translation until the Teubner series republished the original texts very recently. The only adequate lexicon of critical and rhetorical terms is still Ernesti's, originally published in the eighteenth century and recently reprinted, but it is far from perfect. This is all the more regrettable in that Liddell-Scott-Jones is not very good in this area. We are now somewhat better provided on the Latin side,[13] but a good Greek lexicon in this field is very much needed.

A good deal of valuable work was done in the intervening years, such as that of Jensen and Sudhaus on Philodemus in Germany,[14] and a number of books and articles by Rostagni[15] and his school in Italy, but the actual texts of some of the Greek critics are still hard to come by. During the last and the present decades, however, there seems to be a renewal of interest in England and North America, particularly as regards Longinus[16] which, one hopes, will rescue that Greek critic, perhaps the greatest in all antiquity, from the inexplicable neglect from which he has suffered since the early nineteenth century. Certainly *On the Sublime*, or, as I prefer to call it, *On Great Writing*, deserves to be included in any classical student's reading list, and no student of criticism and its history can afford to neglect him.

There are, except for Longinus, good reasons for this lack of interest in the post-Aristotelian critics, and one of them is their concentration on style and the perhaps excessively intellectual and analytic approach of ancient critics generally. Much is absent from ancient criticism which we should expect to find there. The ancients seem to have felt that great writers were quite capable of expressing their meaning clearly to their audiences, directly, without intermediaries. There is very little in the ancient critics of any period about purpose or meaning, about imagery, symbolism, levels of meaning—these and other aspects of poetry which are not easily subjected to intellectual analysis are nearly completely ignored, and of course the unconscious mind had not yet been dis-

---

[13] By Heinrich Lausberg's *Handbuch der Literarischen Rhetorik*. (München 1960).

[14] Chr. Jensen, *Philodemus über die Gedichte, fünftes Buch* (Berlin 1923). S. Sudhaus, *Philodemi volumima Rhetorica*, 2 vols. (Leipzig 1902-6), reprinted (Teubner).

[15] A. Rostagni, *Scritti Minori*, 3 vols. (Turin 1955), and *Anonimi del Sublime* (Milan 1947).

[16] D. A. Russell's edition, *Longinus On the Sublime* (Oxford 1964), and his translation. See also my translation: *Longinus on Great Writing* (Bobbs Merrill, 1957), and a number of articles.

covered. Although the Greeks were very conscious of the importance of the emotions in the fifth and fourth century, they were
living in the first age of reason. Aristotle is very Greek when he
insists that clarity (σαφήνεια) is the first and essential quality of
any speaking or writing,[17] the only quality to which he is willing
to apply the term *aretê* or virtue. With that deceptive simplicity
of his he argues that, since language is a means of communication,
if you fail to make your meaning clear, you have obviously failed
in the art of expression. Without clarity, other qualities are of no
value.

This assumes that all poetry and prose have, or should have, a
precise meaning to convey. One remembers that wicked little
comment of his about ambiguity, that it is to be avoided unless it
is deliberately intended, "which is what people do who have
nothing to say but pretend that they have; such people usually
write poetry, as Empedocles did."[18]

It is then not surprising that when Aristotle in the *Poetics*[19]
comes to the aspect of poetry which concerns the expression of
thought, he should refer us to the *Rhetoric*, implying thereby
that the means to be used are the same in poetry and prose. He
never explains the difference except on two points: the poet may
use more ornate language, and of course he writes in verse (that
is, in regularly recurrent metrical patterns), but Aristotle himself
sees that this is not so important for, as he says, though Empedocles writes in verse, his work is that of a physicist.[20] Aristotle wants
to differentiate different kinds of literature by "the nature of the
imitation," or, as we might put it, "the nature of the genre," but
he does not achieve this very successfully, nor indeed attempt it
for most genres. Nor does any later critic clearly differentiate
poetry from prose, but for this we can hardly blame them, since
we have found no satisfactory account of the difference.

This neglect of what we might call the more spiritual side of
poetry and this concentration on style in the post-Aristotelian critics is what we call the "rhetorical" slant in ancient criticism, and it
is real enough; yet it has often been exaggerated. It is well known
that the theoretical study of the art of expression began with the

---

[17] *Rhet*. III, 2,1 (1404b 1-3).   [18] *Rhet*. III, 5 (1407a 32-35).
[19] *Poetics*, ch. 29.   [20] *Poetics*, ch. 1 (1447b 17-20).

fifth-century sophists, when the growth of democracy ensured power and influence to the man who could sway an assembly or a popular court. Hence a demand for the art of public speaking, which all the sophists tried to teach. We know that the first textbooks on oratory were slanted for use in the lawcourts and studied the types of arguments and other ways to influence a jury or assembly. By the time Aristotle wrote, this language study was already nearly a century old and had developed a highly technical vocabulary. All the post-Aristotelian critics were trained in oratory and criticize from this point of view. Moreover their approach is apt to be very theoretical in that they state their theories of style and then apply their formulae to particular authors (as Dionysius does) or, worse, use their authors merely to illustrate their theories and categories. Even Aristotle does this in his *Rhetoric*. Here I should like to quote a passage from A. M. Guillemin[21] which I feel throws a great deal of light on ancient critical methods:

> The attitude of modern criticism towards literature is very different from that which it adopts to the fine arts. When a book is in question we attach the greatest importance not only to its formal beauty but also to the value of its thought and feelings, to its subject, its content. To consider only the author's procedures, his style, is to be literary in the worst sense of the word. Yet we adopt a quite different attitude to the products of the fine arts. Here successful technique is the first consideration; interest in the subject or content betrays a lack of education! ... The ancients handled literary criticism much as we handle art criticism. Their criticism may lack certain features, but it was certainly not false criticism.

Mme Guillemin is speaking of the late first century A.D. in Rome, when emphasis on the techniques of expression had become even more dominant, and, in spite of the efforts of Cicero and Quintilian, the theories of the teachers of speech had become oversubtle and very highly sophisticated. Her main point, however, applies from the fourth century B.C. on. It helps to explain how, between Plato and Longinus, so little is said about the mind of

[21] A. M. Guillemin, *Pline et la Littérature de son Temps* (Paris 1929), p. 64.

the writer and so much about his style, figures of speech and thought, sentence-structures, prose rhythms and the like.

But let us not exaggerate, and above all let us not be prisoners of our own translations. When we speak of the "rhetorical" slant of ancient criticism, we are affected by the modern dislike of "rhetoric," which is in any case not the equivalent of ῥητορική or *eloquentia*. It is always the common words which are the hardest to translate; even when the basic meaning is identical (which it very rarely is) the associations of the words are quite different. (This is one good reason why courses in translation should always be taught by people who know the originals.) Θεός is not equivalent to God or even a god, ψυχή is not the same as soul, and so on. When the words can be transliterated we are on slippery ground indeed! What confusion has not been caused in discussions of Platonic philosophy by speaking of the theory of Ideas, for of course Plato's ἰδέαι are not ideas at all. So too when we render ῥητορική by rhetoric. Ῥητορική meant the art of speech and the whole of it, the art of reasoned speech, the *Logos* which, as the ancients were never tired of repeating, distinguishes man from the other animals. And *Logos* is itself untranslatable since it means word, speech, phrase, expression, as well as reason itself, and refers to content as well as to form.

From this point of view, the whole educational system of Isocrates which aimed at producing men who, as he put it, could speak well on great subjects (which also meant writing) seems at times based on a confusion of the different meanings of the word *Logos*. The system, and also the confusion, were inherited by the Romans, and we must not be misled by words to think that mere rhetoric, in our sense of the word, was the aim of their education. Isocrates certainly was no mere rhetorician; he wanted to develop character and a social conscience, and so, quite explicitly, did Cicero and Quintilian. If they are all a bit vague as to how this is to be achieved, I am not at all sure that we are any more clear or explicit.

It is a pity that the ancient texts dealing with this art of expression are commonly referred to as "rhetorical works" even when written by such literary scholars as Dionysius and Demetrius, or even by a philosopher like Aristotle.

Granted that ancient critics largely concentrated on style, granted that in doing so they were at times inclined to approach literature as a treasure house of illustrations of their own theories, and that this was the chief weakness of ancient criticism, yet even their formulae have a good deal of sense to them: choice and structure of content; choice of words and word-arrangement, if we must take the analytic approach, is a sensible formula; so too purity of language, lucidity, appropriateness, and a degree of ornamentation, are not a bad list of essential qualities. Moreover, their rigidity in the use of their formulae has often been exaggerated.

Take for example the notorious formula of the three styles, the simple, the grand and the intermediate, according to which we are told in some of our text-books that the ancient critics classified their authors. (And we may note in passing that they were well aware that the simple style of the fireside chat is just as much a matter of art as the grand and impressive.) No extant Greek critic, at least before Roman times, does in fact use the formula, in its full sense, which includes all aspects of style. Dionysius of Halicarnassus, who is always quoted as doing so, in fact has no overall formula, though he does speak of three styles or types of word-choice and three types of word-arrangement, but these do not correspond and cannot be telescoped into an overall formula. Moreover, and this is the point I want to stress here, he is very much aware of the limitations of his formulae, as he shows when he introduces his three styles of word-arrangement:[22]

> Word-arrangement is of many different kinds, and these cannot be brought under any general classification or precisely enumerated. It is an individual thing like personal appearance, and each of us has his own style of word-arrangement. The same is true of painting: all painters use the same colours but each one mixes them in his own way which differs from the others. So in prose and poetry we all use the same words, but each of us uses them in his own way. However I think there are three generic distinctions, and only three. . .

and he then proceeds to describe them: the austere, the flowery, and the plain. Where we do find the formula of three styles in its

[22] *On Word-Arrangement*, ch. 21 *ad init.*

full sense, as in Cicero and the *Rhetorica ad Herennium*, it is always made clear that the good orator must be able to use each style at the appropriate time.

Then let us take the rhetorical formula of imitation or *mimêsis*. This has nothing to do with the Platonic formula of art as imitation of nature of which we shall speak later, but refers to the imitation or emulation of great speakers or writers. Dionysius here too has a highly relevant passage on two kinds of *mimêsis* in his essay on Dinarchus:[23]

> Imitation is related to the models in two different ways: the first is a relationship which develops naturally if one remains in close contact with the model for a long time and lives with it; the second resembles it but results from the application of rhetorical rules. About the first kind there is little one can say; of the second one can say only that all the models have a natural grace and charm of their own, while the contrived imitations, even if they are as perfect as imitations can be, always have something laboured and unnatural about them. . . .

Quintilian goes to great pains to direct the reading of his pupils, but in a long chapter on *imitatio* he has nothing but contempt for those who merely imitate the rhetorical devices of their models and think that to write like Cicero it is necessary only to end a clause with *esse videatur*.[24] In this matter of *imitatio* or *mimêsis* the ancient critics have, I think, often been unfairly dealt with by modern commentators. Longinus too has a great passage on the inspiration to be derived from contact with great writers of the past.

The formula of qualities can also be too mechanically applied, as it is by Dionysius in an early work from which he quotes a comparison of Herodotus and Thucydides.[25] He uses it better in his essay on Lysias, and once more he shows himself aware of the limitations of his own formula where, discussing Lysias' charm (χάρις) he says:[26]

> . . . It is admirable and defies definition; it is equally obvious to the layman and the expert, but most difficult to explain and hard for even the most able writers to attain. . .

---

[23] *Dinarchus*, ch. 7.
[24] X, 2.
[25] *Letter to Pompey*, ch. 3.
[26] *Lysias*, chs. 10-12.

and he then goes on to declare that many other kinds of beauty cannot be theoretically accounted for; one senses the beauty but cannot explain it or define it; only by long practice can one train oneself to recognize it, but still without being able to give any rational or theoretical explanation of it. Quintilian too has much to say about the limits of what can be taught. All ancient critics insist that a beautiful style is due to three things: natural talent, theory, and continual practice, and that of these three only the second, i.e. the theory (*ars* or τέχνη) can be taught.

Some of these ancient critics were teachers of oratory, others had received a rhetorical education and they were at times the victims of what I call formula-itis but, if we read them with more sympathy than they often receive, we shall find them much less rigid, much more conscious of their limitations than they are often thought to be, and therefore much more interesting.

Moreover the teachers of speech have, it seems to me, been blamed somewhat unfairly. If the more imaginative, general and spiritual aspects of literature were largely ignored after Aristotle, that was hardly their fault. The teachers of speech had a job to do and they did it well, with the result that the average educated Greek and Roman, especially in the classical Roman centuries, could use their own language a good deal more ably, it seems to me, than the average graduate of our universities. The art of speech is certainly not the whole of higher education, as some of the ancients were inclined to think, but it is still an important part of it.

The blame for the neglect of the more general qualities of literature must surely be at least shared by the philosophers, for, as far as our evidence goes, the various schools of philosophy after the fourth century made no substantial contribution to the study of these more general aspects of poetry or literature. They left it to be dominated by the students of style, whose own studies, in part perhaps for this very reason, became more and more technical and complicated.

Yet if the orator remained *the* prose artist throughout these centuries, this may not be due only to the rhetorical slant of ancient criticism. Literature was always spoken, and the orator was the speaker par excellence. He may even at times have appeared to be the true heir of the oral poets, for he seemed to be composing as he went along.

With the orator this was mostly an illusion; we know that Demosthenes was a poor extempore speaker, and the speeches of most of the orators were most carefully prepared, even committed to writing and memorized. But then oral extempore composition may well often have been an illusion with the epic poets themselves, with whom all Greek literature began. In saying this I do not for a moment mean to deny the oral techniques of composition —the repetitions, the formulaic phrases, the epic epithets and the rest—which we all know and recognize in Homer, or the capacity of the epic poets to compose as they recited. But surely they did not do so every time. When an epic poet had composed a highly successful lay, he would surely repeat it on other occasions. Indeed he might well spend years working on variations of the main lays in his repertoire, and one imagines that this is how long epics, like the *Iliad* and the *Odyssey*, were born, before alphabetic writing was in general use.

I have in this lecture tried to point to some general attitudes to literature on the part of the Greeks generally: the belief in the universal appeal of poetry and the great influence it had on their society, the instinct for dramatization and some results of it, how long their literature, both prose and poetry, retained its oral nature at least to the extent of being read aloud, and the sensitivity to its sound throughout antiquity, the feeling that the poets were teachers of their people and were expected to face their social responsibilities. I have also discussed certain common features of ancient criticism which the modern student may find obstacles to sympathetic understanding.

It may well be that, because of the obvious differences due to our modern mass media of communication, we are entering an era wherein the spoken word and the human voice may again attain a greater importance, and literature, in some sense, become more oral again, with a new emphasis on some kind of catharsis of the human emotions. We cannot here go into the full implications of this change, and for the present we must leave them to our experts in mass media of communication. However, we may well express the hope that, in expounding their own theories and helping us in "understanding the media," our experts in communication may remember Aristotle's advice that in any form of communication by means of words spoken or written, lucidity is the one and essential virtue.

II. SPECIFIC QUESTIONS

TODAY, I INTEND to deal with two or three well-known ancient theories in Plato and Aristotle, which continue to provoke a good deal of controversy and misunderstanding. I hope we may at least clear up some of the latter.

We shall begin with Plato's notorious theory of art as "imitation" of phenomena, upon which his ban on poetry in the *Republic* is largely based. This theory has often been interpreted far too literally, as if a kind of photographic copy was all that the poet, painter or sculptor was able to create, and we shall see that for this misinterpretation Plato himself must share the blame.

It is important to realize that the word *mimêsis* and its cognates, imitation and to imitate, had already been applied both to poetry and the fine arts before Plato. We find it in a Homeric hymn, where it is usually translated "to mimic," but the meaning may well be wider.[1] It is there applied to a choral song. Herodotus uses it three times, once of a carving which "imitated" a corpse and was circulated at banquets in Egypt as a kind of *memento mori* for the guests.[2] The word is also found in the Hippocratic treatise *On Diet* where it is also applied to sculpture.[3] In the *Memorabilia* of Xenophon we have the report of a conversation of Socrates with a sculptor who argues he can only "imitate" the physical, but Socrates argues that he can represent the soul to some extent, since he can imitate the physical or outward manifestations of emotions and the like.[4]

Finally, there is an interesting use of the word in Aristophanes, where the rather precious poet Agathon is introduced in women's clothes because he is writing an ode for a women's chorus and the dramatist must identify himself with his characters, and, as he says, "what we do not have, 'imitation' will find for us."[5] The point of the somewhat dubious jokes about Agathon is greatly

---

[1] *Hymn to Apollo*, 158.

[2] Herodotus, II, 78. A similar use is found at II, 86, 2; II, 169, 5; and III, 37, 2. All these refer to sculpture. These examples are quoted by T.B.L. Webster's "Greek Theories of Art and Literature down to 400 B.C." in *CQ.* 33 (1939), 166-179. He also discusses other words of similar meaning.

[3] Hippocrates, *On Diet*, 21, quoted by Webster.

[4] *Memorabilia*, III, 10.

[5] *Thesmophoriazusae*, 148.

enhanced if Aristophanes is playing on the meaning of a semi-technical word commonly applied to poetry, as he probably is.

Add to this that Plato himself, in the *Laws*,[6] introduces the idea of mimêsis as a truism: "now everybody will agree to this about mousikê (poetry and music), that all its creations (ποιήματα) are imitation and image-making. Will not all agree to this, poets and audience and actors?—Certainly." We thus have mimêsis or imitation applied to poetry in a general sense, and in the same sense Plato also applies it to music and even to architecture,[7] which also must imitate good character, and here, obviously, direct imitation is impossible.

It is interesting to note that Plato uses the word in this general sense in the third book of the *Republic*,[8] before he has attached any special meaning to mimêsis, where he says that the poet must not 'imitate' Zeus displaying excessive sorrow at the death of Hector and Sarpedon. Obviously, no one had ever seen Zeus weeping. The criticism here is that this is *not true* of the gods. "Represent," and "representation" are obviously better translations here, and I would use them throughout, but this might seem to shirk the problem, and sometimes "imitation" is the more obvious translation. The essential meaning surely is that art must be true to life.

To understand the attacks on the poets in the *Republic*, we should remember that already in the *Apology* Socrates had found that poets could not explain their own poetry. He concluded that they composed not with knowledge but through inspiration. We should also remember that inspiration or possession by a god might well be a doubtful blessing to a Greek: think of Phaedra in the power of Aphrodite or Agave possessed by Dionysus and killing her own son.

We should remember further that in the *Ion* the rhapsode of that name is also shown to rely on inspiration, and Plato describes the process of poetic communication in a vivid simile (533d-e):

It is no art or craft which enables you to talk well on Homer, but a divine power which moves you, like the power of a magnet. This not only attracts iron rings but imbues them with its own

---

[6] *Laws*, III, 668b 9–c 2.
[7] *Republic*, III, 401b–c.
[8] *Rep.* 388c.

magnetic power, so that sometimes a long chain of such rings are suspended from one another; and the power of attraction in all of them derives from the magnet.

So the Muses inspire men, and the inspiration is passed on to others, till we have a whole chain of men possessed.

It is this communication of inspiration, i.e. of strong emotion or ecstasy, from the poets through the actors or rhapsodes to their audiences, uncontrolled at any point by reason or knowledge, of which Plato was always afraid, especially in the education of the young but also in its influence upon the community at large.

As the intellectual heir of Socrates and the apostle of a new type of education based on reason and knowledge, Plato was bound to challenge the claims made on behalf of the poets and their place in the educational system. As great a believer in the importance of early training as any modern psychologist,[9] he condemns not only Homer's tales about his gods but also the uncontrolled behaviour of his heroes. Such passages must not be heard by children or by free men who must have the courage to prefer death to disgrace (387b).

With the principle of censorship thus firmly established, Plato turns to literary forms, and it is now that he uses the term mimê-sis in the special sense of impersonation.[10] We spoke yesterday of the Greek's fondness of dramatic presentation by direct speech, because it is more vivid and secures a more intense emotional response and identification. This is precisely why Plato is afraid of it. A wave of intense emotion sweeping over twenty or thirty thousand spectators in a Greek theatre must have been almost tangible in its intensity. Plato must often have felt it, and because we become what we imitate (or impersonate),[11] he was afraid of it. He believed that to impersonate many characters on the stage, or to identify with them (like the rings in the *Ion*) could undermine our character and the control of our emotions in real life. For this reason he forbad the dramatization of any evil character on the stage. The 'imitative' poets must go. When we meet one

We shall do him reverence as before someone wondrous and

---

[9] e.g. *Rep*. II, 377b, and cf. *Laws*, 791 ff.
[10] From 392d.   [11] 395c 7.

delightful . . . we shall anoint him with myrrh, crown him with wreaths—and send him away to another city. (398a)

Not quite all poetry is banished. Hymns to the gods, encomia of virtuous men, even dramatization of good men and their deeds, can stay. This does not satisfy us at all, but at least it means, as Plato thought, that poetry could still fulfill an educational function.

We are not satisfied, nor should we be, but we should at least recognize that, as so often, Plato is raising for the first time, at least theoretically, a very important social problem, that of the censorship of art, and of literature in particular, a problem which still worries every civilized state. His answer is clearly unsatisfactory and Aristotle will already improve on it, but a completely satisfactory solution still has to be found two thousand years later.

The issue was obviously important to Plato and he returns to it in the tenth book. Meantime he has established his metaphysical theory of Forms and his psychological theory of the three main parts of the human soul, reason, feelings and passions. He now tries to use both theories to confirm and support his banishment of most poets from his city. He makes it perfectly clear that this is still his purpose both at the beginning of the discussion (595a) and when, at the conclusion, he says that it is therefore right to refuse to admit the poets and their poetry (605b and 606e) and denies that Homer educated Greece.

The psychological argument offers little difficulty. It merely re-states emphatically the dangers of the drama's appeal to the uncontrolled passions which reside of course in the lowest part of the soul, without any direction from the reasoning part which should govern the soul. There are many conflicts in the human soul, but "mimetic" poetry is of no help, since the highly passionate states of the soul are better material for tragedy and more pleasing to the mob (604e). Witnessing and enjoying highly emotional displays on the stage and "feeling with" the tragic or comic characters undermines our self-control.

Nor need we be disturbed by Plato's denial of knowledge to the poets. There is no doubt that the feeling that the poets were the teachers of men had led to exaggerated claims on their behalf. As Plato puts it: "we hear from some people that they have knowledge of all the crafts, of all human things pertaining to virtue and vice, and of things divine."[12] He will not bother the poets about knowledge of the crafts (he had already done so in the *Ion*), but what of the claim that they know strategy, government and the way to educate men? Can they show any city they have governed, any individuals even whom they have educated, as the Sophists can?

The reference to the Sophists should warn us that there is irony here, for of course to Plato the Sophists had no knowledge either. He does not pursue the argument very far; the whole of the *Republic* is an argument for the need of philosophic knowledge of the Forms for the governor or the educator. I suspect some irony too where he says that if the poets had the necessary knowledge to make things instead of only imitations of them, they would obviously have better things to do than to write poetry (599b).

It is the metaphysical argument at the beginning of Book X which has really caused all the trouble. Having, in the central books, established the Forms as the only objects of true knowledge, the only constant and true realities, Plato now uses the following illustration: There is a Form of bed and this is made by God (or the divine, for ὁ θεός is generic when used in this way); the carpenter, with his eye on this Form, makes a physical, actual bed; the painter then can only make a picture or imitation of this, and a one-sided one at that; so his product is at two removes from the truth. This of course is again a different meaning of mimêsis, and it seems to assert that art (for the poet is put in the same position as the painter) can do no more than imitate or represent particular things.

If we take this illustration literally it creates a lot of problems. Nowhere else in Plato do the gods create the Forms, which are eternal; it is very doubtful whether there are Forms of artefacta elsewhere in Plato; nor is it suggested elsewhere that carpenters or artisans have any knowledge of the Forms. These are problems for the philosophers, but they do suggest that in using this illustration Plato may not be altogether serious. Moreover, we have seen that he himself uses mimêsis in other and more general senses.

[12] 598e ff.

In any case, it is admittedly dangerous to attach too much importance to a particular detail in a Platonic myth or illustration. The artist is here put below the artisan; in the myth of the *Phaedrus* he is definitely put above him in the scale of lives, and this should warn us to be careful not to attach too much importance to this particular illustration in the *Republic*, which is far too often treated as if it were the only thing Plato had said about poetry and the only meaning he had ever given to the word mimêsis. In any case, as a recent scholar has put it: "Plato's order can be accepted without seeming to constitute any very impressive indictment of art, except we confine its reference to anyone who may have thought that artists are necessarily well informed and sound in their judgments on domestic science."[13]

The argument, however, which seems to me conclusive against taking the bed and painter illustrations too seriously in its detail is that this interpretation of mimêsis cannot possibly apply to music and architecture, for example, yet Plato clearly says more than once that these arts too are a form of imitation. We must therefore distinguish between what I have called the general meaning of mimêsis and the particular and special meanings in which it may be used in a particular passage, for a special purpose.

It is true that Plato is somewhat more severe towards art in the tenth book than in the third; he seems, for example, to exclude all drama, though somewhat hesitantly, but essentially his attitude is the same in both discussions, and, while passages can be quoted from the *Republic* itself which seem to imply another kind of art, in which the painter, for example, does know the Form and could make a picture of a man more beautiful than any man who ever existed, it remains true that in his actual discussions of art and poetry he never allows the artist to imitate the Forms directly. It seems clear that art was, to Plato, less important than life, however useful it may be in training the emotions before the age of reason. The *Symposium* shows how important the love of beauty is in the education of the philosopher, but in the ascent from the

---

[13] See N. R. Murphy, *The Interpretation of Plato's Republic*, p. 225. In this chapter, "Plato's treatment of art," Mr. Murphy quite rightly points out that Plato refuses to recognize that art has "a province of its own of a serious kind" or any "independent standard of rightness"; in the next section I am also indebted to him.

love of physical beauty, through the realization of the beauty of laws and institutions, to the full realization of the Form of beauty itself, no kind of art is mentioned. In the *Phaedrus* too it is the beauty we see in the actual world which leads us gradually to a perception of higher beauty (250c). In both dialogues the ascent to supreme beauty is only another aspect of the ascent to the understanding of truth and the Good. Nowhere does Plato envisage an aesthetic divorced from knowledge of Reality and Goodness, and, perhaps for this reason, he never allows the arts, not even poetry which he loved, a place in the ascent of the philosopher through love of truth, beauty and goodness.

Democritus' saying that the successful poet is out of his mind, possessed by a god, and that there are no sane poets on Helicon[14] is often contrasted with the Platonic position and his fear of a purely emotional appeal. And yet Plato says almost the same thing in the *Phaedrus*, where the myth, like the *Symposium*, is a supreme vindication of passion and emotion. Socrates there says (244d) "the madness which comes from the gods is a finer thing than human sanity," and he continues (245a):

> The third kind of madness comes from the Muses. It lays hold of a gentle and virgin soul, rouses and inspires it to song and poetry . . . and whoever comes to the gates of poetry without the Muses' madness, believing that technical skill will make him an adequate poet, is ineffectual himself and the poetry of this sane man vanishes before that of those who are mad.

"Madness which comes from the gods" expresses mythically what Plato would in more sober prose describe as passion controlled by reason, so that there need be no contradiction with the *Republic*, though there is certainly a change of emphasis and a more sympathetic attitude to poetry.

It is in the *Phaedrus* too that Plato makes some positive contributions to criticism. He lays down the principle that every discourse, whether poetry or prose, must be like a living organism in which every part has its proper place and function. He also lays down a definite method for the scientific study of 'rhetoric', which includes an analysis of different kinds of arguments and a study of

[14] Horace, *Ars Poetica*, 285-7.

human psychology—a method which, as has often been observed, Aristotle closely followed in his *Rhetoric*.

There is also a pleasant passage on the difference between art and mere technique. It would be ridiculous, he says, to claim to be a doctor because one knows the effect of every medicament but does not know when to apply them, or claim to be a musician if one only knows one's notes. And Socrates continues (268c 5):

> What if a man came to Sophocles or Euripides and said that he knew how to speak at length on trifling subjects and briefly on important ones, that he could at will make pitiful or frightening speeches, threatening speeches and so on, and that in teaching these things he taught how to compose tragedies?
> —I think, Socrates, that they would laugh at anyone who thought that tragedy was anything less than the organization of those elements together so that they harmonize with each other and with the whole work.

Here Plato recognizes that the great tragedians *are* masters of an art or craft and puts them on a par with Hippocrates as a doctor and Pericles as a statesman. So in the *Sophist*, in an elaborate diaeresis or classification in the hunt for the Sophist, we have one kind of mimêsis by voice and gesture (this must include dramatic presentation) which makes images intended to look like the original, though not exact copies, and this involves knowledge of the model.[15] This too implies a craft or technê, and the knowledge that goes with it is even more extensive.

Plato's final discussion of poetry is in the second book of the *Laws*, and he uses the word mimêsis freely in what we have called the general sense. There is a good deal of emphasis on the importance of poetry in training the young, but now Plato adds another function which we may call the recreational function: even after one has been taught to take pleasure in the right things, the good result of this training is apt to be disturbed in the hurly-burly of life and (653d):

> the gods, taking pity upon the race of men and its labours, established the round of divine festivals as a rest, and gave them

[15] *Sophist*, 267c-d.

the Muses and their leader Apollo and Dionysus as fellow celebrants, so they might be restored . . . .

Dionysus is of course the god of drama, whether tragic or comic, and poetry and music now have two functions: the training of the emotions in childhood, and the restoration of this emotional stability in maturity. This passage should not be forgotten when dealing with Aristotelian catharsis.

The imitative arts are now to be judged by three criteria: pleasure (only it must be the pleasure of the right people), the correctness of the imitation (which includes consistency of characterization, appropriate language and the like, and is at least an artistic criterion, however crudely expressed) and thirdly, as always, the social and psychological, i.e. the moral aspect. Plato still refuses to call καλόν, beautiful or well done, any poem which does not pass this last test, although he now adds that the poet need not be aware of this last factor (670e), only he must then obey the lawgiver as to whether his work will be performed.

So we have these meanings of mimêsis in Plato: first, the general meaning that art imitates life, and this sense did not originate with him; second, impersonation, which also includes emotional identification on the part of the spectator, and, thirdly, the special sense used in the metaphysical illustration of the painter and the bed.

When Aristotle, at the beginning of the *Poetics*, states, not as a point to be established but as a starting point to be argued from, that epic, tragedy and comedy, dithyrambic poetry, the music of the flute and the lyre are forms of imitation, as are painting, sculpture and dancing, the last of which by rhythm alone imitates character, sufferings and actions, one naturally assumes that he is using the word mimêsis in the same general sense we found in Plato and elsewhere. And so, I believe, he is, both there and throughout the *Poetics*, except once (1460a 8) where he uses it in the sense of impersonation.

Many commentators who are keen to endow Aristotle with a purer aesthetic than Plato's, have tried to find differences and of course have done so. The latest of these is John Jones who, in his book *On Aristotle and Greek Tragedy*, has developed a rather elaborate theory.[16] As far as Plato is concerned he bases himself entirely on the illustration of the painter and the bed used in the tenth book of the *Republic*, although he says himself that "Plato's argument is so unworthy . . . that one suspects him of knocking it hastily together in order to give himself a chance to attack art *en passant* from the standpoint of his central doctrine of Ideas." This, we have seen, is probably exactly what Plato did.

Observing that Plato never allowed that a poet or other artist might imitate the Forms directly (which is quite true, when Plato is actually discussing art) and that for Aristotle the Form is indwelling, Mr. Jones then goes on to say as regards the theory of Aristotle:

> The artist, who may or may not know what he is doing, is concerned with the intelligible essence, the Form, in a manner which distinguishes him both from philosophers and from ordinary men. His activity is the contemplation of a Form by the rendering of it into the medium of his art.

This is indeed attractive, the only difficulty being that there is no evidence at all that Aristotle had any such theory, and Mr. Jones quotes none. The same is true, I fear, about his ingenious theory that when Aristotle defines tragedy as an imitation of an action, this action or *praxis* is to be distinguished from the story or plot, *the mythos*, as the Form is to be distinguished from the "dramatic medium."[17] The distinction between action and plot can indeed be maintained, but Aristotle nowhere (as Mr. Jones admits) calls the *praxis* or action a Form. Indeed it is doubtful whether in the *Poetics* he is thinking about Forms at all.

Aristotle was thoroughly familiar with all that Plato wrote and with a good deal that he said as well, and he is much less inclined to overemphasize the one illustration of the painter and the bed than are most modern commentators.

To understand Aristotle it is necessary to realize that in working out his own theories he always has those of his predecessors in

---

[16] John Jones, *On Aristotle and Greek Tragedy* (London, 1962), pp. 21-24. Mr. Jones' discussions of particular tragedies are interesting and often illuminating, but I cannot agree with his interpretations of the *Poetics*.

[17] Jones, *op. cit.*, pp. 24-29.

mind, especially those of Plato. He may accept or reject them, correct or refine them; he may even at times misrepresent or misunderstand them, but he always has them in mind. This is very obvious in other parts of his philosophy; it is also, I believe, very true of his literary theories.

He accepts, as we have just seen, the Platonic theory of art as imitation, in its general sense. He also inherits from Plato the theory that any kind of discourse must have an organic unity or, as he puts it with deceptive simplicity, must have a beginning, a middle and an end. Unity of plot is most important and indeed it is the only unity he insists on; and from this principle of unity it follows that every event must follow those before it as probable or necessary, i.e. be conditioned by what went before, and that similarly every character must be consistent and act in a manner probable or inevitable.

He also accepts the Platonic insistence on censorship in the last book of the *Politics*, the only place where he discusses mousikê from the point of view of its educational and social effects, and it is important to realize that mousikê throughout this discussion means (as it usually does) both poetry *and* music, not music only, as it is usually translated. This is obvious where he says that the music of the flute must not be used in education because you cannot utter words when you play it, and also elsewhere.[18] In the *Politics* he very obviously adopts Plato's moral approach. This he also, I believe, accepts in the *Poetics*, but he corrects some of Plato's exaggerations. Where Plato forbids all impersonations of evil on the stage, Aristotle refines this and says that the moral effect should take into account the play as a whole, as well as the particular character and circumstances. The moral effects of poetry are not discussed as such in the *Poetics*, but this does not mean that Aristotle has changed his mind. Many have tried to empty the *Poetics* of all moral implications but they have not, in my opinion, been at all successful. There is no pure aesthetic in Aristotle any more than in any other Greek critic or philosopher.

We saw that to the educational function of poetry Plato had, in the *Laws*, added a recreational function which aimed at the resto-

[18] See my *Aristotle on Poetry and Style* (Bobbs Merrill, The Library of Liberal Arts, 1958), p. XIII and note 10.

ration of emotional balance. In the discussion of the *Politics* Aristotle adopts both of these and adds a third, its contribution to the life of leisure, though he unfortunately does not elaborate upon the last, but we must remember his definition of leisure as the time which remains after work and after recreation.[19]

It is exclusively in connection with the recreational function of mousikê that Aristotle speaks of catharsis in the *Politics*, and there the meaning is quite plain. Emotional people have their emotions whipped up by certain types of mousikê, as some people are driven to a kind of frenzy by certain orgiastic music and then undergo a kind of purge which restores their emotional balance.[20] No one disputes that this is the meaning of the word catharsis in the *Politics*, and Aristotle refers us to the *Poetics* for a further discussion of it.

We do not possess that further discussion, but the word does occur at the end of the famous definition of tragedy in the sixth chapter of the *Poetics* where we read that "tragedy is an imitation . . . which through pity and fear achieves the catharsis of such emotions." Two main interpretations have held the field; the word catharsis means a cleansing, a purifying; it is either an Orphic and religious metaphor, i.e. the purification of such emotions, or a medical metaphor (as in the *Politics*) and the meaning then is "a purgation of such emotions." The first meaning, purification, has nowadays been largely abandoned, partly because of the use of the word in the *Politics*, and in part also because neither pity nor fear are considered desirable states in the *Rhetoric*, and Aristotle does not know any disinterested or pure pity. He defines pity in the *Rhetoric* as a kind of pain which we feel at seeing someone who does not deserve it suffer evil of a destructive or painful kind, an evil which we fear may come upon ourselves or someone dear to us, and when this evil seems near.[21]

The interpretation of catharsis as a kind of purge is strengthened, I think, if we remember the highly emotional atmosphere of Greek drama and the Greek theatre, of which we spoke yesterday, and the passage about the recreational function of poetry in

[19] *Politics*, VIII, 1 (1337b 32–1338a 13).
[20] *Politics*, VIII, 7 (1341b 33–1342a 29); cf. *Laws*, VII (790c 5–791b 2).
[21] *Rhet.* 2,8 *ad init.*

the *Laws*, as well as the fact that the rousing and quietening of the emotions, especially of pity and fear, by the power of the spoken word had been a subject of study ever since Gorgias. The rhetoricians had written books about it. Against this background it seems clear that the phrase in the definition must refer to the emotions of the audience.

Recently however, two distinguished scholars have presented a quite different interpretation of the sentence. Professor Gerald Else translates as follows:[22]

> an imitation . . . carrying to completion, through a course of events involving pity and fear, the purification of those painful or fatal acts which have that quality.

Professor Kitto, in a paper published last year,[23] in effect accepts the second part of this interpretation, but not the first. He recognizes that the pity and fear must be those of the audience, and that the simple words "through pity and fear—δι' ἐλέου καὶ φόβου —cannot mean "through a course of events, etc.," but must mean by arousing pity and fear. With this I agree, and I think any unprejudiced reader of the Greek words would. But Kitto does accept the translation of catharsis as the purification of the tragic events.

Both these scholars want us to ignore the use of catharsis in the *Politics* in interpreting the *Poetics*, and both insist that the catharsis in the *Politics* is purely musical. As I have already stated, I believe that mousikê in the passage of the *Politics* should be taken to include poetry, and "the Muse of the theatre," of which Aristotle there speaks, must surely include tragedy. This I had already argued, and I believe proved, without any reference to the definition of tragedy in mind.[24] If I am right, then the two passages largely deal with the same phenomenon; and in any case they deal with very similar ones.

I must also disagree with Kitto when he identifies *diagôgê* with recreation and separates cathartic mousikê from recreation. Aris-

---

[22] *Aristotle's Poetics, The Argument* (Harvard 1957), p. 221.

[23] H.D.F. Kitto, "Catharsis" in *The Classical Tradition*, Literary and Historical Studies in Honor of Harry Caplan, edited L. Wallach (Cornell University Press, 1966), pp. 133-147.

[24] See note 18 above; Kitto, p. 134; Else, p. 440.

totle in the *Politics* clearly states[25] that mousikê has three functions: the educational (also called ethical), the recreational, and that which contributes to the life of leisure (*diagôgê*) which we might call the cultural. Further the use of cathartic mousikê is restricted to the second function, the recreational. Nor do I see that it is necessary to the traditional interpretation to consider catharsis as the final cause of tragedy.

One may well admit that if one separates the last ten words of the famous definition from all contemporary thought, spins intellectual cobwebs about them in this isolation, and forgets about the use of catharsis in the *Politics* (though why should we? for I note that Professor Else does not hesitate to use other works of Aristotle to interpret the *Poetics* elsewhere[26]), then these last five words could mean "the purification of such events," that is, events which stir up pity and fear, though this, I think stretches the meaning 'such' (τοιούτων) a good deal more than the traditional interpretation does, i.e. "the purgation of such emotions."[27] Else and Kitto then immediately ask us: What emotions?, as many others have done. I confess I see no difficulty here; it may be anger or indignation, or any of the many emotions that may be aroused in the course of a tragedy, emotions which may reach a high degree of intensity but which of themselves, unless we feel the specifically tragic emotions of pity and fear, will not be purged. Tragedy may arouse a great many emotions, but *unless it stirs up pity and fear in the audience there will be no catharsis*. Mere anger or indignation and the rest may indeed be very intense, and they may yield to yelling at the movies or to smashing your TV set, but not to the purging of "such emotions," whereas the tragic mixture of pity and fear will, or so Aristotle thought. Nor do I understand what exactly is meant by the purification of the act. Oedipus may be purified in the sense that he is not responsible for

[25] See, for example, VIII, 9 (1341b 38): καὶ γὰρ παιδείας ἕνεκεν καὶ καθάρσεως . . . τρίτον δὲ πρὸς διαγωγὴν. . . .
[26] For example, pp. 433 ff.
[27] In *Politics*, VIII, 7 (1342a 12), Aristotle has just been speaking of the medicinal catharsis (ὥσπερ ἰατρείας τύχοντας καὶ καθάρσεως) and then goes on: "Necessarily this very same thing is experienced by those who feel pity and fear, and emotional people generally. And by others in so far as each is subject to *such emotions*" (καθ' ὅσον ἐπιβάλλει τῶν τοιούτων ἑκάστῳ. . . .), an even looser use, which here too includes emotions in a wide sense.

his incest, and therefore to be pitied, but is the incest itself purified in any reasonable sense? Else says: "We have said that the purification of the *pathos*, the exculpation of the hero's motive from polluted intent, is precedent to our feeling pity for him." The exculpation of the hero's intent is a quite different matter and a very necessary one, but why the purification of the act? Even if we felt that, a Greek would not. For him the pollution was almost a physical thing, which in cases of unintentional homicide was thought to cling to the instrument of death, and even when the doer was exculpated, the instrument of death has been known to be tried and cast outside the boundaries of the state.[28]

Professor Kitto (p. 144) is somewhat more sophisticated. He emphasizes that among the distressful events the tragic mimêsis makes a strict choice as to which are proper subjects of tragedy (quite true, and Aristotle makes this very clear); then the playwright must stick to what is relevant. As he puts it "the action presented in art is more unified, more logical, more significant, more serious and philosophic than an event in real life." All this is true, good Aristotle, and undisputed. Kitto proceeds:

> an action in real life necessarily has indefinite origins and an indefinite end. Besides, this, if it has its penumbra of the uncertain, contingent, purely accidental. Artistic representation, on the other hand, of its nature, removes such fuzziness; it leaves everything clearcut and significant. Therefore, when Aristotle says that the mimesis performs a catharsis of the distressful events, I suggest that it was this kind of cleaning up that he meant; the mimesis clears away everything but what is meaningful, and because all is now meaningful it can without revulsion enter our minds and bear fruit. . . . It works this catharsis of events by evoking our pity and fear. . . .

This last sentence seems to put the cart before the horse. Admittedly, Aristotle wants every detail to be relevant, he says so clearly enough elsewhere, and it makes sense to say that this complete meaningfulness makes it easier to evoke pity and fear, but

---

[28] See Demosthenes, *Against Aristocrates* (XXIII), 76, and other passages in D. M. MacDowell's *Athenian Homicide Law in the Age of the Orators* (Manchester. U.P. 1963), pp. 85-89.

how is this complete relevance to be achieved *through pity and fear?* That does not seem to make sense. The relevance is achieved by the writer before his play is ever put on the stage, and pity and fear are the result, not the cause. Kitto's argument does not seem logical even though catharsis by itself could well mean this cleansing of events—but not in the context.

"The purgation through pity and fear of such emotions" may not be a very satisfactory description of the emotional state one finds oneself in when witnessing a great tragedy, though "such emotions" are the emotions aroused by the tragedy. Commentators have had a lot of fun with the phrase and said that one does not go to the theatre to be purged, and that this is not the end of tragedy. Aristotle never says one should or that it is. Richard Eberhardt, a poet and dramatist, is quoted by Kitto (p. 134) as saying:

> My emotions of pity and fear were not purged . . .
> What I felt was that my whole being was purged.

Aristotle's phrase may not be perfect, but it does not seem to me to be much more indefinite than this one and if we remember that he says that, through feeling pity and fear, we feel purged of all the emotions which the tragedy has stirred up in us along with pity and fear itself, i.e. such emotions, then it seems to me that most modern descriptions of the result of tragedy are no more adequate. We have a curious way of expecting from Plato and Aristotle perfect answers to problems to which we have ourselves not found the solution. At any rate, "the purgation, through pity and fear, of such emotions" seems to me much more adequate than "the purification or the cleansing of such events."

Let us now turn briefly to the tragic hero and the tragic flaw, terms which are much more familiar in modern than in ancient criticism, and here I had better translate the famous passage (52b 34-53a 12). Aristotle has been discussing the kind of events which will evoke pity and fear, and he says:

> In the first place, *good men* must not be seen suffering a change from prosperity to misfortune, for this is not fearful or pitiful but shocking. Nor must *wicked men* pass from misfortune to prosperity as this is the most untragic of all; nothing happens

as it should, it is neither popular[29] nor fearful nor pitiful. Nor again must *a thoroughly wicked man* pass from prosperity to misfortune; such a plot may be popular, but it does not arouse pity or fear. We feel pity for *the man* who does not deserve his misfortune, we feel fear for *someone* like ourselves; neither feeling is here involved.

This leaves us with *the one* in between.[30] *Such a man* is one who is neither outstanding in virtue or righteousness, nor is it through wickedness and vice that his change to misfortune takes place, but through a hamartia; he is of those who are of great repute and good fortune, like Oedipus or Thyestes, and the famous *men of such families.*

You will note that Aristotle switches from the plural to the singular and I have faithfully followed him, for Mr. John Jones, remarks, quite truly, that most commentators and translators use the singular throughout, thus introducing here the tragic hero who, he maintains, does not exist in the *Poetics*.[31] This is an exaggeration. Aristotle uses the plural when he is describing the kind of people who are *not* proper characters of tragedy, but he uses the singular throughout the sentence where he describes the man who is, until the very last when he says that such a man must be among the great of the earth, like Oedipus or Thyestes, and the famous men of such families. This last plural is not, I think, significant. The most one could reasonably maintain is that Aristotle does not specifically say that the tragedy must be about one main character, and might therefore admit tragedies which are not, and there obviously are such. One might also add that he lays some emphasis on the "house" or family, and that this is apt to be of more importance in Greek tragedy than in modern, which it quite obviously is. So far Mr. Jones is right.

To say, however, that the tragic hero has actually been imported

---

[29] For this meaning of φιλάνθρωπον see Daniel de Montmollin's article "Le sens du mot φιλάνθρωπον dans la *Poétique* d'Aristote," *Phoenix*, 9 (1965), pp. 15-23.

[30] Since Aristotle says that we should feel both pity and fear, that we feel pity for one who does not deserve his fate and fear for someone like ourselves, so that the tragic character must be both, I cannot follow Else's rendering of ὁ μεταξύ as one "between the undeserving sufferer and the sufferer who is like us" (p. 377). Nor should we identify the undeserving with the completely good man, since Aristotle has dismissed the latter as not tragic.

[31] Jones, pp. 11-20.

into the *Poetics* and that Aristotle did not have him in mind, is not, I think, a fair interpretation of the passage. That he had him *mainly* in mind I have no doubt whatever.

Let us now turn to the 'hamartia,' the famous "tragic flaw." The best tragic character is clearly stated to be neither saint nor villain. (Homer knew this, and his greatest hero, Achilles, certainly does not behave like a perfect hero.) Further, he should not deserve his misfortune, so that we can pity him, and he should be a man like ourselves, so that we can feel fear; his tragedy should come about through some hamartia. The trouble, of course, is the ambiguity of that word. Its general meaning is to miss one's target; it frequently means wrongdoing or sin; it can also mean an error or mistake, though generally some kind of responsibility lies with the doer of the deed.

It has generally been thought that the hamartia must be *either* a flaw of character which makes the tragic character morally responsible for his tragedy, *or* a simple mistake which brings the tragedy about but implies no moral responsibility. The first interpretation was unsatisfactory: scholars have found it impossible to find a moral flaw in Oedipus for example (though some commentators write as if, had he only not been so impatient, he might have lived in happy incest with his mother for the rest of his life). Aristotle does not say that there is any moral responsibility. Hence the present fashion is rather to take hamartia to refer to a mere mistake or error.

Professor Else adopts this translation, then argues that it is a mistake due to ignorance, usually of the identity of the person later to be recognized. Then he goes on to say that the hamartia *is* that ignorance (pp. 379 and 383).

He relies largely upon Aristotle's discussions of voluntary and involuntary actions in the *Ethics*. In one passage he finds that some involuntary actions are due to ignorance of the particular circumstances, and that these win pity. In another passage the word hamartêma is used to describe a certain kind of injurious action due to ignorance, δι' ἄγνοιαν. Incidentally, elsewhere in the *Ethics*, as Else also notes, Aristotle uses hamartia to describe actions due to wickedness. So the only fair conclusion from all this is that hamartia and hamartêma can describe *either* a wicked act *or* a mistake, which we knew before we started, and does not help much. Nor are we entitled to identify the action due to ignorance with ignorance itself. Hamartia cannot be equated with ignorance, and δι' ἁμαρτίαν is not the same as δι' ἄγνοιαν.[32] The difficulty is that if hamartia is a mere mistake, unless there is something in the character of the man, which caused it or made it likely, it is hard to see how the tragedy could conform to Aristotle's other requirement that every event or incident should follow the other as probable or inevitable.

We are here once more in danger of being unduly confined by our own translation. When we speak of a flaw of character, our word refers to moral character almost exclusively. But this modern divorce between moral character on the one hand, and brains or even physique on the other, is quite foreign to Aristotle and to Greek thought generally,[33] and we shall come nearer to his meaning if we take hamartia as a flaw or weakness in the *personality*: it may be moral, intellectual or physical; it might even be an error, provided there be something in the personality which makes this error probable or inevitable. It implies no moral responsibility, but it accounts for the tragedy, and thus makes it dramatically satisfying. There is no moral flaw in Oedipus, but there is a certain obstinacy and impatience which causes the discovery, and through which the tragedy may be said to happen. In any case there must be some flaw, for otherwise the man would be a perfect personality and therefore (to Aristotle) not a proper tragic character.

There are many other important and suggestive thoughts about tragedy in the *Poetics* which we have no time to deal with, though none, fortunately, have caused as much confusion and controversy as those we have dealt with. One other confusion we may per-

---

[32] Else, p. 383: "It follows that the tragic hamartia is an ignorance or mistake as to certain details." For the whole discussion see pp. 378-385. The passages from the *Ethics* upon which it is based are III *ad init.* and V,10 (1135a 15–1136a 9), and cf. *Rhetoric*, I, 13 (1174b 4-10). For hamartia in the sense of wicked deed see *Eth*. III, 2 (1110b 29).

[33] This has been pointed out by P. W. Harsh in his article "Ἁμαρτία again" in *TAPA*, 76 (1945), p. 51. Harsh, however, inclines to moral flaw or at least "some degree of culpability" on the part of the hero. Yet he sees very clearly that "such classification (into either error of judgement or ethical fault) involves a false dichotomy between intellectual error and moral fault." Of special interest are the examples he gives of the use of hamartia in tragedy.

haps clear up in passing, though it is not, or should not be, controversial, and that is the difference between peripety (περιπέτεια) and the change of fortune, which Aristotle calls *metabasis*. The latter occurs in all tragedies, the former, peripety, has a quite different meaning, and refers to a reversal or change of direction, which occurs only in the best tragedies. By this Aristotle means that things which are going in one direction suddenly develop in another. He himself refers to the Oedipus scene where the messenger from Corinth is about to free Oedipus from his fear of parricide and incest by showing him he is *not* the son of the Corinthian king and queen, but in so doing sets in motion the chain of revelation which shows that he has already committed both sins.

Aristotle refers us to the *Poetics* not only for a discussion of catharsis which we do not have, but also for a discussion of the laughable, which we do not possess either. Both may have been in the lost second book, if it was ever written. Comedy as a subject, hallowed by custom and religion as it was, seems to have embarrassed the philosophers. There are a couple of casual references in Plato, who does not want his citizens to act in it (or perhaps even write it if μιμεῖσθαι covers both) and one interesting passage in the *Philebus*.[34] After mentioning the mixed pleasures of tragedy—"we enjoy it, yet we weep"—Plato goes on to say that pain is also involved in the pleasures of comedy, for a kind of envy or spite (φθόνος) is always present which makes us laugh at the misfortunes of others. He then adds that ridicule is closely related to the lack of self-knowledge, for the proper butt of comedy is the man who does not know himself, who does not know his own limitations, in relation to his ability, his wealth, appearance or the like, provided only—the proviso is important—that he is not so powerful that fear displaces laughter. Thus, the passage concludes, pain is mixed with pleasure, not only in dirges and tragedies, but in "the whole tragedy and comedy of life." Plato does not elaborate.

In the *Poetics* we have only the short description of comedy (one can hardly call it a definition) in the fifth chapter, where Aristotle is mainly concerned to contrast it with tragedy:

Comedy . . . is an imitation (mimêsis) of men who are inferior

---

[34] Philebus, 48a–49c. The other references in Plato are *Rep.* 606c and *Laws*, 816e.

but not altogether vicious; the ridiculous being a kind of ugliness. It is a sort of *flaw* (ἁμάρτημα) and ugliness; an ugliness which is painless and not destructive.

The ugliness which is not painful reminds us of the butt of comedy who must not be too powerful; and the comic flaw which is not painful or dangerous parallels the tragic flaw to some extent. Note, however, that there is no mention of a comic catharsis.

In a discussion of the laughable, Cicero makes one of his characters say that he had found no worthwhile discussion on the subject by any Greek writer, only collections of jokes.[35] This makes it pretty certain that none by a prominent writer was extant in his day. I may mention in passing a very late and undated Greek little treatise which, because we have so little on comedy, has attracted much attention, the so-called *Tractatus Coislinianus*. I do so in order to warn you that there is no justifiable reason to build upon this an Aristotelian theory of comedy, as has sometimes been done. It gives a confused definition of comedy which seems to be an attempt to apply to comedy the Aristotelian definition of tragedy. It also contains a list of ways to provoke laughter which may or may not go back in part to Peripatetic sources, but that is all.

I have spent most of my time today on a few specific theories, and have not dealt with some quite important works of ancient critics, such as those of Dionysius of Halicarnassus, in particular his masterpiece on *Word-Arrangement*, and above all the work of Longinus. I have done so in part because I have dealt with these at some length elsewhere,[36] and partly because the particular theories which I have dealt with here—Plato's theory of art as "imitation," Aristotle's catharsis and the tragic flaw—are continually referred to in modern discussions of criticism, and very frequently misinterpreted.

There are two contrary trends about the two philosophers today. On the one hand Plato seems to be blamed for everything, without being given the benefit of any doubt; on the other hand Aristotle is nearly always highly praised, but the temptation to read modern theories into his text is almost irresistible after centuries of scholarly debate. The only way to avoid these tendencies is to keep

[35] *De Oratore*, II, 217.
[36] See my *The Greek and Roman Critics* (Toronto 1965).

the Greek texts continually before us when discussing them, to be sure of what they said and what they meant, even if we cannot all agree. In this connection I like to remember a saying of Aristotle himself, also from the *Poetics*:[37]

> The proper method of criticism is the opposite of that mentioned by Glaucon who says that critics start with certain assumptions, for which they have no good reason. Then they condemn the writer out of hand, arguing on the basis that he said what they think he said, which they do not like.

This certainly applies to the critics of Plato. It also applies to commentators on Aristotle, except that in his case I would add:

> Or they praise him on the assumption that he said what they think he said, which they like very much. Only he did not say it.

[37] Ch. 25 (1461b).

4

Justinian and
the Imperial Office

BY GLANVILLE DOWNEY

Delivered February 12 and 13, 1968

JUSTINIAN AND
THE IMPERIAL OFFICE

ACH OF THE three reigns that may be described as epochs
in the history of the Roman empire, those of Augustus,
Constantine and Justinian, constituted both an end and a
beginning. Constantine and Justinian were the heirs of Augustus,
but in addition to the powers and functions established by the
first *princeps*, these sovereigns inherited the additional powers,
duties and responsibilities that from time to time became attached
to the imperial office. Moreover, Constantine and Justinian found
themselves called upon to deal with situations and problems that
had come into existence since the time of Augustus. Thus it was
that both Constantine and Justinian, inheriting the established
traditions of the imperial office, shaped that office to meet the
needs of their times. Finding at their disposition both a tradition
and what we might call an apparatus of rulership, each of these
sovereigns left his own distinctive stamp on the monarch's role.

If with this in mind we follow a well established scholarly
tradition and take the reign of Justinian (A.D. 527-565) as
marking both the end of the Late Roman Empire and the beginning of the Byzantine State, we shall see in the imperial
office, as it was filled by this remarkable man, both the essential
continuity that had been maintained throughout the five hundred
years since the reign of Augustus, and the creative activity through
which Justinian set out to use his office to realize in its complete
form the Christian Graeco-Roman society that Constantine had
inaugurated. The imperial office of Justinian represented a direct
and continuous transmission of *potestas* and *auctoritas* from the
rule of the first emperor, but the Roman world had changed in
five hundred years and it was Justinian's task, as heir of Augustus,
to rule a changed world. It may be useful to take the opportunity
offered by these lectures to try to pick out the elements of the
continuity of the imperial office, and the indications of the unity
of Justinian's plans for his reign, that show what the task of a
Roman emperor was five hundred years after the death of
Augustus.

The variety and the spectacular nature of the events of his long career have had the result that there are several pictures of the reign of Justinian in circulation today, and that, as in the case of some other bold and active monarchs, Justinian may run the risk of being famous for the wrong reasons. Indeed, his fame exists today on several different levels. To some readers who are not otherwise seriously concerned with Roman History, Justinian is well known as the husband of Theodora. Procopius' *Secret History* will always find readers who will not go on to read the other sources or even the serious modern accounts; and these readers will enjoy thinking of Justinian as the wicked emperor of Procopius' scabrous gossip, alleged to have been seen seated on the throne in the form of a demon, or walking about the palace at night carrying his head in his hands.[1] To the common man, it is an admired prerogative of monarchy to be wicked, and Justinian, in Procopius' distorted view, possessed excellent qualifications for distinction here.

Above this elementary level of Justinian's popular reputation, there is another aspect under which he has become notorious, even among some scholars, for the wrong reason; and here, in the rectification of a false tradition, we may find a clue that will help us toward a judicious assessment of Justinian's conception of his own task as emperor.

To some students it has seemed a blot on Justinian's character that in A.D. 529, only two years after he became sole emperor, he "closed" the schools of Athens in which classical Greek philosophy was still being taught. Gibbon described this episode in terms that had the effect of establishing a definitive judgment on the emperor's action: "Justinian suppressed the schools of Athens, and the consulship of Rome."[2] We may suspect that this is an instance in which Gibbon's literary craftsmanship lent unmerited, though elegant, support to his detection of a stage in the decline and fall. In fact Gibbon linked two actions that otherwise might have been taken to represent two different kinds of motives, and he brought them together under the idea of suppression which

[1] *Anecdota* 12.14-27; 18.1, 36-37; 30.34.
[2] *History of the Decline and Fall of the Roman Empire*, ed. J. B. Bury (London 1897-1902) 4.261.

might convey the image of arbitrary and tyrannical action. Justinian is presented as having done away with two of the most characteristic institutions of the ancient world, one intellectual, the other political. There may also be a further suggestion, to any who might be predisposed to perceive it, that it was Christian bigotry that was responsible for the suppression of a last remnant of the philosophy of Hellas. Lovers of ancient Greece might take this moment to mourn the end of one of the great traditions of the human spirit, and to think of Justinian as the agent in this termination of an era.

At the same time we must remember that in the eyes of Justinian there was justification for his action, in that it was the duty of a Christian emperor to eliminate paganism and assure the salvation of his people through the universal acceptance of Christianity. One of the best known programs of his reign was the systematic persecution of pagans, Jews and Samaritans, and the closing of the schools of philosophy in the ancient home of pagan Greek philosophy was surely a logical part in the care of a Christian emperor for the spiritual welfare of his people. In this sense, Justinian was merely completing a process of the Christianization of the Roman state that had begun under Constantine. In reality the episode provides an instructive insight into the emperor's conception of the duties of the Christian monarch. It has not always been taken into account that even after the closing of the schools of Athens, Greek philosophy continued to be taught elsewhere during Justinian's reign. The career of John Philoponus, the celebrated Aristotelian commentator at Alexandria, does not seem to have been hindered by governmental restriction, and there is ample testimony to the work of the flourishing schools at Gaza in Palestine, where Greek literature and philosophy formed the basis of the curriculum.[3]

[3] On the work of John Philoponus and on scholarly activity at Alexandria, see H. D. Saffrey, "Le chrétien Jean Philopon et la survivance de l'école d'Alexandrie au VIe siècle," *Revue des Études Grecques*, 67 (1954), 396-410; M. V. Anastos, "The Alexandrian Origin of the Christian Topography of Cosmas Indicopleustes," *Dumbarton Oaks Papers*, 3 (1946) 73-80; *idem*, "Aristotle and Cosmas Indicopleustes in the Void," *Prosphora eis Stilpona P. Kyriakiden* (Thessalonika, 1953), 35-50 (*Hellenika*, Parartema 4). On scholarship in Palestine, including Gaza, see G. Downey, "The Christian Schools of Palestine: A Chapter in Literary History," *Harvard Library Bulletin*, 12 (1958), 297-319, and *Gaza in the Early Sixth Century* (Norman, Oklahoma, 1963).

What our evidence indicates is that Justinian's action at Athens had to do primarily with the manner in which Greek philosophy was being taught there. The scholars who were engaged in philosophical study and teaching at Alexandria and at Gaza were Christians, and their teaching was presented in a Christian context. At Athens, on the contrary, the teachers were themselves pagans, and it was this that concerned Justinian. The extant testimony indicates that what Justinian did was to require that the teachers at Athens become Christians so that they might offer their instruction within the larger framework of Christian doctrine, as their colleagues at Alexandria and Gaza were doing. Conversion of the teachers would presumably have satisfied Justinian's desire to complete the Christianization of the intellectual life of the empire. As it happened, the professors at Athens found themselves unable to renounce their faith and so had to give up their teaching.[4]

This episode shows us, in the first place, that one of Justinian's major concerns as emperor was to assure unity of religion and culture that in the ancient world had political importance. The Emperor Julian the Philosopher, faced with a similar political problem, had forbidden Christians to teach the Greek classics on the ground that Christian teachers, by the method of their instruction, might corrupt the minds of the pagan youth. Justinian saw danger, not in the teaching of classical philosophy as such, but in its being taught by pagans who might by their method of presentation corrupt the minds of Christian youth. Justinian conceived it to be one of the duties of the Christian monarch to make sure that the intellectual activity of his realm conformed in all respects to Christian doctrine. Just as Christians because of their religion had been regarded as politically subversive in the pagan Roman empire, pagans in the Christian Roman empire could only be regarded as subversive, in that they were unable to form an organic part of the Christian community and state. The conflict between Christianity and paganism had been a clash be-

---

[4] On the closing of the schools in Athens, see G. Downey, "Justinian's View of Christianity and the Greek Classics," *Anglican Theological Review*, 40 (1958), 3-12, and "Julian and Justinian and the Unity of Faith and Culture," *Church History*, 28 (1959), 3-13.

tween two different kinds of unity of religion and culture. Out of this conflict there had grown a new kind of unity of religion and culture—the new Christian unity which took over and transformed the Greek heritage. It was Justinian's task to see that this process was completed and that the new unity, of which the imperial office itself was a part, was firmly established. Justinian considered that he was called to rule a state that had come to represent the harmonious and active blending of various traditions, Roman and Greek, pagan and Christian. The process of the combination of these elements had begun when the conversion of Constantine the Great inaugurated the Christian Roman Empire. It was a process that could not have been carried out at once in all details and important work remained for Justinian to do.

For his task Justinian inherited an impressive tradition of power and authority which for five hundred years had been building up what might be called the official personality of the Roman emperor. It was a personality that each emperor inherited; indeed it was a personality that existed in itself, for history had shown that it was true, as Tacitus has written, that princes were mortal, but the Roman state was eternal.[5]

While there did not exist a written constitution in which the emperor's powers and responsibilities were defined, these powers and responsibilities were constantly set forth in different kinds of media that were intelligible to all the citizens of the empire. The imperial dress and insignia, the elaborate ceremonial of the court which in fact had something of a liturgical character, the official titulature in documents and on coins and inscriptions, the language of the panegyrical addresses which had to be offered to the sovereign on state occasions, all combined to define the life and work of the ruler of the greatest state in the civilized world, who was in effect the symbol of the Roman state and the Roman people. The emperor came to be regarded as the source of law; in effect, in the Greek phrase which had first been used of the Hellenistic kings, he was the *nomos empsychos*, the law incarnate. The Emperor Augustus had been presented with a golden shield on which were inscribed the names of four virtues, *virtus, clem-*

5 Tacitus, *Annals* 3.6.5.

entia, iustitia, pietas,[6] which were supposed to be *par excellence* the qualities that had enabled him to save the state from civil war and create its new government. Following that precedent, a whole catalogue of official virtues and personal qualities became connected with the emperor's person, such as clemency, constancy, piety, justice, moderation.[7] When the ruler possessed these virtues, his reign was characterized by the fortunate conditions described in other inscriptions on the coins, such as peace, liberty, security, happiness, concord, equity. The frequent inscription "providence" alluded both to the forethought exercised by the emperor and to the divine providence which protected and fostered his reign. The emperor was described as eternal just as the Roman Empire was traditionally spoken of as eternal.

Beginning with Pliny's elaborate panegyric of Trajan, a well developed literary tradition of panegyric, in Greek and Latin, prose and verse, celebrated the emperor's achievements and virtues. The well exercised theme of the honorific address to the emperor built up a corpus of laudatory and admonitory thoughts that grew in number and in complexity as successive panegyrists displayed their ingenuity. Alongside the catalogue of imperial virtues appeared the list of imperial benevolences which likewise were commemorated on the coins. Mottoes such as *vota publica, concordia, aeternitas Aug., felicitas Aug., congiarium, liberalitas, libertas restituta, vota suscepta, fides exercituum, disciplina Aug.,* all reminded the people of the special qualities and activities of the rulers.[8]

It would have been difficult for either the panegyrist or the

---

[6] *Res Gestae Divi Augusti,* c. 34.2.

[7] See M. P. Charlesworth, "*Providentia* and *Aeternitas,*" *Harvard Theological Review,* 29 (1936), 107-132; idem, "The Virtues of a Roman Emperor: Propaganda and the Creation of Belief," *Proceedings of the British Academy,* 23 (1937), 105-133; idem, "*Pietas* and *Victoria*: The Emperor and the Citizen," *Journal of Roman Studies,* 33 (1943), 1-10; Harold Mattingly, "The Roman 'Virtues,'" *Harvard Theological Review,* 30 (1937), 103-117. For convenient lists of the blessings, virtues and qualities, see, for example, Michael Grant, *Roman Imperial Money* (London, 1954), 156-175, and P. V. Hill, J. P. C. Kent and R. A. G. Carson, *Late Roman Bronze Coinage, A.D. 324-498* (London, 1965), indices, pp. 34-35, 108-111.

[8] For a convenient collection of this evidence, see Harold Mattingly, *Roman Coins from the Earliest Times to the Fall of the Western Empire,* second edition, reprinted (London, 1962), 144 ff.

emperor to escape from the discussion of the imperial virtues. To us these virtues come as well worn themes, whether they are to be considered as the desirable attributes of the private individual or the necessary equipment of the sovereign; but to the citizens of the empire these were matters of public concern since they affected the welfare of the Roman state and the Roman people; and the virtues for which the ordinary man ought to strive took on imperial proportions in the case of an all powerful sovereign.

The panegyrics were taken sufficiently seriously to make it possible for the speakers on occasion to make use of their opportunities to convey rebuke and admonition in the form of praise. This could be done in public, and in the presence of high dignitaries. The emperor could be praised, pointedly, for virtues which everyone including himself knew he did not possess, and, if he were intelligent, he would take the hint.

Each new emperor was saluted in this way and the greetings continued throughout his reign. To the modern reader the repetitions of the themes might seem tedious, but the panegyrics served a real purpose. Because there was no written constitution, each emperor had a certain freedom to interpret the nature of his office—and many emperors added to their powers. Once an emperor had acquired a new power, it would have been difficult to deprive him of it. Thus the panegyrics had real significance as popular statements of what was expected of the emperor, and what the limitations as well as the possibilities of his office were considered to be. The rulers' conduct was under constant observation, and they must meet certain standards if they wished to retain the loving obedience of their subjects.[9]

This is what we might call the ideological apparatus of the imperial office that Justinian inherited. He was fortunate in having had an apprenticeship during the nine-years' reign of his uncle Justin I (A.D. 518-527) when he was in fact the power behind

---

[9] See, among other studies, L. K. Born, "The Perfect Prince according to the Latin Panegyrists," *American Journal of Philology*, 55 (1934), 20-35, and the same scholar's chapter "Ancient Theories of Statecraft," in his *The Education of a Christian Prince* (New York, 1936) 44-93 (Columbia University, *Records of Civilization*, No. 27, reprinted, New York, 1965). For a comprehensive account of the activities of the panegyrists and of their presentation of political theory, see Francis Dvornik, *Early Christian and Byzantine Political Philosophy: Origins and Background* (Washington, 1966), especially volume 2.

the throne, possessed of influence but not responsibility.[10] During this period Justinian had the opportunity to observe and to make plans, and the promptness with which he set on foot certain projects such as the codification of the law after he became emperor shows that he had some very definite ideas about what he intended to do.

What use, then, do we find him making of the "apparatus"— constitutional tradition, political theory, iconography, ceremonial, and what we might call the vocabulary of propaganda and public relations, such as the traditional themes of literary panegyric and the mottoes on the coins? Justinian was a person of scholarly and literary interests, and he must have been well acquainted with the literary panegyrics, for example of Themistius and the *XII Panegyrici Latini*, which were much admired. As a conscientious ruler he would consider carefully what use he might make of all this material.

It is evident, of course, that Justinian in effect did not employ the full resources of the traditional publicity that had been developed before his time. The coins bear only a few mottoes, and there are extant none of the panegyrics of the traditional type. It is possible of course that such were written but have not been preserved; there must have been many panegyrics from all periods of the empire that did not achieve, and doubtless did not deserve, the admiration of generations of readers. But as we shall see later in our study, the panegyrics that we do possess from Justinian's reign are so different from the traditional laudatory addresses that we shall be justified in supposing that panegyrics of the conventional style may not have been in favor with the emperor, or that they did not possess the literary merits of the pieces that have been preserved.

This does not mean, of course, that Justinian was not careful to maintain the essential titles that proclaimed his power. In his

[10] On Justinian's role during his uncle's reign, see A. A. Vasiliev, *Justin the First: An Introduction to the Epoch of Justinian the Great* (Cambridge, 1950; *Dumbarton Oaks Studies*, 1). The standard work on Justinian's reign will now be Berthold Rubin, *Das Zeitalter Iustinians*, of which the first volume has been published (Berlin, 1960). Pending completion of this work, the same scholar's earlier work, *Prokopios von Kaisereia* (Stuttgart, 1954), should be consulted.

inscriptions he is *Dominus noster Iustinianus perpetuus Augustus*.[11] In his laws he declares himself to be *nomos empsychos*, "animate law."[12] On the coins we miss the rich vocabulary employed by some earlier emperors, but two important phrases are retained on most of the issues, *Victoria Augustorum* and *Gloria Romanorum*. The mint of Antioch alone continued to use the traditional legend *Concordia*.[13]

At the same time that the coins portray Justinian as a Roman emperor in the ancient tradition going back to Augustus, they show him as a Christian ruler. The cross portrayed in the field and the sceptre surmounted by the cross which the emperor holds both proclaim the tradition, established as the ideology of the Christian imperial office under Constantine the Great, that the Christian Roman emperor was the vice-gerent of God on earth, that the Christian empire was a *mimesis* of the kingdom of heaven, that the earthly ruler in his earthly realm was a counterpart of God the ruler of heaven, and that the earthly ruler was chosen for his task by God and guided by divine inspiration through communication from the Holy Spirit.[14]

By the time of Justinian the emperor was able to take advantage of certain traditional terms which embodied in the same word both pagan and Christian imperial ideology. For example, when Justinian in official inscriptions was given the traditional epithet *piissimus*,[15] he could be thought of as *pius* in two senses, both the official *pietas* of his pagan Roman predecessors and the *pietas* of the loyal Christian sovereign whose *pietas* had to be all the greater because his office was divinely ordained. One such term that conveyed both a pagan attribute of the emperor and a Christian quality was *philanthropia* or love of mankind. The fourth-

---

[11] H. Dessau, *Inscriptiones Latinae Selectae*, no. 832.

[12] Justinian, *Novella* 105.2.4. See Dvornik, *op. cit.*, 716-723, and A. Steinwenter, "Nomos empsychos. Zur Geschichte einer politischen Theorie," *Anzeiger Akad. der Wissenschaften, Wien, phil.-hist. Kl.*, 83 (1936), 250 ff.

[13] A. R. Bellinger and Philip Grierson, eds., *Catalogue of the Byzantine Coins in the Dumbarton Oaks Collection and in the Whittemore Collection*, vol. 1 (Washington, 1966), pp. 66, 76, 135; W. Wroth, *Imperial Byzantine Coins in the British Museum* (London, 1908), vol. 1, p. 60.

[14] See Dvornik, *op. cit.*, 611 ff.

[15] Dessau. *loc. cit.*

century pagan panegyrist Themistius, in competition with Christian panegyrists, developed the theme of *philanthropia* as the sum of all the virtues and the highest attribute of the Roman sovereign. In Christian literature, including the prayers in the Divine Liturgy which were familiar to every Christian in the realm, *philanthropia* was an attribute of God and of Christ. Thus when Justinian in his laws declared that his rule stemmed from his *philanthropia* toward his subjects, he was recalling both the pagan and the Christian origins of his office.[16]

Apparently Justinian considered it unnecessary to revive, on his coins and inscriptions, the full vocabulary of the traditional descriptions of the imperial office. In view of his scholarly interests and his repeatedly expressed admiration for the usage of former times—concerning which he used such phrases as *veneranda vetustatis auctoritas*[17] and *inculpabilis antiquitas*[18]—we might expect that if he had wished to employ the full catalogue of imperial virtues he would have done so. Evidently he considered that the titles and mottoes that he did use were sufficient.

It is in the area of panegyric that we find a distinctive style of literary propaganda that has deservedly achieved a place both in the history of literature and in the evidence for Justinian's activities. The literary history of his reign shows that Justinian like Augustus saw the value of support of his plans by literary men, and it is evident that he gave substantial encouragement to men of letters—witness among other writings the histories of Procopius and Agathias and the poems of the Greek Anthology that were composed during his reign—and there are preserved three panegyrical compositions, by Deacon Agapetus, Paulus Silentiarius and Procopius of Caesarea, that are quite different from the conventional honorific addresses to the emperor and are literary creations in their own right.

The little treatise of Agapetus, who is described as a deacon on the staff of the Church of St. Sophia in Constantinople, is

---

[16] See G. Downey, "*Philanthropia* in Religion and Statecraft in the Fourth Century after Christ," *Historia*, 4 (1955), 199-208, and Dvornik, *op. cit.*, 686, 713.

[17] *Novella* 23.3.

[18] *Novella* 8, iusiurandum.

unusual among imperial panegyrics in both form and contents.[19] The treatise was addressed to Justinian shortly after his accession (§34). Following the long series of lengthy and majestic imperial panegyrics, both Latin and Greek, Agapetus' little book is refreshingly brief. An individual feature of Agapetus' plan of treatment is the arrangement in seventy-two brief paragraphs, each devoted to a particular topic. The number seventy-two recalled the number of the disciples of Jesus as recorded in one tradition of the Gospel of Luke (10:1), though another tradition gave the number as seventy. The arrangement in paragraphs provided a further opportunity for literary elegance in the form of an acrostich formed by the initial letters of each line which spelled the salutation to the emperor and the author's name and title, this being a device, characteristic of the literary taste of the time, that would have been pleasing and flattering to Justinian.

Most of the paragraphs consist of two sentences, often a relatively longer introductory sentence in which a theme or proposition is stated, followed by a shorter conclusion. The reader would be reminded at once of the style of the Book of Proverbs in the Old Testament. By adopting this style, Agapetus indicated the moralizing and religious purpose of his treatise, and also perhaps suggested a connection between his own work and the authority conveyed by the supposed authorship of the Book of Proverbs by Solomon.

Each of Agapetus' sayings or paragraphs is brief enough to be easily grasped and easily remembered, and the sequence of the sayings is carefully arranged. While the official imperial virtues are enumerated and discussed, Agapetus is careful throughout to remind Justinian that he is not only the emperor of the Romans but a Christian individual, and the advice and admonition are directed both toward the conduct of the ruler and toward his responsibilities as a human being. In a number of instances,

---

[19] Migne, *Patrologia graeca*, 86, pt. 1, cols. 1163-1186. There is an English translation of parts of the treatise in Ernest Barker, ed., *Social and Political Thought in Byzantium from Justinian I to the Last Palaeologus: Passages from Byzantine Writers and Documents* (Oxford, 1957), 54-61. After these lectures were written, a valuable study of Agapetus was published by Patrick Henry III, "A Mirror for Justinian: the *Ekthesis* of Agapetus Diaconus," *Greek, Roman and Byzantine Studies*, 8 (1967), pp. 281-308.

advice on public and on private conduct is arranged in alternating paragraphs—a device that tends to alleviate the monotony that might attach to the rehearsal of such well known themes.

The choice of material shows equal care and learning. Having given himself the framework of seventy-two paragraphs or sayings, Agapetus did not produce a list of seventy-two different themes, but chose several topics for repeated treatment in different parts of the work. The leading theme that he presents, first of all in the opening paragraph, is that the ruler must honor God because he is the source of the ruler's power, and the earthly *basileia* is described as the likeness of the heavenly *basileia*. Here the concept καθ' ὁμοίωσιν, "according to the likeness," is introduced, to be repeated later in variations, for example in the paragraphs in which it is said that the man who comes to know God is made like to God (§3), and that the ruler is an image (*eikon*) of God who must imitate God (§§21, 37), the imitation being in the form of good works (§45). The concept of ὁμοίωσις θεῷ was a familiar theme of Christian philosophy, which had borrowed the phraseology from Plato.[20]

A concept that appears almost as frequently is the *philanthropia* of the emperor toward his subjects (§§6, 20, 40, 50). The mention of this divine gift to the Christian ruler would recall to the emperor and to the hearers and readers of the treatise the frequent passages in the Divine Liturgy in which *philanthropia* appears as one of the most important attributes of God and of Christ.[21]

It is not necessary in this place to list all of the Christian virtues that Agapetus discusses. Piety (*eusebeia*) is recalled constantly (§§5, 11, 13, 15, 58, 68), and the mind of the ruler is described as the mirror of the glory of God (§§9, 24). The most prominent of the qualities that the emperor must exhibit toward his subjects, justice (§18), self-control (§§18, 68), good will

---

[20] On this important doctrine, see Johannes Quasten, *Patrology*, III (Utrecht and Westminster, Maryland, 1960), 292-293, citing among other studies H. Merki, *Homoiosis theo: Von der platonischen Angleichung an Gott zur Gottähnlichkeit bei Gregor von Nyssa* (Fribourg, 1952).

[21] See the passages in the Liturgies of St. Basil and of St. Chrysostom in the edition of F. E. Brightman, *Liturgies Eastern and Western*, Vol. I: *Eastern Liturgies* (Oxford, 1896), pp. 309, line 19; 310, 19; 312, 4; 312, 26; 313, 31; 317, 11; 315, 6; 318, 10; 324, 6; 338, 10; 342, 17; 343, 18; 344, 14.

(§§19, 35), pity (§23), forethought (§46), gentleness (§§50, 52) and the like are enumerated.

One of the most interesting features of the treatise is the way in which Agapetus employs concepts which were well known in classical thought. In the third paragraph the Delphic precept "know thyself" is introduced as a "divine teaching." Those among Agapetus' audience who had had a classical education would be reminded of the occurrences of this precept in Greek literature,[22] though the phrase also occurred (in a specialized application) in the Septuagint version of the Song of Songs, 1:8.

There are clear reminiscences of Isocrates, whose influence on all this type of literature was considerable.[23] In §17 Agapetus brings together two well known precepts, one classical, the other Christian. Here Justinian's reign is declared to be that time which was predicted, when either philosophers rule, or rulers are philosophers. This is the well known dictum of Plato,[24] which Agapetus introduces with the phrase προεῖπε τις τῶν παλαιῶν, "one of the men of ancient times proclaimed . . ." Then he goes on immediately to quote the phrase from Proverbs (1:8) that "the fear of God is the beginning of wisdom." These thoughts were not a novelty in the vocabulary of imperial panegyric; Themistius, for example, made use of the dictum of Plato;[25] but by his easy quotations of the Delphic precept and of Plato, which some members of his audience would be pleased to be able to identify, Agapetus gave his treatise an air of elegant learning. But in spite of these touches of classical learning, Agapetus' treatise is primarily an expression of the church's concern for the emperor, conveying the church's teaching on the imperial office in which it is emphasized (as Apagetus writes, §21) that "In his body the ruler is like every man, in his office he is like God." God

[22] On the text and tradition of this and the other Delphic precepts, see W. Dittenberger, ed., *Sylloge Inscriptionum Graecarum*, ed. 3 (Leipzig, 1915-1924), No. 1268.
[23] See B. Keil, "Epikritische Isokratesstudien," *Hermes*, 23 (1888), 367-369. On other sources of Agapetus, see K. Praechter, "Der Roman Barlaam und Joasaph in seinem Verhältnis zu Agapets Königsspiegel," *Byzantinische Zeitschrift*, 2 (1893), 444-460.
[24] Plato, *Republic*, 473 C.
[25] Themistius, *Or.* 17, 214 A.

has given the emperor the rule of the world (§30) with great power; he must imitate the giver of the power so far as he can (§37). Thus he must imitate God's mercy, since he is God's image (*ibid.*). It is the ruler's duty to guard the laws, since he has no one to compel him to guard them (§27). The emperor rules the *kosmos* (§25) and thus is the only true ruler in the world with divine authority and divine guidance.

Agapetus' treatise presents a much more detailed and more extensive portrait of the ideal Christian monarch than any of the panegyrics offered to Justinian's Christian predecessors which are extant; and we must emphasize once more the way in which the panegyrist deals with both the private life and the official life of the emperor. A political and moral treatise in this form would run the risk of sounding like a catechism; but Agapetus' little work has a warm and friendly tone that saves it from this danger.

Another panegyric of Justinian constitutes one of the most important literary sources for his reign—a distinction not achieved by most imperial panegyrics. This is Procopius' work on the buildings of Justinian, which we are safe in assuming was commissioned or at least inspired by the emperor himself. The style and length of the first book of the work, which is devoted to the emperor's building activities in Constantinople, suggest that this part of the work was delivered orally in the presence of the emperor.[26]

Justinian was the most active and lavish builder of all the emperors since Constantine the Great. The provision for his people of magnificent public buildings and strong fortifications was a traditional excellence of the ancient sovereign, regularly praised in panegyrics and recorded in imperial biographies.[27] Procopius' work indicates that Justinian had a well planned building program in Constantinople and throughout the empire. In writing his treatise, Procopius evidently had access to official records.[28] Illustrating the generosity and power of the emperor in the enumeration of his extensive undertakings, Procopius shows the emperor

---

[26] G. Downey, "The Composition of Procopius, *De aedificiis*," *Trans. Amer. Philol. Assoc.*, 78 (1947), 171-183.

[27] See, for example, *Res Gestae Divi Augusti*, ch. 19-21 and app. 2-3; Suetonius, *Life of Augustus*, 29-30; Pliny, *Panegyric of Trajan*, 51.

[28] G. Downey, "Justinian as a Builder," *Art Bulletin*, 32 (1950), 262-266.

as endowed with creative imagination, wisdom and technical skill which surpass those of the most eminent architects and engineers of the day. What was of real significance and satisfaction for Justinian himself was Procopius' emphasis on the religious importance of Justinian's construction of churches and other religious buildings, notably of course the Church of St. Sophia. Thus while the theme of the panegyric is the emperor's buildings of all kinds, the work records and praises the emperor's piety and zeal both as a religious individual and as a sovereign anxious for the spiritual welfare of his people.

Another panegyric that tells us much about Justinian as a Christian emperor is Paulus Silentiarius' learned and ornate description of St. Sophia in verse.[29] Like Procopius' monograph on the buildings, Paulus' poem has the form of an *ekphrasis*, or literary description of a monument, a form much admired in postclassical Greek literature.[30] The greater part of the poem is a brilliant description of the church and its decorations; but again like Procopius, the panegyrist takes care to describe the overwhelming spiritual impression the building made on those who entered it. The purpose of Paulus' poem was ultimately spiritual, and he closed with an account of the deeply religious character of the emperor who brought this church into being.[31] Paulus cites the gospels in depicting the devotion of the emperor.[32]

Procopius and Paulus show us an aspect of Justinian's activity and of his conception of his imperial office that must have been very important to the emperor, as to his subjects. Our own first thought of St. Sophia is likely to be of the architectural marvel of the building; indeed, if it were not still standing, we might be less concerned with its marvellous character, for it would be difficult to visualize it adequately even from the skillful descriptions of Procopius and Paulus. But Justinian did not build the

---

[29] The *ekphrasis* is edited, with a valuable introduction and commentary, by Paul Friedländer, *Johannes von Gaza und Paulus Silentiarius: Kunstbeschreibungen Justinianischer Zeit* (Leipzig and Berlin, 1912).

[30] G. Downey, art. "Ekphrasis," *Reallexikon für Antike und Christentum,* IV (1959), cols. 921-944.

[31] Vv. 917-920.

[32] Compare vv. 46-47 with Matt. 6:12 (cf. Friedländer's note *ad loc.*), and vv. 56-57 with Matt. 5:44. Cf. Rubin, *Das Zeitalter Iustinians,* p. 430, note 404.

church simply as an architectural *tour de force*. It was that, of course, but its real purpose was to provide a splendid setting for the Divine Liturgy which was the central and essential service of the Greek church. Here St. Sophia indeed had a unique purpose, for it was not only intended to be the most magnificent church in existence, but was to serve as the emperor's church and the cathedral of the patriarch of the capital, that is, the church which was to be the place of the celebration of the Holy Communion which was the sacramental act that united the people of the Christian Roman Empire, in which both emperor and patriarch played a role, the emperor in this case acting both as emperor and as an individual member of the Christian community. Every celebration of the Divine Liturgy, in every church in the empire, was a declaration of the religious basis of the Christian Roman state. In the case of St. Sophia the setting of the Liturgy had a special significance since the church was an offering of the emperor in which he was to perform official actions in his capacity as vice-gerent of God on earth. The building of the church was part of his service as vice-gerent; in building it he was providing the proper surroundings for the celebration of the Divine Liturgy which was the corporate act of the Roman people. It was the description of Justinian in this aspect of the discharge of his office that was the ultimate purpose of the panegyrics of Procopius and Paulus.

Our study thus far has considered two kinds of evidence for the nature of the emperor's office under Justinian, namely the traditional concepts that Justinian himself cited, *nomos empsychos* and *philanthropia*, and the panegyrics of Agapetus, Procopius and Paulus Silentiarius. The panegyrics may be taken to reflect at least in general terms the emperor's desires and interests; but we also possess a text emanating from Justinian himself that records, almost certainly in the emperor's own words, Justinian's own view of the relationship between the imperial office and the church. This pronouncement is of particular value to us because it is conveyed in terminology chosen by the emperor.

Justinian was a literary emperor, and we are safe in assuming that many of the *Novellae*, which were supplements to the Code, were written by the emperor himself. Procopius tells us that

Justinian took pleasure in writing many of his own state documents in Greek, and in reading them aloud in public in spite of what Procopius and others considered his provincial accent[33] (who could have told the emperor that his accent needed improvement?); but having been born in a Latin-speaking region of the empire, Justinian had Latin as his original literary language, and indeed the *Novellae* may be thought to show a distinctive—and forceful—style.

Our text is the famous *Novella* VI, which was issued in A.D. 535, among the several new pronouncements which were intended to serve as prompt supplements to the Code, the second and revised edition of which had been published on November 16, A.D. 534.

This decree is concerned with the ordination of bishops, priests and deacons, and in the preface the emperor takes the occasion to define the position of the priesthood in the state and the relationship between the imperial office and the priesthood. Justinian opens the preface as follows: "The things of greatest importance among men are the gifts of God, given from on high by his love for mankind, namely priesthood (*sacerdotium*) and the imperial office (*imperium*). The first renders service in divine matters, the other governs and takes anxious care for the earthly aspects of human life. Both proceed from one and the same origin, and both make human life fairer. Therefore nothing will be a matter of greater concern to rulers than the honorable position of the clergy, especially since the clergy continually pray to God on behalf of the rulers. If the priesthood is blameless in every respect, and is confident of its relationship with God, and if the imperial office rightly and fittingly adorns the polity that has been entrusted to it, there will be an auspicious harmony which will bestow every good thing upon the human race. We therefore have the highest concern both for the true doctrines of God and for the honorable position of the clergy, and we believe that if they keep that honorable estate, there will be given to us, through it, the greatest good things as a gift from God, and we believe that we shall hold firmly the things we now have, and obtain the things that have not yet come to us. All things will be done

---

[33] Procopius, *Anecdota*, 14.3-4.

fairly and fittingly, if the beginning of the undertaking is worthy of God and pleasing to him. We believe that this will be the case, if observance is maintained of the holy teachings (*regularum*) which were handed down by the apostles, those witnesses and servants of the word of God, who are justly praised and revered, and which have been guarded and interpreted by the holy fathers."

This document deserves our careful attention, especially in view of the frequently repeated criticism of Justinian, that he indulged in tyrannical and unwarranted interference in the affairs of the church. We must notice in the first place that Justinian is careful to speak of *imperium* and *sacerdotium*, not *imperator* and *sacerdotes*.[34] It is not easy to render Justinian's *imperium* and *sacerdotium* in English; the context indicates that *imperium* is employed here in the sense of the imperial authority, and that *sacerdotium* has the collective meaning of the priestly order or priestly state; one might think of the term as meaning the priestly class. This question of translation emphasizes the fact that Justinian is careful not to use the term *ecclesia* in this place.

What seems clear is that Justinian, in considering the best way to express the relationship that we, in language that has modern connotations, call the problem of church and state, spoke in terms of component and function. *Sacerdotium* and *imperium*, he declares, proceed from the same divine source and form a partnership in the life of mankind, specifically in the life of the members of the Christian Roman Empire. When both components are functioning in their true form of excellence, the result is harmony (*consonantia*). Since the imperial office has traditionally been endowed with the means for the physical protection of the state and for the maintenance of the good order and welfare of the people, the *imperium* is responsible for the prosperity and well being of the *sacerdotium*.

Such is the ideal state of affairs. Everyone realized that this involved the harmonious collaboration of an *imperium* embodied in an *imperator* who might be subject to human weaknesses, and of a *sacerdotium* composed of *sacerdotes* who in spite of ordination and consecration might on occasion have to struggle with

[34] The terms used in the Greek text are ἱερωσύνη and βασιλεία.

worldly thoughts that might arise even in connection with their spiritual occupations.

Justinian's reign illustrates the problems that could come to both *imperator* and *sacerdotes* in the discharge of what they considered to be their respective duties. In addition to his duty toward the church, the Christian Roman emperor had the duty of promoting and maintaining the physical welfare of the state. Given the new kind of responsibility of governing a Christian empire, the Emperor Constantine had declared repeatedly, in edicts and letters, that the safety and prosperity of the state depended on the continued existence of religious truth and harmony among the subjects of the state, for God would rightly punish a state that harbored religious strife and error.[35] Such an idea had been familiar in the days of the pagan Roman Empire, whose people constantly reminded themselves that the prosperity of the empire depended on the continued favor of the gods of Rome, which must be secured by right worship. Constantine's successors had repeated his declaration, and Theodosius the Great had taken the logical step of issuing laws that made religious error a crime against the state—that is, a crime against the Roman people.[36]

Justinian thus inherited the grave duty of the maintenance of orthodoxy and the elimination of heresy and paganism (which included Judaism and Samaritanism). The church itself, of course, had this mission, but in terms of reconciliation and conversion, not of punishment; and in a matter that was a basic task of the church there could arise questions of how far the emperor should go in his duties. The scope of our present inquiry will not permit a detailed investigation of Justinian's theological activities and of the nature and degree of his involvement in the administrative affairs of the church; but it has been essential to review the emperor's carefully considered statement in the preface to *Novella* VI because of the importance of this document for our understanding of the imperial office and in particular for its bearing on the subject of what has been called Caesaropapism, a concept that

[35] See Dvornik, *op. cit.*, 635 ff.
[36] See Noel Q. King, *The Emperor Theodosius and the Establishment of Christianity* (Philadelphia, 1960), 28 ff.

has become notorious in the modern criticism of Justinian and his program.

Here we have an example of modern scholarship impelled to debate a historical problem that did not exist in antiquity, certainly not in the terms in which modern scholars have seen a supposed problem. The word Caesaropapism, meaning the unwarranted interference of the emperor in the internal affairs of the church on a regular basis, is in fact a word created in modern times for a specific purpose. Neither this word nor anything like it is found in the ancient writers, who would surely have used such a term if they had thought it called for. The recent studies of Professor Deno J. Geanakoplos[37] will excuse us from a detailed rehearsal of the controversy in modern times between those who find Caesaropapism in the history of church and state in Byzantium, and those who argue that Caesaropapism in the modern sense of the word did not exist in Byzantium since it was the emperor's duty to protect and promote the welfare of the church, and since the occasional attempts at really unwarranted interference, such as Justinian and some later emperors certainly did undertake on several occasions, never had lasting results. The church was too vast an institution to be permanently affected by attempts at domination by the secular authorities.

One of the difficulties that scholars have introduced into the study of this subject is that they have supposed that they have seen, in the Eastern Empire and the Byzantine church, a situation which is in fact characteristic of the relationship of church and state in the West, which was actually different from the relationship prevailing in the East. If we are to speak of Caesaropapism, we must also be prepared to speak of the concept in reverse as Papalocaesarism, for it is notorious that just as an emperor might on occasion dictate to the church, there were other times when,

[37] "Church and State in the Byzantine Empire: A Reconsideration of Caesaropapism," *Church History*, 34 (1965), 381-403; *Byzantine East and Latin West* (New York, 1966), 55-83; "Church Building and 'Caesaropapism,' " *Greek, Roman and Byzantine Studies*, 7 (1966) 167-186. Reference may also be made to a review by G. Downey of P. R. Coleman-Norton, *Roman State and Christian Church* (London, 1966) which is to appear in the *American Journal of Philology*.

emperor and patriarch being in different positions of strength, the patriarch dictated to the emperor, quite successfully.

It has seemed appropriate to dwell at some length on the theme of *imperium* and *sacerdotium* because a proper understanding of Justinian's pronouncement is essential if we are to appreciate correctly the emperor's conception of his office—which was also the conception that the emperor expected his subjects to accept. It is true that Justinian did proceed in high-handed fashion in some matters which in principle ought to have been the sphere of the church, especially the formulation of doctrine; but then in the Monophysite controversy the emperor was faced with a religious disorder of the gravest proportions, which constituted a political problem that justified efforts at solution of the most vigorous kind. Any emperor endowed with the energy and the intense intellectual activity of Justinian would have been impelled to attempt to solve a problem that the church itself had been unable to deal with satisfactorily.

The separation in modern times of what we call church and state, and the divorce of religion and culture that often results, may have made it difficult for us to visualize in all its significance the unity of religion and culture of the ancient world, pagan as well as Christian. Libanius, a leading pagan figure at Antioch in the fourth century, declared that "literature and the worship of the gods are twin sisters,"[38] and with appropriate alteration the same could be said of the society of the Christian Roman Empire. When this is the normal conception of the relationship between religion and culture, and between religion and "secular life," the result is an emergence of a specific type of community—a Christian *polis*, or a *civitas Dei*—in which the specific activities of the government, the church, and the citizens are all thought of as working together to form one harmonious whole. Perfect harmony might not be possible at all times, but this would not affect the validity of the concept.

It is this conception of the Christian community that lies behind Justinian's picture of *imperium* and *sacerdotium*, including the emperor's role with respect to both components. We realize

[38] Libanius, *Or.* 18.157.

for example that the emperor visualized St. Sophia as a special church because it was there, in the most magnificent church of the empire, which faced the imperial palace across the Augustaeum, the main square of the capital, that *imperium* and *sacerdotium* were brought together as the emperor in his official capacity took part in the Divine Liturgy.

There remain further texts which will illustrate the imperial office of Justinian under other aspects. One of these is the splendid gold medallion found in Caesarea of Cappadocia in the middle of the eighteenth century and presented eventually to the Bibliothèque Nationale, from which it was stolen and melted down in 1831.[39] Fortunately a facsimile had been made for the British Museum (fig. 1). On the obverse the emperor as commander in chief appears in armor, with a plumed helmet; his title is *Dominus noster Iustinianus perpetuus Augustus*. On the reverse the medallion portrays the victorious emperor on horseback in military dress conducted by winged Victory, epitomizing the majesty and power of the imperial office expressed in the inscription *Salus et gloria Romanorum*, "The Salvation and Glory of the Roman People." The victorious emperor, leader of his people in both peace and war, was one of the oldest themes of the iconography of the imperial office; Justinian's medallion, for example, recalls similar medallions of Constantine the Great.

This is a massive gold medallion, intended for limited circulation, not a coin, and it commemorates a special occasion, possibly the triumph of Belisarius over the Vandals in Africa. To appreciate its full significance we must recall the inscriptions *Victoria Augustorum* and *Gloria Romanorum* which appear on the regular issues of Justinian's coins.[40] In the first place, we notice that the mottoes represent two components of the state, the emperor and the people, and that the themes displayed in connection with each component are different. In the case of the coins which refer to the emperor alone, it is *victoria*, in the phrase *Victoria Augus-*

---

[39] The medallion is reproduced by W. Wroth, *Catalogue of the Imperial Byzantine Coins in the British Museum* (London, 1908), frontispiece of volume I. There is an excellent reproduction in John W. Barker, *Justinian and the Later Roman Empire* (Madison, Wisconsin, 1966), Pl. 1 (facing p. 158), with a note on the medallion and its history, pp. 286-287.

[40] See above, note 13.

FIG. 1. Facsimile of gold medallion of Justinian

torum, while in the case of the people, that is, the state as a whole, it is *salus* and *gloria*, in the phrases *Salus et gloria Romanorum*, or *Gloria Romanorum*. Since it is the emperor who is the leader and defender of the people it would seem that it is the *victoria* of the emperor that provides and assures the *salus* and *gloria* of his subjects.

How these abstractions are to be rendered in English is not altogether as simple as it might at first seem. *Victoria* is not only a specific victory but the quality of victoriousness, or the ability to triumph over enemies, which was one of the important qualities of the official personality of the Roman emperor. In the *victoria* coins the monarch is shown attended by the goddess of victory, who is represented in the familiar type of the classical winged figure, with an important change in some of the representations in which the goddess carries a long cross.

In the case of *salus* and *gloria* we are dealing with ideas that are in their nature more complex than the idea of *victoria*. Both concepts appear on the coins of the earlier emperors. *Salus* has two shades of meaning which may occur separately or together, one being safety or security, the other salvation, that is, what we might think of as a static condition of safety or a positive action resulting in salvation.

Gloria is of course a much more general term, with a number of shades of meaning.[41] Often it is the sum of several conditions or qualities. In literary usage it describes magnificence and renown, of either an individual or a ruler or a people, and it also denotes pride, whether justified or not justified, and even vainglory. Sometimes it is linked with the equally general concept of *virtus*, as in the epitaph of Publius Cornelius Scipio (*honos fama virtusque gloria atque ingenium*),[42] or in a passage in Tacitus' *Annals* concerned with Tiberius (*gloria ac virtus*).[43] *Gloria* is specifically an attribute of the ruler, illustrated in several passages of Pliny's *Panegyric of Trajan*.[44] In the same panegyric, *gloria* is brought

---

[41] See the article *gloria* in the *Thesaurus Linguae Latinae*.
[42] *C.I.L.* 6.1288 (Dessau, *I.L.S.* 4).
[43] Tacitus, *Annals*, 4.33.6.
[44] Pliny, *Panegyric of Trajan*, 3.3, 4.5, 4.6, 8.2, 8.3, 10.3, 10.6, 24.5, 28.1, 63.1, 70.8, 85.5, 86.6.

back by the emperor as a result of victory in war.[45] There are various ideas that cluster about the idea of the *gloria* of the emperor, such as *fama, civium pietas, libertas,* and *immortalitas.*

For the Romans of the pagan empire, *gloria* was an idea rich in meaning, linked as it was with the idea of the greatness and the eternity of the empire. *Salus* and *victoria* were conditions that were essential to the existence of *gloria.* However, by the time of Justinian, *salus* and *gloria* had come to have additional meanings in the form of Christian connotations. These are illustrated, for example, in a book familiar to Justinian and his Latin-speaking subjects, the Apocalypse of John, in which *gloria* and associated ideas are illustrated frequently, especially in the acclamations and prayers. *Gloria* is an essential attribute of God and of Christ. In the Apocalypse it is associated with the ideas of *potestas, honor, virtus, divinitas, sapientia, fortitudo, benedictio. Salus,* representing Greek *soteria,* appears less often, but in one passage, an acclamation addressed to God (19:1-2), *salus* and *gloria* are linked, as they are on the gold medallion of Justinian, while in another passage (12:10) *salus* is linked with *virtus, regnum Dei* and *potestas.*[46]

Thus the empire of Justinian enjoyed a *salus* and a *gloria* which recalled not only the ancient traditional *salus* and *gloria* of the Roman people but the even richer *salus* and *gloria* of divine origin that Christianity had brought into the world. And we must notice another important token of the significance that these words had for Justinian and his subjects. The coins and the medallion speak of the *salus* and *gloria* of the Romans. The word is *Romani,* not *S.P.Q.R.* or *res publica.* Here again we may see the union of the *sacerdotium* and the *imperium* to which, together, the *salus* and the *gloria* belonged.

It appears, further, that Justinian was not content to be depicted only in the traditional iconography of the victorious emperor on horseback conducted by winged Victory. We hear of another equestrian statue of Justinian as the victorious leader of

---

[45] *Ibid.* 16.3.

[46] In addition to the passages cited above, see the following passages in the Apocalypse of John: 4:11, 5:10, 5:12, 5:13, 7:12, 19:1-2, 19:7.

his people which was much more widely known among his subjects as a whole than the image on the medallion since this statue stood on a tall column in the center of the Augustaeum. Procopius describes the statue in a well known passage of the treatise on the emperor's buildings:[47]

Before the Senate House there was a market-place called the Augustaeum . . . There there is a column of extraordinary size, composed of large stones in circular courses . . . And finest brass, cast in panels and garlands, covers the stones on every side . . . On the summit of the column stands a gigantic bronze horse, facing toward the east, a very noteworthy sight. He seems about to advance, and to be splendidly pressing forward. Indeed he holds his left fore foot in the air, as though it were about to take a forward step on the ground before him, while the other is pressed down upon the stone on which he stands, as if ready to take the next step; his hind feet he holds close together, so that they may be ready whenever he decides to move. Upon this horse is mounted a bronze figure of the emperor, of colossal size. And the figure is habited like Achilles, that is, the costume he wears is known by that name. He wears half-boots and his legs are not covered by greaves. Also he wears a breastplate in the heroic fashion, and a helmet covers his head and gives the impression that it moves up and down [i.e., as if the horse were in motion], and a dazzling light flashed forth from it. One might say, in poetic speech, that here is that star of Autumn. And he looks toward the rising sun, directing his course against the Persians. In his left hand he holds a globe, by which the sculptor signifies that the whole earth and sea are subject to him, yet he has neither sword nor spear nor any other weapon, but a cross stands upon the globe which he carries, that emblem by which alone he has obtained both his empire and his victory in war. And stretching forth his right hand toward the rising sun and spreading out his fingers, he commands the barbarians in that quarter to remain at home and to advance no further.[48]

[47] Procopius, *Buildings*, 1.3.12, abridged and adapted from the translation of H. B. Dewing with the collaboration of G. Downey in the Loeb Classical Library edition of Procopius, vol. VII (London and Cambridge, 1940, reprinted with additions and corrections, 1961).

[48] On the significance of this statue in the iconography of the imperial office, see Richard Brilliant, *Gesture and Rank in Roman Art: The Use of Gestures to Denote Status in Roman Sculpture and Coinage* (New Haven, 1963), 184-185 (*Memoirs of the Connecticut Academy of Arts and Sciences*, vol. 14).

It may seem unusual to think of the sedentary and scholarly Justinian represented in the armor of the colorful Greek hero of the Trojan War, but Justinian could claim kinship in his role of defender of the empire against another race of oriental barbarians. What is important for our present inquiry is the emperor's choice of a representation of himself as Achilles. We may perhaps appreciate the significance that would have attached to such a representation if we try to imagine, for example, Augustus or Constantine the Great choosing to be represented as Achilles on horseback in the square in front of the imperial palace.

Justinian might be described, if we may employ a modern phrase, as the complete Roman Emperor, personally involved and active in politics, theology, law, education, art and architecture. We think of his career in terms of the universal scope of the activity of some of the earlier sovereigns, notably Augustus. Justinian was not being active just for the sake of being active, indeed more active than his immediate predecessors; he was bringing to fulfilment the development of the Graeco-Roman Christian state through contributions which completed, and on occasion surpassed, those of his predecessors. His actions all tended toward the building up of a new kind of Graeco-Roman Christian community. The codification of the law was not simply a necessary revision and reorganization of a vast body of jurisprudence that had become unmanageable for the jurists; it was the creation, in a new form, of the law which was to govern the new community. The closing of the philosophical schools at Athens was not simply the elimination of pagan instruction which was a danger to the whole community; it was a logical final step in the establishment of the new type of professional Christian scholarship that was the kind of scholarship that was essential in the new community.

There is a Renaissance drawing of an equestrian statue in Constantinople which has been identified with the statue described by Justinian, reproduced e.g. by Brilliant, *op. cit.*, 183, and as the frontispiece of the Loeb Classical Library edition of the *Buildings* of Procopius. However, the Renaissance artist indicated that the statue was a statue of Theodosius, and there has been some question whether the drawing should be taken to represent the statue of Justinian described by Procopius; see Brilliant, *op cit.*, 184-185, and P. W. Lehmann, "Theodosius or Justinian? A Renaissance Drawing of a Byzantine Rider," *Art Bulletin,* 41 (1959), 39-57: In either case, the drawing is valuable testimony to the imperial iconography.

The representation of the emperor "in the armor of Achilles" on the column in the Augustaeum was an effort to illustrate the emperor as heir of the ancient Greek tradition of kingship as well as the successor to the Roman emperors.[49] This statue placed Justinian in the Greek heroic tradition illustrated by well known statues, executed in the eastern provinces, which show Roman emperors under the aspect of Greek royalty and divinity.[50] A notably philhellene emperor such as Hadrian played a prominent part in this expression of the significance in Greek lands of the Roman imperial office. The Roman Empire had always been an empire of two worlds, Greek as well as Latin, and Justinian ruled Greek speaking lands in which the Greek religious and intellectual tradition formed the basis of daily life.

There are well known traces of Justinian's activities—some of them not altogether fortunate—as a theologian. We must remember that he was also a student of history. His writings testify to his regard for the example of ancient times, which as we have noted he speaks of as *inculpabilis antiquitas*. He cites the *veneranda vetustatis auctoritas*.[51] His task was the renewal of the Roman Empire, the *renovatio imperii Romani*. The Mediterranean was to become once more *mare nostrum*, "our sea." The ancient physical extent of the empire had significance as the sign of the empire's power, and so the recovery of the lost territories was an essential part in the placing of the Roman state once more in its true position of power in the world. In all this program Justinian directed his policies on the basis of the past history of Rome since it was his duty—and his privilege—to bring the diminished empire to a condition in keeping with its past tradition. Today we see Justinian as a rather spectacular figure, representing a milestone in ancient history and in the history of European and Slavic monarchy. We must remember that he stood in a long line of emperors in a political tradition in which the imperial office was

[49] Achilles was descended from Zeus: Homer, *Iliad*, 21.187; cf. Dvornik, *op. cit.*, 148.

[50] G. M. A. Hanfmann, *Roman Art* (Greenwich, Conn., n.d. [1964?]), Nos. 55, 56, 58; Jale Inan and Elisabeth Rosenbaum, *Roman and Early Byzantine Portrait Sculpture in Asia Minor* (London, British Academy, 1966), Pl. 19, no. 1 (Hadrian); Pl. 41, no. 4.

[51] See above, notes 17-18.

thought of as greater than the incumbent. The imperial office was a symbol of the sovereignty of the Roman people, forming a part of the basis for his belief in the power of Rome which logically produced the conviction that Rome was eternal.

Justinian as we have seen inherited the pagan and the Christian traditions of his office. He was not endeavoring to build up the imperial office for his own aggrandizement. In the political tradition of that time, only a monarch could do certain kinds of things for his community, and the community needed the things that its sovereign could do for it. God was the creator and sustainer of the world, and the emperor, as the earthly image of God, had an official role in his realm as creator and sustainer; and the Roman political tradition, with its absence of a written constitution, made it possible for an emperor of unusual endowments to achieve the personal ascendancy that Justinian possessed—in more than sufficient measure, as some of his subjects thought.

We may return now to two of our principal themes. The choice of Holy Wisdom for the dedication of the principal church in the imperial capital had been the choice of Constantine the Great—very likely at the suggestion of his ecclesiastical advisers such as Eusebius of Caesarea—but the name may be thought to have taken on a special meaning in the light of Justinian's program. As the emperor inspired and directed by God, Justinian both needed and received the wisdom (*sophia*) from above that God gave to those who asked for it (James 1:5). The wisdom of God, embodied in Christ, "the power of God and the wisdom of God" (I Cor. 1:24), could be thought of as both the symbol of Justinian's program and the central expression of the role of Constantinople as the splendid imperial capital that Justinian was bringing into being. It is not an accident that the central places of worship in both classical Athens and Christian Constantinople, the Parthenon and St. Sophia, both represented the sovereignty of divine wisdom. In the city of Athena, wisdom and learning had been regarded as things of greatest importance. As the city of the Holy Wisdom of God, Constantinople acknowledged that all wisdom and all achievement come from God. Justinian the vice-gerent of God was the heir of Augustus the *pontifex maximus*.

Justinian had brought Athens and Jerusalem together in his Constantinople, which was to be the complete Christian *polis* in which the emperor and his court, the church, and the university and literary circle around the emperor served as a creative force in the same way that the classical Greek *polis*, as analyzed by Aristotle in the *Politics*, had served as a creative force for its people. It is clear, of course, that Justinian's political and military undertakings were not always soundly conceived, and he spent the substance of the empire injudiciously. At the same time he created an image of the imperial office that formed a landmark in the history of monarchy.

5

Lykourgan Athens: 338-322

BY FORDYCE W. MITCHEL

Delivered April 9 and 10, 1968

LYKOURGAN ATHENS: 338-322

SOMEONE once expressed his dislike for the then strange sounds of Richard Strauss' music and displayed his preference for earlier, more familiar musical modes with the following jingle:

> Wenn Richard, dann Wagner;
> Wenn Strauss, dann Johann!

The title "Lykourgan Athens" will probably evoke a similar response in an audience in which even the classicists instinctively feel that the noun which should naturally follow the adjective "Lykourgan" is "Reforms" (with reference of course to the Great Rhetra and the hoplite revolution in archaic Sparta); and that the adjective which most suitably precedes "Athens" is "Periklean" (with sympathetic overtones of Parthenos, Parthenon, Propylaia and Imperialism).

But our Lykourgos was no Spartan, but an Athenian—and a reformer in his own right; he had nothing at all to do with his shadowy Spartan namesake—unless we choose to search for the roots of Lykourgos' admittedly conservative outlook and program in his early association with Plato's Akademy, where to express admiration for the Spartan mirage was at least a fashionable gambit.

Closer, of course, is the connexion between the "Athens" of Lykourgos and the generally more familiar Athens of Perikles. It was the same city—in direct lineal descent and separated by roughly one hundred years. But it was a completely different ballgame.

The defeat of the Greek allies on the field at Chaironeia in 338 at the hands of King Philip and his Macedonians had indeed not deprived Athens of her freedom—not at least in our sense of the word freedom. The Athenians still enjoyed complete autonomy in the conduct of their local affairs, their navy was intact and still formidable, their control of Samos had been confirmed by Philip, and the Boiotian territory of Oropos, on Athens' northeastern frontier facing the island of Euboia, had been ceded by the Macedonian in compensation for the loss of territories in the northern Aegean.

But, in so far as the Greek concept of freedom embraced not only freedom for oneself and for one's state, but also the right to dominate others,[1] the Athenians must have felt that their ancient freedom had been sharply curtailed; most of them must have been pained by the contrast between the happy memory of the Athenian empire of the fifth century and the stark reality of Athens' present condition as an unwilling partner in the League of Korinth, which they recognized as Philip's instrument of domination over Greece and of his proposed Panhellenic crusade against Persia.

This humiliating condition was not the result of a sudden reversal of fortune, nor was the defeat at Chaironeia entirely unforeseeable. The decline in Athenian power had set in at least as early as the 350's with the successful revolt of the allies in the Social War. The events of the following decade down to 340, including Philip's aggressions in the Northern Aegean and his advance into central Greece, had given the Athenians small cause to preen their feathers. Philip's agents and sympathizers in the assembly had pointed out the futility of resistance. Demosthenes, who had been Athens' most sanguine 'hawk' during the 340's, was himself aware, at the time of the final showdown, of the "too late and too little" aspect of the allied counteroffensive and realized how heavily the hope of victory depended on pure luck when he went into the battle with the words 'Agathê Tychê' (with Good Fortune) emblazoned on his shield. And so the decision at Chaironeia was less sudden than final, less unexpected than shocking.

That the shock was indeed profound we learn from Lykourgos' speech in condemnation of Leokrates (spoken some eight years after the event) and from the fragmentary evidence concerning the emergency measures proposed at that time; the army had been shattered, one thousand Athenians had fallen, two thousand more had been taken captive, and the rest had escaped only by disgraceful, headlong flight; the city was filled with the panic-stricken folk from the countryside who had come in with their flocks and herds. The old men and the boys, those too old or too young to have gone to Chaironeia, now manned the walls as the last line of defense, while the walls themselves were being frantically repaired

---

[1] J.A.O. Larsen, "Freedom and its Obstacles in Ancient Greece," *CP*, 57 (1962) 230-234.

and strengthened. To meet the manpower shortage, an illegal proposal was made to free the slaves and to enfranchise the resident-
aliens who were able and willing to bear arms. Stern measures
were taken against the fainthearted who sought safety in flight
from the city. The Athenians had every reason to expect an almost
immediate attack on the city, and they were determined to make
a last-ditch stand.

That the expected blow never fell was due more to Philip's
decision to offer irresistibly generous terms than to Athens' will
to resist armed invasion. The decision to offer peace was most
probably based on military and diplomatic expediency. Philip was
too great a general to risk a battle when the same ends could be
achieved through diplomacy. He was well aware of how much it
would cost in men, materiel and time to storm or reduce by siege
a determined, fortified city which still controlled its access to the
sea, and he also knew he would gain far more credit among the
Greeks in general by offering generous terms than by sending in
his victorious army to overwhelm a famous Greek state. Thus we
may judge that Athens' determined stance and energetic activities
in the days following Chaironeia, albeit they may somehow have
sweetened the terms of the offer, had little or no effect on Philip's
ultimate decision to offer peace.

But the stiffened attitude did have an effect, and a lasting one,
on Athens itself. The will to resist had not been broken, and this
will—coupled as it was with the grim and humbling lessons of
Chaironeia (especially the chagrin for the two thousand who surrendered and the shame for the rest who had taken to their heels)
—produced a healthy reaction. We might even say that the Athenian reaction over the next sixteen years should be expressed in
Toynbeean terms, as a response to the "stimulus of hard knocks."

That this response should in many ways take the form of out-
right imitation of the fifth century is hardly surprising, for even
before the defeat, when the Athenians were voting on measures
in the Assembly, they had been continually invited to recall the
famous accomplishments of their forefathers and urged "to look
at the Propylaia of the Akropolis, to remember the sea-fight at
Salamis, and the ancestral tombs and trophies."[2] But *now* the chief

[2] Aeschin. II. 74.

difference was that they were inspired to make the necessary sacrifices and to take the requisite actions which they had previously
been too selfish to make.

There were other differences, of course, some of them forced on
the Athenians by the exigencies of the times, others resulting from
changed ideology. These will figure in tomorrow's lecture—the
form and content of the Athenian response to the "stimulus of
hard knocks," but today we are more immediately concerned with
the initial stimulus itself—the shock of Chaironeia which has already been described—and with the reasons why this reaction
should have been kept alive and active throughout the Lykourgan
period and even afterwards. The reasons are to be found in the
subsequent activities of Alexander in Greece and in the news from
Asia. To these events we must turn very briefly.

In spite of certain recent (and in my opinion, wrongheaded)
attempts to show that Alexander sought to buy Athenian friendship by initiating the plan to restore the Golden Nikai with a personal donation[3] and to curry favor by adopting Athenian types on
the obverse and reverse of his own gold staters,[4] it still appears that
all he managed to produce in the minds of *most* Athenians was a
hostile reaction and a steady hatred for himself in particular and
for the Macedonian hegemony in general. A. R. Bellinger, in
accepting the theory of Alexander's role in the restoration of the
Nikai, reminds us "that not all Athenians were his enemies; doubtless he had more friends than we know, and perhaps he thought
he had more friends than he did."[5] Less elegantly but with equal
assurance one might answer that there were few Athenians who
would not have preferred Alexander dead; the friends we do not
know could not have been politically active, and Alexander was
too intelligent a man to have thought that all the men on his pay-
roll were his friends. At least Bellinger has the candor to admit
that there are grounds for "skepticism as to such cordial relations
between Alexander and Athens in 336" when he says that it "is

[3] The theory is H. A. Thompson's (*HSCP*, Suppl. I [1940] 183-210; esp.
206-207), seconded by D. B. Thompson (*Hesperia*, 13 [1944] 174-209; esp.
177), and dubbed a "daring conjecture" by A. R. Bellinger, *Essays on the Coinage of Alexander the Great* (New York, 1963) 13.

[4] S. Perlman, *Num.Chron.*, ser. 7, 5 (1965) 57-67.

[5] *Op.cit.* (note 3 above) 13.

foreign to general historical probability."[6] To that I would add the suggestion that the whole theory of Alexander's role in the restoration of the Nikai is based on a chronological impossibility.

But our concern is not with Alexander's feelings toward Athens, but with the Athenians' continuing attitude toward Alexander and the Macedonians, for this is what determined the shape and force of their reaction. We must not forget how the Athenians offered thanks for the good news of Philip's assassination, voted honors for his murderer[7] and vainly placed their hopes on the outbreak of a dynastic struggle between Alexander and Attalus;[8] how cowed they had been by the unexpected invasion of northern Greece by the young king at the head of a loyal army.[9] Again they had rejoiced at the false rumor of Alexander's death in the wilds of Illyria[10] only to be thrown into panic by his swift march into Boiotia —and stunned by the savage destruction of Thebes.[11]

Now the true implications of membership in the Korinthian League became clear when Alexander gained sanction for his barbarous act by having it approved by the League. At least Athens was not represented on that occasion, but she had to take desperate and shameful measures in her effort to avoid sharing the fate of Thebes: they despatched a congratulatory letter to Alexander for his "victory"[12] and bitterly attoned for their false start in the uprising by condemning their general, Charidemos, to exile as a warmonger.[13] They dared not refuse the required contingents (which were in fact no more than hostages)[14] for the expeditionary force against Persia, in spite of the fact that their former generals, now in exile, and an untold number of fellow-citizens were fighting as

---

[6] *Idem.*

[7] Aeschin. III. 77; Plut. *Dem. XXII*; *Phoc.* XVI. 6.

[8] Diod. XVII. 3. 2, 5. 1 with Welles' note *ad loc.* in *LCL.*

[9] Aeschin. III. 161; Diod. XVII. 4. 4-9.

[10] Arr[ian, *Anabasis*] I. 7. 2-3; Aelian, *VH* XII. 57.

[11] Arr. I. 9. 9; Diod. XVII. 14; Plut. *Alex.* XI. 5-6; Justin, XI. 3. 7-4. 12.

[12] Diod. XVII. 15; Arr. I. 10. 2-5.

[13] Arr. I. 10. 6; cf. H. Berve, *Das Alexanderreich auf prosopographischer Grundlage* (München, 1926) II, no. 823 (cited hereafter as Berve II). Another general, Ephialtes, along with a comrade, Thrasyboulos, went into exile, perhaps voluntarily. Cf. Berve II, nos. 329 and 378. All three subsequently served on the Persian side.

[14] Diod. XVII. 22. 5; these twenty ships were kept in service long after the other "allied" naval contingents had been disbanded.

mercenaries in the Persian army, whose ablest leader, Memnon of Rhodes, belonged to a family whose members had received honors at Athens for their benefactions.[15]

Clearly the sympathies of the Athenians were with Alexander's opponents, nor could they have been fooled into believing that they stood to benefit materially from Alexander's quasi-liberation of Asia Minor where the cities gained a "freedom" which Badian has compared to "that of Victor Emmanuel III, who was popularly said to be free to do everything Mussolini wanted."[16] Isokrates' scheme to open up the Great King's lands to Hellenic colonization had already been scuttled by Philip, when he substituted revenge as the motive for the crusade against Persia.[17] Thus the news from Granikos caused no joy in Athens, and the dedicatory inscription which accompanied the three hundred Persian panoplies intended for Athena was offensive ("Alexander son of Philip and the Hellenes except the Lakedaimonians [dedicate these spoils] from the barbarians who inhabit Asia"),[18] not only for its intended slap at the still independent Spartans but also for the probably unintentional sarcasm of ascribing to the Greeks what had been, as everyone knew, an almost purely Macedonian victory. At any rate the spoils served only to remind the Athenians that their friends had been defeated and that many of their fellow countrymen, captured after the battle, had been sent as slaves to work in the mines of Macedon.[19] As Alexander advanced down the coast of Asia Minor toward Miletos and then laid siege to the city, the Athenians took the risk of allowing the Persian fleet to take on supplies at neighboring Samos.[20] Since this very fleet was attempting to relieve the beleaguered city, surely the Athenians did not rejoice at the city's fall—nor at the destruction of Halikarnassos,

[15] Berve II, no. 497; M. Tod, *A Selection of Greek Historical Inscriptions*, II (Oxford, 1948) no. 199 with commentary (cited hereafter as Tod II).

[16] E. Badian, "Alexander and the Greeks of Asia Minor," in E. Badian, ed., *Ancient Society and Institutions* (Oxford, 1966) 49.

[17] For Isokrates' panhellenic scheme see his *Panegyricus* and *Philip*; cf. U. Wilcken, *Alexander the Great* (New York, 1967) 19-21 (Isokrates' plan) and 34-38 (Philip's subversion of it).

[18] Arr. I. 16. 7.   [19] Arr. I. 16. 6; 29. 5-6; III. 6. 2.

[20] Arr. I. 19. 8.

among whose chief defenders stood their ex-general Ephialtes and his comrade Thrasyboulos.[21]

Somewhat later, in 331, one final episode occurred which forced upon the Athenians an agonizing choice between what the large majority must have felt to be the honorable course of action and what their good sense told them would be a disastrous course. In that year King Agis of Sparta,[22] the only major Greek state which had abstained from the decision at Chaironeia and by virtue of her abstention had managed to avoid membership in the League of Korinth, chose to make his move. He had been active in lining up allies and in hiring mercenaries with money donated by certain Persian admirals with whom he had established a kind of alliance both before and after the battle of Issos.

Naturally he hoped for and sought Athenian support. They in turn were clearly interested and had brought the matter as far as launching a number of ships and debating whether or not they would vote the money to man them, when suddenly they had second thoughts on the whole scheme. They certainly made the sensible decision—for the time was not ripe and they had not yet recovered from the losses of 338; they also remembered that Alexander held a great number of Athenian hostages—both the crews of the twenty triremes which the king had retained at the time he had dismissed the rest of the 'allied' fleet and the unfortunate men who had been sent to the mines after the battle of the Granikos. But sensible as the decision was, there was the lurking suspicion in the minds of many that it had not been in the tradition of Marathon and Salamis, and that they had left the Spartans in the lurch. There were political repercussions for a year following.[23]

The Athenians were now truly alone—with Thebes destroyed and Sparta knocked out—alone with their bad consciences and with ever increasing feelings of frustration and helplessness in the face

[21] The siege and destruction of Halikarnassos: Arr. I. 20. 2-23. 6; the parallel account of Diod. XVII. 23. 4-27. 6 emphasizes the parts played by Ephialtes and Thrasyboulos; cf. note 13 above.

[22] The most recent account of Agis' war, marred only slightly by an exaggerated notion of Agis' genius and a consequent misunderstanding of Demosthenes' role, is that of E. Badian, *Hermes*, 95 (1967) 170-192.

[23] The most famous was the process "On the Crown" between Aischines (III, *Against Ktesiphon*) and Demosthenes (XVIII, *On the Crown*). Further below.

of the waxing power of Macedon. Their really last hope was that
something unforeseen would happen to Alexander—even as it had
to Philip—and the young king's habit of exposing himself con-
spicuously in the front line of battle made this hope a very real
one. But actually it was Alexander's complete withdrawal from
the scene that allowed the reaction against him in Greece to grow,
that caused the spirit of resistance to develop and ripen into a revolutionary movement. For his famous πόθος (longing) and dreams
of conquest took him farther and farther afield until he had disappeared beyond the horizon of the known world into regions
from which men had good reason to hope he would never return.
By the time he did in fact, and contrary to expectation, return from
the East in the spring of 324, several states had already gone too
far to pull back without fear of reprisals. But the king did not
return to quash the upstarts in person; he actually aided the revolutionary movement, first by delaying in Babylon, whence he
increased the existing discontent by issuing the order to restore all
exiles, and then by suddenly dying—just in time to escape, as
Ernst Badian once put it *per litteras*, "one almighty row." By his
final act Alexander probably anticipated, but surely precipitated,
the Hellenic war for which Athens had been quietly preparing
herself for some fifteen years.[24]

The story of Athens during this period is actually an account of
Lykourgos' administration, and therefore the age rightly bears
his name. For his were the policies which gave both form and
content, both purpose and meaning to the Athenian response to
the Macedonian conquest and subsequent domination of Greece.
We will come to know Lykourgos more fully through a study of
his program and influence, but for the rest of the hour I would
like to discuss the man himself, whose patriotic zeal fired a defeated, dispirited people to make an effort far beyond their
strength, and the other men whose cooperation or opposition in
the so-called coalition government helped change, ever so briefly,

[24] For the overall situation at the time of Alexander's death see E. Badian,
"Harpalus," *JHS*, 81 (1961) 16-43, reprinted in G. T. Griffith, *Alexander the
Great: The Main Problems* (Cambridge, 1966) 205-233. For Athens' alliance
with Aitolia and whether it preceded the news of Alexander's death see the dis-
cussion in L. Moretti, *Iscrizioni storiche ellenistiche*, I (Firenze, 1967) no. 1
(Vol. 53, Biblioteca di studi superiori).

the course of Athenian history. In my discussion I will emphasize what seem to me the shortcomings of the now generally accepted view that the coalition government was made up of four distinct factions—promacedonian conservatives, promacedonian radicals, antimacedonian conservatives, and antimacedonian radicals—and that the promacedonians had a free hand in foreign affairs while the antimacedonians ran things at home. This theory is at once too complicated and too simple.

DRAMATIS PERSONAE

LYKOURGOS son of Lykophron of the deme Boutadai[25] was born of the priestly clan of the Eteoboutadai and was himself an hereditary priest of Poseidon-Erechtheus, a proud office still attested in the second century A.D. in a family in which the name of Lykourgos and that of his granddaughter Philippe still survived.[26] The office explains in part Lykourgos' extraordinary religiosity, his special concern for the cults in the Erechtheion and at Eleusis, and for the cult of Poseidon in Peiraieus, as well as his general interest in the revival of all the ancestral cults in Attika. His immediate ancestors had been prominent in the late fifth century when his like-named grandfather had been lampooned by Aristophanes[27] and his father murdered by the Thirty Tyrants[28]— a heritage which may account for Lykourgos' loyalty to the democratic ideals, albeit his ideal was the moderate democracy which was popular in the third quarter of the fourth century and took its origin, not from the fifth-century tradition, but from the legendary king, Theseus.[29] Larsen has taught us that the hallmark of the

[25] F. Dürrbach, *L'orateur Lykurgus* (Paris, 1890); J. Kirchner, *Prosopographia Attica* (Berlin, 1901) no. 9251 (cited hereafter as *PA*); Berve II, no. 477; Kunst, *RE*, 30 (1927) 2446-65, no. 10. The *Life of Lykourgos* which appears among the pseudo-Plutarchian *Lives of the Ten Orators* is cited as [Plut.] *Mor.*, and the speeches are cited from the edition of J. O. Burtt, *Minor Attic Orators*, II (*LCL*).

[26] This seems likely if not certain from the stemma published by E. Kapetanopoulos, *Arch.Eph.*, 1964 (appeared 1967) 120-123. The latter-day priest of Poseidon-Erechtheus was Ti. Klaudios Demostratos Sounieus, the son of Klaudia Philippe, the daughter of Lykourgos Palleneus.

[27] [Plut.] *Mor.* 843E.   [28] [Plut.] *Mor.* 841B.

[29] A. E. Raubitschek, "Demokratia," *Hesperia*, 31 (1962) 238-243; *AKTE des IV. internationalen Kongresses für griechische und lateinische Epigraphik* (Vienna, 1962) 332-337.

conservative democracy was that more of the important officials were elected and fewer selected by lot; these officials were still responsible to the People for their actions and the Assembly remained active in making decisions on policy.[30] This is precisely the form of Athenian democracy described by Aristotle and honored by the outgoing Councillors in 333/2 by a bronze statue of Δημοκρατία which was set up in the Agora.[31]

In keeping his faith in democracy Lykourgos had to resist some of the notions to which he was exposed as a young man attending lectures at the Akademy, but the Platonic influence can be discerned in his abiding concern both for the training of the youth and for faith in the gods as the proper basis of civic life. But it was his own moral quality which earned him the reputation for honesty so great that the People entrusted him with the financial administration of the whole state for three four-year periods,[32] and for a wisdom which allowed his proposals to be accepted with a minimum of opposition.

Of Lykourgos' public life before ca. 340 we know nothing; it was then that he began to accompany Demosthenes and Polyeuktos on embassies seeking aid for the approaching war with Philip.[33] At any rate his reputation as an honest and able administrator was already established before he was elected to supervise the public finances—an office he assumed in midsummer 338/7 shortly before Chaironeia.[34] It is ironic that one who probably owed his election, and indeed the creation of his extraordinary office, to the war-time

[30] J.A.O. Larsen, "The Judgment of Antiquity on Democracy," *CP*, 49 (1954) 1-14, esp. 3, where he gives the cardinal features of popular government, and 7-9, where he discusses the conservative trend, including the direct election of the more important officials, in the latter part of the fourth century. Larsen is not alone in his failure to recognize the real purpose of Eukrates' so-called Law against Tyranny passed in 337/6 (p. 9).

[31] See note 29 above.

[32] Cf. Diod. XVI. 88. 1: διοικήσας δώδεκα ἔτη; [Plut.] *Mor.* 841B, 852B; ταμίας ἐπὶ τρεῖς πεντετηρίδας.

[33] [Plut.] *Mor.* 841E.

[34] This is the generally accepted date based on [Plut.] *Mor.* 841B-C and the statement of Aristotle (*Ath. Pol.*, 43. 1) that such offices ran from one Panathenaia to the next, that is, for four years beginning Hekatombaion 28, 338/7. Cf. *TAPA*, 93 (1962) 213-229, esp. 220-221 with notes 19 and 20, and 223-224 with note 22; where there is confusion between *quadrennia* and *pentetêrides*, it is easier to stick with the Greek and remember that the Panathenaic *pentetêrides* during Lykourgos' period of influence extended from 338/7 to 334/3, from 334/3 to 330/29, from 330/29 to 326/5.

crisis, should have gained lasting fame as the financial administrator of, and the moving spirit behind, a program of peace-time recovery.

DEMOSTHENES of Paiania should need no introduction. His staunch opposition to Macedonian aggression remained unchanged after the debacle at Chaironeia, and his popularity with the People was, if anything, stronger than ever.[35] Nevertheless he played for the most part a secondary role in the Assembly, where he let his friends introduce his proposals,[36] while he served the state as Grain Commissioner, Commissioner of the Festival Board, and as Superintendent of Walls for his own tribe, Pandionis.[37] Early in 336/5 he placed himself and his city in serious jeopardy when he grossly underestimated the capabilities of the youthful Alexander and gratuitously proposed honors for Philip's assassin and a thank-offering for the glad tidings. Again in 335/4 the false rumor of Alexander's death in Illyria caused him to foment rebellion and to use Persian gold to arm the Thebans for their fatal resistance. In this case he very nearly led his city into sharing the fate of Thebes and was himself among the ringleaders whom the king demanded to be given up to him. Alexander relented only on the plea of Demades and Phokion, who had been unwavering advocates of the peace and were allowed to go bail for the future conduct of their colleagues.[38] Whatever deal was made at that time was thereafter honored by the more volatile antimacedonians, now convinced that peace was the only sensible policy. Demosthenes was the only prominent Athenian (although there were doubtless others less well-known) who came out in favor of the ill-starred uprising of Agis, and even Demosthenes seems to have done little more than make a characteristically rash statement in the beginning and then, as Plutarch tells us, "cowered down."[39] This initially favorable response by Demosthenes is not mentioned in a recent attempt to

[35] Demosth. XVIII. 248-250, 285-288.   [36] Aeschin. III. 159.

[37] Aeschin. III. 24-27; Demosth. XVIII. 113.

[38] See note 12 above plus Plut. *Dem.* XXIII. 5, *Phoc.* XVII. 2-5. The references to this episode have been collected and discussed, convincingly I believe, by Berve II. no. 762.

[39] Plut. *Dem.* 24. 1. Plutarch may have known no more about D.'s role than what he had read in Aeschin. III. 165-167.

picture Agis as a military genius who would have led the Greeks to victory but for the lack of Athenian support which was allegedly withheld by Demosthenes because he was still piqued about the lack of Spartan help at Chaironeia.[40] The arguments used to excuse Sparta's earlier refusal are even less convincing when, turned inside out, they are used to denounce Athens when it was later her turn to refuse. The military situations were not all that different; if Antipater's forces were weaker than those of Philip, so was Greece north of Attika less able to resist. An alliance with Sparta in 331 could have had but one certain result—the utter devastation of all Attika. The best explanation of Demosthenes' "cowering down" is that he was under oath to those who had saved his life to be quiet, that peace was the official policy of his government and that the Athenians had made a realistic appraisal both of Agis' chances and of their own potential.[41]

DEMADES of Paiania, a fellow-demesman and perhaps a cousin of Demosthenes,[42] was a very different type of man. He came from modest circumstances and had enjoyed neither the philosophical

[40] Badian, *op.cit.* (note 22 above) 172: "Politically, Sparta's failure to join Demosthenes' alliance [in 338] had only one serious consequence: it offended Demosthenes." This tendentious statement ignores not only D.'s initially favorable response to Agis' request for aid, but also the fact that D. was at this time playing a secondary political role. It was Demades and sober second thoughts that prevented the manning of the ships. Phokion, too, would have advised against belligerency.

[41] Like Badian, both Aischines (III. 165-167) and Deinarchos (I. 34-36) try to make Agis' defeat look like a lost opportunity for the Athenians and to pin the whole blame on D. as though the decision was his alone. Although both these speeches are full of rhetorical distortion and try to put D. in the blackest light possible, neither goes so far as to claim that he *opposed* the sending of aid in the ekklesia, but only that he was ineffectual and equivocating. Aischines was speaking not long after the defeat and death of Agis and was trying to turn the public embarrassment over Athens' inglorious role against D.; he purports to quote D. directly and draws a vivid picture of his actions which must have been still fresh in the minds of the jurymen; he represents his opponent (167) as boasting that he had set the Lakonian uprising in motion and caused the Thessalians and Perrhaibians to revolt, and then turns to mockery and ridicule; but the report of what D. actually said, little and ineffectual as it was, was clearly in favor of Sparta and resistance, and that is a far cry from saying that he was against the Spartan alliance in 331 as a "consequence of the Spartan decision in 338" (Badian, 173).

[42] E. Badian, *JHS*, 81 (1961) 34, note 134. Recent works on Demades are: P. Treves, "Demade," *Athenaeum*, 11 (1933) and V. De Falco, *Demade Oratore*[2] (Napoli, 1954); for the epigraphical evidence see Al. N. Oikonomides, *Platon*,

education nor the oratorical training of his wealthier colleagues.[43] His native talent must be reckoned all the greater, therefore, for he was admittedly one of the foremost orators of his day.[44] But as one might expect of a self-made man, he was an utter opportunist. He cared not a whit for Athens' past glory and conducted the affairs of state, as he himself said, as though he were piloting a shipwrecked vessel; and he had no qualms about moving decrees which would have been deemed unworthy of a still sovereign state, so long as the state stood to gain thereby.[45] And the state did gain, for the success of Demades' many negotiations at the Macedonian Court derived in large measure from the friends and influence he had acquired by moving honorary decrees for important Macedonians while doing no material damage whatever to Athens.[46]

He had a ready tongue—and indeed it was to this that he owed his rise to prominence, for he was among the two thousand prisoners taken at Chaironeia and had the courage to stand up to Philip when the latter had broken off a drunken revel to come gloat over his Athenian captives.[47] Having won the king's favor in this unexpected way, Demades was vaulted into a leading position by being sent to Athens with Philip's terms of peace. But his outspoken way is also the cause of his bad reputation, for many of his sayings are preserved merely because they are witty and, since they appear in our sources out of context, make him appear to have been a venal scoundrel. Scholars have repeated these remarks, along with the calumnies of his opponents, and allowed Demades to condemn himself out of his own mouth.[48] We are rarely asked to consider his own assertion: "Yes, I have changed my policy, but in doing so I have spoken only against what I have

---

6 (1956) 105-129 plus S. Charitonides, *Hesperia*, 30 (1961) 32, line 144; Demades' role as Military Treasurer is discussed by F. Mitchel, *TAPA*, 93 (1962) 213-227 with corrigenda in *AJA*, 76 (1966) 66.

[43] References in A. Schaefer, *Demosthenes und seine Zeit*[2] (Leipzig, 1886) III, 21, notes 1 and 2. Cited hereafter as Schaefer III[2].

[44] Plut. *Dem.* X. 1.

[45] Plut. *Phoc.* I. 1. Cf. F. Blass, *Die attische Beredsamkeit*[2] (Leipzig, 1898) III. ii., 277, note 3. Cited hereafter as Blass III[2].

[46] Tod II. nos. 180 and 181 with commentary; Oikonomides, *op.cit.* (note 42 above) nos. 7-10, 20 and 23.

[47] Diod. XVI. 87.

[48] For example: Blass III[2], ii. 273-278; Schaefer III[2], 20-24, and esp. 211.

said, never against the interests of the state."[49] In labelling Demades a promacedonian it is convenient to forget that he often
rose in the Assembly and spoke off-the-cuff in support of Demosthenes when the latter had been shouted down.[50]

Demades played a much greater part than is generally recognized in the internal administration of the state, for as the elected
Treasurer of the Military Fund for the quadrennium 334/3-330/29
he was second only to Lykourgos in importance and acted not
just as a disburser of money, but as a supervisor of many other
matters, some of which had previously been the province of the
Festival Board and others which were directly related to Lykourgos' program of reform and recovery, e.g., the restoration of the
golden Nikai.[51] He further cooperated with Lykourgos in keeping
Athens at peace in 331, when the ill-timed rebellion of Agis had
the People inflamed and ready to send ships to support the Spartans.[52] Lykourgos and Demosthenes were in very difficult positions
for they both knew—although Demosthenes was carried along at
first—that Athens was not ready for war, but it was plainly impossible to discuss the facts in public. This would have been tantamount
to admitting that war was indeed the ultimate aim of Athenian
policy, only to see the debate degenerate into a squabble about
whether it should come now or later. To make matters worse
Demades had on hand in the Military Treasury the enormous sum
of a hundred and sixty talents which had just come in from Lykourgos' successful prosecution of Diphilos for illegal mining practices.[53] There had not yet been time to allocate the money to the
several projects then under way, and Demades, when asked, had
to admit that the Athenians did indeed have the money to man
the ships; "But," he said, "I had planned to give each of you fifty
drachmai for the Festival of the Pots, and if you would rather
spend the money for this other purpose, you must provide for the
festival from your own pockets."[54] That was the end of the war

[49] Plut. *Dem.* XIII. 2.
[50] Plut. *Dem.* X. 5.
[51] Cf. *TAPA*, 93 (1962) 219-223 with *AJA*, 76 (1966) 66.
[52] For the date see K. J. Beloch, *Griechische Geschichte*[2] (Berlin and Leipzig, 1922) III. i. 646. Cited hereafter as Beloch III[2].
[53] [Plut.] *Mor.* 843D-E.
[54] Plut. *Mor.* 818E-F; *Cleom.* XXVII. 1 with the MSS. reading: πρῳρατεῦσαι.

talk, and Lykourgos and Demosthenes were off the hook. Understandably it was something they never talked about later.[55]

Demades' activity as an orator was by no means confined to moving decrees in honor of the Macedonians (although the necessity for such decrees was recognized at the time, and he was given a free hand unless he went too far and proposed *proxenia* for such an out-and-out scoundrel as Euthykrates of Olynthos).[56] He was also active in the settlement of some problem concerning Lemnos,[57] the regulation of naval affairs, and the development of the commercial area of the Peiraieus.[58] Sometime after 330 he is found among the envoys who went with Lykourgos to Delphi to celebrate the Pythais and to dedicate a bronze tripod;[59] in 329/8 he was one of the commissioners elected (again with Lykourgos) to supervise the celebration at the Amphiaraion, and in the next year he was one of the private individuals who contributed to the dedication set up there by the Council of Five Hundred.[60] He was also a member of the Council sometime in the 330's according to a recently published Bouleutic list. But, if Larsen's redating of the list to before 341/0 is correct, we have the earliest evidence of Demades' public service in the years prior to Chaironeia and his encounter with Philip.[61]

[55] A.H.M. Jones (*Athenian Democracy* [Oxford, 1957] 34) has rightly identified the half-*mna* distribution from the spoils of the Diphilos-case, attributed to Lykourgos, with the distribution in like amount attributed to Demades at the time of Agis' uprising. This was a special, in fact unique, distribution and, since it was during Demades' tenure as Military Treasurer, had nothing to do with the Festival Fund, as argued by J. J. Buchanan, *Theorika* (Locust Valley, N.Y., 1962) 80-81, 84.

[56] For the alleged necessity see Hyp. *Phil.* 5-6 and Souidas, *s.v.* Demades; for the indictment of Demades and for his proposal in favor of Euthykrates, see J. O. Burtt, *Minor Attic Orators*, II (*LCL*) 576-580.

[57] In 337/6; cf. E. Schweigert, *Hesperia*, 9 (1940) 325-327, no. 35.

[58] Cf. Oikonomides, *op.cit.* (note 42 above) nos. 12, 17-19.

[59] Cf. W. Dittenberger, *Sylloge Inscriptionum Graecarum³* (Leipzig, 1915-24) no. 296 (cited hereafter as *SIG³*). D. M. Lewis (*BSA*, 50 [1955] 34) would date the Pythais to 326/5 and connect it with the dedication to the new temple at Delphi, but the matter is far from certain. It should be emphasized that a Pythais was motivated by specific events in Athens altogether unrelated to Pythian years and events in Delphi. Demades received *proxenia* at Delphi, perhaps on this very occasion; cf. *SIG³*, no. 297.

[60] Cf. *SIG³*, no. 298 = *IG*, VII. 4254. It was probably a statue.

[61] Cf. S. Charitonides, *Hesperia*, 30 (1961) 30-57, esp. 32, line 144; J.A.O. Larsen, *CP*, 57 (1962) 104-108.

One must conclude that Demades was a thoroughly useful citizen and, after all, a patriot. His alleged venality was certainly less well known to his fellow-citizens, who elected him to an office of high public trust, than to scholars, who, beginning with Plutarch, have taken too literally some of his own brash sayings and the malicious slanders made by his adversaries in court speeches. Although one could never believe that Demades and Lykourgos were close friends, they obviously got along.

PHOKION is the most puzzling figure of the period and deserves the fullest treatment because his position has been most consistently misinterpreted. He is supposed to have headed a conservative, aristocratic faction which dominated Athenian foreign policy and advocated submission to Macedon as a means of gaining support in their struggle against the democrats at home. One may well doubt the existence of any such faction, but this is not the place to re-examine the picture of the whole party structure which is found in the standard works today.[62] It must here suffice to call attention to the anachronistic inappropriateness of attaching modern class and party labels, which indicate general and fixed differences in principle and policy, to men who readily changed sides on specific issues and acknowledged personal enmity as their main reason for attacking a particular political measure.[63] It is but a short step beyond this to point out the absurdity of supposing that a 'promacedonian party' could have operated openly in the sullenly hostile political climate of Athens in the 330's and 320's. 'Promacedonian' was at that time a dirty word which, along with accusations of bribery, cowardice and questionable ancestry, was leveled indiscriminately at any opponent whatever without regard for accuracy. It was applied most often to the advocates of peace because it so happened that the only sensible course for Athens

---

[62] For the classic statement of the four-party structure (see above, page 11) see: J. Beloch, *Die attische Politik seit Perikles* (Leipzig, 1884) 249-250, followed by W. S. Ferguson, *Hellenistic Athens* (London, 1911) 7f.; Beloch IV². i. 52-56; W. W. Tarn, *CAH*, VI (Cambridge, 1927) 440; G. Glotz-P. Roussel-R. Cohen, *Histoire Grecque*, IV (Paris, 1938) 196-198; Th. Lenschau, *RE*, 30 (1941) 458-473, esp. 465.

[63] Cf. R. Sealey, *JHS*, 75 (1955) 74-81; *Historia*, 5 (1956) 178-203; *AJP*, 79 (1958) 71-73 (all three now reprinted in *Essays in Greek Politics*, New York, 1967); S. Perlman, *Athenaeum*, 41 (1963) 327-355.

to follow coincided with the policy which the Macedonians hoped she would follow, and those who allowed themselves the dangerous luxury of expressing their antimacedonian sentiments in public naturally ridiculed those who steadfastly held to the only safe course. But there is no credible evidence that either Phokion or Demades had other than patriotic motives for what they proposed or that they talked peace only to gain favor with the Macedonians. It was, of course, inevitable that they should gain Macedonian favor once their position became known and that Phokion should from time to time find himself the rallying point for a few men with baser motives, but both men demonstrated their devotion to Athens on many occasions, and it is inconceivable that either one should have acted as the head of a party (had any such existed) whose interests were opposed to those of the state.

As for Phokion himself, he was hardly an aristocrat. Only because of his innate nobility and his alleged youthful association with the Akademy does Plutarch doubt the tradition of his humble origin.[64] But against this doubt must be weighed the tradition itself, and that Phokion lived his whole life in ostentatious poverty, refused to contribute to a public sacrifice on the grounds that he was a debtor,[65] and as far as we know never performed a single liturgy. He remains furthermore, the one prominent figure of the later fourth century whose demotic is still unknown. It was to his friendship with Chabrias rather than to birth and position that Phokion owed his early military training and his promotion to a command.[66]

This early training under a competent general made Phokion the nearest thing to a professional general the Athenians had, at least for their citizen soldiery, and they elected him to the office repeatedly in spite of his open contempt for the People, his refusal to seek office and his reluctance to lead them out to fight. When he did go out, however, as he did to relieve Megara and Byzantion[67] and to defend Euboia and the Paralia,[68] he proved himself a competent general and enjoyed such success that he could boast that during his long tenure as general the Athenians had been buried

[64] Plut. *Phoc.* IV. 1.
[66] *Ibid.* VI. 1-VII. 2.
[68] *Ibid.* XII-XIII, XXV.
[65] *Ibid.* IX. 1.
[67] *Ibid.* XIV-XV.

in private tombs (rather than in public monuments for the war-dead).[69]

But Phokion was a most cautious general, and this caution in military matters, when translated to the *bema*, became a policy of quietism which has been interpreted as being promacedonian. Actually he had two basic rules which can be deduced from all his actions and sayings: 1) Never fight until every possibility of negotiation has been exhausted; and 2) Not even then unless victory is assured or one's back is to the wall. He had little confidence in those whom he led, and even against the Boiotians he advised the Athenians to fight with words in which they were superior, not with arms with which they were inferior; and against Alexander he advised them that they should either be superior in arms themselves or friends to those who were.[70] He was kept on the bench both at Chaironeia and at Lamia because the Athenians feared that he would accept Macedonian offers to negotiate a peace.[71] But it was Phokion's extreme caution as a general, not his alleged promacedonian policy, that made him always advise a course of peace and quiet. Although he had advised negotiating with Philip before Chaironeia and afterwards was a leading figure in the group which accepted the mild terms of the peace, he opposed the Athenians' making a military alliance with Philip without knowing first what would be expected of them. And in 322 he was quick to lead out the homeguard to defend the Paralia against the Macedonian invaders under Mikion. One concludes that, although he was often opposed to those who earned the name of patriot by advocating war,[72] he was no less a patriot than they.

AISCHINES of Kothokidai is well-known because of his persistent opposition to Demosthenes, and the facts of his life can be learned from a judicious reading of his own speeches and those of his opponent.[73] He was, however, but a minor character in the story

---

[69] *Ibid.* XXIII. 1.   [70] *Ibid.* IX. 4, XXI. 1.

[71] In 338/7 Phokion was serving with the fleet (*Ibid.* XVI. 1-2); in 322/1 he was general of the countryside and, after the death of Leosthenes, was passed over in favor of Antiphilos (*Ibid.* XXIV. 1-2).

[72] E.g. Polyeuktos Sphettios (*Ibid.* IX. 5); Demosthenes (*Ibid.* XVII. 1); Leosthenes and Hypereides (*Ibid.* XXIII. 1-2).

[73] See also Guenther Ramming, *Die politischen Ziele und Wege des Aischines* (diss. Erlangen, 1965).

of Lykourgan Athens, and only a few specific points need to be discussed.

It is generally agreed that he was no traitor—this was the verdict of a handy majority of the ancient jury which heard the case, and it is accepted by the majority of modern scholars without question. He was, nevertheless, gullible where Philip was concerned; nor did he foresee the consequences of his eloquence before the Amphiktyonic Council at Delphi.[74] Those who would make Aischines over into a far-sighted statesman must be classed with the less than twenty percent of the jury who voted with him to condemn Ktesiphon.

If Aischines helped the Macedonian cause, he did so unwittingly, and it cannot be concluded that he was a member of a promacedonian 'party' or that he was a supporter of Phokion simply on the grounds that he called upon Phokion for support when he was on trial for treason,[75] or because he was included among those who were sent to accept Philip's terms of peace. In the first case an important part of Aischines' defense rested on his distinguished military record, and it was only natural that he should call upon the man who had been general at Tamynai where Aischines had been twice decorated for valorous conduct.[76] Phokion was famous for defending even those who opposed him,[77] and his support of Aischines shows only that he recognized a good soldier and considered him innocent of the charge. Nor does Aischines' inclusion in the embassy after Chaironeia[78] prove any close connexion with Demades and Phokion: Demades was sent because he had come from Philip in the first place;[79] Phokion, because he was commander-in-chief and was known to have favored negotiation even before the battle;[80] and Aischines, because he had been cordially received by Philip on a previous occasion, and his

[74] Aeschin. III. 106-128; Demosth. XVIII. 145-149.
[75] Aeschin. II. 170; 184.
[76] *Ibid.* 169.   [77] Plut. *Phoc.* X. 2, 5.
[78] Aeschin. III. 227; Demosth. XVIII. 282.
[79] Diod. XVI. 87; Demosth. XVIII. 285; Souidas, *s.v.* Demades (probably from [Demades], *On the Twelve Years*, 9).
[80] Plut. *Phoc.* XVI. Phokion's participation in this embassy is nowhere attested but is a logical inference both from his extraordinary position in the Athenian state after Chaironeia and from the courtesy and favor shown him by Philip thereafter. Cf. Nepos, *Phoc.* I. 3; Plut. *Phoc.* XVII; Schäfer III². 25, note 1.

well-known personal enmity toward Philip's chief antagonist was, under the circumstances, an asset. There is no indication that the members of this *ad hoc* embassy continued to cooperate with one another after the embassy's business was done. To Demades alone fell the chore of maintaining good relations with the leading Macedonians, and Aischines' war against Demosthenes was a private affair, receiving no support as far as we know from his former colleagues. Nor can Aischines himself be linked with the obscure sykophants who hounded Demosthenes in the hectic period which followed the peace.[81]

In his famous indictment of Ktesiphon in 336, Aischines may have had the support of a certain Diodotos,[82] but when the case was reinstituted in 330 it was nothing but a pettifogging attempt to use the public embarrassment over the Agis affair as a means to seek personal revenge for an old wrong, and he went it alone. We hear of no friends at the bar, and among the jurymen they were so few that the prosecutor was caught in his own web. And finally there was no one but his intended victim who rallied to his side in defeat. For what the story is worth, it was Demosthenes who overtook him as he was sneaking away and offered him the amount of his fine.[83] The notion that the suit was staged by the 'friends of Macedon' to deal a shrewd blow to their opponents is contradicted by the outcome.[84] A 'party' which could neither muster a fifth part of the votes nor give comfort to a 'member' who had suffered in the line of duty was no party at all. On the other hand it is not surprising to find an orator bringing a public suit because of personal enmity, and in Aischines' case at any rate it is not surprising that he vainly overrated his own ability to persuade and entirely misjudged the man and the occasion.

HYPEREIDES of Kollytos was a man of wealth and family who performed many liturgies and in his youth had been Lykourgos' contemporary at the Akademy.[85] He was Phokion's equal in personal integrity, Demades' in physical indulgence,[86] and Demosthenes' in unrelenting opposition to Macedonian domination. His

---

[81] Demosth. XVIII. 249.
[83] *Ibid.* 845E-F.
[85] [Plut.] *Mor.* 848D.
[82] [Plut.] *Mor.* 846A.
[84] Tarn, *CAH*, VI. 446-448.
[86] *Ibid.* 848F (probity); 849D-E, Athen. VIII. 341e (sensuality).

position vis-à-vis Macedon made him a natural associate of Lykourgos and Demosthenes, but he maintained a certain independence of action. Contrary to the *communis opinio*, which sees him as a fiery radical democrat at home, and eager for an early showdown with Macedon, he seems to have pursued a conservative internal policy, while his cautious approach to the Macedonian problem kept him out of trouble until the very end.

He was the prime, and successful, prosecutor of the infamous Philokrates in 343,[87] and proudly listed his victim's property for confiscation,[88] while Demosthenes failed to convict Aischines on a similar charge. And he was elected by the ultra-conservative Areiopagite Council, in the place of Aischines, to represent Athens before the Amphiktyonic Council in the dispute with Delos.[89] In the days following Chaironeia he courageously proposed measures, which were clearly unlawful, to meet the manpower shortage, viz., to place even the Council of Five Hundred under arms,[90] and to grant citizenship to any non-citizens and freedom to any slaves who were able and willing to bear arms in the city's defense.[91] These were emergency measures to which Athens had had recourse in the past, and so were neither unprecedented nor radical.[92] Although the financial loss to certain rich slaveholders could have been stiff, it would not in any case have been recurrent, while the dilution of the festival distributions through the creation of new citizens would have been a blow much harder to bear for the many poor— and the dilution, moreover, would have continued year after year. On the whole it is better to consider the measures as war-time expedients, devoid of political implications.

There is no indication that Hypereides was implicated in the crisis of 335[93]—and this is strange indeed for one who is supposed to have been a hot-headed antimacedonian of the radical party. His name does not appear in the list of eight ring-leaders—the list said

---

[87] Hyp. *Eux.* 29-30.

[88] B. D. Meritt, *Hesperia*, V (1936) 393-413, no. 10; esp. lines 45-50, 101-115 with commentaries.

[89] Demosth. XVIII. 134; [Plut.] *Mor.* 850A.

[90] Lycurg. *Leoc.* 36-37.

[91] *Ibid.* 41; [Plut.] *Mor.* 849A.

[92] Cf. A. Diller, *Race Mixture Among the Greeks Before Alexander* (Urbana, 1937) 111-112; 148.

[93] Cf. Berve II, no. 762.

by Plutarch to have derived from "the majority and most reliable writers"[94]—whom Alexander demanded after the destruction of Thebes, and his speech in defense of these very men is a further indication that he was not one of their number.[95] Nor is there any sign that he had any part in stirring up the People at the time of Agis' rebellion. It may be that Hypereides was politically inactive during the late 330's, but it is more likely that he was independently pursuing a more cautious policy in foreign affairs.

But Hypereides *was* active as an advocate. His defense of Euxenippos against an accusation in which Lykourgos supported the prosecutor[96] has been taken as "the first sign that the radicals were passing definitely into opposition; they had desired war, and thought that the government had neglected a favorable opportunity."[97] But there is no evidence either that Hypereides was warmongering in the 330's or that any of his policies were radical or demagogical. The speech for Euxenippos is actually a defense against a typically demagogical attack which derived from personal enmity and employed the usual sykophantic smoke-screens— bribery, promacedonism and prejudice against a wealthy man.[98] Lykourgos' secondary support of the prosecution (Hypereides' reference to him is anything but hostile) can be explained simply— the deeply religious old man truly believed that Euxenippos had played false in reporting the oracular dream and that he had allowed Olympias, the Macedonian queen-mother, to make a dedication to Hygieia at the Amphiaraion.[99]

Finally the speech contains two incidental items which are of primary importance in interpreting the relationships between the leading statesmen. First it should be noted that Hypereides had played a prominent part in defending, sometime around 331/0, the Athenians' embellishment of the shrine at Dodona against the sharp protests of Olympias.[100] The restoration of the image of

---

[94] Plut. *Dem.* XXIII.   [95] [Plut.] *Mor.* 848E.   [96] Hyp. *Eux.* 12.
[97] Tarn, *CAH*, VI. 446.   [98] Hyp. *Eux.* 21-22, 32, 39.
[99] Al. N. Oikonomides (*Neon Athenaion*, I [1955] 57-58) has argued persuasively that Euxenippos was an official of the cult of Hygieia at the Amphiaraion, having himself set up the cult image, and that he was a proxenos of the Oropians. This would explain why it was he who gave Olympias permission to dedicate the *phiale* and perhaps why his 'vision' in the sacred precinct was in favor of the god.
[100] Hyp. *Eux.* 24-26.

Dione in response to Zeus' oracle must have been a matter close to Lykourgos' heart, and Hypereides' part in the affair is proof of his continued support of Lykourgan policy in the face of Macedonian opposition.

Secondly Hypereides refers to the magnanimity of the People in acquitting certain mining magnates who had been falsely accused of malpractice in the working of the mines. The acquittals, he says, had dispelled the fear which had for a time discouraged exploratory cuttings, and now had caused a renewed interest in mining and an increase in public revenues, which certain orators had spoiled by misleading the people and imposing tribute on the lessees.[101] The 'fear' of which he speaks must be connected with the aftermath of Lykourgos' successful prosecution of Diphilos, when his success and the enormous sum involved brought on a rash of sykophantic prosecutions which threatened to cut off a major source of revenue. To judge from Hypereides' spirited discussion of the cases, it seems possible that he had played a significant part in stemming the tide of meritless accusations and had thus helped to increase the annual revenue, which was yet another primary aim of the Lykourgan program. The imposition of 'tribute' on the mine owners is a different matter. Here Hypereides argues from the rich man's point of view against what certain orators had proposed. Since the proposal was a scheme to raise money, one of the orators was very likely Lykourgos, and Hypereides' objection shows a genuine difference of opinion.[102]

But a difference of opinion about one economic measure does not show that Hypereides had "passed definitely into opposition" to the Lykourgan program. Else it would be hard to explain why Hypereides appears as the defender of Lykourgos' sons (who had been cast into prison after their father's death) against the charges of Menesaichmos who, if there were any truth in the traditional party labels, would have been Hypereides' chief ally.[103]

When, however, the Harpalos affair had split the governing group wide open and the Areiopagite Council had handed down its indictments, Hypereides was chosen to prosecute the case not

[101] *Ibid.* 34-36.
[102] *Ibid.* 37. See below, page 33 and note 126.
[103] [Plut.] *Mor.* 842E; cf. Hyp. frg. 118 (Kenyon).

only because he had received no bribe himself,[104] but probably because the Council insisted on his election even as it had done nearly ten years earlier in the Delian affair. His long-standing friendship with Demosthenes, to which he refers in his speech,[105] was obviously shattered, but soon afterwards, on the outbreak of the Hellenic war, they again made common cause[106] and they were completely reconciled shortly before their deaths in exile.[107]

A summary of the preceding character sketches of the leading statesmen suggests that the governing of the city was throughout the Lykourgan Period in the hands of a conservative group within which the ideological differences were less than is generally supposed and personal dislikes did not prevent cooperation on essential matters of external and internal policy.[108] The elimination of an active promacedonian faction from the scene allows us to draw a different picture of the political developments. It is a picture in which the only treason was a terrible name with which the zealous and doctrinaire Lykourgos labelled the faintheartedness of a few unfortunate individuals; the fierce recriminations in the courts were the results of personal enmities and rivalries of long standing. If there was any tension over the problem of the peace, it was not indeed whether it should exist, but what use should be made of it and whether the accommodation to Macedonian hegemony should be total and permanent or merely token and temporary. As for the internal reforms, they seem to have encountered little or no opposition and were not a matter of controversy; they included proposals such as support for religious institutions, the revival of patriotic spirit and renewal of civic pride and responsibility, and public works—all measures that are as immune to political attack as 'Mom and apple pie.' Within the group there was no one so conservative that he hoped to overthrow the democracy or to use Macedonian support to impose oli-

104 *Ibid.* 848F.

105 Hyp. *Dem.* frg. 6, coll. 20-21 (Kenyon).

106 [Plut.] *Mor.* 849F, reading *Demosthenes* with the MSS. instead of Xylander's gratuitous *Leosthenes*.

107 *Ibid.* 849A-B.

108 Cf. Perlman, *op.cit.* (note 63 above), who maintains that the orators were all of the same economic class, i.e. middle and upper middle. A.H.M. Jones, *op.cit.* (note 55 above) 35-37, suggests that even the ordinary citizens who attended assemblies and sat on juries were reasonably well off.

garchy in order to safeguard the interest of his class; at the same time there was no one so liberal that he did not realize that the People had to be guided with a tight rein.

Most important, there was no one who was not first of all a patriotic Athenian, and, therefore, desirous of seeing his city strong and independent, able to defend herself and her commerce, and to benefit her friends. Not one of them would have objected to any measure which was designed to make the young men ready to stand firm in the battle line and the men of substance to contribute their wealth to the city; to restore stability and integrity to the government and to the administration of the fiscus; to promote the development of industry, commerce and agriculture which was now possible under the general peace; to revitalize the citizens' pride in the city and their reverence toward the gods; or to reassert Athens' cultural leadership and to make her again the adornment of Greece.

Each of these measures could be seen separately for what it was, recognized as good and carried out by some specific action—that is, by collecting money and supplies, by constructing ships and commissioning buildings, by passing laws and reforming the administrative machinery, by reviving festivals and restoring temples, by training the youth and so forth. As was said, not one of the leading statesmen could have been strongly opposed to any of these—which is not to say that they all appreciated the way in which the several projects were related one to another or that they would have understood what Lykourgos meant if he had tried to explain the purpose of his overall program as he himself must have conceived it: that the citizens should become once again the "lovers of Athens" and Athens herself, "the school of Hellas."

II. THE PROGRAM

Those of you who survived yesterday's lecture will recall that we joked about the title of the series: "Lykourgan Athens," but did not specifically justify it. The fact is that Lykourgos son of Lykophron of Boutadai is the only Athenian after Perikles who so effectively dominated his city's policies and left such an indelible mark upon the city, its institutions and buildings, that his twelve year period of influence rightly bears his name. Today we will see that so many of the things that were accomplished or attempted during this period appear to have been initiated in conscious imitation of the Periklean Golden Age, that I hope you will agree that we are justified in calling it (in analogy to the terminology of Roman history) the "Silver Age of Lykourgos." His is the comprehensive program of reconstruction, reform and revitalization that is the substance of today's lecture.

The most obvious place to begin a description of Lykourgos' program is in the area of financial administration, for the one government office he is known to have held himself and to have continued to influence was concerned with the fiscus, and we may guess that it was in large part through the control of funds that Lykourgos was able to put his stamp on the many several projects and programs. He was also famous for increasing the state revenues, but unfortunately we know more about how he spent money than how he raised it[109]—or indeed about what the official powers of his office may have been.[110]

What does seem clear is that the Athenians, in the critical period before the battle of Chaironeia, created a special, super-office with extraordinary powers and tenure for a man in whose ability and integrity they had an unusual confidence. Lykourgos probably took office as Administrator of the Revenue (ὁ ἐπὶ τὴν διοίκησιν) at the time of the Great Panathenaia, just weeks before the battle,[111] and at the same time the regular office of Treasurer of the Military

[109] A. M. Andreades, *History of Greek Public Finance*, I (Cambridge, Mass., 1933) 376-378.
[110] Cf. B. D. Meritt, *Hesperia*, 29 (1960) 2-4, no. 3. S. Markianos (*GRBS*, 10 [1969] 325-331) has solved the vexing problem of Lykourgos' periods in office during his twelve years of financial administration.
[111] See preceding note and note 34 above.

Fund (ταμίας τῶν στρατιωτικῶν) was assumed by Lykourgos' brother-in-law, Kallias of Batê;[112] it is probable, but less certain, that Demosthenes was elected as one of the ten Directors of the Festival Fund (οἱ ἐπὶ τῶν θεωρικῶν).[113] It seems that the whole financial administration had thus passed into the hands of men who favored the militant policy then being pursued.

This policy was completely reversed by the battle, but the same men remained in office for the rest of the quadrennium. And Lykourgos, although his office was not renewable, nevertheless managed to have friends elected to succeed him, so that he actually administered the city's finances for a period of twelve years, 338-326. From an inscription honoring Xenokles of Sphettos,[114] one of Lykourgos' friends who succeeded him in office, we learn that the office itself was probably concerned chiefly with the *merismos* (the allocation of funds to those agencies authorized by law to spend it) and probably concerned also with the disposal of the Surplus (τὰ περιόντα) either for distributions or for projects. It seems likely that the Administrator's authority placed him above the Military Treasurer and the Festival Board, but it was helpful to have in these positions men who would be sympathetic and cooperative. What other prerogatives the Administrator may have enjoyed we cannot say, for Aristotle does not even mention the office, but it is safe to assume that he had *eisodos* in the Council (with the right to make proposals) and that he sat *ex officio* on the several boards, both regular and special, which disbursed state funds.

Although the title was new, the idea of concentrating the administration of all public resources into the hands of a single individual was not. In the decade or so prior to and just after the Peace of Philokrates (346), the Athenians had allowed Euboulos of Probalinthos, a man who like Lykourgos enjoyed a special reputation for honesty and ability, to control the public finances by channeling the Surplus through the Festival Board, *not*, as some have thought, to squander them on distributions, but to reserve them for many useful projects of defense and improvement.[115] The

---

[112] [Plut.] *Mor.* 842F.

[113] Cf. Buchanan, *op.cit.* (note 55 above) 72, note 1.

[114] Meritt, *loc.cit.* (note 110 above).

[115] Aeschin. III. 25; cf. G. L. Cawkwell, *JHS*, 83 (1963) 47-67.

only difference was that Euboulos had spent money to make Athens strong in the face of Macedonian aggression but apparently had tried to avoid using this strength in a showdown, whereas in Lykourgos those who felt that Philip must be stopped now or never found a man who was Euboulos' equal in integrity and ability and, furthermore, was willing to expend all his own energies and all the resources of the state in a decisive struggle against Macedon. But the mere fact that the state *had* resources for war, and that in the panic which followed the news of the defeat the Athenians judged their city able to withstand a siege, shows that Lykourgos' predecessor had been active in repairing walls, building ships, and even in securing the water supply which, despite Demosthenes' sneers, was surely a *sine qua non* for a beleaguered city.[116]

It is ironic that Lykourgos, the advocate of military action (as distinct from mere preparedness), should so soon have been forced by the course of events to adopt the more passive policy of his predecessor, and that by pursuing it successfully he should have achieved his lasting fame, while Euboulos should have been held responsible for the defeat at Chaironeia because of his ill-advised strategy of meeting the Macedonian menace only in Greece and because he allegedly squandered resources and corrupted the citizens with festival distributions. But there were no such abuses in the festival distributions, and Philip's victory must be credited to his own military genius and to the strength of his new style army, rather than blamed on the pacifists. Furthermore, the soundness of Euboulos' projects (specifically those which had been suspended with the outbreak of the war) receives the highest vindication from the fact that Lykourgos included them in his more extensive program, i.e. when he resumed the repair and modernization of the city's defenses, the storing up of weapons, the construction of

---

[116] Demosth. III. 29 with scholia (Dindorf, VIII. 133); cf. [Demosth.] XIII. 30. Likewise D.'s snide reference to τὰς ἐπάλξεις ἃς ἐκονιῶμεν tries to belittle very worthwhile work on the walls; whether the walls were heightened with mudbrick battlements or sheathed in the same material against heavy artillery, the new additions certainly needed to be stuccoed as protection against the weather. It is unnecessary to suggest an earlier date for *IG* II² 244 to prove that Euboulos' administration had a care for the city's defenses; Cawkwell, *op.cit.* (preceding note) 66, note 109.

triremes, and the work on the naval arsenal and shipsheds in Peiraieus and the Telesterion in Eleusis.

If Lykourgos achieved a more noteworthy success in increasing the state revenues, it is to be explained by the fact that he was operating in a period of enforced and uninterrupted peace, while the smaller financial recovery under Euboulos' administration was achieved in a period when peace, even after 346, was only relative and hard to maintain. At any rate it must be remembered that peace, with all its promotion of agriculture, industry and commerce, was the essential ingredient of financial recovery, no matter who was administering the fiscus, and that the task of keeping the peace was as much of a concern for Lykourgos in the years after Chaironeia as it ever had been for Euboulos in the years before.

Peace, then, was the basic element of Athens' recovery, which, as we saw yesterday, also received a significant boost from the "stimulus of hard knocks," nor should we omit to mention the benefits which still accrued to Athens from the excellent harbor, docking facilities and market buildings which had been built in the preceding century with the tribute of empire and from the trading and banking habits which had been established in those happier days and still continued to swell the income of Athens' now tributeless fiscus.[117] But a great share of the credit goes to Lykourgos himself for his skillful economic and political exploitation of the peace through exercising the powers of his administrative position and of his own personal prestige. For the growth of the annual revenue to an average of 1200 T. over the twelve year period did not just happen;[118] and the differences between Lykourgos' administration and that of Euboulos were not just quantitative, but qualitative.

The first goal in the program of financial recovery was to conserve what revenue there was and to see that it did not evaporate through inefficiency and useless distributions. The Festival Board did not after Chaironeia recover the important functions it had performed in the days of Euboulos; Lykourgos preferred to continue to channel the Surpluses through the Military Fund for the sake of greater efficiency and also perhaps to signal an official shift

[117] Cf. A. French, *The Growth of the Athenian Economy* (London, 1964) 175.
[118] Andreades, *op.cit.* (note 109 above) 377 and note 4.

away from free distributions to a program of public works which would increase employment[119]—this last would have been in clear imitation of Perikles who, according to Plutarch, wished to give the people a share of the public income but not for sitting still and doing nothing.[120] At any rate the Festival Board was officially divested of its broad powers by the Law of Hegemon (probably in 336/5), which may have gone further and regularized all the Lykourgan changes in the financial administration which till then had been on a *de facto* basis. The efficient, centralized administration, planning on a quadrennial basis, eliminated the losses due to the inexperience of annually changing boards, and Lykourgos' indictments against wrongdoers, written "with a pen dipped not in ink but in death," put an end to graft.

The second goal would have been to stimulate the growth of the peace-time economy. Lykourgos got the ball rolling by borrowing in his own name, but on behalf of the state, the sum of 250 T. We should note the startling implication that the stock of Lykourgos & Co. was higher than that of Athens herself.[121] Chance has preserved only a fraction of what measures he took personally to generate tax revenue by encouraging economic activity, but we do know that Lykourgos was responsible for sending out a naval patrol to protect commerce from pirates and that, when the patrol had achieved its mission, he came forward to move a decree in honor of the general, Diotimos.[122] To insure a steady grain supply it was necessary to have a care for the happiness and well-being of foreign corn dealers, and so we find Lykourgos moving decrees to grant *enktesis* to Egyptian and Kyprian merchants so that they might build temples to and worship their native gods in Athens.[123]

[119] Cf. Mitchel, *op.cit.* (note 42 above) 224-225, esp. note 37.

[120] Cf. Plut. *Per.* XII. 5-7.

[121] Andreades, *loc.cit.* (note 118 above) and note 1.

[122] *IG* II² 1623, lines 276-308, is a decree of 335/4 to send out the general Diotimos with two fast new ships. It is known from [Plut.] *Mor.* 844A that Lykourgos passed a decree in the following year to honor Diotimos. The decree survives as *IG* II² 414a, as restored by E. Schweigert, *Hesperia*, 9 (1940) 340-341. The later colony to the Adriatic was also to guard against pirates. The decree, moved by Kephisophon son of Lysiphon of Cholargos, is typically Lykourgan; cf. Tod II. no. 200.

[123] Cf. Tod II. no. 189 and J. Pečírka, *The Formula for the Grant of Enktesis in Attic Inscriptions* (Praha, 1966) 59-61. There were many foreigners in Athens at this time not only for trade, but for refuge from Macedonian oppression; cf. Diller, *op.cit.* (note 92 above) 112. It may have been at this time that a law

Note how closely the economic motives of the mover are related to his abiding interest in religion. The founding of a colony on the Adriatic some ten years later is in line with the other commercial goals; the decree authorizing the expedition is typically Lykourgan in tone and was moved by one of Lykourgos' chief supporters, Kephisophon of Cholargos; the name of the Founder, Miltiades of Lakiadai, is significant in that it allows us to suggest that Athens was trying to replace the lost territories in the Thracian Chersonnesos which had been colonized in the sixth century by a like-named *oikistes*.[124] Not surviving are the *poletai* lists which might have shown the dip and recovery in mining activity which is attested by the "new cuttings" and "restored confidence" to which Hypereides refers in his defence of Euxenippos.[125]

The imposition of "tribute" on the mining magnates, which Hypereides mentions in the very next paragraph, may have been nothing more than a temporary change in the law which would require mining lessees to include their mineholdings in their assessment ($\tau\acute{\iota}\mu\eta\mu\alpha$) for the surtax ($\epsilon\grave{\iota}\sigma\phi o\rho\acute{a}$).[126] Could it be that Lykourgos was struggling with that seemingly ageless problem— how to increase the tax-take without stifling the growth of economic activity? He could (and did) continue the special ten talents *eisphora* levied on resident aliens and paid annually between 347/6 and 323/2 to help with the construction of the naval arsenal and shipsheds,[127] but he could not increase and extend such taxes indefinitely without running into trouble.

Recourse was had to a cleverer method which went beyond pure economic policy and involved other areas in the overall program,

was passed setting forth general regulations for granting *enktesis* to foreigners; cf. W. K. Pritchett, *Hesperia*, 15 (1946) 159-160, no. 16. Pečírka, *op.cit.*, 140-142, warns that we cannot be certain of the date at which the clause κατὰ τὸν νόμον began to be used in grants of *enktesis* but states that it was common in the majority of such decrees in the last third of the fourth century.

[124] See note 122 above.

[125] Hypereides (*Eux.* 36) indicates that there was considerable activity ca. 330, but the *poletai* lists that chance has preserved suggest rather that there was a drop in mine leases under Lykourgos after a sharp increase under Euboulos; M. Crosby, *Hesperia*, 19 (1950) 189-312, esp. 190, note 3; cf. R. J. Hopper, *BSA*, 48 (1953) 200-254.

[126] Cf. R. Thomsen, *Eisphora* (Copenhagen, 1964) 243-245: the mines were state property and untaxable, but the lessee's mills and workshops were private property and, although they were usually exempt, *could* have been taxed.

[127] *IG* II² 505, lines 1-30.

such as the revitalization of civic pride, patriotism and religious feeling. The method was to persuade a wealthy man to assume responsibility for a specific project. He would act as supervisor and 'angel' for the project, and, when the funds provided by the state proved insufficient to finish up the job in a fashion commensurate with the new standards of excellence, he would make up the difference from his own pocket and, of course, receive public recognition for his generosity (*epidosis* as distinct from *leitourgia*).

This plan can be seen in operation in the great rebuilding of the walls which got under way on the motion of Demosthenes at the end of 338/7[128] and continued at least into the next year.[129] The fortifications were divided into ten sections and each section made the responsibility of a single tribe. The tribe in turn elected its own supervisor who received ten talents from the state and became responsible for the finances of the project. Demosthenes provided 100 *mnai* on his own,[130] and we may safely assume that he was not the only member of Pandionis who contributed either money or services and that Pandionis was not the only tribe to conduct its business in this way. By exploiting the recent fear, playing upon patriotic feelings and introducing the spirit of competition, Lykourgos (who appropriated the money) and Demosthenes (who introduced the bill and set the patriotic example) were able to finish considerably more wall than would have been possible under a typical public works project.

Other public projects which were carried out partially at private expense include the Panathenaic stadium and the temple of Apollo Patroos in the Agora. In the first case Lykourgos persuaded a certain Deinias to donate the property, a steep and useless ravine south of the Ilissos river and west of the Ardettos hill,[131] and got the job done in time for the celebration of the Panathenaia of 330 through the generosity of Eudemos of Plataia, who provided a thousand yoke of draft animals for the work of leveling the ravine and bringing in the stone for the retaining wall (*krepis*) around the race

128 Aeschin. III. 27-31.

129 *IG* II² 244 concerns the walls of Mounichia and Etioneia. The date 337/6 is based historically on the known activity at this time and epigraphically on the "litterae aetatis Lycurgeae propriae." The date is accepted by F. G. Maier, *Griechische Mauerbauinschriften*, I (Heidelberg, 1959) 40, but needlessly questioned by Cawkwell (see note 116 above).

130 Aeschin. III. 17.   131 [Plut.] *Mor.* 841D.

course and possibly for the semicircular southern end, or '*theatron*.'[132] And in the second case when word came from the Delphic god that the altar, which was to stand in front of Lykourgos' new temple of Apollo Patroos, then abuilding in the Agora, had to be covered with gold, Neoptolemos of Melitê promised to do it.[133] We now know that this wealthy and public-spirited individual, in addition to his other well-known public services, was mainly responsible for the reconstruction, in his home deme, of the temple of Artemis Aristoboulê ("with the best advice"), which had been built by Themistokles after the battle of Salamis to commemorate his victory.[134] The renewal of this little shrine in the third quarter of the fourth century fitted in with Lykourgos' aims—it was a reverent and pious act and it called to mind an event which was a matter of great national pride. The private contributions of men like Eudemos and Neoptolemos were obviously an important factor in the success of Lykourgos' financial administration, but, and this is no less important, they were also expressions of faith in Lykourgos' integrity and program, and we may assume that he had more than money on his mind when he came forward himself to move the decrees in their honor. The list of private contributors could be greatly expanded if time permitted.

A series of laws regulating religious expenditures, the primary purpose of which was presumably to insure that sacrifices and cult practices could be carried out according to ancestral custom, made for more efficient, long-ranged budgeting of the central fiscus. By earmarking specific revenues for specific festivals, it was also guaranteed that the funds, which had previously been frittered away through lack of regulation, would be carefully administered and used for public functions. Lykourgos' own law which dealt with regulations for the festivals, the fund from the sale of the victims' hides, and the making of suitable cult vessels for the processions is well known,[135] but the law concerning the Lesser Pana-

---

[132] Tod II. no. 198. Further economies were effected by transferring surplus beams from Philon's arsenal to the board in charge of the stadium; *IG* II^2 1627, lines 382-384.

[133] [Plut.] *Mor.* 843F. For the temple see H. A. Thompson, *Hesperia*, 6 (1937) 77-115; for an illustration and discussion of the altar, see esp. 110-111; for the date of the temple, 102-104.

[134] J. Threpsiades-E. Vanderpool, *Arch.Delt.*, 19 (1964) 26-36.

[135] *IG* II^2 333.

thenaia deserves mention at this point because of the important new fragment which tells how the festival was to be financed.[136] Athens had recently acquired the territory and harbor of Oropos, including the shrine of Amphiaraos, and the lands had been parcelled out among the ten tribes. But a certain area called *Nea* (New Land) was reserved for leasing, and the income (amounting to 47 *mnai*) was specifically set aside for the Lesser Panathenaia.[137] The mover of the law, Aristonikos of Marathon, was a supporter of the Lykourgan program both now[138] and later when he was executed along with the other antimacedonians after the Lamian war. His father Aristoteles had moved the so-called "Charter" of the Second Athenian League in 378/7.[139]

One last financial reform is worthy of mention in this brief survey. Athens was one of the latest mints on the mainland to strike a regular bronze coinage, and it was Lykourgos who at this time led the city to adopt a mature monetary system (and thus to conserve silver) by issuing a fiduciary coinage. Contemporary with the first series of Athenian bronze is a series with Eleusinian types and legend which reflects Lykourgos' personal interest in the mysteries, and were struck to focus attention on Athens' one great Panhellenic festival and particularly on the celebration of 335, the first during Lykourgos' administration.[140] Perhaps used as a "festival coinage" these little bronze tokens helped bring home again some of the silver Athens was spending abroad.

We must pass over, without even cataloging, the many military constructions and expenditures by which the Athenians tried to prepare their city to defend her independence. Military preparations—arsenals, shipsheds and ships; walls, forewalls and moats; forts, stockpiles of missiles and the 'war chest'—were terribly important and must have consumed the lion's share of the budget,

---

[136] D. M. Lewis, *Hesperia*, 28 (1959) 239-247. This fragment is the upper part of *IG* II² 334 = *SIG*³ 271. *Hesperia*, 7 (1938) 295, no. 20 is also concerned with the management of a major festival; the mention of a musical contest makes the Greater Panathenaia a possibility.

[137] Cf. L. Robert, *Hellenica*, 11 (1960) 189-203.

[138] E.g. he supported Lykourgos' decree to send out ships against the pirates (note 122 above), probably by adding a rider specifying that the ships be "fast, new and shipshape."

[139] All references in Lewis, *op.cit.* (note 136 above) 241, commentary on lines 3-4.

[140] J. P. Shear, *Hesperia*, 2 (1933) 246.

even as in a modern state, but it was far more important to prepare the minds, hearts and bodies of the men who would have to put all these things to use. The conduct of the Athenian troops at Chaironeia must have suggested that the typical hoplite was in need of 'repair' as much as any wall.

Toward this end, and at the level where the effort would be most effective, an annual outlay of some 40 talents[141] was budgeted for the ephebic corps to pay the expense of the ephebes, their leaders, trainers and equipment. The spate of ephebic honorary decrees and monuments belonging to the Lykourgan period[142] (in contrast to the one decree definitely known to have been passed in all the years prior to Chaironeia)[143] surely indicates a new approach to the existing practices, whatever they may have been, concerned with the training of the eighteen- and nineteen-year-old youths for military service and citizenship. In order that they might learn to stand firm in the battle line and be obedient to their officers, they were not only taught the skills of handling weapons and drilled in hoplite warfare, but were also subjected to a program of intensive indoctrination in patriotism. They were introduced to the religious bases of their civic life and took an active part in the religious festivals, many of which served to remind them of Athens' glorious past. The taking of the ancestral oath[144] was made over into an impressive ceremony. The ephebic tribes were modelled on the actual tribes, with elected cadet officers called taxiarchs and *lochagoi*, not just in imitation of the regular army organization but as a preparation for that part of civil life and responsibility which centered in the tribe. It is possible that those who had held cadet offices constituted a kind of reserve from which to draw experienced candidates for the annually elected or appointed tribal offi-

[141] The amount, suggested by W. S. Ferguson, *Hellenistic Athens* (London, 1911) 10, is a likely approximation derived by multiplying the estimated annual enrolment of cadets and officials by the per capita allotments mentioned by Aristotle, *Ath. Pol.*, 42. 3.

[142] To the list of nine given by F. Mitchel, *TAPA*, 92 (1961) 347-357, esp. 348-349, add two more published by Ch. Habicht, *AM*, 76 (1961) 143-148, nos. 2 and 3. Also *IG* II² 2970 has been dated to 334/3 by F. Mitchel, *Hesperia*, 33 (1964) 349-351.

[143] In 361/0; cf. M. Mitsos, *Arch.Eph.*, 1965, 131-136.

[144] Tod II. no. 204. For corrigenda and more recent discussion see G. Daux, "Deux stèles d'Acharnes," in *Charisterion eis A. K. Orlandon*, I (Athens, 1964) 78-84.

cers; and they met together and voted 'tribal' decrees to honor their officers and others who had been helpful.[145]

Although the *epheboi* seem to have spent most of their first year down in Peiraieus and most of the second in the frontier forts, it is tempting to associate the contemporary refurbishing of the Theseion in the SW portion of the Agora with some intent to provide an appropriate ephebic center near the administrative heart of the city. This suggestion is based not only on Theseus' reputation as the founder of democracy and as *the* Athenian youth *par excellence* but also on the close association of the Theseion with the building complex now identified as the Library and Gymnasium of Ptolemy—a known center of ephebic training in later centuries.[146] But perhaps we should wait for the archaeological dust to settle before we conjecture too much.

We are on somewhat firmer ground when we connect Lykourgos' building of the wrestling school and of the gymnasium in the Lykeion with the need to provide better places to drill and train.[147] The Lykeion had been the traditional muster point and athletic field for at least two centuries and possibly already had a gymnasium of sorts, but the Lykourgan buildings, with their landscaping and trees, must have transformed the old drill field and *dromos* into a beautiful park,[148] and it is no wonder that Aristotle (who returned to Athens in 335) chose, probably with Lykourgos' encouragement,[149] to open his school there. Certainly Lykourgos himself took special pride in these buildings, for it was in front of the *palaistra* that he set up a stele recording all his official acts to

[145] Cf. *TAPA*, 92 (1961) 347-357.

[146] Cf. H. A. Thompson, *AJA*, 69 (1965) 177; *Hesperia*, 35 (1966) 40-48. The building has also been identified as the Heliaia; cf. R. E. Wycherly, *Athenian Agora*, III (1957) 145-146. See also note 164 below.

[147] [Plut.] *Mor.* 841D.

[148] J. Travlos, Πολεοδομικὴ Ἐξέλιξις τῶν Ἀθηνῶν (Athens, 1960) 90-92 and Plate III. Cf. also E. Vanderpool, *Arch.Eph.* (1953-54) 126-128.

[149] The facilities of the Lykeion are the only real link between Aristotle and Lykourgos. The latter was primarily interested in education and was not enough of a philosopher himself to have been caught up in the rivalries between Plato and Isokrates (he studied with both, *Mor.* 841B) or between Xenokrates and Aristotle; although he was a friend and supporter of the former (*Mor.* 842B-C), it was the Peripatetic Demokles who defended his sons when they were accused after his death (*Mor.* 842E).

be an example to the young men (probably ephebes) who trained there.[150]

The foundation of an 'ephebic college' with its buildings and with its curriculum designed to instruct young men in the ideals, loyalties and duties appropriate to a citizen of a free state was to last—not without changes to be sure—to the very end of pagan antiquity, and ephebic dedications are to be found among the latest surviving Athenian documents.

The efforts to renew political faith in the *polis* and to revive patriotism and civic pride did not stop, unfortunately, with the training of the ephebes. Lykourgos took punitive action against their elders who were guilty, at least in *his* eyes, of unpatriotic conduct: he condemned Lysikles, one of the generals at Chaironeia, for his part in the disaster, and Autolykos the Areiopagite for having so despaired of the city's ability to withstand siege that he had sent his family away into safety;[151] his speech against Leokrates, a citizen who had fled the city after Chaironeia and had returned after eight years, is a sermon on patriotism and preserves, no doubt, the sincere convictions of the speaker, but it is a bit frightening to learn that he failed only by a tie vote to secure conviction. On the brighter side of the ledger we find that Lykourgos himself and his supporters were generous in proposing honors to those whose actions showed them to have been public benefactors. They began appropriately with those who had given their lives at Chaironeia and whose ashes were buried in the Kerameikos beneath an imposing monument of fifth-century type hard by the tomb of the heroes of the fifth-century disaster at Koroneia[152]—in a ceremony for which Demosthenes spoke the *epitaphios*.[153] Thereafter the Athenians proudly offered sanctuary and special privileges, even as they had done earlier in their struggle against Sparta, to those allies and friends who had become victims of a promacedonian

[150] [Plut.] *Mor.* 843F.

[151] *Ibid.* 843D; Lycurg. *Leoc.* 53; Diod. 16. 88.

[152] D. W. Bradeen, *Hesperia*, 33 (1964) 55-58, no. 16. For the epigram see Tod II. no. 176.

[153] Demosth. XVIII. 285-289. The preserved *Epitaphios* (Demosth. LX) has been despised since antiquity, but its authenticity has been defended in modern times; cf. A. Lesky, *History of Greek Literature* (London, 1966) 605, with note 1.

reaction in their native states.[154] They commonly voted honors not only to donors of large sums, but to public officers and priests who had carried out their jobs honestly and well.[155] Such public-spirited recognition of patriotic actions was as beneficial to the bestowers as to the receivers—and perhaps more so.

One of the major problems faced by a conservative democratic leadership which hoped to revive public spirit and patriotism was to encourage broad participation in the government while avoiding the excesses of radical democracy. The People had to have some stake in the polity (other than the distributions and pay for attendance at courts and assemblies) if they were to become willing to support it and to make sacrifices for it. Aristotle's account of the Athenian polity during the Lykourgan period describes just such a broad-based democracy;[156] and the many contrasts he draws between former and contemporary practices shows that he knew of many changes which had taken place since the restoration of democracy in 403, some of which were surely Lykourgan. Without entering into the discussion of why Aristotle failed to identify the reforms he mentions and failed even to mention still others,[157] attention may be called to certain minor changes in governmental procedures, the purpose of which seems to have been to broaden participation—and hence to increase interest and to share honor and responsibility—in the operations of the government. For instance, the Co-chairmen of the Assembly came to be listed in decrees along with the Chairman who actually put the motion to the vote;[158] and it is likely that the role of the Arbitrators in deciding minor disputes received some stimulus at this time.[159] The shift from expensive bronze dicasts' tickets (*pinakia*) to cheap ones of boxwood,

---

[154] Cf. Tod II. no. 178; Diller, *op.cit.* (note 92 above) 112.

[155] E.g. the secretary *kata prytaneian, Hesperia,* 7 (1938) 293, no. 19; the priest of Asklepios, *Hesperia,* 28 (1959) 169-174, no. 1. Both are from the first year of peace, 337/6.

[156] *Ath. Pol.* 42-69.

[157] But see J. Day, M. Chambers, *Aristotle's History of the Athenian Democracy* (Berkeley, 1962) 188-189.

[158] S. Dow, *Hesperia,* 32 (1963) 335-365. IG II² 547, dated to 324/3 by W. K. Pritchett and B. D. Meritt, *Chronology of Hellenistic Athens* (Cambridge, Mass., 1940) 2-4, mentions *symproedroi* within the decree and is perhaps a regulation.

[159] All the dated *diaitetai* lists come after 330. IG II² 1927, which has been dated earlier, is known only from Chandler's copy.

which took place ca. 330,[160] was probably a move to make it easier for citizens to participate in jury service.

The most common place of Assembly during the Lykourgan period was probably the theatre of Dionysos on the south slope of the Akropolis, and Lykourgos himself is generally given the credit for extending and building the stone auditorium, much of which remains in place.[161] The front row of thrones, if they are not Lykourgan, are at least faithful copies of fourth-century originals. The stone stage building doubled as a platform for orators, and Aischines, at least, must have felt right at home. Behind and below the stage building appeared a stoa for the comfort of Assemblymen and theatre-goers alike. The theatre was also the scene of the impressive ceremony in which the ephebes, at the end of their first year of training, passed in review and received their "sacred arms." It is difficult to think of a better example of the interlocking purposes of the several facets of the overall program—encouraging the citizens to participate in political, religious and cultural activities, providing an impressive spectacle which involved the youngest year-class and furnishing gainful employment for the building trades.

But this was not the end of Lykourgos' plans to encourage the active participation of all the citizens in making public decisions. Archaeology has disclosed a grandiose scheme, begun late and never finished, to remodel and enlarge the Pnyx (in other words, to make it less of a 'Pnyx'). The auditorium itself was extended to seat more people more comfortably; two large stoas (set at an angle to one another and joined by an ornamental gateway) were started on the terrace above the auditorium and faced it; they would have provided shelter from the sun and rain, and shops to sell food and drink; thus they would have been a great convenience to those who came in from some distance to attend the meetings. These stoas were the first of such great size to be started in Athens and may have expressed a competitive response to the great South Stoa built in Korinth by Philip and Alexander for meetings

[160] S. Dow, *BCH*, 87 (1963) 653-687; cf. *Ath. Pol.* 63. 4. See now J. H. Kroll, *The Bronze Allotment Plates of Fourth-Century B.C. Athens* (Harvard diss., 1968).
[161] A. W. Pickard-Cambridge, *The Theatre of Dionysus in Athens* (Oxford, 1946) 134-174.

of their League. The whole complex was centered on a large altar (probably of Zeus Agoraios) directly above and behind the speakers' platform (*bema*), so that the meetings would be under the protection of the god.[162]

A few years ago it appeared that what Lykourgos had done or begun for the benefit of those who attended the Assembly he had also tried to do for the jurors who sat all day in the lawcourts. The building complex at the SW corner of the Agora was labelled 'Heliaia,'[163] and the cloister-like building known as the Square Peristyle (in the NE corner, and lying partially under the Stoa of Attalos) was associated with the lawcourts on the basis of the bronze ballots found amid the ruins of the Peristyle's predecessor on the same site. Both these structures had undergone enlargement and remodelling which was dated archaeologically to the second half of the fourth century and associated with the Lykourgan building program. Today[164] the 'Heliaia' has been replaced by the 'Theseion' (mentioned above) and the Square Peristyle is being identified as the Leokorion, a shrine to the legendary daughters of Leos who gave their lives to save the city in a time of peril. Their sacrifice was a popular subject in Lykourgan Athens and was referred to at least twice in contemporary speeches.[165] Their shrine was surely one of those holy places visited by the ephebes as they began their two-year tour of duty, and its refurbishing at this time is to be related less to the building program than to the program to revive civic pride and patriotism.

Closely related to the program of civic regeneration was a program of religious reforms. It is hardly surprising that one of Plato's pupils should have believed that faith in the gods was basic to good citizenship or that, finding himself in a position of influence, he should have sought to bind men to their *polis* by

---

[162] R. L. Scranton-H. A. Thompson, *Hesperia*, 12 (1943) 291-301.

[163] As late as 1962 with the publication of *The Athenian Agora*[2] (Athens, 1962) 106-108, 204-208. See above, page 38 and note 146.

[164] That is, 1968. In 1970 Professor Thompson and "*opinio communis* of the Agora Staff" have again come to favor the identification of the SW complex as the Heliaia; cf. *Hesperia*, 39 (1970) 117, note 10. It is well to remember that the name of an Athenian building was often unrelated to its use. In the present context it makes little difference whether Lykourgos was providing for the jurors or the ephebes.

[165] Phokion, as reported in Diod. XVII. 15. 2, and Demosthenes, in his *Epitaphios*, 29.

making it again the center of their spiritual lives. Lykourgos' own deep religious involvement was inseparable from his devotion to the state and can be detected in his speeches, in his financial administration, in his concern for specific cults, in his building program and in his personal participation. The material for discussion is exceedingly rich, but there is time to mention only the most important, that which is concerned with the 'ancestral' worship.

The most important cult of all, of course, was that of Athena Polias, whose priestess belonged always to the clan of the Eteoboutadai, as did the hereditary priest of Poseidon-Erechtheus, which office was held by Lykourgos himself.[166] Mention has already been made of the laws which regulated and earmarked funds for the Panathenaic festivals, so that they might be celebrated with time-honored pomp and ceremony; and of the special commission elected to be in charge of making gold and silver processional vessels and ornaments for the maidens who carried baskets in the parade. The commissioners in charge of the processional vessels also saw to the restoration of the golden *Nikai*, and another board made recommendations concerning the restoration of a statue of Athena Nike which had been dedicated to commemorate naval victories *ca.* 425.[167] Lykourgos himself was largely responsible for the construction of the Panathenaic stadium, which greatly increased the possibilities of spectator participation at the contests. It was probably at this time that the small sanctuary and altar, identified as belonging to Zeus Phratrios and Athena Phratria, was built just south of the Royal Stoa in the Agora (emphasizing with cult worship the goddess' role as guardian of the purity of the citizenry and reminding each citizen of the religious basis of his citizenship),[168] and that the newly cleared water-moat was designated Athena's own, thus placing the whole city under divine protection.[169]

---

[166] [Plut.] *Mor.* 843A-C, E-F.

[167] Cf. *IG* II² 403, which is probably Lykourgan.

[168] H. A. Thompson, *Hesperia*, 6 (1937) 104-107; photograph of altar, 106.

[169] The inscription which both identifies the *telma* and dedicates it to the goddess was found *in situ* near the Dipylon; cf. G. Gruben-K. Vierneisel, *Arch.Anz.*, 79 (1964) 414. The lettering is, in my opinion, fourth century. The *telma* extended at least to the Diochares Gate where another stretch of it came to light during construction work in Syntagma Square; cf. J. Travlos, *Arch.Anz.*, 55 (1940) 165; *idem, op.cit.* (note 148 above) 75-78; J. Threpsiades, *Arch.Delt.*, 14 (1960) 25-27.

In a cave on the northwest slope of the Akropolis Pythian Apollo had sired Ion, the eponymous father of all Ionians, and hence the Pythian god was called Apollon Patroos by all Athenians.[170] His worship was re-emphasized by Lykourgos not only because he was counted an ancestor, but because his help was needed in deciding fine points in the religious reforms.[171] His new temple, cult image and gilded altar in the Agora have already been mentioned, and Lykourgos' special interest in the cult is attested by his going as one of the *hieropoioi* who led the Pythiastic procession to Delphi sometime after 330.[172] It has been convincingly argued that the famous Akanthos Column in the Delphi Museum is an Athenian dedication of about the same time and that the three dancing maidens are daughters of Kekrops and Aglauros.[173] Their roles in Athenian mythology and ritual are peculiarly appropriate both to Lykourgos' family interest in the cult of Erechtheus and to the Kreousa-Ion story. The emphasis on 'paternal' Apollo, Poseidon-Erechtheus and other cult places associated with the old aristocracy on the north side of the Akropolis may have been something of a counterweight to that great building on the south side which was a monument to the ideals of Periklean democracy.[174]

Another religious innovation of the time was the establishment of the cult of Demokratia. Perhaps since 403 the Athenians had annually celebrated the liberation of Athens and the restoration of democracy with sacrifices on the 12th of Boedromion,[175] but in 333/2 the Council of Five Hundred, on leaving office, dedicated what must have been a cult image of Demokratia in the Agora[176]— and in the following two years the goddess received sacrificial offerings.[177] The deification of Demokratia was literally an expression of faith in a political ideal and at the same time a graphic illus-

---

[170] Cf. Demosth. XVIII. 141.

[171] He was certainly consulted before Lykourgos drew up his law on religious reforms; cf. *IG* II² 333, lines 24-25; P. Foucart, *BCH*, 7 (1883) 391-392. We have already noticed the Athenian interest in the oracular shrines of Zeus at Dodona and of Amphiaraos at Oropos. For the interest in Ammon see C. J. Classen, *Historia*, 8 (1959) 349-355; A. M. Woodward, *BSA*, 57 (1962) 5-13.

[172] *SIG*³, no. 296. For the dating problem see note 59 above.

[173] J. Bousquet, *BCH*, 88 (1964) 655-675.

[174] *Ibid.*, 662.

[175] Cf. L. Deubner, *Attische Feste* (Berlin, 1932) 39.

[176] See note 29 above for both the inscription and a discussion of the cult.

[177] *IG* II² 1496, lines 131-132, 140-141.

tration of the way in which Lykourgos thought that religious belief should be basic to life in the *polis*. Although the cult was new, Demokratia herself was 'ancestral'—since she had been introduced to Athens by Theseus.

Lykourgos' policies toward the sanctuaries at Eleusis and Oropos had a more practical bent, which is not to say they were less sincere. The former was the center of one of the oldest and most revered cults in all Greece, and the one Athenian festival which attracted throngs of people from beyond the borders. The sanctuary was spruced up, the walls were repaired[178] and work was pushed forward on Philon's portico on the west side of the Telesterion.[179] These projects made the sanctuary more beautiful for the goddesses as well as for the visitors, and the latter were doubtless pleased by the addition of a horse race to the customary contests of the festival.[180] The ancestral custom of collecting 'first fruits' for the goddesses was revived in time for the collection to take place for 329/8[181] and a tower was repaired to receive the offerings.[182] This revival may have been partially a return to ancestral custom for its own sake, but it was also a religious reaction to the growing grain shortage (the 'first fruits' were to insure good crops) and the income from the sale paid the expenses of the sanctuary during a very active year.

In the same year the Ploutonion, a small temple built in a cave to the right of the Sacred Way when one has entered the sanctuary, was given its finishing touches[183] and marks a revival of the god's role not only in the enactment of the mysteries[184] but as a giver of agricultural wealth.[185] At the Eleusinion in Athens Plouton was feasted as he reclined on a couch, by a committee of wealthy citizens chosen by the hierophant—and this was done specifically in response to an oracle.[186] Both the sacred feast and the renewal of the temple are probably to be connected with an oracular response to a question about the famine.

---

[178] *IG* II² 1672, lines 23-28. [179] *IG* II² 1675.

[180] *IG* II² 1672, lines 258-261. [181] *Ibid.*, lines 263-288.

[182] *Ibid.*, line 291. [183] *Ibid.*, lines 168-187.

[184] G. Mylonas, *Eleusis and the Eleusinian Mysteries* (Princeton, 1961) 146-149.

[185] He received 'first fruits' along with the goddesses. *IG* II² 1672, line 182.

[186] *IG* II² 1933.

The cult of Amphiaraos at Oropos posed a problem not of restoration (for he was not a native Athenian deity) but of assimilation. Hypereides' defence of Euxenippos preserves an amusing picture of the complicated mess which resulted from Athenian efforts to integrate the land of Oropos by distributing parts of it among the tribes.[187] Here it must suffice to point out that the god's reputation as an oracle was the basic cause of the trouble, for Lykourgos could not afford to affront Amphiaraos by enquiring at Delphi about the ownership of the disputed territory;[188] but recourse to divination by dream in Amphiaraos' own sanctuary only laid Euxenippos open to charges of impiety and bribery.

But in the affairs of the sanctuary itself the Athenians fared better. In 333/2 they crowned Pytheas of Alopeke for repairing the sacred spring and for furnishing it with a proper inlet and underground drains.[189] In the following year they crowned the god for the care he had shown for the health and safety of the Athenians and others who had come to his shrine, and on the same day they honored the noted antiquarian, Phanodemos of Thymaitidai, who had served that year as *nomothetes* for matters pertaining to the sanctuary.[190] He had succeeded in legislating a quadrennial festival to be supervised by elected *epimeletai* who were to lead a sacred procession to Oropos and conduct a festival which included horse racing, stunt-riding and the usual athletic contests. Phanodemos himself served with Lykourgos and others on the board when four years later (329/8) this festival was actually celebrated.[191] He had also legislated the sacrifices to be offered to Amphiaraos and to the other gods in the sanctuary,[192] and further had found funds, just as Lykourgos had done in other cases, to carry out the sacrifices and "for the construction of the sanctuary."

Unfortunately none of the extensive remains can be definitely labelled Lykourgan, in spite of the epigraphical evidence of building activity, and it must suffice to mention, as a measure of Athenian interest in the site, that at least one ephebic tribe spent enough

---

[187] Hyp. *Eux.* 16.

[188] Cf. Hypereides' suggestion after the fact, *Eux.* 15.

[189] *SIG³*, no. 281.   [190] *SIG³*, no. 287 = *IG* VII 4253.

[191] *SIG³*, no. 298.

[192] Cf. Paus. I. 34. 2-5 for a description of the cult practices and a list of the 'other gods.'

time there to set up their class dedication in the sanctuary,[193] and that, sometime between 338 and *ca.* 330, Meidias and Thrasylochos of Anagyrous (Demosthenes' enemies) dedicated statues there (the latter's made by Leochares).[194] The use of the demotic rather than the ethnic on these dedications shows that the Athenians considered themselves masters of Oropos, and the subsequent erasure after 322 is eloquent testimony of the Oropian reaction to this latter-day Athenian imperialism.[195] The Athenian occupation lasted fifteen years, but it was undoubtedly the most brilliant period in the history of the sanctuary thanks to Lykourgos' leadership.

Finally one comes to the most famous festival of all—that of Dionysos—and to what is, for us at any rate, Lykourgos' most important revival. More important than the rebuilding of the theatre itself (mentioned above) was Lykourgos' decision to preserve Athens' rich dramatic heritage by having definitive copies made of the works of the three great tragedians and by requiring the actors to use these canonical texts.[196] The Athenians were further reminded of their heritage by the bronze statues of Aischylos, Sophokles and Euripides which Lykourgos had set up in the theatre.[197] He also put new life into the performances of comedy with a law which increased the number of actors eligible for the leading roles, while the institution of a choral competition at the feast of Poseidon in Peiraieus must have stimulated an improvement in choral performances generally.[198] The success of the policy of official encouragement may be measured by the number and magnificence of the choregic monuments which were set up at this time and immediately afterwards, beginning with the monument of Lysikrates (335/4) on the Street of the Tripods[199] and ending with those of Nikias and Thrasyllos (320/19) in the sanctuary of Dionysos.[200]

---

[193] B. Leonardos, *Arch.Eph.*, 1918, 73-100.

[194] M. Mitsos, *Arch.Eph.*, 1952, 181, no. 13; 188, no. 15.

[195] *Ibid.*, 183.

[196] [Plut.] *Mor.* 841F.

[197] *Idem.* The famous Lateran Sophokles is considered a copy of the Lykourgan original. The statues of Aischylos and Euripides are discussed by G.M.A. Richter, *Greek Portraits*, IV (1962) 24-29. Lysippos' statue of Sokrates which stood in the Pompeion (Diog. Laert., II. 43) was probably commissioned during the Lykourgan period.

[198] [Plut.] *Mor.* 842A.   [199] *IG* II² 3042.

[200] *IG* II² 3055 and 3056 respectively.

Next to his financial administration Lykourgos was most famous in antiquity for his building program, and in modern times he has been considered the only Athenian "worthy, from the point of view of the adornment of the city with stately buildings, to be compared with . . . Pericles."[201] And yet, as we have seen, the program did not exist merely for its own sake—each project was undertaken for a specific purpose and was connected in some way with the defence of the city, its frontiers and harbor; the establishment of new cults and festivals or the revival of the old; the encouragement of attendance at public meetings and ceremonies; the training of the youth or some such thing.

The continual activity did, however, produce some general results. It created a need for all sorts of materials and services, and hence many jobs for the poorer classes—artisans and unskilled laborers, and it must have rectified the conditions to which Xenophon refers when he urges the restoration of temples, the repair of the walls and docks,[202] and the sensible use of vacant areas within the city.[203] The project on the Pnyx cleared away the slums which had encroached on that area by the mid-forties,[204] and to some extent the program removed the contrast, of which Demosthenes had earlier complained,[205] between the lavish splendor of private dwellings and the drabness of public buildings. In undertaking such an ambitious program the Athenians must have felt that they were emulating their ancestors, of whom they were envious as well as proud,[206] competing with the Macedonian building of Korinth and Olympia, and simply catching up with other cities where stone theatres and large stadia had existed for a long time. Only if we stop to consider that Athens had completed no significant building since the Erechtheion and the temple of Athena Nike, can we duly appreciate the Lykourgan building program; only by viewing the achievements of all the programs combined can we appreciate the honor with which later ages—not just the next gen-

[201] Andreades, op.cit. (note 109 above) 377.

[202] Xen. Vect., VI. 1.

[203] Ibid., II. 6. According to Xenophon 'sensible use' might have included allowing metics to acquire such property, but neither Euboulos nor Lykourgos went so far; cf. J. Pečírka, Eirene, 6 (1967) 23-26.

[204] Aeschin. I. 81-82.

[205] Demosth. III. 29; [XIII.] 28-30.

[206] Ibid., XXII. 76-78.

eration[207] but well into Roman times[208]—regarded the man who was mainly responsible.

In all this activity there is nothing to indicate that Athens was deliberately preparing to initiate a war of revenge against Macedon to recover her lost possessions. There is much, on the other hand, to suggest that under the strong and skillful guidance of Lykourgos she made the most of the unprecedented peace to recover her strength and pride and to renew those manifestations of vigorous public life which had in the past made Athens great, famous and admired. Military strength was only a part of the great tradition, and under Lykourgos military preparedness was only a part of the overall program—the other parts being pursued for their own worth. It was in part only incidental that all elements of his program contributed toward military preparedness, in that they stimulated the patriotism and devotion to the state which made men again willing to make the personal sacrifices which were necessary if Athens was to hold on to what she had and resist further interference in her internal affairs.

In 323/2 the war came on because of just such interference. As far as the Athenians were concerned their possession of Samos was an internal affair, and it had received Macedonian confirmation.[209] Alexander's 'exiles decree' was precisely the kind of thing they were prepared to resist if negotiations failed.[210] They had been angered by Alexander's demand for deification[211] and enflamed by the Harpalos affair which had shown their inability to grant sanctuary to a citizen and benefactor, and had blasted the political

---

[207] IG II² 457 and 3776.   [208] Ibid., 4259.

[209] Cf. Diod. XVIII. 56. 7; Beloch III². i. 572.

[210] Diod. XVIII. 8. 6-7; F. Mitchel, Phoenix, 18 (1964) 13-17.

[211] J.P.V.D. Balsdon (Historia, 1 [1950] 363-388 = Griffith, Problems [see note 24 above] 179-204) has shown that contemporary evidence of Alexander's own request for deification is indeed slim, but both the king's disturbed state of mind toward the end of his life (cf. E. Badian, AUMLA, 17 [1962] 80-91 = Studies in Greek and Roman History [Oxford, 1968] 192-205; A.H.M. Jones, CR, 63 [1949] 122) and his reference to Philip as his 'so-called' father (Plut. Alex. XXVIII; J. R. Hamilton, CQ, n.s. 3 [1953] 151-157 = Griffith, Problems, 235-241) lend support to the view of Ch. Habicht (Gottmenschentum und griechische Städte [München, 1956] 17-36) that Alexander merely suggested, rather than demanded, deification in connexion with honors for Hephaistion. C. Edson (CP, 53 [1958] 61-65) in his review of Habicht concludes that, even if it was only a suggestion, "the fact remains that the initiative came from the king himself."

association, now bereft of Lykourgos' steadying influence, which had been so effective in keeping the peace.[212]

But the outbreak of war was by no means precipitous; they sought to negotiate and stalled for time while they looked about for allies who like themselves had grievances, and they watched with interest the deteriorating relations between Alexander and his officers, particularly Antipater.[213] And as they inventoried the ships in Peiraieus, counted the money and arms on the Akropolis, and reviewed the year-classes which had matured since 338 and had been trained and indoctrinated more thoroughly than any classes before, it is no wonder that they felt confident of their own strength. The sudden death of Alexander only cinched the matter.

History has condemned the Hellenic war as a forlorn effort and taken Athens' humiliation as an excuse to characterize the Lykourgan reformation as an unsuccessful attempt to turn the clock back. But many an underdog has come out on top; and the Greek defeat at Krannon was not inevitable, but can be ascribed to specific errors in planning and strategy.[214] The fact that Athens had once again stood at the head of a coalition of Greek states fighting against a foreign (and in their eyes, barbarian) domination was far more important than the fact that they lost. The defeat at Krannon left no glorious tradition as had the victory at Marathon, but the subsequent characteristic readiness to strike a blow in the name of freedom (whatever the *real* motive) without carefully weighing the odds beforehand, and the tradition, even in the face of repeated devastations and penalties, of persistently supporting the weaker and therefore losing side in resistance to imperial aggrandizement are not without a certain nobility. One need only recall the third century struggles of Athens against Antigonos Gonatas and Philip V; the city's support of Rome against Macedon, of Mithridates

[212] Cf. E. Badian, *op.cit.* (note 24 above) section 4.

[213] *Idem.* Also cf. *Phoenix*, 18 (1964) 13-17, for further discussion of Alexander's relationship to Antipater.

[214] Errors in planning would include too much concentration on building obsolescent triremes and on training hoplites instead of native rowers, for as much money as Lykourgos had stored up, it was not enough to compete with the gold of looted Asia when it came to hiring rowers on the open market. It was bad strategy for Leosthenes to demand unconditional surrender at Lamia and for Antiphilos not even to attempt to prevent the defeated troops of Leonnatos from linking up with Antipater's army in retreat from Lamia after the siege.

against Rome; its luckless choice of Brutus over Octavian and Antony, of Antony over Octavian. For its resistance to the demands of the Byzantine emperor the medieval village was punished by Viking mercenaries who left their 'runish' marks upon the lion guarding the harbor;[215] and modern parallels may be found in the Greek war of independence and in the defiant Ὄχι of 1940.

As for the overall program, it cannot be discounted as ineffectual simply because of the military defeat or on the grounds that the reforms were not lasting. Although many changes were either wrought by later governments or imported from the Hellenistic east or the Roman west, although many of the buildings were left unfinished or suffered alterations or destruction in later times, still the men of the Lykourgan period left a definite stamp both on Athens and on classical antiquity. It was they who first canonized not only the texts of the tragedians (thus showing the way to the Alexandrians) but also the historical traditions of the preceding centuries—including such items as the ephebic oath, the oath of Plataia and the decrees of Miltiades and Themistokles—which modern scholars find so difficult to reconcile with earlier documents. Their version of things was different, just as their version of democracy was different—but it was *their* version of the latter (opposed alike to radical democracy, tyranny and oligarchy) which was exportable to the new cities of the Hellenistic world[216] and not without influence on the political theory of the Roman empire,[217] whence it passed into the western tradition.

Reference has already been made to the vitality of the *ephebeia*, and with it must be mentioned the philosophical schools which were started about the same time with semi-official encouragement and enjoyed an equally long run. Nor can we dismiss as a hopeless rearguard action Lykourgos' attempt to restore the democratic spirit and the worship of the ancestral gods—not if we consider

[215] The lion now guards the Customs House in Venice; cf. Holger Arbman, *The Vikings* (London 1961) Pl. 67.

[216] E.g. the revived city of Priene used Athenian legal and constitutional forms, and maintained close cultural, religious and diplomatic ties with the mother-city. Cf. F. Hiller von Gaertringen, *Inschriften von Priene* (Berlin, 1906) x, xiii-xiv.

[217] Cf. J. H. Oliver, *Demokratia, the Gods, and the Free World* (Baltimore, 1960) 164; Raubitschek, *AKTE* (note 29 above) 337.

that Athens longer than any other Greek city preserved her democratic forms, even under the late empire, and remained a bastion
of paganism (albeit with a greatly increased pantheon) in an increasingly Christian world until finally her schools and her cults
had to be destroyed by the imperial decree of Justinian.

Lykourgos was not only a builder, but a restorer and, in the
best sense, a 'classicizer.' He looked for what was good in Athens'
past—whether in literature or law, religion or architecture—and
sought to preserve and imitate it. For Athens he was the founder
of the classical tradition, and if the tradition had not begun to crys-
tallize under Lykourgos in the 330's and 320's, one may well ask
when and under whom it would have had its start? Between
Lykourgos and Hadrian there was little chance, and by Hadrian's
time, what would have been left? One concludes that the ready
modern acceptance of Thoukydides' prophecy, concerning the fame
which would accrue to Athens in later times because of her ruins,
rests in good part (excluding only the glories on the Akropolis) on
Lykourgan activity. But Lykourgos' values were not those of the
materialistic historian; thanks to his efforts more was preserved
than Thoukydides had imagined, and Athens is remembered for
other reasons and her fame rests on foundations even more solid
than those of her architectural wonders.

6

Ostracism at Athens

BY EUGENE VANDERPOOL

Delivered April 30 and May 1, 1969

OSTRACISM AT ATHENS
I. THE OSTRACA

Y OU ARE all no doubt familiar with the institution of ostracism, that law under which any Athenian suspected of wanting to set himself up as a tyrant or dictator might be sent into exile. Passed as part of the legislation of Kleisthenes in the late sixth century B.C., it remained on the books at least until the time of Aristotle in the second half of the fourth century B.C. Its practice, however, was limited to a much briefer period. The first ostracism took place in 487 B.C. and the last in about 417 B.C.; it is limited, that is, to a period of seventy years which falls within the fifth century and corresponds roughly with the period of Athens' greatness.

Ostracism was an honorable exile. The person banished had to leave the country for ten years but returned at the end of that period in full possession of his property and civic rights. The idea was rather to clip the wings of the too ambitious man than to ruin him permanently.

Designed originally as a safeguard against tyranny, it very soon turned into a weapon of party warfare. The Athenians, ever keen and quick in political matters, were not long in discovering that here was an excellent way of getting rid of a political opponent. Only the first three ostracisms, we are told, were specifically directed against "friends of the tyrants." Thereafter, as far as we can judge, the reason was rather party politics. The culmination came in 417 B.C. when Hyperbolos was ostracized under such scandalous circumstances and with such obvious manipulation by the political parties that the Athenians saw that the voting had been rigged and the law circumvented. Although it apparently remained on the books, the law from that time on was a dead letter.

The procedure in ostracism was roughly this. Each year in the sixth prytany, that is during the winter, at one of the popular assemblies the question was put "Is there need to hold an ostracism this year?" No names were mentioned. The question was simply put in general terms. If the vote was negative, the matter was dropped and could not be brought up again until the following year at the same time. If it was affirmative, however, arrangements were made for the voting to be held two months later in the eighth prytany, that is, in the early spring.

The voting took place in the Agora, the main public square of the city, and a part of the square was specially fenced off for the purpose with a wooden fence. Ten gates were left, one for each of the ten tribes, and the voters entered through the gate of the tribe to which they severally belonged. The nine archons and the boule supervised the voting. Tribal and deme officials must have been stationed at each gate to identify those who presented themselves as being members of the tribe and as citizens eligible to vote. The voters then passed through the gate, casting their ballots with the inscribed side turned down as they went in. They presumably were required to remain within the enclosure until all the votes had been cast as a precaution against double voting. When all the votes were in, they were counted by the officials, and whoever had the most, provided at least 6000 votes had been cast, had to leave Attica within ten days for a period of ten years.

But it is not about the institution of ostracism that I want to speak in these lectures; it is rather about the ostraca themselves, the ballots used in the voting. These ballots have been found by the hundreds at the Agora and more recently by the thousands at the Kerameikos just outside the city walls. They have added considerably to our knowledge of the history of ostracism and they are also of interest in themselves in a variety of ways. What I have to say will be based mainly on the finds at the Agora (about 1250 ostraca in all), but I will occasionally add a few points that have been made public about the recent great find of over 4500 pieces from the Kerameikos. I will refer also to some of the previous finds from the Kerameikos, of which there are several hundred, and to the remarkable group of 190 ostraca against Themistokles from the North Slope of the Acropolis. The total number of ostraca now known is probably around 6500. Much of what I say will not be new, but as the published reports are scattered through journals over the last thirty years or more, it may be opportune to pull them together.

The Greek word *ostrakon* has two meanings, a shell and, by

analogy, an earthenware vessel or a fragment of such a vessel, which may often resemble a shell. Scholars of earlier generations were in doubt as to which of these two meanings was intended in the case of ostraca used in voting at an ostracism, and George Grote's words in his classic *History of Greece*, written just over a hundred years ago, illustrate their uncertainty: "The process of ostracism was carried into effect by writing upon a shell or potsherd the name of the person whom a citizen thought it prudent for a time to banish; which shell, when deposited in the proper vessel counted for a vote towards the sentence." There is no longer any doubt, of course, for since Grote's time thousands of actual ostraca have been found and none is a shell; all are potsherds.

These potsherds are found in a great variety of kinds, shapes and sizes and they come from all sorts of pots. About 40% are from plain jars or pitchers. Semi-glazed kraters or lekanai form another very large category, about 23% of the whole. This very common type of pot was the standard mixing bowl of the period and must have been in use in every household, rich or poor. Pieces of broken ones will always have been ready to hand, and their firm finished surfaces with dull black glaze inside and glaze wash outside make them ideal for writing. Fragments of fine black-glazed vases of various shapes make up the third large category, about 27% of the whole. Skyphoi, kraters, amphorae and the like are found, but by far the most common of the black-glazed shapes is the kylix. Frequently the foot of the kylix is used, and these are of particular interest because, being small and compact, their profile is often preserved and this profile is sufficiently distinctive to be identifiable and datable. Some 75 Agora ostraca are from the feet of kylixes as are 122 of the 190 from the North Slope group.

The remaining 10% shows considerable variety. Eight Agora ostraca are on fragments of red-figured vases (figs. 1 and 66). There are some twenty on black-figured sherds (figs. 3 and 4), and occasionally a fragment of a geometric or proto-Attic pot is used. Others are fragments of lamps, of pithoi (fig. 7), of terracotta water pipes, of wellheads (fig. 12), and even of roof tiles (figs. 6, 58, 60). Almost any sherd would do.

In size they vary somewhat, though all are such as can be held conveniently in the hand. One is extremely large and heavy (fig.

7): it is a fragment of a pithos some 6 inches long, 4 inches wide, and 1 inch thick. It weighs 1 pound 2½ ounces, and would have been even more effective as a brickbat than as a ballot!

Let us now consider what was written on these potsherds. Basically, of course, it was a name, the name of the person the voter thought should be banished; but, as we shall see, people had rather different ideas of what constituted a name and, furthermore, they did not always confine themselves merely to the name but added epithets and accusations and curses and even caricature sketches. Now a citizen's name in fifth century Athens was made up of three parts, his own given name, his father's name, and the name of the deme or district in which he was registered (figs. 7, 8, 58). This last element, the demotic, had just recently been added as a part of the reforms of Kleisthenes. Kleisthenes had in fact wanted all citizens to be identified simply by their demotics, not by their patronymics at all, so as to eliminate the distinction between the old families and the new citizens. In practice, however, the innovation was slow in catching on. The full name is seldom used on ostraca, and the name with demotic alone is found rather infrequently (fig. 9). The name alone is also found, but not very commonly (fig. 16). More often we find simply the name and patronymic according to the old fashion (fig. 10). This is natural enough, of course, for everyone is first of all the son of his father, but it applies more particularly in the case of members of the old aristocratic families. Kimon, for example, is always "the son of Miltiades" and never "of the deme Lakiadai." Aristeides is always "the son of Lysimachos" and only once do we find an abortive attempt to write the full name.[1] Kallixenos is 240 times "the son of Aristonymos" and only 5 times "of Xypete"; twice his name appears in full. Hippokrates is 111 times "the son of Alkmeonides"

---

[1] See the ostracon illustrated in figures 41 and 42. The demotic was Alopeke-then which is also attested in the literary tradition, Plutarch, *Aristeides*, I, 1; Plato, *Laches*, 180, c, d. I do not know how to explain the demotic ek Koiles reported from the Kerameikos by F. Willemsen, *Deltion*, 23, 1968, *Chronika*, p. 28. According to the publication there are 32 Aristeides ostraca (in fact the number is now over 50, as Mr. Willemsen kindly informs me). Only one, however, has the full name, Aristeides Lysimachou ek Koiles; the rest have simply name and patronymic. As it is hard to imagine that there was another Aristeides, son of Lysimachos, from Koile, different from the well-known Aristeides, I can only suppose that the Koile demotic is a mistake on the part of the writer of the ostracon.

and 14 times "of Alopeke"; there is no instance of the full name. By contrast, the exclusive or predominant use of the demotic is rare. The one case where we have a clear-cut instance of it is likewise an exceptional case. Menon, son of Menekleides of Gargettos, is identified 68 times by his demotic (fig. 11), but only 9 times by his patronymic and 4 times by his full name.[2] But this Menon was not a native-born Athenian. He came from Pharsalos in Thessaly and had been granted Athenian citizenship in return for having aided the Athenians at Eion near Amphipolis. So it is probably more natural that he should be known as a Gargettian. His father would not be generally known, and he himself would prefer to be called a Gargettian so as to emphasize his newly acquired citizenship. In other cases where we find the demotic preferred the persons involved are unknown and the number of instances are too few to allow any conclusions, though the suggestion that people from the country demes were more likely to be identified by their demotics than the city people perhaps has something in its favor. Boutalion of Marathon has six demotics (figs. 12 and 13) and one patronymic. Acharnion of Xypete, a large deme in the city area lying somewhere between Athens and Piraeus, has three demotics only.[3] Habronichos, son of Lysikles of Lamptrai, appears 4 times on the ostraca with his demotic and once with the name alone. His patronymic is used in the texts of Herodotos and Thucydides, but not on the ostraca.[4] There are also seven singletons, people represented by one ostracon apiece, who are identified by their demotics.[5]

This overwhelming predominance of the patronymic makes the case of Themistokles all the more interesting. Among the Agora

[2] Werner Peek, *Kerameikos*, III, *Inschriften, Ostraka, Fluchtafeln*, pp. 62-78; F. Willemsen, *A.M.*, 80, 1965, pp. 113-121, and *Deltion*, 23, 1968, *Chronika*, pp. 28-29; A. E. Raubitschek, *Hesperia*, XXIV, 1955, pp. 286-289; W. B. Dinsmoor, *Hesperia*, Suppl. V, pp. 142, 144 and 161-163. My statistics do not include the more than two hundred Menon ostraca mentioned in Willemsen's 1968 article for which no breakdown is available.

[3] *Hesperia*, Supplement VIII, pp. 394-395.

[4] *Hesperia*, Suppl. VIII, p. 395 ("Andronichos"); A. E. Raubitschek, *Classical Review*, LXX, 1956, pp. 199-200; M. Chambers, *Classical Philology*, LIV, 1959, pp. 42-44; F. Willemsen, *A.M.*, 80, 1965, pp. 106-107.

[5] Charias Paianieus (*Hesperia*, Suppl. VIII, pp. 396-397); Eupolis Thoraieus (here, figure 18); Laispodias of Koile, a city deme (*Hesperia*, Suppl. VIII, p. 400); Onomastos Konthyleus (here, figure 44); Panaitios Agrylethen (here, figure 43); Philokydes Lamptreus (*A.M.*, 80, 1965, p. 108); Sokrates Anagyrasios (here, figure 9).

ostraca, which come from a variety of deposits and so probably give a good cross section, there are 148 with the name plus patronymic, Neokleous (fig. 14), and again 148 with the name plus the demotic, Phrearrhios (fig. 15). Besides these there are 5 with the full name (figs. 7 and 8) and 5 with the name Themistokles alone (fig. 16). How are we to explain the unusually large number of demotics? Surely not, I think, in terms of Themistokles' social status; you will recall that, although on his father's side he belonged to the noble family of the Lykomidai, his mother was a foreigner; this made him technically a *nothos*, as people of mixed parentage were called, but did not affect his citizenship status. The explanation is to be sought rather in the character of Themistokles himself. It seems to me that Themistokles must have deliberately cultivated the use of the demotic; that he wanted to be known as "the Phrearrhian" rather than as "the son of Neokles"; and that he did this in order to increase his popularity among the common people. This would be quite in keeping with his character. He was the man who knew everyone by name.[6] Remember too how he is portrayed in the anecdote at the beginning of Plutarch's *Life*. According to this, Themistokles, whose mother was a foreigner, used to exercise at the Kynosarges gymnasium which was frequented by boys of mixed parentage but not by full-blooded Athenians. Themistokles, however, persuaded certain well-born youths to join him at Kynosarges and thus is thought to have removed the distinction between the two groups. Here, surely, we see a true politician at work at the grassroots level. He knows everyone by name, and he himself wants to be known by the popular, not the snobbish, designation.

Over and above the simple name, what occurs most frequently perhaps is the article. We find it seven times with the patronymic, as "Aristeides ho Lysimachou" (fig. 17), and three times with the demotic, as "Boutalion ho Marathonios" (fig. 13) and "Eupolis ho Thoraieus" (fig. 18).

Some voters, in order to leave no doubt as to the purpose of the ballot, added the word *ito*, "go," after the name: "Themistokles, son of Neokles, out with him" (fig. 19). There are four such ostraca in the large group from the North Slope of the Acropolis.

---

[6] Plutarch, *Themistocles*, V, 4.

An ostracon from the new Kerameikos find says sarcastically "This ostracon is in honor of Themistokles Phrearrhios."[7]

One voter really let himself go and wrote a little poem[8] (fig. 20). The ostracon is one against Xanthippos, son of Arriphron, the father of Pericles, who was ostracized in 484 B.C. It reads:

$$X\sigma\acute{a}\nu\theta[\iota\pi\pi\sigma\nu \ \tau\acute{o}\delta\epsilon] \ \phi\epsilon\sigma\grave{\iota}\nu \ \grave{a}\lambda\epsilon\iota\tau\epsilon\rho\grave{o}\nu \ \pi\rho[\upsilon\tau]\acute{a}\nu\epsilon\iota\upsilon\nu$$
$$\tau\acute{o}\sigma\tau\rho\alpha\kappa[\upsilon\nu \ \text{'}A\rho\rho\acute{\iota}]\phi\rho\upsilon\upsilon\sigma \ \pi\alpha\hat{\iota}\delta\alpha \ \mu\acute{a}[\lambda]\iota\sigma\tau\text{'} \ \grave{a}\delta\iota\kappa\hat{\epsilon}\nu.$$

"This ostracon declares that Xanthippos, son of Arriphron, is the most guilty of the accursed prytanes."

I follow Adolf Wilhelm's interpretation, which has also been adopted by Meiggs and Lewis, but others have been suggested and are perhaps possible. None is really sure. The difficulty lies in the exact form the writer intended for the words "aleiteron prytaneion," and hence his exact meaning; but whatever the meaning, the reference escapes us.

Another man added a curse to his ballot, which was apparently directed against Hippokrates, son of Alkmeonides (fig. 21). The name Hippokrates can be read in the second line, badly spelled, with the pi roughened to phi and the kappa roughened to chi: Hiphochratous. The first line is very badly written and hard to interpret, but I think we should see in these letters the words ma and tisin; ma, an exclamation, tisis, vengeance; in other words "Ma, vengeance to Hippokrates." I like to think of the writer of this ostracon as an old bearded peasant from the back country of Attica who had a grudge against Hippokrates and who came to town on Ostracism Day to have his revenge. As he prepared his ostracon one can almost hear him muttering in a voice as thick as his beard "Ma! tisin Hiphochratous!"

The normal way of the writing on the ostraca is from left to right and from the top line down. This was normal practice in fifth century Athens, just as it is with us today, and most of the ostraca are written in this way. Sometimes, however, they are

---

[7] Mentioned in *A.J.A.*, 71, 1967, p. 295.

[8] A. E. Raubitschek, *A.J.A.*, LI, 1947, pp. 257-262; O. Broneer, *A.J.A.*, LII, 1948, pp. 341-343; E. Schweigert, *A.J.A.*, LIII, 1949, pp. 266-267; Adolf Wilhelm, *Anz. Akad. Wien*, 1949, pp. 237-243; Russell Meiggs and David Lewis, *Greek Historical Inscriptions*, p. 42; H. Schaefer, *R.E.*, s.v. Xanthippos (follows Raubitschek).

written retrograde, i.e. from right to left (fig. 22). This backward writing had long been outmoded at Athens even in the early fifth century B.C., and if it is still found on a few ostraca we may assume that they were written by old men who had learned their letters in an earlier generation, or possibly by left-handed persons to whom backward writing came more naturally. Sometimes they are written in what is called boustrophedon (fig. 23), the way the oxen turn when plowing—over and back—another old-fashioned way of writing. Another example is partly boustrophedon, but the writer has first followed around the edge of the sherd and has only gone into reverse when he started back across the bottom (fig. 24). Sometimes the lines are written from the bottom up (figs. 16, 17, 25), a curious system of which there are a few examples even on stone inscriptions though always for short texts, tombstones, dedications and the like.[9] And sometimes the writing just rambles (fig. 26).

The spelling too is sometimes atrocious, as on an ostracon of Kallixenos (fig. 27), written retrograde with both names misspelled and finally left unfinished; or on another (fig. 28) for which no reasonable name has been suggested, though the second line seems to be playing with the demotic Cholargeus.

But lest anyone think the ancient Athenians had a monopoly on bad spelling, let me remind you what appeared on some of the ballots in the Minnesota primaries in March 1952 when Dwight D. Eisenhower's name was written in by a large number of voters. I quote from *Time* magazine of March 31, 1952:

"When the clerks began to tabulate the vote, they discovered what the voters had written: Dwight D. Eisenhower, Eisonhauer, Eausonhower, Isenhower, Eneshower, Izenour, Ikenhouer, Ike."

It was doubtless intended that the ostraca should be prepared by the voters themselves. Each citizen would take a potsherd and write on it the name of the person he wanted to see ostracized, scratching the name on the sherd with a sharp pointed instrument. In practice, however, many people would no doubt be unable to cope. Some would be illiterate or nearly so. Others would be un-

---

[9] The *locus classicus* for this phenomenon on stone inscriptions is Adolf Wilhelm, *Beiträge zur griechischen Inschriftenkunde*, pp. 3ff. For ostraca see also W. Peek, *Kerameikos* III, p. 61.

certain as to just what was required. Others still would be too busy or too lazy to find a suitable sherd and inscribe it. It seems reasonable to suppose, therefore, that on Ostracism Day many scribes would set up booths or tables at various points in the Agora and along the roads leading to it. They would be ready, for a small consideration, to sell you a sherd with the name of your "candidate" already written on it. These scribes would probably have prepared beforehand sherds with the names of the leading "candidates" of the day, which, although never officially announced, must have been generally known. But they would also be ready with blank sherds on which to write any other name the voter might wish. This can be illustrated by two ostraca of Kallixenos written on the foot of a krater (fig. 29). The two pieces are evidently from the same pot and in fact actually join one another. They were found in different deposits about 200 meters distant from one another. These, of course, since they bear the same name, might have been prepared by political opponents of Kallixenos rather than by professional scribes, but at the Kerameikos there are several instances of ostraca that join one another but have different names written on them; three times a Megakles ostracon joins a Themistokles ostracon, once Megakles joins Mnesiphilos and once Kimon joins Themistokles.[10] These must be the work of scribes.

Political groups too must soon have discovered that it was expedient to have a lot of ballots with the name of their opponent ready on Ostracism Day to be handed out to wavering voters and to persons who for one reason or another had not provided themselves with ostraca. Nothing illegal was involved, of course; they were just trying to make it easy for people "to vote the right way." We may recognize such a lot in the group of 190 ostraca all with the name of Themistokles found in 1937 in a well on the North Slope of the Acropolis. I illustrate a few of these ostraca (fig. 30) and I think you will agree that those in the top row were all written by one hand, those in the second row by another and those in the lower row by a third hand. Fourteen hands have been recognized in this group, and I think it is

---

[10] B.C.H., 92, 1968, pp. 732-733; Deltion, 23, 1968, Chronika, pp. 28-29, pl. 19 a and c.

clear that these ostraca were prepared all at one time by one of the anti-Themistokles parties to be handed out on Ostracism Day. Notice that the material is the same in all the cases illustrated in figure 30—kylix bases. Of this big lot of 190 (fig. 31) no less than 122 were on kylix bases, the rest on skyphos bases or small bowls, imperfectly fired, and other miscellaneous sherds. What probably happened was that one of the anti-Themistokles parties decided to prepare some ballots to be handed out on Ostracism Day. The party heelers assigned the job of collecting sherds very sensibly decided to go to the source—a potter's shop—and get them from his dump of broken or discarded pots. The kylix bases appealed to them as highly suitable, and they collected as many as they could. They also took some skyphos bases, some misfired bowls and other pieces. With this material they went back to party headquarters. Other heelers were summoned, were shown the pile of sherds and were told to sit down and write the name of Themistokles on as many pieces as they could. On Ostracism Day each took as many sherds as he could conveniently carry, went down to the Agora and circulated among the crowds, handing out his ready-made ostraca to any who wanted one. The party workers had been over-optimistic and had made more ostraca than they had been able to distribute, perhaps more than they were able to carry with them to the Agora. Some were left over, and I think it is probably these leftovers that were discarded in a deep well near the party headquarters to stay there until they were dug out again in the excavations of the 1930's.

This group of ostraca, like all we have looked at so far, is made in the orthodox manner, the name being scratched on the sherd with a sharp instrument. This is the obvious, natural way to write on a sherd. It is slow and tedious, however, and where a lot of ostraca are to be made, whether by a scribe or by a party, painting is clearly a much quicker and simpler method. One has only to set oneself up with the necessary paint and brush or ink and pen, and then the job goes quickly. Only six painted ostraca have been found thus far. Two of them are rather special, having been made by potters; the letters are large and are done in glaze paint which has been fired. Of these, more tomorrow. More typical, probably, are the four done in dilute paint or ink which, not having been fired, has faded. The fact that the writing on such ostraca tends to fade probably accounts for the small number that have been found. The earliest of these are from the middle of the fifth century and bear the names of Perikles (fig. 33), Thucydides, son of Melesias, and Kallias, son of Didymias (fig. 57), but the most interesting is that of Hyperbolos, son of Antiphanes (fig. 32), the last person to be ostracized. We need hardly hesitate to say that this ostracon was made to order for the coalition that was formed to oust Hyperbolos.

In the matter of letter forms, spelling and pronunciation of ancient Greek, the evidence derived from the ostraca is of first-rate importance. We have here original documents that can be closely dated, written by average citizens, where there is seldom any attempt at formal correctness such as we find in official inscriptions on stone, and where there is no chance of later change or emendation which often takes place in the transmission of our literary texts. Here, and in the other informal graffiti on potsherds, we find, to adapt a phrase of Mark Twain's, "Greek as she is spoke." The ostraca are particularly valuable because we find the same names repeated over and over, and we are thus better able to judge what is a mere slip of the pen and what is a mistake that may be due to real misunderstanding and where some linguistic principle may be involved.

I can only give a few examples of this sort of thing. The name of Themistokles as we find it in our literary texts and in inscriptions of later classical times is spelled Themistokles, that is, with tau in the third syllable (fig. 24), and this is undoubtedly the correct spelling when one takes into account the derivation of the name. On the ostraca, however, it is almost always spelled Themisthokles, with theta in the third syllable (figs. 7, 8, 14, 15, 16 etc.), i.e. by metathesis of aspiration. Among the Agora ostraca there are no less than 293 instances of theta and only 14 of tau. One man has written tau and theta on top of one another (fig. 35), and another has put in both for good measure, Themisthtokles (fig. 34). It seems clear then that in Themistokles' own day his name was generally written with theta in the third syllable and was no doubt so pronounced.

The name of Kallixenos' father, Aristonymos, is normally and correctly spelled with upsilon in the penult, Aristonymou (fig. 45). This is found in 103 instances. In 9 cases, however, we find iota instead of upsilon (fig. 36). The phenomenon is not confined to this word, however, but occurs also in the demotic Xypetaion where we have 2 instances of Xiphet-(fig. 38), against 3 for the correct Xypet-(fig. 37). We conclude, therefore, that the sounds of upsilon and iota were sufficiently close to cause confusion to some people. The pronunciation of upsilon was therefore probably more like ü than ou.

The sign later used for omega (Ω) sometimes appears on ostraca of the early and middle fifth century (fig. 39). It never represents omega, however, but is always used for the impure diphthong ou of the genitive ending. This phenomenon is very rare on stone inscriptions in Attica. The ostraca show, however, that it was by no means uncommon in the first half of the fifth century B.C. Statistics, based on ostraca found at the Agora, show that the omega sign was used for the omicron-upsilon of the genitive ending in 18 cases as against 242 for the normal o, that is about 8% of the time. This shows, I think, that some people were attempting to represent by a separate letter the special sound of the impure ou of the genitive ending. There are also 9 cases where the diphthong is written out in full, ou (fig. 40), as later became normal. The norm at the period of which we are speaking is a simple o.

Another case where contracted and uncontracted forms of the same ending occur side by side is to be found in names in —kles. These names appear in the contracted form —κλές (i.e. —κλῆς) in 198 instances (figs. 19, 30, 35). This is the standard form of classical times. But we find the uncontracted form also —κλέες (i.e. κλέης) no less than 43 times (figs. 8, 14, 16, 25), and this is the form in which we find these names in the pages of Herodotos. This uncontracted form for names in —kles continues in occasional use down through the fourth century B.C.

In the matter of the gemination of consonants, that is the use of a double instead of a single pi in a name like Hippokrates or a double instead of a single lambda in a name like Kallixenos, there is a clear trend towards the double. There are 216 instances of the double consonant, which was later to become the standard spelling, as against 121 instances of the old-fashioned single form among the early fifth century ostraca at the Agora.

Evidence of this sort when properly tabulated and interpreted should be of great interest to philologists.

Then there is the matter of letter forms: crossed or dotted thetas, three or four barred sigmas (and even five barred sometimes!), Attic or Ionic gammas or lambdas, and the like. This is a topic of lively interest to epigraphists, and the ostraca and other graffiti will eventually supply a large amount of statistical data bearing on it. This is not likely, however, to be of much help in the dating of official inscriptions on stone, for these, as is well known, lag considerably behind popular usage. Suffice it to say here that, although Ionic forms appear sporadically in the sixth and early fifth centuries, it is after the Persian Wars that real encroachment begins. From the second quarter of the fifth century they appear frequently alongside the old Attic forms, they gain ground steadily, and well before the end of the century they are found almost universally. We shall see some examples of this as we go along.

All this brings up the general question of literacy. What do the ostraca tell us about literacy in fifth century Athens? Obviously the very existence of a law such as the law on ostracism presupposes that the electorate was largely literate, that the legislator knew that most of the citizens would be able "to take an ostracon and write on it the name of the person he thought should be banished."[11] If in fact many resorted to scribes or accepted hand-outs from the political parties, this is as much a matter of convenience as anything, considering the difficulty of finding a suitable sherd and implement and of writing on an intractable medium. But there are enough ostraca which are obviously "home made" to show that many individuals had a go themselves at making their own ostracon. Their writing is sometimes halting and erratic, their spelling bad; they often leave the names unfinished. On the other hand they sometimes write more than was required, adding an invective or an accusation, even going so far as to write a little verse or draw a caricature.

This brings us finally to a consideration of what is probably the most famous and best known story about ostracism, Plutarch's anec-

---

[11] The quotation is from Plutarch, *Aristeides*, VII, 5.

dote about Aristeides and the illiterate peasant.[12] You will remember how the story goes. It is the day of the ostracism. The Agora is crowded. People have poured into the city from all sides to cast their votes. An illiterate or semi-literate man is having trouble preparing his ostracon. He comes up to Aristeides, not recognizing who he is but seeing that he is an educated man, and asks him to write the name of Aristeides on his sherd. Aristeides, not letting on who he is, asks the man what he has against him, to which the man replies: "Nothing; I do not even know the fellow, but I am tired of hearing him called 'The Just'."

On the ostracon illustrated in figure 41, and which the drawing, figure 42, shows more clearly, the name of Aristeides is written quite neatly though faintly along the upper edge. Then a start was made in uncertain characters on the patronymic, Lysimachou, but this was abandoned half way through. Next a start was made on the demotic, Alopekethen, but there is confusion towards the end and it too was left unfinished. Finally the ostracon appears to have been taken in hand by a person who knew what he was about. The halting second and third lines were scratched out and the father's name Lysimachou was written underneath in clear, firm characters.

It would be too much to claim that this is the very ostracon referred to in Plutarch's anecdote, although with a few changes in detail the anecdote could be made to suit it. It does, however, illustrate admirably the difficulties experienced by illiterate voters and so aids us in visualizing the scene and makes the anecdote more vivid.

[12] Plutarch, *Aristeides*, VII, 7-18.

II. SOME HISTORICAL POINTS

ESTERDAY we looked at ostraca mainly with an eye to what was written on them, how it was written, and what sort of sherds were used. Today I want to consider them as historical documents and show how they can sometimes be used to add substantially to our knowledge of Athenian history.

Among the ostraca discovered to date we have pieces bearing the names of every person known from the ancient authors to have been ostracized or even involved in an ostracism with the exception of Nicias, about whom I will speak later, and Kleisthenes and Miltiades, son of Kimon, whose ostracisms are imaginary. Besides these many other names occur on the sherds that are not mentioned in the literature in connection with ostracism. Some of these people like Leagros, son of Glaukon, are very well known. About fifty ostraca with the name of Leagros are reported from the big Kerameikos lot of 1966-67.[13] For others, tentative identifications can be suggested. For example, Panaitios Agrylethen might possibly be the Panaitios who was *kalos* on so many early red-figured vases; but he might equally well be someone quite other. In fact, even the name is not perfectly sure: the one ostracon on which it appears (fig. 43), is broken at the left, and if only a small sliver is missing at the upper left corner there might be no room to restore a pi, and the name might be Anaitios instead of Panaitios. I think, however, that Panaitios is to be preferred. Other names appearing on ostraca, like Onomastos Konthyleus, are completely unknown (fig. 44). We should not, however, just for this reason disregard them. These people must have been somehow in the public eye, must have held some position or other to have been voted against; and they may, of course, turn out to be people of considerable importance as happened in the case of two men, a certain Kallixenos and a certain Kallias, whose stories I will now outline for you.

Among the very first ostraca to be discovered in the Agora excavations, back in 1932, were two with the name Kallixenos Aristonymou (fig. 45).[14] We searched in the history books and proso-

---

[13] *B.C.H.*, 92, 1968, p. 732; *Deltion*, 23, 1968, *Chronika*, pp. 27 and 29, and pl. 19, d.

[14] For a fuller discussion of what follows see the article "Kallixenos the

pographies for some mention of this person, but in vain; we found none. His name was not recorded. From the circumstances of discovery of the two ostraca and the type of pottery used for them we could, however, date him quite closely, for it was clear that these votes had been cast in the late eighties of the fifth century B.C. Thus from this first discovery we already had important basic information about the man.

As the years passed the excavations brought to light many more ostraca with the name of Kallixenos, there are now over 260 of them, and it became clear that we had to do with a person of some prominence. His ostraca were usually found in association with those of Themistokles and Aristeides and also of a certain Hippokrates, son of Alkmeonides, who, like Kallixenos, was otherwise unknown. Among these ostraca were several with the designation Kallixenos Xypetaion (figs. 37 and 38), that is, Kallixenos of Xypete. Xypete was a large deme in the city area lying somewhere between Athens and Piraeus. That this Kallixenos of Xypete was the same as Kallixenos son of Aristonymos we learned from two fragmentary ostraca on which both the patronymic and the demotic appeared. We thus had the man's full name, Kallixenos Aristonymou Xypetaion.

We were also given a glimpse of what he looked like, although rather a sketchy one! One of the voters, not content with writing merely the name, decorated his ballot with a drawing showing a head in profile to the right—a bearded head wearing some sort of wreath or crown (figs. 46 and 47). There can be little doubt, I think, that this sketch is intended to represent Kallixenos, although as a likeness it is probably not much better that the surreptitious drawings that school children sometimes make of their teachers. Our artist-voter, who apparently had time and talent to spare, went on to fill in the remaining vacant spaces with a branch and a fish, the head of which can be made out in the lower left corner.

When the study of the whole lot of Kallixenos ostraca was taken up a number of other interesting points emerged. A fragment of an ostracon, though broken at right and left, was still sufficiently well preserved to enable us to establish an important fact (fig. 48).

Alkmeonid," by G. A. Stamires and E. Vanderpool in *Hesperia*, XIX, 1950, pp. 376-390.

The first line on this sherd reads . . . meon . . . , the second . . . lixen . . . , the third . . . isto. . . . The second and third lines are clearly to be restored Kallixenos Aristonymou. But what of the first line? I think there can be little doubt that we have here the family name of the Alkmeonidai, probably in the genitive plural. The whole text is therefore to be restored ['Aλκ]μεον[ιδôν Καλ]-λίχσεν[ος 'Aρ]ιστο[νύμο]. Kallixenos thus belonged to the great and well known Alkmeonid family, a family that was deeply involved in the political strife of the age, and one that had many enemies; hence it is not surprising to find an attempt being made to ostracize him.

If further confirmation of Kallixenos' connection with the Alkmeonid family were needed, we might recall that in an earlier generation Megakles the Alkmeonid, married Agariste, daughter of Kleisthenes, tyrant of Sicyon. Agariste's grandfather was called Aristonymos. The use of the name of a Sicyonian ancestor in the Alkmeonid family would be quite normal and is indeed paralleled in the case of Kleisthenes the legislator.

The large number of votes against Kallixenos (there are now over 260) indicates that he was a prominent figure and that a considerable portion of the populace thought he should be ostracized. There is evidence too that feeling against him ran high: on one ostracon the voter wrote *Kallixenos ho prodotes*, Kallixenos, the traitor (fig. 49).

Next we may look at a curious piece that comes from the handle of an oinochoe and has painted on it in large black letters a name that must be restored as Kallixenos (fig. 50). That it was used as an ostracon I think there can be no doubt, for it was found in a large deposit of ostraca, the largest yet found at the Agora, over six hundred pieces, of which about 165 were against Kallixenos. But this is no ordinary ostracon. It is not even an ordinary painted ostracon, for it is painted in the glaze used for decorating vases. Clearly then it is the work of a potter. I once thought that it must have been written on the complete vase when the vase was made and so have been part of the decoration. Its use as an ostracon would have been a second use. I thought that the inscription might originally have read *Kallixenos kalos*, Kallixenos is fair, and I allowed my fancy to speculate on how a vase that had been made as a gift for the fair Kallixenos in his youth was later turned into a ballot designed to send him into exile. But this romantic explanation will not do. Among the many ostraca found lately at the Kerameikos there is one with the name of Menon which is painted in this same sort of black glaze and it is painted on a simple sherd and not in any way that could be considered decorative.[15] It is merely a case of a potter making an ostracon for himself in the easiest possible way; and so must our Kallixenos piece be.

What date are we to assign to the Kallixenos ostraca, and can we say whether Kallixenos was actually ostracized or not? These are the historical questions that we must now try to answer. The general date, I think, is sure. A deep well or shaft in which the fill had gathered slowly over a period of several years produced at a depth of about 8½ to 9 meters three ostraca with the name of Megakles. Megakles, you will recall, was ostracized in 486 B.C. A couple of meters higher up were two ostraca of Kallixenos along with one of Themistokles and one of Hippokrates, son of Alkmeonides. There were also three ostraca of Aristeides, one with those just mentioned and two still higher up at a depth of about five meters. The fill in this part of the well, between nine and five meters, seems therefore to have gathered in the eighties of the fifth century, between 486 when Megakles was ostracized and 482 the year of Aristeides' banishment. The ostracophoria in which Kallixenos was involved should fall within this range.

Now ostraca with the names of Kallixenos, Themistokles and Hippokrates, son of Alkmeonides, are commonly found together at the Agora. There are usually a few Aristeides ostraca along with them. One might argue, therefore, that these groups belong to the year 482 when Aristeides was banished, and that the bulk of the Aristeides ostraca had been sorted out in the counting to make sure they were the largest number and then discarded elsewhere. A few odd pieces remained with the residue which was mostly dumped along the road leading out from near the Tholos at the southwest corner of the Agora. But this suggestion is rather involved, and besides it would mean that there were four major "candidates" at the ostracism of 482. It is better, I think, to suppose that these ostraca date from 483 B.C. and that the Aristeides

---

[15] *Deltion*, 23, 1968, *Chronika*, p. 28, and pl. 19 e.

ostraca that are found with them belong to the scatter vote of the year; a number of other names are found, such as Kydrokles, son of Timokrates.

This supposition, however, raises another problem. There are three big groups in which the names of Kallixenos, Themistokles and Hippokrates, son of Alkmeonides, occur, one group of 605 ostraca, another of 172 and a third of 41: a total of 818 ostraca in all. If we subtract 212 which are too fragmentary to be read with certainty, we are left with 606 ostraca. Of these 245 are against Themistokles, 217 Kallixenos and 97 Hippokrates; there are only 12 Aristeides, 9 Kydrokles and 26 with various other names. This means that Themistokles has the largest number of votes by a slight margin, and he has this margin in each of the groups. If, therefore, our groups give a representative sampling then Themistokles must have received the largest number of votes. But Themistokles was not ostracized in the four eighties. His turn did not come until about ten years later. We are forced then to suppose that the requisite 6000 votes were not cast and the ostracism was void. Alternatively we may assume that our sampling is not typical and that Kallixenos did in fact receive the largest number of votes and so was ostracized. It does not seem possible to decide with certainty.

Another case where it will be possible to write a similar "biography" of a previously unknown man is that of Kallias, son of Kratios. Two ostraca with this name were found at the Agora in the nineteen thirties and they could be dated in the eighties of the fifth century.[16] Nothing was known otherwise about the man, and the ostraca were assigned to the scatter vote of one of the ostracisms of those years. Two or three years ago, however, in the excavations of the German Archaeological Institute at the Kerameikos a large dump of ostraca was found. Among them were nearly 800 with the name of this Kallias whose deme was found to be Alopeke. On four of these ostraca Kallias is designated as *ho Medos*, "the Mede," and on another there is a caricature sketch of a man in Persian garb, with cap, trousers and pointed shoes. He is thus characterized as a friend of the Persians and, as the Persians were giving

---

[16] *Hesperia*, Suppl. V, pp. 141 and 161. One of the two is published there, the other merely mentioned; I illustrate it here, figure 51.

support to the former tyrants, he will also be a friend of the tyrants. He is therefore almost certainly the victim of the ostracism of 485 B.C. when Aristotle tells us that following Hipparchos and Megakles a third friend of the tyrants was banished, without, however, giving his name. The above facts are culled from news reports.[17] When the whole lot is published, it will no doubt be possible to fill out the picture further as we have just done with Kallixenos.

Thus these two men, Kallixenos, son of Aristonymos of Xypete, and Kallias, son of Kratios of Alopeke, about whom nothing whatever had previously been known, have turned out to be important figures in Athens at the time of the Persian Wars, and have been brought back, entirely through the agency of the ostraca, if not into the full light at least into the half-light of history. We are forcefully reminded of what gaps exist in our knowledge of Athenian history.

We turn next to Alcibiades the elder.[18] Here we have to do with a well-known man who is reported to have been ostracized—one source even says that he was ostracized twice but this is not to be trusted—and the problem here is not one of identifying the person and deciding whether he was ostracized or not, but of determining the date and if possible the cause of his ostracism. Our literary sources give no clue on either point, but the discovery of several ostraca allow us to bring some archaeological evidence to bear on the problem.

Now we said that we know from ancient authors that the elder Alcibiades *was* ostracized. Since we also know that his grandson, the famous Alcibiades of the later fifth century, was also a "candidate" in his day, when Hyperbolos was banished, the first problem in the case of each ostracon with the name Alcibiades is to decide if possible which of the two is meant, the grandfather or the grandson. Both men had the same name, Alcibiades, son of Kleinias of Skambonidai, so other criteria must be sought. The shapes of the letters, particularly lambda and sigma, and the use of epsilon or eta for the long vowel in the last syllable of name or demotic offer the readiest means of distinction, and when the old

---

[17] *A.J.A.*, 71, 1967, p. 295; *B.C.H.*, 92, 1968, p. 732.
[18] *Hesperia*, XXI, 1952, pp. 1-8; XXXVII, 1968, pp. 117-118 and 398.

Attic forms are used the ostracon may with some confidence be assigned to the elder Alcibiades (fig. 52) whereas when Ionic forms appear (fig. 53) it is more likely that the younger Alcibiades is meant. The type of pottery and the circumstances of finding of the individual ostraca may sometimes offer additional criteria. Using these data the eleven Alcibiades ostraca that have been found thus far have been divided up, eight to the elder and three to the younger.

The date of the ostracism of the elder Alcibiades is not known. Modern scholars used to place it in 485 B.C. when, as Aristotle tells us, the third "friend of the tyrants" was ostracized without, however, naming him. The arguments for placing his ostracism in this year are only of a general nature and are not very compelling or convincing. In fact, it comes down to nothing more than putting a loose name in an empty slot. But now there is some new evidence. We have just seen that the year 485 B.C. is almost certainly to be given to another person, Kallias, son of Kratios, and that 483 B.C. is the year when Kallixenos was a leading "candidate." This fills all the available years in the four eighties and leaves no room for the elder Alcibiades. His exclusion from the four eighties had already been suggested by archaeological observations. A considerable amount of fill dating from the time of the Persian destruction of Athens in 480 B.C. has been dug in the course of the Agora excavations. This fill often contains ostraca, and the names of all the persons known or supposed to have been ostracized in the four eighties have been found in such fill, namely Hipparchos, Megakles, Kallias, Xanthippos, Kallixenos and Aristeides. The names of many other persons who were doubtless "candidates" in these years have also appeared. No ostracon with the name of Alcibiades has yet been found in pre-Persian fill, however. This is negative evidence, of course, and is perhaps not decisive by itself. It does, however, suggest quite strongly that the ostracism of the elder Alcibiades did not take place in the four eighties.

But there is some positive evidence as well. Two of the ostraca which must be assigned to the elder Alcibiades are kylix bases. Although it is of course not possible to date these to an exact year, we can say that they are of a type that does not appear before the Persian invasion but which is in common use in the second quarter of the fifth century, i.e. from about 475 to about 450 B.C. One of these kylix bases (fig. 54) is of exceptional importance. Dateable by its shape in the second quarter of the fifth century it was found in a deposit of this very period in which the pottery runs down to but hardly beyond the middle of the century. The lambdas on this ostracon are of Ionic form, not Attic, and if we did not have the evidence of the circumstances of finding we should have been inclined to assign this piece to the younger Alcibiades, assuming that an old sherd had been used, as frequently happens. Other ostraca and graffiti show us, however, that Ionic forms begin to appear with some frequency in the second quarter of the fifth century; for example, ostraca of Kimon who was banished in 461 B.C. occasionally have the Ionic lambda. This fact, combined with the other evidence, allows us to date this ostracon with complete assurance in the second quarter of the century. The type of pottery prevents it being earlier, the circumstances of finding prevent it being later. As it seems fair to assume that it was used on the occasion of his own ostracism and not on some other occasion when his name may have been up, for example at the ostracism of Kimon, it follows that his ostracism is to be dated in the second quarter of the fifth century B.C.

In order to test this conclusion and, if possible, pin the event down more precisely within this quarter century we must see what is known about the career of this elder Alcibiades. There is not much, but what there is seems to fall in the four sixties. One point is suggestive. Alcibiades the elder had once been proxenos of the Spartans at Athens, but he renounced the position. This is generally believed to have taken place in connection with the affair of Ithome when Athenian troops which had been sent under the command of Kimon to aid the Spartans at the request of the Spartans themselves were ordered home again by the Spartans before the siege was over. This insult to Athens caused a wave of anti-Spartan feeling, as a result of which Kimon was ostracized in 461 B.C. Alcibiades, the Spartan proxenos, tried to save himself by renouncing the proxeny, but the gesture was ineffective, or came too late. In the following year, the spring of 460 B.C., we may safely assume that he followed Kimon into exile.

Two ostraca with a new name, Dieitrephes, son of Euthoinos,

(fig. 55) were found recently.[19] They came in association with two ostraca of Alcibiades the elder, and the fill in which the four ostraca were found was of the second quarter of the fifth century B.C. This provides welcome support for the date 460 B.C., already suggested for the ostracism of Alcibiades. It also gives an approximate date for the Dieitrephes ostraca. There is no reason to suppose, of course, that Dieitrephes was ever ostracized; the ballots are best thought of as belonging to the scatter vote of Alcibiades' or Kimon's year.

This Dieitrephes, son of Euthoinos, belonged to a well-known Athenian family. His brother Hermolykos distinguished himself at the battle of Mykale in 479 B.C. and fell near Karystos a few years later. One of his sons, also named Hermolykos, set up an offering on the Acropolis made by the sculptor Kresilas. Another son, Nikostratos, is mentioned several times as a general in the Archidamian War; he fell at Mantineia in 418 B.C. His grandson Dieitrephes is perhaps best known as the leader of the Thracian mercenaries who sacked Mykalessos in 413 B.C.

The discovery of the name of Dieitrephes' father, Euthoinos, on the ostraca allows us to make a small correction in our texts of Herodotos, for Euthoinos is mentioned in Herodotos, IX, 105, as the father of Hermolykos. The manuscripts of Herodotos, however, give several variant forms of the name, Εὔθοινος, Εὔθυνος and Εὔθονος, and modern editors have chosen now one, now another form. The ostraca settle this discrepancy in favor of Εὔθοινος, and our texts of Herodotos should be corrected accordingly.

There is another small historical point on which the ostraca have shed light, the ostracism of Kallias, son of Didymias. This Kallias is known to us as a great athlete, a pankratiast. He won a series of victories at all the great games, at Olympia in 472 B.C., at Delphi twice, at Isthmia five times, at Nemea four times, and at the Great Panathenaic Games at Athens. Two monuments celebrating his victories have survived to our day, one at Olympia, the other on the Acropolis.[20]

This is the only connection in which we hear of Kallias, son of

[19] *Hesperia*, XXXVII, 1968, pp. 118-119.
[20] E. Curtius und F. Adler, *Olympia*, V, *Die Inschriften*, bearbeitet von W. Dittenberger und K. Purgold, no. 146; *I.G.*, I², 606; A. E. Raubitschek, *Dedications from the Athenian Akropolis*, no. 164.

Didymias, except for a passing mention in the oration against Alcibiades, which has come down to us among the works of Andocides (IV, 32), where it is stated that he was ostracized in spite of the fact he had won victories at all the great games and so had brought glory to Athens. As this oration is usually not regarded as a very reliable historical source, and as athletes generally do not make politicians, the ostracism of Kallias has generally been rejected, there being no other reference to political activity on his part.

But there are now three ostraca with his name which shows that he was at least involved in an ostracism. Two of them are normal ones with incised inscriptions (fig. 56), but the third is a *painted* one (fig. 57). This suggests that he was not merely voted against by a few people, but that there was a concerted campaign against him. There is, therefore, no longer any real reason to doubt that he was ostracized.

The date of the ostracism is not known exactly. The letter forms on the ostraca would suit a date around the middle of the fifth century. About 450 B.C., or soon after, Kallias set up his dedication on the Acropolis celebrating his athletic victories. This act of self-advertisement, done long after the victories had been won and when Kallias was already a mature man in his forties or fifties, may well indicate political ambitions. We may assume, therefore, that Kallias was a rival of Perikles and that he was ostracized in the course of Perikles' drive for power which culminated in 443 B.C. with the ostracism of Thucydides, son of Melesias. His ostracism may therefore be placed in one of the immediately preceding years.

The case of Menon is similar. The only record of his ostracism is an entry in the lexicon of Hesychios where we read: "Some say that Menon was ostracized." There are now over 300 ostraca with his name, almost all from the Kerameikos, so there is no doubt that he was in fact ostracized.[21]

We have already commented on his name, Menon, son of Menekleides, of Gargettos, and have noticed the predominant use of the demotic in referring to him. We said that he was a Thessalian from Pharsalos who had been granted Athenian citizenship for having aided the Athenians at Eion in 477 B.C. with three hundred horse-

---

[21] Bibliography above, note 2.

men. He fell from favor twenty years later when a Thessalian cavalry force that had again come to aid Athens turned traitor at the battle of Tanagra in 458 B.C. Menon's ostracism should follow in the spring of the following year, 457 B.C. It is significant that one of the ostraca calls him a traitor. Another epithet that is used of him is ἀφελής. It occurs on three ostraca recently found at the Kerameikos.[22] Just what is meant by it is not clear. The word means artless or simple in a good sense, bold or brazen in a bad sense. Probably the bad sense is intended, but just what the writer had in mind is not clear.

We move down now to the later fifth century and will consider the case of Kleophon.[23] Kleophon is well known from references in the historians, orators and comic poets. He was a demagogue, a brash, loud-mouthed fellow, a sort of latter day Kleon. He was known as the lyre maker, much as Kleon was known as the tanner. Our sources are insistent on this side of his character and they tell us nothing of his family except that his mother was a foreigner. A late writer, Aelian, moralizing on famous men of obscure origin, says "one could not readily name the fathers of Hyperbolos, Kleophon and Demades, although they became leaders of the popular party of Athens." All this has led modern historians to assume that he was of lowly birth; one speaks of him as "a man without a family," another as a slave.

We now have four ostraca with the name of Kleophon, one of which gives his full name (fig. 58), and we learn that he was the son of Kleippides and of the deme Acharnai. This allows us to identify as his father Kleippides, son of Deinias, who was a general in 428 B.C. Kleippides too was voted against in an ostracism, probably that of 443 B.C. when Thucydides, son of Melesias, was ostracized, and we have 27 ostraca with his name, some of which give the demotic, Acharneus, which clinches the identification. All were found at the Kerameikos. We see then that Kleophon was not of obscure birth but belonged to an Athenian family of some prominence, even though he himself may have been a bad lot.

A brother of Kleophon's has also become known through a handsome ostracon (figs. 62-63) with the name of Philinos, son of

[22] A.M., 80, 1965, p. 118.
[23] Hesperia, XXI, 1952, pp. 114-115; and XXXVII, 1968, p. 120.

Kleippides.[24] The name is incised on the under side of the base of a bowl with incised decoration which may be dated about 430-420 B.C. This is probably the Philinos mentioned without patronymic or demotic in the sixth oration of Antiphon who was successfully indicted for theft of public funds. So both Kleippides' sons went wrong.

The ostraca against Kleophon and his brother Philinos must have been cast in the year of the ostracism of Hyperbolos, the last ostracism ever held and the only one recorded in this general period.

I close, then, with a small point about this last ostracism. I will not discuss the problem of date on which the ostraca have shed no light. The traditional date is 417 B.C., but 418, 416 and 415 have also been proposed.

The complicated political dealings that took place on the eve of this ostracism are variously reported. According to one version it was Alcibiades and Nicias who joined forces to oust Hyperbolos. According to another there was a third man involved, Phaiax. But still another version, attributed to Theophrastos, maintained that it was Alcibiades and Phaiax who were striving against one another and that Nicias was not involved.[25]

No large groups of ostraca from this last ostracism have yet been found, but there are 19 individual pieces that can be assigned to it. These have been found widely scattered, mostly at the Agora, a few at the Kerameikos. Of the known protagonists, we now have 4 ostraca of Phaiax[26] (figs. 59-60), 3 of Alcibiades (fig. 53), 2 of Hyperbolos (figs. 32 and 64-65), *none* of Nicias. Of other names that can be associated more or less certainly with this ostracism we have 4 of Kleophon, 3 of Hippokles, son of Menippos (fig. 61), known to have been a general in 412 B.C., and one each of Philinos, Phileriphos, and Charias of Paiania.

This is obviously too small a number on which to base any general conclusions, but the absence of Nicias ostraca is none the

[24] *Hesperia* XXIII, 1954, pp. 68-71.

[25] 1: Plutarch, *Aristeides*, VII; 2: Plutarch, *Alcibiades*, XIII; [Andocides], IV, 2; 3: Plutarch, *Nicias* XI, and, less positively stated, *Alcibiades* XIII.

[26] The best preserved example is from the Kerameikos, W. Peek, *Kerameikos* III, pp. 78-80, no. 149; J. Kirchner, *Imagines inscriptionum atticarum*[2], no. 38. The ostraca give the demotic for the first time.

less striking. Could it be that these few scattered sherds, like straws in the wind, indicate the trend, and that Theophrastos was right in saying that when Hyperbolos was ostracized it was Phaiax, not Nicias, who was striving against Alcibiades? We will watch with more than usual interest for future discoveries of ostraca dating from this last ostracism which may help us decide this point.

From these few examples I have shown, I hope you have seen something of the varied interest of the ostraca. These little pot-sherds with a name scrawled on them are very personal, very human documents and bring us very close to the average citizen. We find him struggling with his writing and his spelling, uncertain often even as to the direction in which his writing should run. We find him giving vent to his feelings, calling out "vengeance" or "traitor," we find him killing time either doodling a portrait of Kallixenos or writing a little verse about Xanthippos.

But we are also brought very close to the great events of Athenian history. History is people, and the more we learn about the people who made history, the better we will understand the history of their times. The ostraca have proved an unexpectedly rich source of information about the people whose names they carry. We learn about their family connections, we get hints of why they were being voted against, we can work out the date of their ostracism and so fit it into the general history of the times. And quite apart from all this, it is always a moving experience to read on these potsherds the great names of fifth-century Athens, of Themistokles, of Aristeides, of Kimon, and of Perikles.

NOTES ON THE ILLUSTRATIONS

(Numbers preceded by P are Agora inventory numbers. Numbers preceded by AO are North Slope inventory numbers. The objects identified by such inventory numbers are all in the Stoa of Attalos Museum.)

Fig. 1. Fragment of a red-figured mug (oinochoe shape 8 A); by the Painter of Berlin 2268. See on Figure 2.

Fig. 2. Ostracon of Kallixenos Aristonymou. The writing is on the inside of the red-figured mug fragment, Figure 1. P 17620. *Hesperia*, XVII, 1948, pp. 185-186, pl. 66,1.

Fig. 3. Fragment of a black-figured amphora, probably Panathenaic, showing the knee and shield of a running hoplite. Part of the shield device, an extended forearm and hand, is preserved (in white now much faded). Used as an ostracon against Hippokrates, son of Alkmeonides. Notice how the writing follows neatly around the edge of the shield. P 15593. Not previously published.

Fig. 4. Rim of black figured calyx krater. See on Figure 5.

Fig. 5. Ostracon of Aristeides Lysimachou. The writing is on the inside of the krater rim illustrated in Figure 4. Notice the double sigma in the name. P 20399. Not previously published.

Fig. 6. Ostracon of Hippokrates Anaxileou. The sherd is a roof tile of Laconian type with dull red glaze. The suggestion that this Hippokrates was the victim of 485 B.C. (*Hesperia*, XXI, 1952, p. 8) must be withdrawn in view of the far stronger "candidacy" of Kallias Kratiou as described below in the second lecture. P 2702. *Hesperia*, XV, 1946, p. 272, pl. 25,6.

Fig. 7. The largest ostracon. It bears the name of Themistokles Neokleous Phrearrhios. P 15727. Not previously published.

Fig. 8. Ostracon of Themistokles Neokleous Phrearrhios. P 9950. This ostracon has been illustrated frequently in general histories and handbooks.

Fig. 9. Ostracon of Sokrates Anagyrasios. P 20325. *Hesperia*, XIX, 1950, p. 337, pl. 105 c.

Fig. 10. Ostracon of Xanthippos Arriphronos. P 6107. *Hesperia*, X, 1941, pp. 2-3.

Fig. 11. Ostracon of Menon Gargettios. P 14578. Not previously published. Note the Ionic gamma.

Fig. 12. Ostracon of Boutalion Marathonios. P 6133. Mentioned, *Hesperia*, XV, 1946, p. 272, note 14, but not previously published. The ostracon is a fragment of a drum-shaped terracotta wellhead like those published in *Hesperia*, XVIII, 1949, pp. 114-127.

Fig. 13. Ostracon of Boutalion Marathonios. P 5004. Mentioned, *Hesperia*, XXXVII, 1968, p. 118, but not previously published. Note that the name has been written twice over, the first effort in the bottom line having been crossed out. The article is used before the demotic.

Fig. 14. Ostracon of Themistokles Neokleous. P 17138. Not previously published.

Fig. 15. Ostracon of Themistokles Phrearrhios. P 18621. Not previously published. Note the use of the dative case.

Fig. 16. Ostracon of Themistokles. P 15498. Not previously published.

Fig. 17. Ostracon of Aristeides ho Lysimachou. P 16871. Not previously published.

Fig. 18. Ostracon of Eupolis ho Thoraieus. P 23059. Not previously published. The letter forms indicate an early fifth century B.C. date.

Fig. 19. Ostracon of Themistokles Neokleous with the word ITO added. AO 49. *Hesperia*, VII, 1938, pp. 233-234.

Fig. 20. Metrical ostracon of Xanthippos Arriphronos. P 16873. For bibliography see above footnote 8.

Fig. 21. Ostracon of Hippokrates with curse. P 15594. *Hesperia*, Suppl. VIII, p. 403, no. 18.

Fig. 22. Ostracon of Xanthippos Arriphronos written retrograde. P 4692. Not previously published. The patronymic was originally written with a single rho, but a second was later crowded in.

Fig. 23. Ostracon of Themistokles Phrearrhios, written boustrophedon. P 2441. Not previously published. Mentioned as a late example of boustrophedon writing by Henry R. Immerwahr in "Book Rolls on Attic Vases" p. 42, note 3 (the inventory number is wrongly given as P 2241). This article is in

Classical, Mediaeval and Renaissance Studies in Honor of Berthold Louis Ullman, ed. Charles Henderson, *Edizione di Storia e Letteratura,* 93, Rome, 1964.

Fig. 24. Ostracon of Themistokles Neokleous, written boustrophedon. P 19836. Not previously published. Mentioned by Immerwahr, *loc. cit.* above, under Fig. 23.

Fig. 25. Ostracon of Megakles Hippokratous written from the bottom up. P 17965. Not previously published. Notice the use of the dative case.

Fig. 26. Ostracon of Themistokles Phrearrhios with rambling script. P 5964. Not previously published. The writer wrote the name retrograde along the lower edge of the sherd then turned it around and started back with the demotic but doubled around again in a curious curl.

Fig. 27. Ostracon of Kallixenos Aristonymou. P 9967. *Hesperia,* XIX, 1950, p. 386, no. 19.

Fig. 28. Ostracon of a man from Cholargos (?). P 17222. Not previously published. The name in the first line seems to be in the accusative case and reads either—parea or—padea.

Fig. 29. Two joining ostraca of Kallixenos Aristonymou. At left P 17915 + P 19209; at right, P 22992. Neither has been previously published.

Fig. 30. Nine ostraca of Themistokles Neokleous from the big group found on the North Slope of the Acropolis: see *Hesperia,* VII, 1938, pp. 228-242. Top row, left to right, AO 122, AO 109, AO 95. Hand A. Characteristic are the crossed thetas and the dividing line separating name and patronymic. Middle row, AO 101, AO 27, AO 35. Hand E. Characteristic is the small writing with thin strokes and with the bottoms of the letters towards the outer edge of the sherd. Notice also the thetas with a single vertical stroke making them look like phis. Bottom row, AO 104, AO 77, AO 64. Hand C. Notice particularly the Y-shaped strokes inside the thetas.

Fig. 31. The big group of the Themistokles ostraca from the North Slope of the Acropolis as exhibited in the Stoa of Attalos Museum. *Hesperia,* VII, 1938, pp. 228-242. About 40% of the group is shown, including kylix bases (with a sample kylix in the middle), skyphos bases at the lower right, small bowls, imperfectly fired at the lower left, and various odd fragments on the second shelf up.

Fig. 32. Painted ostracon of Hyperbolos Antiphanous. P 12494. *Hesperia*, VIII, 1939, p. 246.

Fig. 33. Painted ostracon of Perikles Xanthippou. P 21527. *Hesperia*, XXI, 1952, p. 113 and XXII, 1953, p. 99.

Fig. 34. Ostracon of Themistokles Neokleous. P 15461. Not previously published. The patronymic was abbreviated.

Fig. 35. Ostracon of Themistokles Phrearrhios. P 5958. *Archaeology*, I, 1948, p. 81.

Fig. 36. Ostracon of Kallixenos Aristonymou with iota in the penult of the patronymic. P 15473. *Hesperia*, XIX, 1950, pp. 383-384, no. 12.

Fig. 37. Ostracon of Kallixenos of Xypete. P 15493. *Hesperia*, XIX, 1950, p. 388, no. 27.

Fig. 38. Ostracon of Kallixenos of Xypete with iota in the first syllable of the demotic. P 15600. *Hesperia*, XIX, 1950, p. 388, no. 26. The last three letters are on the other side of the sherd.

Fig. 39. Ostracon of Hippokrates Alkmeonidou with omega in the genitive ending. P 6885. Not previously published.

Fig. 40. Ostracon of Hippokrates Alkmeonidou with the genitive ending written out in full. P 17648.

Fig. 41. Ostracon of Aristeides Lysimachou Alopekethen with corrections. P 5976. Mentioned in *Hesperia*, V, 1936, p. 39, but not previously illustrated.

Fig. 42. Drawing of the ostracon illustrated in figure 41.

Fig. 43. Ostracon of Panaitios Agrylethen. P 19810. Not previously published. The letter forms suggest a date in the early fifth century B.C., probably the four eighties.

Fig. 44. Ostracon of Onomastos Konthyleus. P 17647. Not previously published. The circumstances of finding suggest that this ostracon is part of the scatter vote of the ostracophoria of 483 (?) B.C. See *Hesperia*, XVII, 1948, pp. 193-194.

Fig. 45. Ostracon of Kallixenos Aristonymou. P 2734. *Hesperia*, XV, 1946, p. 272, no. 8. A second inscription, the number 50, should belong to a previous use either of the sherd or of the kylix since there is no parallel for a number on an ostracon. See *Hesperia*, XXV, 1956, p. 20, under number 82.

Fig. 46. Ostracon of Kallixenos with portrait. P 7103. *Hesperia*, XIX, 1950, pp. 377 and 389, no. 29.

Fig. 47. Drawing of the ostracon illustrated in figure 46.

Fig. 48. Ostracon of Kallixenos the Alkmeonid. P 15799. *Hesperia*, XIX, 1950, pp. 377-378, and p. 389, no. 30.

Fig. 49. Ostracon of Kallixenos the Traitor. P 3786. *Hesperia*, XIX, 1950, pp. 378-379, and pp. 389-390, no. 32.

Fig. 50. Painted ostracon of Kallixenos. P 17960. *Hesperia*, XIX, 1950, pp. 379-381, and p. 390, no. 34.

Fig. 51. Ostracon of Kallias Kratiou. P 15706. Mentioned in *Hesperia*, Suppl. V, p. 141, under no. 29.

Fig. 52. Ostracon of Alcibiades the Elder. AO 194. *Hesperia*, IX, 1940, pp. 247-248, no. 296 and XXI, 1952, p. 2, no. 2.

Fig. 53. Ostracon of Alcibiades the Younger. P 7310. *Hesperia*, XXI, 1952, p. 3, no. 7.

Fig. 54. Ostracon of Alcibiades the Elder. P 18537. *Hesperia*, XXI, 1952, pp. 1-2, no. 1.

Fig. 55. Ostracon of Dieitrephes Euthoinou. P 27691. *Hesperia*, XXXVII, 1968, p. 118, no. 4.

Fig. 56. Ostracon of Kallias Didymiou. P 4622. *A.J.A.*, XXXIX, 1935, p. 179.

Fig. 57. Painted ostracon of Kallias Didymiou. P 5946. Not previously published.

Fig. 58. Ostracon of Kleophon Kleippidou Acharneus, P 27594. *Hesperia*, XXXVII, 1968, p. 120, no. 6.

Fig. 59. Ostracon of Phaiax Erasistratou Acharneus. P 373. Not previously published. The writer used the Ionic xi at the end of the name but apparently did not trust it to give the sound he wanted and added a sigma after it for good measure, remembering the old Attic chi sigma combination.

Fig. 60. Ostracon of Phaiax Erasistratou. P 17293. Not previously published.

Fig. 61. Ostracon of Hippokles Menippou. P 2948. Not previously published.

Fig. 62. Ostracon of Philinos Kleippidou. P 23548.

Fig. 63. Stamped decoration on the floor of the black-glazed cup-kotyle used as an ostracon of Philinos. See above on figure 62.

Fig. 64. Ostracon of Hyperbolos Antiphanous. P 18495. *Hesperia*, XVII, 1948, pp. 186-187; *Archaeology*, I, 1948, p. 81.

Fig. 65. Drawing of the inscription on the ostracon of Hyperbolos, fig. 64.

Fig. 66. Red-figured decoration on the floor of the cup used as an ostracon of Hyperbolos, see above on figure 64.

ILLUSTRATIONS

For notes on illustrations

see pages 245–50

1

2

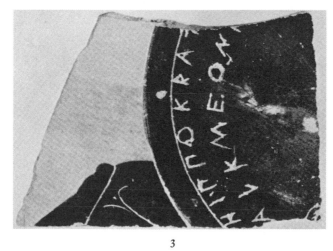

3

4

5

6

8

9

10

11

12

13

14

15

16

17

18

19

20

21

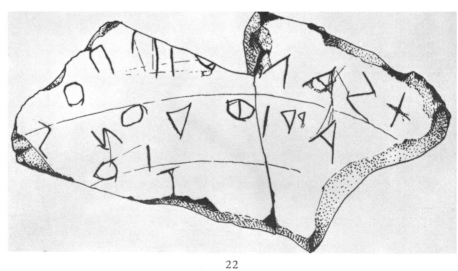

22

23

24

25

26

28

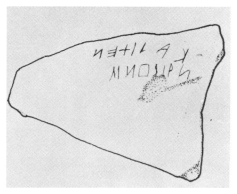

27

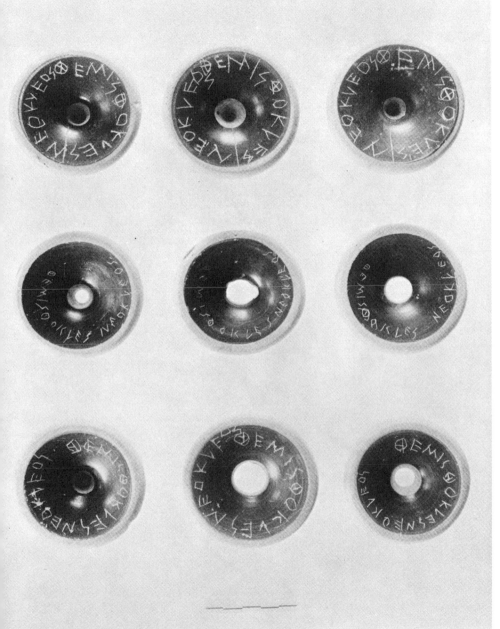

31

32

33

34

35

36

37

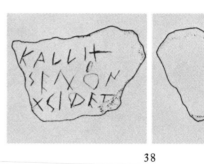

38

39

40

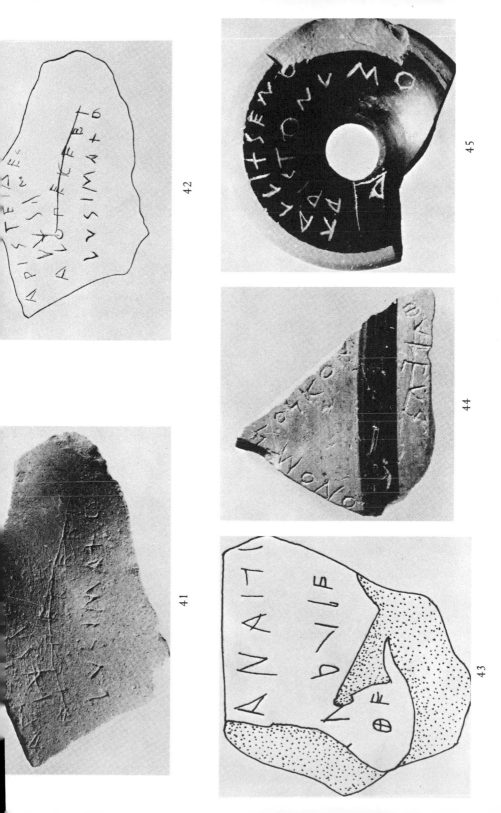

41

42

43

44

45

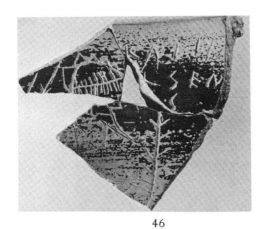

46

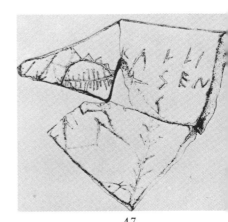

47

48

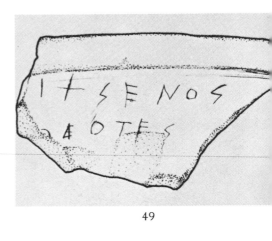

49

50

51

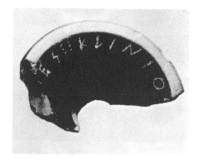

52

53

54

55

56

57

58

59

60

61

62

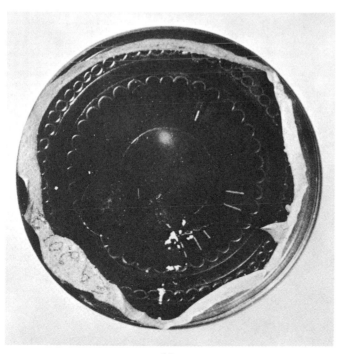

63

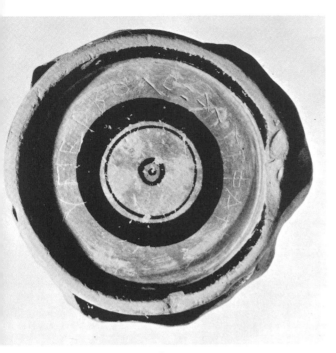

64

65

66

7

Titus Quinctius Flamininus

Philhellenism and *Realpolitik*

BY E. BADIAN

Delivered April 8 and 9, 1970

TITUS QUINCTIUS FLAMININUS

PHILHELLENISM AND *REALPOLITIK*

I

I T IS an honour to be asked to address you here, in what has become one of the most distinguished series of lectures in our field. Especially as, unlike some of my predecessors, I have no new discoveries to put before you: I am strictly a historian, that is to say a dealer in *crambe repetita*. However, our age—the age of image-makers and image-breakers; of Camelot and the credibility gap—is not one that needs to be told at length about the importance of the characters, aims and methods of politicians, and the image they reflect in the minds of their contemporaries and successors.

Granted that the task is worth the effort, there are few men in Roman history who more deserve the historian's scrutiny than T. Quinctius Flamininus. For it was he who laid down the principles of association between Rome and the Greeks of the Greek homeland and the lines on which Roman expansion in the East was to proceed. His importance was fully recognized in his own day: his statues abounded in the cities he had liberated;[1] he was the first Roman (and for a long time the only one) to whom a cult was established, which Plutarch still saw flourishing;[2] and he was one of the select few men of the middle Republic who was made the subject of one of Plutarch's *Lives* on the strength of all this.

I have been told that it is my duty, in this first lecture, to trace the historiography of my subject. Inevitably, within the limits imposed, I must do so in a cursory manner, especially since it would be wrong to confine the survey to learned works read only by the few; but the effort is in any case worth making, and the fate of a great man's fame has lessons to teach us about those who interpret it. I shall therefore proceed with my allotted task, picking out what points of interest I have time for.

Flamininus' memory seems to have faded in later antiquity, and renewed interest in him is surprisingly recent. In the fourth cen-

[1] See *RE*, s.v. 'Quinctius,' col. 1094; Chamoux, *BCH* 89, 1965, 214f.
[2] Plut. *Flam.* 16.

tury A.D., the author of the work *de uiris illustribus*, which survives among the works of Aurelius Victor, entered him as "Q. Flaminius" and, to make his error plain, described him as the son of the consul who fell at Trasimene (51). Although everyone of importance in and after the Renaissance read Plutarch and Livy (who suffice to disprove the story), this was accepted, wholly or partially, by a surprising number of the men who, right down to the nineteenth century, concerned themselves with Flamininus. Zedler's great German *Lexicon*, in the first half of the eighteenth century, lists him as "Flaminius" and, of course, merely reproduces a summary of the sources (basically Livy and Plutarch); and as late as 1842 the *Britannica* still manages to list him under the wrong name. But in the 18th century, in any case, there is no sign of ancient history in the modern sense. Such real interpretation as there was— Gibbon and his predecessors in his field, and the isolated figure of Beaufort, whom even Niebuhr originally did not know (or, at least, mention)—does not seem to have reached what we regard as the central periods of Roman history. The great *Encyclopédie* does not enter names as such; but one can pick him up (misnamed) under "Isthmiens, Jeux"—a summary of Livy's account of the great scene at the Isthmia of 196 (misdated 194) is prefaced with the remark that the Romans there pushed their generosity (or was it wise policy, the author wonders—but does not stay for an answer) to the furthest point by giving 'authentic freedom' to the whole of Greece.

One expects a time-lag between scholarship and encyclopaedias: we shall come back to this. But at the time, the experts were little better. Rollin's *Roman History* (part of his world history), hailed as a masterpiece in eighteenth-century France, where it began to appear (1739) shortly before his death and was completed by other hands after, was still reprinted, both in the original and in English translations, over a century later: generations learnt the history of Rome from it. Rollin does no more than to reproduce Livy, adding conventional laudations. The entry in Michaud's *Biographie universelle* (vol. 15, 1816) is clearly based on Rollin, laudations and all.

One cannot help feeling surprised at the long ignorance of, and at the absence of the least interest in, the period of Roman expan-

sion in the East and its central character, both among educated laymen and among scholars. Scipio Africanus (with no surviving *Life*
by Plutarch) was on everybody's lips.[3] He appears four times in
Dante,[4] as one of the conventional great Romans, set in parallel
even with Augustus. He gained entry—with many of Plutarch's
heroes—to Petrarch's book on famous men, and Petrarch wrote a
long heroic poem (the *Africa*) about him, in a fever of youthful
excitement. But not Flamininus. Machiavelli, who might well have
found something of interest in a scrutiny of Flamininus' career,
shows no interest in him.[5] And there appears to be no mention of
him in Bayle's *Dictionary*, in Bossuet, in Saint-Évremond, in Mon-
tesquieu—yet these men had their views on Roman history. In
England, the first edition of the *Encyclopaedia Britannica* (1768)
does not know him, though it knows Scipio. The third (completed
1797) for the first time has an entry, long and laudatory. It may
well be based on Rollin, but goes beyond him in an effort at historical interpretation; thus, of the Isthmian proclamation: "This
celebrated action procured the name of Patrons of Greece to the
Romans and insensibly paved the way to universal dominion." The
point was well taken, for an eighteenth-century gentleman. Naturally, he finds nothing wrong with the obvious political motive:
he takes it for granted, as Polybius did. It was left for a nineteenth-
century scholar to deny it. He concludes by stating that Flamininus
(if that *was* his name!) "had imitated with success the virtues of
his model Scipio": again the paramount place that Scipio had
usurped in the tradition is made clear. (Needless to say, the sources
provide no reason to credit him with taking Scipio for a model.)

The *Britannica* is worth following a little further. Like all encyclopaedias, it expects a certain longevity from its articles, especially those not dealing with scientific discovery; and though this

[3] For the complicated question of the *Lives* of the two Scipios, see (most conveniently) Ziegler, *RE*, s.v. 'Plutarchos,' coll. 696f., 895f., 949f. These *Lives*, in
any case, disappeared early and cannot have been known even to the earliest
mediaeval scholars.
[4] *Inf.* 31, 116; *Purg.* 29, 116 (with Augustus); *Par.* 6, 53 (with Pompey);
27, 61. (Dante did not know Plutarch: see Ziegler. *op.cit.* 949.)
[5] Machiavelli was specially interested in Plutarch. See the letter quoted by
R. Ridolfi, *Vita di Niccolò Machiavelli*[2] (1954), 88 and n. 18 (p. 404). He clearly
used the parallel *Philopoemen* (*Princ.* 14: cf. *Philop.* 4). Yet he has only incidental
references to Flamininus, none profound (*Princ.* 24; *Disc.* 2, 4 [=*Livy* 32,34];
letter of Dec. 20th, 1514 [Alvisi 155], to Francesco Vettori [=Livy 35,49, *fin.*]).

aspect has recently been increasingly criticized, it is by no means new. One effect of this is to increase the time-lag between scholarly controversy or discovery and its reflection in the encyclopaedia article: at times, it will entirely obscure what has come and gone before any editor got round to noticing it. Of course, small revisions are made, especially if they shorten the entry—as editors remind their contributors in stern advisory notices. And small revisions can be revealing. The best example of this, perhaps, is not in the *Britannica*, but in the *Americana*, which deserves a moment's attention.

Francis Lieber's great first edition (1831, modelled on the latest Brockhaus in his native Germany) does not include an entry for Flamininus—which is characteristic, as we have seen. It is also unfortunate. The pupil of Niebuhr and friend of Ranke, penetrating thinker and (at his best) superb writer, would have been well fitted to write an interesting article, had he himself been interested. Our hero's first appearance in America, however, was reserved—as far as I can see—for Appleton's *New American Cyclopaedia* (1860). The short and factual entry is significant only for one sentence: "By pretending that his object was to remove from Greece the Macedonian yoke [was this written by a German?] he detached many of the Greek states from Philip." This appeared in the new edition of 1873. In 1903 (as far as I have been able to trace it) the *Americana* was revived by Frederick Converse Beach. However, his introduction ignores all previous American efforts in the field. Surveying encyclopaedias from "Zeidler" [*sic*: surely at second hand!] to the *Britannica*, he regretfully concluded that none of them were useful for Americans or for anyone outside the leisured upper class: he was therefore publishing an original American encyclopaedia, written entirely by "specialists" who "are not only experts but brilliant writers as well." After all this, it is sad to see that the entry on Flamininus is almost a verbatim reproduction of that in the Appleton *Cyclopaedia*, including the sentence quoted. In 1911 a new *Americana* appeared, now published by the *Scientific American* and still edited by Beach. His introductory claims are even more bombastic: he has been assisted by more than two thousand of the most eminent scholars and authorities in America and Europe; the work is again entirely new (not even a reference to his own effort of 1903) and "no existing source of information has been relied upon" [*sic*]. On his authors' stylistic merits, he waxes quite lyrical. However: the entry on Flamininus is unchanged. As a matter of fact, it had a great future. The new *Americana* became established and in due course proudly announced its early nineteenth-century foundation; the article on Flamininus was touched up in style (the Teutonicism eliminated), and a new endpiece written to cover Titus' career after his return to Rome from his campaign. But there, essentially, it still is, a hack piece of mid-nineteenth-century compilation, with only one really major change: for "pretending," somewhere along the way, someone substituted "promising." The last trace of individuality was eliminated.[6]

Let us return to the *Britannica*. The next major edition was the seventh (1842). The entry is entirely rewritten (the subject called "Flaminius"), in an exuberantly laudatory style keeping, in parts, almost *verbatim* to the sources: "The mildness of his manners, his affability, and constant regard to the strict rules of justice gained him the hearts of all who approached him." The only flaw is the mission to Prusias that led to Hannibal's death—it is better not to believe it. "We would fain believe that he did not tarnish his character by conduct so utterly unworthy of it." The rewriting was not worth the effort: verbose and uncritical, the entry is no improvement on that of fifty years earlier. It is significant only in showing, in simple and naive form, a kind of wishful thinking that appears, at a more sophisticated level, in some later scholarly writing and that, as we shall see, is still found in present-day work and helps to make the subject of our investigation significant in the study of the scholarly—and the human—mind. In fact, the article was soon felt to be unsatisfactory: in the eighth edition (1855) it is withdrawn and a stopgap substituted. German scholarship was penetrating.

It is interesting that all this could be going on in England at a

---

[6] On Lieber, see *Dict. of Amer. Biogr.* 11, 236f. On the Appleton *Cyclopaedia*, see R. Collison, *Encyclopaedias*[2] (1966), 187f.; on the *Americana*, ibid. 184— inaccurate and unhelpful (e.g., the 1903 edition has been altogether missed). Charles A. Dana's editorship of the *Cyclopaedia* provides a distant connection with Buffalo! I should like to thank my friend Professor G. W. Bowersock for helping me with some dusty researches into encyclopaedias—a subject that repays further study.

[Added in proof: The 1970 edition of the *Americana* has come up with a new—signed—article; unfortunately no real improvement on its long-lived predecessor.]

time when even the art of the encyclopaedia, in Germany, had already reached professional standards that have perhaps never been surpassed. It was in 1813—just before the Battle of Leipzig, he tells us—that J. S. Ersch was commissioned by the publisher J. F. Gleditsch, of that city, to edit a general encyclopaedia of the arts and sciences. The result—after an intermission caused by international events—was the *Allgemeine Encyklopädie* edited by Ersch and J. G. Gruber: a work that Collison[7] has rightly called "the greatest Western encyclopaedia ever attempted," even though, like other great human endeavours, it was never completed. The article on Flamininus, in volume 45 of the first Section (published 1847), covers eleven double-column pages; and though it is obvious that some interpretations that we take for granted (and that in fact rest on combination) are not yet known to the author, he has very thoroughly collected the evidence available to him and built up a complex and sophisticated picture: perhaps over-impressed by the laudatory passages in Plutarch on Titus' justice, gentleness and Hellenic culture, the author notes that he was not above taking action contrary to humanity or morality where the interests of Rome appeared to require it; and he makes this unquestioning Roman patriotism the keynote of Titus' character, and the winning of the Greeks to Roman rule his real achievement. Presumably this may be taken as representing the state of German academic opinion about the middle of the century, just before Mommsen began writing.

The entry in Ersch and Gruber is undoubtedly the best treatment in a non-specialist work ever attempted. There is no proof that, in this respect or in others, the *Britannica* took any notice. But German scholarship as such, *via* British scholarship, was bound to have an indirect effect, even on an institution not given to learning from its peers. The great ninth edition (1878) presents a new and more professional article, written by a scholar clearly familiar with

---

[7] *Op.cit.* 182. Though his history of this work is mostly accurate, as far as I have been able to check it, he fails to mention Gleditsch, the optimistic publisher who stimulated its inception. Around 1831 the work—inevitably!—was taken over by F. A. Brockhaus. The volumes concerned give no explanation of the change. Gruber's introduction to vol. 2 is worth reading as an attempt to classify and subdivide human knowledge: like the work as a whole, it is (though a failure) a magnificent monument of the human spirit.

recent scholarly work on the subject. (We shall meet his sources in detail later.) After a competent survey, he makes his own views plain in his summing up: "There seems no doubt that Flamininus was actuated by a genuine love of Greece and its people. To attribute to him a Machiavellian policy . . . is absurd and disingenuous. There is more force in the charge that his Hellenic sympathies prevented him from seeing the innate weakness and mutual jealousies of the Greek states of that period, whose only hope of peace and safety lay in submitting to the protectorate of the Roman Republic." The liberation of Greece, if a mistake, "was a noble and generous mistake, and reflects nothing but honour on the name of Flamininus." You may be puzzled by that word "disingenuous": it may be *absurd* to believe in the Machiavellian policy; but why "disingenuous"? The answer is illuminating; but permit me to mystify you a little longer.

The entry survives unchanged into the next major edition (the eleventh, of 1911). In the next full edition (the fourteenth: 1929) it is still there, with only one or two small changes: the words "and disingenuous" have been removed, as has the final statement about the noble mistake. One would like to think that this was done by a man of good taste and good sense, aware of what had been written by scholars in the preceding fifty years; alas, I suspect it was due to the Editor's usual injunction to save some space on unimportant entries. In any case, in this new form, the article written for the 1878 edition survived the Second World War as it had the First, and was still there in 1962, unaffected by nearly a century of scholarship.

It is only in the last few years that a signed article by a major scholar (H. H. Scullard) has been substituted.[8] The surprising feature of it is that it still draws heavily, in spirit, on its superseded predecessor: "His idealistic philhellenic policy had been implemented with great skill in diplomacy and war, and he had enabled the Romans to establish a protectorate over an autonomous Greece, *whose local jealousies he may have underestimated*" (my italics:

[8] Since the *Britannica* no longer produces numbered editions, but "markets" its product annually, with slight changes each year and trade-in offers for used sets, it has become practically impossible to see each year's "model," and I may be a year or so out. I first found Scullard's article in the 1964 edition.

compare the ninth edition, quoted above).[9] This is where the *Britannica*—i.e., educated non-specialist opinion in English-speaking countries—stands today, unaffected by waves of controversy over Flamininus' character and policies, of which the general reader can find no inkling. What is perhaps most surprising is the lack of any reference to Scullard's own considered scholarly judgment. Let me quote from his great work on this period: "Shallow and vain, ambitious and domineering, he lacked that soundness of character and loftiness of soul which were felt by all who came into personal contact with Africanus."[10] The bland tradition of the encyclopaedia has covered it all, leaving no trace of critical evaluation.

With this by way of transition,[11] let us turn to the scholars. Flamininus was bound to arouse the interest of Niebuhr, the first and one of the greatest. Niebuhr was an eighteenth-century gentleman, with a good deal of political experience in the Napoleonic wars; when he chose to be critical, he had no illusions. He speaks of Flamininus' "policy of making the Greeks little and the Aetolians weak," and he duly notes fear of Antiochus as a motive for the "liberation." After enunciating the strange notion that the Romans ought really to have established a federally constituted state in Greece, he continues by observing that their "only thought was how they might reduce those countries to a state of dependence."[12] As a realistic historian, he takes this for granted and implies no disapproval. And as (in part) influenced by Hegel—it is here that the influence of Hegel begins to appear—he knows that Rome

[9] No argument is advanced for this statement, and it is difficult to see on what it can be based, except for the Mommsen tradition as reflected in the earlier *Britannica*.

[10] *Roman Politics* (1951), 101. Cf. 120: "Flamininus was more vain, shallow and pretentious, seeking applause and intriguing for power, consumed by ambition." And see n. 45 (below) with text: Scullard has in fact done much for our understanding of Flamininus.

[11] There are, of course, many other encyclopaedias one might look at, and I have looked at all those accessible and intelligible to me, in German, Spanish, Italian, Greek and Russian. But this enquiry must be limited to what is characteristic and what affected the English-speaking tradition. Unfortunately I did not have access to the early editions of the German Brockhaus, on which the original *Americana* is based. (Later issues contain nothing of any importance.) The *Italiana*, which is so often valuable on Classical subjects, has a disappointing article by De Sanctis, based on his equally disappointing treatment in *Storia dei Romani* 4, 1.

[12] *Lectures on Ancient History* (ed. and transl. L. Schmitz, 1852), 3, 392f.

was destined for conquest by the *Zeitgeist* and applauds Flamininus as its instrument, while full of contempt for the contemporary Greeks, whose degeneracy was one of the axioms of Hegel himself. Niebuhr heaps scorn on the Aetolians, "a people whose territory was not larger than the canton of Bern, and who yet could have been mad enough to think themselves the equals of the Romans."[13] The cause of this madness is "the character of the southern nations who, though unable to do anything, fancy that they can do everything." (He fails to tell us why the difference of about three degrees of latitude between Rome and Aetolia should be decisive in this respect.) Flamininus is highly praised for his moderation in responding to this insufferable arrogance of the weak unconscious of their proper station: "it was lucky for the Greeks that in spirit and education he was a Greek"—in proof of which, the epigrams quoted by Plutarch are adduced.[14] "Any other general, who was not actuated by that love of the Greeks, . . . would have regarded such conduct very differently. Flamininus . . . had the glorious mission to deliver Greece." He goes on, in this very context, to admit that the Romans were "by no means just" towards the Aetolians, who were entitled to the cities that Philip had taken from them; but "Quinctius Flamininus, at least, seems to have acted from very pure motives."[15]

It is sad to see the pioneer of scientific history a prey to absorbed Hegelian prejudices, interrupted by twinges of conscience. The result is that enthusiasm for the generous victor can totally blind him to the facts that he knew as well as anyone. "This noble moment of enthusiasm," he says of the Isthmian proclamation, "afforded Greece a happy period of fifty years."[16] Nor is this a casual lapse:

[13] *Lectures on Roman History* (Transl. Chepmell and Demmler, 1855), 2, 160. This passage is not in Schmitz's third edition (n. 15, below).

[14] *Ibid.* 162. This same "southern vanity" appears as an object of pity rather than blame in *Lectures on Ancient History* (n. 12, above), 3, 392.

[15] *Lectures on the History of Rome*[3] (ed. and transl. L. Schmitz, 1853), 2, 170f. On the Senate's Greek policy he makes the singular statement that "it would be unfair to inquire into their motives"!

[16] Ibid. 171-2. The twinge of conscience appears sporadically in Niebuhr's treatment of this question. Cf. the remark about Antiochus, and especially, in *Lectures on Anc. Hist.*, 3, 397, the admission that "serious history" must concede that Flamininus could and should have overthrown Nabis in 194. It is clear that Niebuhr realised that his benevolence (see n. 15) was an unaccustomed departure from serious history.

he goes on to comment what a long span fifty years constitute in a human lifetime. Polybius must have turned in his grave.

It would have been interesting to have Droysen's considered views on our subject. Droysen, of course, was much more of a convinced Hegelian than Niebuhr would ever have admitted to being and was on the side of the future against the past.[17] But he totally rejected the German idealization of Classical Greece, to which Hegel had never demurred. He regarded it as "utopian and unhistorical"; he disapproved of a biological model in which the flowering of Classical beauty was followed by "nothing more than fading and degradation, nothing but an age of barrenness, of nauseous putrefaction."[18] Unfortunately his account stopped at the Roman conquest. Perhaps he could not reconcile his two opposed premises and—like Mommsen, who could not kill off his Caesar— could not bear to see his Hellenistic world overrun by the barbarians; particularly since it was a necessary step in God's purpose and, being on the side of the future, he could not have disapproved.

Mommsen's views are on record, and were momentous.[19] He inherited Niebuhr's picture of Flamininus as the Greek by inclination and education, who brought Greece fifty years of happiness by acting, from the purest motives, in the spirit of the age. Unlike Niebuhr, he was not blinded to the facts of those years. He therefore proceeded to stand the picture on its head. Since, clearly, there were *no* fifty years of happiness, Flamininus could *not* have been fulfilling the demands of the *Zeitgeist*. He thus becomes a sentimental Hellenist, causing nothing but confusion and suffering, by well-intentioned, but anti-historical, generosity. It is interesting to see how the mistaken idea, causing insuperable antinomies, clamours to be stood on its head: we shall see it happening to Mommsen's own. To Mommsen, expanding Niebuhr, Flamininus "be-

[17] "Sie wissen schon, dass ich Verehrer der Bewegung und des Vorwärts bin; Cäsar, nicht Cato, Alexander und nicht Demosthenes. . . ." (to F. G. Welcker, *Briefwechsel* (ed. R. Hübner, 1929), 1, 66f.).

[18] *Gesch. des Hellenismus*[2] 3, 1 (1878), 173. The geological model that he substituted may not strike the modern reader as much more successful: with the "granite shell" of the Classical age breaking up, "a new soil for richer and more varied development of life begins to form" (ibid. 177). This illustrates the point made in the text, that he could never really fit the Hellenistic age as he saw it into the rather naive Hegelian view of world history that he had chosen to adopt.

[19] References are to vol. 3 of the 1881 edition of Dickson's translation of the *History of Rome*.

longed to the younger generation who began to lay aside the patriotism as well as the habits of their forefathers and, though not unmindful of their fatherland, were still more mindful of themselves and of Hellenism." He opines that it would have been better for Greece if the Roman commander there had been one "who would not amidst literary and artistic reminiscences have overlooked the pitiful condition of the constitutions of the Hellenic states; and who, while treating Hellas according to its deserts, would have spared the Romans the trouble of striving after unattainable ideals."[20] The bitterness of the disappointed German intellectual of 1848 could not speak more clearly: we remember that the *History* was begun in 1850. On the Isthmian declaration, having learnt from his study of the facts and his experience of 1848, he says: "Thoughtful men perhaps asked whether freedom was a blessing capable of being thus bestowed, and what was the value of freedom to a nation apart from union and unity."[21] In the end he defends Flamininus' character and Roman motives (on which this extraordinary interpretation hinges) in a passage of eloquent invective, which shows the strength of his personal involvement—and perhaps the weakness of his case, as he may have suspected it: "It is only contemptuous disingenuousness or weakly sentimentality which can fail to perceive that the Romans were entirely in earnest in their liberation of Greece; and the reason why the plan so nobly projected resulted in so wretched a structure is to be sought only in the complete moral and political disorganization of the Hellenic nation."[22] That ineffectual plan for freedom, nobly conceived, but failing owing to the moral and political disorganization of the nation concerned, is surely one of the most startling examples of history seen in the distorting mirror of the emotionally charged present. It is small wonder that, on completing the work, Mommsen confessed: "I have put what is best and most individual in me into this book."[23] And no wonder that the educated German public found

[20] 240.

[21] 247. Note the way in which the author's reflections are potentially attributed to the characters in the action—a Classical feature of the *History* that helps to make it more enjoyable reading and less reliable history. His summary is worth quoting: "History has a nemesis for every sin—for an impotent craving after freedom as well as for injudicious generosity."

[22] 251f.

[23] Letter quoted by Wucher, *Theodor Mommsen* (1956), 21.

it to its taste. Mommsen, taking Flamininus as he had found him in Niebuhr, could not get away from his (at that time) frequently expressed longing for the firm Prussian jackboot. He had no patience with sophisticated political methods, having experienced their failure, and no sympathy with the defeated; he could not approve of weak scruples in carrying out the God-given task, in creating what the *Zeitgeist* demanded for the ultimate happiness of those concerned. Thus he both created and condemned the figure of Flamininus, the honest but ineffectual sentimentalist. Niebuhr's highly benevolent despot had passed the Hegelian test; Mommsen's weak romantic failed it. At any rate, it was the same test. Thus the figure of Flamininus the sentimentalist had entered scholarly controversy, and had become "relevant" beyond its restricted circle, with an *éclat* in which that great showman would have delighted.

We shall see that Mommsen's was not the only possible interpretation in the light of contemporary experience. His outburst implies the wide acceptance of a more critical interpretation. It is difficult to trace this, as it was probably propounded in lecture-rooms rather than written down in major works. I have found an interesting example of it in an unpremeditated aside by an eminent historian who spent his early years lecturing on ancient history, though (as far as I know) he never wrote a book on this subject. Friedrich von Raumer, writing to Boeckh at the very time when Mommsen was composing his *History*, says:[24] "Titus Quinctius Flamininus was even then using language to disguise truth—like Talleyrand later." A more political approach to the events concerned was obviously not unknown among practising historians. (We must remember that Mommsen, at this time, had had very little training as a historian.) However, Raumer, while eminent and influential,[25] did not write his views down for public consumption, while Mommsen's *History* won immediate acclaim. Between 1861 and 1866, only a few years after it appeared, it was translated into English. And perhaps we may now, for a moment, return to the odd item in the 1878 *Britannica*, which charges certain views with being "disingenuous." I think we can now solve that minor mystery.

[24] Raumer (ed.), *Antiquarische Briefe* (1851), 140.
[25] The most convenient summary of his career and discussion of his importance is in the *Allgemeine Deutsche Biographie* 27 (1888), 403-14.

The word (you may remember) is used by Mommsen's translator, about a decade earlier, in a similar context: "contemptible disingenuousness." Needless to say, it is a slight mistranslation (Mommsen has "Unredlichkeit"), such as we all know will assist the *Quellenforscher*. The word, thus treated, survived in the *Britannica* for a long time: a fitting tribute to Mommsen's overwhelming influence, for good and ill. The whole treatment due to him, as we also observed, survived even longer, indeed for nearly a century; and its echo is recognizably present in the *Britannica* right up to the present day.

In Germany, Mommsen's passionate oversimplification naturally caused scholarly opposition. Again, a wrong judgment was easily stood on its head. Just as it had been clear to Mommsen that the fifty years following the Isthmian proclamation had not been a period of unclouded happiness (hence the need to invert one of the mainstays of Niebuhr's judgment), so it was clear to anyone who looked at the evidence that Flamininus was by no means a naive romantic: inversion of Mommsen's main argument was tempting. Was Flamininus a double-dyed villain, foreseeing and indeed planning the turmoil that was to come in the next fifty years, and perhaps even the Roman annexation after? This, more or less, was the conclusion of Karl Peter, who, in 1863, wrote an essay in reply to Mommsen's view, which he entitled "The Machiavellian policy of the Romans in the time from the end of the Second Punic War down to the Gracchi." In this he sets out to show that the Romans, during the whole of this period, were both imperialistic and cruel, and that they cloaked these vices in a pretence of justice and mercy. He has a good case at times (as, presumably, he would in a lengthy period of any nation's history), especially in the period around the Third Macedonian War. As far as Flamininus is concerned, he does—despite obvious exaggeration of villainous planning—make some valid points: thus, that the war against Nabis was stopped in order to prevent the Achaean League from becoming too strong (though this is perhaps not the whole story).[26] But Mommsen's

[26] The suggestion that the freedom of the Greeks was deliberately proclaimed in order to ensure constant quarrels among them and constant recourse to the Senate is patently absurd and must have helped to ensure the rejection of Peter's views as a whole. He also denies that Flamininus did any more than carry out the Senate's policy, concluding that personal praise for him is irrelevant: this again

History was a passionate masterpiece, while Peter's study was dry and dull—as indeed was the rather superficial *History of Rome*, which he wrote about the same time (1853-69). Mommsen remained in possession.

He had more serious opposition to face, when Wilhelm Ihne produced one of the great Roman histories of the century (rewritten in English by the author himself, 1871-2). His preface to volume 5 is to be recommended as a survey of some of the problems of evidence and interpretation that the ancient historian has to face. Unlike Peter, he genuinely admired Mommsen, and shared with him a passionate rejection of any Rankean claim to total objectivity in historical writing: "A man incapable of feeling sympathy or aversion should not deal with the investigation, certainly not with the delineation, of the acts of moral agents. He may be fit to examine and describe stones [the reference, presumably, is to petrology, not to epigraphy], flowers, or acids, he may solve mathematical problems; but not the great moral problems which are presented by the actions of men."[27] Needless to say, Ihne's history is often sagacious and rarely dull. On Flamininus, his judgment is a masterpiece of balanced exposition, to which any reader will always remain indebted. On this as on other matters, it is time more notice were taken of Ihne's work, and less of Mommsen's *History*, which is—at least for the working historian—the least important of his contributions. Flamininus, says Ihne, "understood the Greek character, and was not inaccessible, like so many other Romans, to Greek views and opinions. But it is a great error to attribute to him . . . a predilection or partiality for the Greeks; a partiality which overruled the calculations of disinterested statesmanship, and made political considerations to depend on sentiment. It is a great error to suppose that he was induced by mere generosity and good will for the Greeks to make concessions which were not entirely in harmony with the interests of Rome. He proved himself throughout to be a cool, clear-headed statesman, keeping always in view the solid

---

seems mere reaction against current views and casts doubt on Peter's real understanding of the whole subject.

[27] P. vii. He goes on to defend himself against the charge of being anti-Roman, stressing that he merely refuses to pay indiscriminate tribute to everything Roman.

advantage of his own country."[28] We might perhaps add, with Polybius: "and his own personal advantage"; but there is no doubt that, both in this general judgment and in his judgment on particular incidents in the story, Ihne is worthy of serious attention by the modern scholar, a century later.

Unlike that of the Germans, nineteenth-century French opinion was not given to hero-worship of Flamininus; perhaps because the tradition of naive philhellenism had never been so strong in that country, perhaps even because the French were politically more mature in their own experience and had had enough hero-worship in their recent history. The standard mid-nineteenth-century history of Rome, by V. Duruy (himself a scholar and educationist, with political experience),[29] was translated into English under Mahaffy's supervision and published both in Britain and in America (1883). His facts concerning Flamininus are not always quite accurate, and his views are firmly hostile, deliberately directed against Mommsen (although he is never named). "Titus Quinctius Flamininus . . . was . . . a member of one of those noble families who had already begun to set themselves above the laws. [He gives no evidence for this judgment.] A good general, a better statesman, pliant and crafty, a Greek rather than a Roman, he represented that new generation who were abandoning ancestral tradition and adopting foreign manners. Flamininus was the true author of that Machiavellian policy which gave up Greece defenceless into the hands of the legions."[30] Larousse's *Grand Dictionnaire Universel*, one of the

[28] 3, 40. In a footnote Ihne defiantly and confidently leaves the reader to make his own reasoned choice between his view and that of Mommsen, part of which he quotes.

[29] He was Minister of Education from 1863 to 1869 and did much to reform French primary and secondary education, against opposition from the Church and the Emperor. See the short entry in the *Encyclopaedia Britannica*. (The *Dictionnaire de Biographie nationale* has not quite reached him yet.) His history of Rome is a French reply to Mommsen.

[30] 2, 1, 99. This provides another interesting example of how a flagrant misinterpretation can be stood on its head and indeed invites this treatment. Compare Duruy's statement quoted in the text with Mommsen (3,240): "He belonged to the younger generation who began to lay aside the patriotism as well as the habits of their forefathers and, though not unmindful of their fatherland, were still more mindful of themselves and Hellenism." It is clear that where Mommsen admired, though (as a historian) he felt obliged to disapprove, Duruy sees nothing but cosmopolitan degeneracy with its deleterious effect on character. The misinterpretation of the facts is carried far beyond Mommsen, and the political passion is equal.

triumphs of nineteenth-century lexicography, is even more out-spoken and takes the "Machiavellian view" to extremes: Rome was afraid of a united Greece, and Flamininus' purpose was simply to split Greece up and sow discord, in order to prepare future an-nexation. He is described as "a good general, but above all a skilful, supple and cunning politician."[31] It was against the background of this critical tradition that the modern historical study of Flamininus and the conquest of Greece took shape and should be understood.[32]

In England, during this period, there is not much to report. The only major historian of Rome, Thomas Arnold, did not get around to dealing with Rome's expansion in the East. Later histories—typically Pelham's *Outlines of Roman History*—mostly take a moderate and sensible line, admitting the genuine admiration of Flamininus and men like him for Hellas and its culture, but recog-nising the basically political nature of the decisions taken. The Oxford and Cambridge dons who wrote on these subjects in the heyday of British Classical education and British imperialism were not carried away to improbable extremes of either enthusiasm or condemnation: the Ionian Islands were a vivid lesson in the pos-sible difference between philhellenism and sentimental policy.[33] However, no really original or significant contribution to the problem seems to have emerged.

In America, 1914 saw the publication of Tenney Frank's *Roman Imperialism*—like most of Tenney Frank's work, idiosyncratic, written mostly from the sources (sometimes read in translation) and with little contact with the mainstream of international schol-arly discussion, especially as written in foreign languages; and, like most of his work, divided between the obviously wrong-headed

[31] The influence of Duruy is obvious; but the author may have read Peter, the only major proponent of this "Machiavellian" view.

[32] Of course, there were different views in France as well. The Didot *Biographie générale* (17,1856) follows, at much greater length, the platitudes of Michaud's *Biographie universelle*—the kind of striking "generic tradition" that we noticed in the case of the *Britannica* and that tends to give encyclopaedic works a ghostly life of their own.

[33] I owe the reference to this parallel to E. D. Steele, of the University of Leeds. See his "Gladstone and Ireland," *Proc. of the Leeds Phil. and Lit. Soc., Lit. and Hist. Section* 14, 1 (1970), 14f. ("Like so many Englishmen of his class in that day, he was a cultured philhellene, but nevertheless considered that the island-ers would be better off as subjects of Queen Victoria" (p. 15). Cf. the long quota-tion from Gladstone's speech of December 16th, 1858, in note 97.)

and the flash of insight illuminating the obviously true. The chapter dealing with the Second Macedonian War and its consequences is entitled "Sentimental Politics": it was Tenney Frank who took this interpretation from Mommsen and popularised it in the English-speaking world. He begins his summary at the end of that chapter with the statement: "It is the fashion to call Flamininus an impractical sentimentalist."[34] It is clear that he had done little serious reading on the subject apart from Mommsen. As we have seen, Mommsen's view never even got near gaining a monopoly among scholars; and the translation of Duruy (not to mention various works from England, minor but well-balanced) should have been available in this country. However, we must presumably take Frank's word for what was fashionable in American lecture-rooms of the time. If so, it shows how little contact with European scholarship (even German) had at that time been established. Frank in fact accepts the view he regards as "fashionable," merely adding that the "generous impulse" on which the policy was based was that of the Senate as a whole, not that of Flamininus alone: it "forgot to count the cost or weigh the consequences." He returns to the tradition of Niebuhr and Mommsen by explaining that "it was not the Senate's fault that the Greeks no longer possessed the capacity to use the gift they had received." This is as perverse as the "Machiavellian" Senate, and by blindly following Mommsen (at least in part through ignorance of the opposition arguments) Frank unfortunately gave the "sentimental policy" a long run in school and university teaching, thereby counterbalancing the wholesome effects of other portions of his book.

Among much else that Frank did not know was a work by a French scholar that had appeared nearly a decade before his own and that (in its preface) had explicitly set itself the task of surveying the different views on Flamininus and Rome's eastern policy and arriving at a judgment. It was in 1905 that G. Colin published his immense tome on Rome and the Greeks in the first half of the

---

[34] 157. He continues: "and there is little doubt that his enthusiasm for the old Greek cry of liberty somewhat blinded him to the larger political needs"—as conceived, obviously, by Mommsen. Note, i.a., the mistranslation of a simple piece of Polybian Greek (Pol. 18, 47, 2) on p. 158, making a statement of alleged fact into a programme. That rendering is found in Shuckburgh.

second century.[35] He amply documents cultural philhellenism in Rome around 200 B.C. and is inclined to accept its influence on policy. In fact, his appreciation of Flamininus is quite generous, though without blindness for his overriding political purpose: indeed, Colin's error was (as Holleaux was later to point out) to antedate and overestimate Rome's imperialistic intentions in the East. But he believes that the Greek cities are better treated than (e.g.) Iberian tribesmen, not to mention Carthage. He also makes the important and (on the whole) valid point—which Tenney Frank, had he known it, would have found congenial—that, while suspicious of great powers, Rome by now had no reason to fear small states, so that generosity did not conflict with political interest. Flamininus therefore eliminated any possibility of suspicion by establishing a balance of powerless states in Greece: by refusing to increase the power of the (at that time) loyal Aetolian allies in the north to the extent that they had expected (i.e. to enable them to take the place of Macedon), or that of the loyal Achaean allies by fighting Nabis to a finish. In fact, this is the "policy of keeping Greece little and the Aetolians weak" that Niebuhr, at his best, had recognised. Like Niebuhr (though in much greater detail and with immense erudition), Colin depicts this as the foundation on which Roman benevolence could then be exercised. His greatest merit, perhaps, is to have drawn attention for the first time (as far as I can see) to the almost inevitable misunderstanding between Greeks and Romans about their respective status: the Romans would take it as a matter of course that the gratitude of the Greeks for their liberation implied future obedience, while the Greeks regarded it as equally natural that the Romans should protect their freedom without expecting anything in particular in return. He rightly notes[36] how Flamininus' letter to Chyretiae takes for granted a right to issue binding instructions and combines this with the statement that the author (or is it Rome?) wants nothing but gratitude and glory—indeed a revealing passage. If I may add a personal note: I came to this work after I had begun to form my own ideas on clientship as a category of Roman thinking in foreign policy;

[35] *Rome et la Grèce de 200 à 146 av. J.-C.*
[36] 169f. For the document, see Sherk, *Roman Documents from the Greek East* (1969), no. 33.

and I found that Colin had, without making that particular connection, for the first time discerned a pattern that I considered valid and important and drawn the right general conclusion about Roman motivations and some of the sources of misunderstanding between Rome and the Greeks.[37]

About the same time Maurice Holleaux was beginning his own researches, which came to be the climax of achievement in the study of these problems. He combined hitherto unparalleled mastery of the evidence (both literary and epigraphical: he did much original work on both), and a characteristic gift for patient and minute analysis of it, with the great historian's ability to see a significant pattern and make it stand out clearly from the accumulation of detail inevitable in serious investigation. Colin had had brilliant intuitions; but his use and scrutiny of evidence left much to be desired, and his important points tended to be diluted in irrelevance. Holleaux was—and, in fact, must remain—unsurpassed in method, in logic and in style.[38] It was fortunate that the editors of the *Cambridge Ancient History* called on him to write the chapters on the Macedonian and Syrian Wars in the eighth volume of that work (1930), with the result that, while much of the history of the Roman Republic in that series is now of largely (shall we say) "historical" interest, these chapters are not likely to be superseded, as far as the English-speaking student is concerned.[39]

Holleaux's main contribution was to a somewhat wider field than concerns us here: that of Roman imperialism in the East.[40] But he naturally often touched on Flamininus, and he devoted one outstanding detailed investigation to him, in 1923.[41] In this, by

[37] Scholars are still making this discovery and claiming it as their own. See, e.g., C. B. Welles, *JJP* 15, 1965, 29 (unaware of all the work done on this question): "I believe that this misunderstanding has been too little emphasized in modern times."

[38] I still believe what I wrote a few years ago (*Studies in Greek and Roman History* (1964), viif.): that his "work on the relations of the Roman Republic with the East will never be improved, except in details to which he did not attend or through the discovery of evidence unknown to him."

[39] For the scholar, they have been superseded by Louis Robert's corrected and annotated edition of the original French text in volume 5, part 2, of Holleaux's *Études d'Épigraphie et d'Histoire grecques* (1957).

[40] For an assessment, concluding that Holleaux's analysis has stood up to all attacks, see Walbank, *JRS* 53, 1963, 1f.

[41] *REG* 36, 1923, 115f.; now *Études* 5, 2, 29f. I have omitted discussion of L. Homo's long articles on Flamininus and Roman policy in *Mél. Cagnat* (1913),

minutely analysing Polybius' account of the negotiations of autumn 198 between Flamininus and Philip V, he showed Flamininus (as indeed Polybius depicted him) making the decision on whether to continue the war depend on his being allowed to be the one who continued it. It is a study in what Polybius called Flamininus' *anchinoia*. Holleaux's conclusion was that Flamininus was prepared to sell, not only either the Greeks or Philip (whichever way things turned out), but Roman political interest, to his private ambition and pride. "Et voilà qui nous fixe définitivement sur la valeur morale du personnage." The charge, which can be read into Polybius, had not previously been made at such length and with such forensic skill, and it introduced a new element into any discussion of Flamininus, since it was soundly based on our only reliable source. Some of the details of the argument could easily be faulted; but the general conclusion seemed irreversible unless Polybius' authority could be shaken. It was no longer merely philhellenism that was the subject of discussion: it was personal character and political loyalty.

Holleaux's views, on the whole, gained acceptance; thus, e.g., by his pupil A. Aymard, who himself, applying Holleaux's method of minute analysis of all known sources and logical deduction from that evidence, sharpened the picture his master had painted of Flamininus' (and Rome's) aims and policies.[42] In England, both Scullard and Walbank accepted these results.[43] In America, Frederic M. Wood tried to overthrow them by the only promising method: he examined various instances in which Flamininus is charged with selfish ambition and concluded that they all go back to hostile interpretation by Polybius, whose hero Philopoemen was Flamininus' embittered enemy; thus the authority of Polybius, in this instance, is highly suspect.

31f.; *RH* 121, 1916, 241f.; 122, 1916, 1f., since they seem to add nothing of major importance and, before long, were superseded by Holleaux's much more influential treatment.

[42] *Les premiers Rapports de Rome et de la Confédération achaienne* (1938), 114f. He presents a picture of carefully planned intrigue, of guarded and ambiguous promises to both Philip and the Greek allies, until the confirmation of Flamininus in command cut the knot and ensured the continuation of the war and a military solution.

[43] For Scullard's view, as expounded in *Roman Politics*, see n. 10 (above) and n. 45 (below) with text. Walbank, *Philip V of Macedon* (1940), 161f. *et al.*

Unfortunately for Wood (and his successors), M. Gelzer was at that very time demonstrating that Polybius' view of Flamininus was in fact favourable![44] This fact—undercutting Wood's whole line of argument—is not really difficult to observe, since Polybius is the main source of all our information, and there is no doubt of the generally laudatory tone of that information in our surviving sources; hence any items that strike us as derogatory cannot be rejected as due to hostility in our principal source. Thus there was no hope of overturning Holleaux along this line of argument. Before long Scullard[45] threw doubts on the validity of Wood's arguments from the political situation; he concluded that "Flamininus doubtless hoped that it would be unnecessary to betray the Greeks, but in the last resort he was probably prepared to urge the Senate to accept Philip's terms rather than to see a rival win that military glory which was almost within his grasp."

This brings us to the major development of recent years, which infused new life into the old controversy, with (as it turned out) rather paradoxical results. In 1954 Günther Klaffenbach published a large fragment of the first treaty between Rome and an Eastern power: the treaty with the Aetolian League made in 212 or 211.[46] In his excellent commentary, Klaffenbach came to the conclusion that, in the light of that treaty, Flamininus' attitude towards the Aetolians can be shown to be cynical and dishonest; he also expressed suspicion about Polybius' treatment of their debate, since the Aetolian case seems to be largely suppressed. His conclusion on Flamininus, since frequently quoted, was: "Alle Mohrenwäsche des Flamininus ist unmöglich."[47]

[44] Wood, "The Tradition of Flamininus' 'Selfish Ambition' in Polybius and Later Historians," *TAPA* 70, 1939, 93f.; Gelzer, "Die Achaica im Geschichtswerk des Polybios," *APAW* 1940, no. 2, 23f. (=*Kl. Schr.* 3 (1964), 145). Pédech's bulky *La Méthode historique de Polybe* touches on the subject (e.g. 220f.), but has nothing to contribute.

[45] *Rom. Pol.* 103, explicitly refuting Wood. (See also Lehmann, p. 25 below.)

[46] *SDAW* 1954, no. 1. The date is not important for our purpose. Klaffenbach opted for 212 and has been followed by Lehmann (below) and others; some have preferred 211. See (most recently) Walbank, *Historical Commentary on Polybius* 2 (1967), 21f.; and my own remarks in *HZ* 208, 1969, 637f.

[47] *Op.cit.* 47, n.1. My own survey of the negotiations with Antiochus (*Studies*, 112f.) may perhaps be mentioned as showing that, whatever one's assessment of Flamininus' philhellenism, it was in any case subordinated to both his personal and his political aims and was used as a means in the achievement of those aims. Essentially this agrees (despite minor differences in details of interpretation) with

The statement that something is impossible tends to challenge people to try it. In the years since Klaffenbach's *editio princeps* there have been dozens of treatments of the inscription—at least as many as of the so-called Themistocles decree. Each has had something to contribute (at least indirectly) to our theme. But there have been only four contributions of major interest to us here— differing in kind and in scope, but sharing the aim of attempting the *Mohrenwäsche* that Klaffenbach had judged impossible; though one of them does end up by admitting that Flamininus was "not, of course, a perfect man."

First, in 1957 there appeared (though it was apparently written by 1952, i.e. it notices the new inscription only cursorily) H. E. Stier's book *Roms Aufstieg zur Weltmacht und die griechische Welt.* It is very much—almost explicitly—a return to nineteenth-century Hegelian canons of judgment, in the light of the German trauma of the twentieth: the moral superiority of the *uictrix causa* is its main principle. The work is pervaded by a passionate belief in the historian's study and its relevance to the present (and indeed to any) age, which makes it fairly comparable, within its more limited field, to Mommsen's *History of Rome.* Stier returns with, on the whole, salutary insistence to positing belief in Polybius' facts as a firm basis for any account of the period; though he himself is perhaps at times tempted, against his own principles, to accept Polybius' interpretations on the same level as his facts. He totally rejects Holleaux's attack, even though this appeared to be based on Polybius; he claims[48] that it is based on mere conjectural filling in of what Polybius himself said no one knew: what happened at a secret colloquy between Philip and Flamininus on the second day of the negotiations of late 198 that form the subject of Holleaux's enquiry. Stier is at pains to show Flamininus not only as a philhel-lene, but as one who let philhellenism play a major part in shaping his policy, even against the opinions of most contemporary Roman politicians. In spirit, as in manner of exposition, it is a return to the thesis of Mommsen. Stier's pupil G. A. Lehmann continued this

---

the view of F. Cassola, in an interesting (but unfortunately, outside Italy, little read) article in which he defends Flamininus' policy from the point of view of expediency (it was, after victory, aimed at gaining Macedonian collaboration) and argues that the Scipios were never opposed to it (*Labeo* 6, 1960, 105-130).

[48] Stier, *op.cit.* 130f.

line in another major work, of a different kind, though closely
based on his master's view:[49] examining the Roman-Aetolian treaty
in great detail, he comes to conclusions about its contents and related
matters, which completely exonerate Flamininus from any charge of
duplicity or dishonesty in his treatment of the Aetolian League. In
a short general discussion of Polybius' presentation of Flamininus,
Lehmann attacks Wood's view of Polybius' hostility to him and
shows (conclusively, I think) that it rests on a basic misunderstanding of ancient attitudes: concern with his personal interests and
dignitas was regarded as legitimate in a Roman politician to an
extent that appears to be inconceivable today. Hence the attempt to
"save" Flamininus from Polybius' "attack" is fundamentally mis-
directed.[50] This is an important contribution to the problem of the
evaluation of ancient attitudes and the errors to which even distinguished scholars are still given in this field. It is clearly applicable
to more than one modern controversy, and what one might call
"Lehmann's principle" should dispose of many traditional and even
celebrated misinterpretations. Those trained in the British public-
school tradition have been particularly given—whether in the case
of Flamininus or in those of other ancient leaders (Alexander and
Caesar are the most obvious cases)—to applying standards absurdly
influenced by their own conditioning, and to regarding as fundamentally hostile any sources (or, for that matter, modern authors)
who depict these men as transgressing Thomas Arnold's code. I am
not implying that moral judgment of ancient men and attitudes is
beyond the historian's proper function: I agree with Ihne that it is
not and cannot be. But it is a very different operation from the
analysis of ancient attitudes to ancient men, and must be kept
strictly separate from it.

In 1963 the article on the Quinctii in *RE* appeared. The section
with which we are concerned, written by Gundel, contains a competent survey of the sources. On the main questions, it on the whole
accepts and transmits Stier's judgments.[51] Thus the "whitewashing"

---

[49] *Untersuchungen zur historischen Glaubwürdigkeit des Polybios* (1967). See
my review, *HZ cit.* (n. 46 above).

[50] Unknown to Lehmann, the same point had been made in a less general way
by Cassola, *op.cit.* (n. 47) 113f. Klaffenbach has corrected Lehmann on a small
point not relevant here: see "Die Sklaven von Elateia," *BCH* 92, 1968, 257f.

[51] There is a useful critical bibliography up to about 1958, when it appears to
have been written. Some later items are added, but have not been much used.

interpretation (to use Klaffenbach's phrase) has become enshrined in the principal standard work.

Most recently (at the time of writing), a small but important article by Balsdon[52]—beautifully written, like all his works—aims at dispelling the charges of dishonesty levelled at Flamininus by Holleaux and (in one instance) by myself. Given to burying inadequate argument under displays of verbal brilliance, it seems to me totally unsuccessful in its main aim, although (as we shall see) it makes many true and important points of detail. One of Balsdon's main weapons is the denial that explicit charges of trickery appear in the ancient evidence. This really contradicts his acceptance of Wood's argument about Polybius' bias against Flamininus (Balsdon, strangely, adds Cato as another biased source!). But it points up his failure to make the distinction that I have called "Lehmann's principle"—that between what we regard as legitimate and what the ancients did—and that between the two processes we have discussed: that of investigating the ancient attitude and that of (if we want to proceed to it) judging both that attitude and the individual or action concerned by our own principles. Homer admired Odysseus far more than most of his modern readers do; but the modern reader has a right to use his own judgment both on Homer's facts and on his attitude. Balsdon's revival of Wood's unhappy theory, itself due to this confusion and long ago disproved by Gelzer and Scullard,[53] was unlucky in that it appeared at the very time when Lehmann was finally burying the principles on which that theory (like Balsdon's own view) is based.

This, then, is where things now stand. Klaffenbach's publication of the treaty of 212/1 has given new impetus to an old discussion.[54] As we have seen, old attitudes have appeared in renovated dress. The most surprising and noteworthy fact is that, contrary to Klaffenbach's expectation, what he regarded as the final proof of Flamininus' dishonest conduct has led to the temporary triumph of

---

[52] *Phoenix* 21, 1967, 177f.

[53] Of whose counter-argumentation Balsdon shows no knowledge, although he cites Scullard in a different connection. He does not mention (or seem to know) Cassola's article. As for Gundel, he cites him with general approval, omitting to note that Gundel (*op.cit.* col. 1061) quotes and accepts the rebuttals of Wood's theory, which Balsdon himself regards as established fact!

[54] For my analysis of the negotiations with Antiochus, see n. 47 (above).

the "whitewashers." Passionately defended by Stier and eruditely by Lehmann, the view of Flamininus as a gentlemanly philhellene is now canonised in Pauly and, never absent from the popular works, has taken possession of scholarship at a new and more sophisticated level. Balsdon's article has seen to it that this development, originating in Germany, is no longer confined to German scholarship. Hegelians among Flamininus' defenders can no doubt congratulate themselves upon the new synthesis. But the time has perhaps come for a new antithesis: the process should not be allowed to continue without further analysis of some crucial points. The historian's duty is often invidious: men are incurably optimistic, stubbornly preferring to believe the best, especially of the victor. Yet that duty must be performed.

1. The Appointment

IT IS A pity that the precise circumstances of Flamininus' appointment are obscure. If we knew more about this, it would be easier to make sense of his Eastern command and his policies. On his family and the earliest stages of his career—a subject on which, despite Livy's efforts, more can perhaps be conjectured than has been—I shall have more to say elsewhere and must refer to my fuller treatment.[2] He came of a Patrician family that had missed the consulship for generations. It had maintained its social eminence (his grandfather, probably, was the one who, as *flamen Dialis*, gave the family a *cognomen*); his brother Lucius was elected to an augurate in 213, probably straight after assuming the *toga uirilis*. It seems to follow that the father—completely unknown except from his sons' filiation —must have held a major priesthood; but he may have died young. This can only be conjecture. Accident could lead to a family's losing power, and it would be a hard struggle to get back to the top.[3]

Titus was probably born late in 229 (perhaps early 228),[4] and we know nothing about his youth: Plutarch, who always delighted in digging out information on his heroes' childhood, found nothing to report. In 208 (when he must already have had at least two years of military service and perhaps more) we find him serving as a military tribune under the great M. Marcellus. During the Hannibalic War, it was—for whatever technical reason—possible to hold this post at the age of about twenty; and we know that ambitious young men tried to do so.[5] In 206 (it seems)[6] he began

[1] Owing to the restrictive conditions of this Lecture Series—inflexibly enforced in my case—it proved impossible to give a rounded picture of Flamininus, as had been the intention. It is to be hoped that my successors will be given the option of extending their exposition to another lecture, so that a subject of major importance can be adequately treated. This lecture concentrates on some crucial incidents from the Macedonian War; though a general assessment—inevitably going beyond the evidence here submitted—is attempted at the end.

[2] "The family and early career of T. Quinctius Flamininus," forthcoming in *JRS* 61, 1971. For the facts and sources see Gundel, *RE*, s.v. 'Quinctius,' no. 45.

[3] Roman annals are full of examples; for an obvious one, see the family of L. Sulla (*RE*, s.v. 'Cornelius,' no. 392; cf. 382 and 302).

[4] Polybius no longer had accurate information on his date of birth. The evidence is surveyed and evaluated in my article cited n. 2.

[5] P. Scipio (the later Africanus) and M. Cato (the later Censorius) are prime

to serve—probably as quaestor: though the date of his quaestorship is not attested, what follows is hard to understand unless he had held the office—under a commander at Tarentum, which had recently been recaptured and needed watching. This commander, whose name appears in Livy as Q. Claudius Flamen, was (I have suggested) more probably a Flamininus, and thus Titus' uncle. After his commander's death Titus stayed on and was asked, in the general shortage of commanders, to take over the garrison, with the rank of *pro praetore*. It was an extraordinary mark of confidence for one so young, and he acquitted himself well. In three or four years in the most Hellenic city in Italy, he showed ability at handling both his soldiers and Greek citizens. It must have been here, as has long been recognised,[7] that he acquired his knowledge of the Greek language and character, which was to make him conspicuous among Roman commanders.

On his return, he might have been expected to go through the offices that were already becoming usual (although not yet required): the aedileship to gain favour, and the praetorship to gain experience. But a young man who had already had praetorian *imperium* for two or three years would find it difficult to descend to an aedileship and, in a sense, take a step backwards in his career. Several men had got, or were getting, to the top without holding the minor curule offices: it was known to be possible for one who had distinguished himself and could muster enough support.[8]

Flamininus had apparently distinguished himself; and it becomes clear that he had attracted the attention of men who mattered. In 201 he was appointed to a ten-man commission to distribute land to Scipio's veterans in southern Italy—country that he knew well.[9] In the following year came a truly extraordinary appointment: while

---

examples: each held the office in his twentieth year, precisely like Titus Flamininus. Cf. Fraccaro, *Opuscula* ii (1957), 218, with my comments, *art. cit.* (n. 2), n. 35.

[6] On what follows see *art. cit.* (n.2), where this view—based on a reinterpretation of the evidence—is argued in detail.

[7] Niese, *Gesch. d. griech. u. mak. Staaten* 2 (1899), 609.

[8] P. Scipio Africanus (consul at thirty) had at least been aedile; P. Sulpicius Galba (*cos.* I 211) had held no curule office (on him, see further below); L. Cornelius Lentulus (said to have held a curule aedileship in absence) returned to a consulship from a Spanish special command in 199.

[9] With all other scholars who have recently touched on this, I follow Livy against Plutarch on the facts of Flamininus' two appointments. See R. E. Smith, *CQ* 34, 1940, 1f.; Tibiletti, *Athenaeum* 29, 1950, 192f.

still on that commission, which had not yet finished its work, he was made one of three commissioners to settle the colony of Venusia —the only man to cumulate two such charges. The result, in political terms, can hardly have been unintended by those who suggested him for these appointments: he gained massive support among veterans, settlers and their families.[10] It was after this, in 199, that he decided to become a candidate for the highest office. This was a decision that, in the Roman social and political order, a young man of thirty could not take by himself, or on the advice of a few coeval friends. It is clear that he had encouragement from men of *auctoritas*: things were working out as some men had been planning. It becomes clearer still when we find two tribunes objecting to his candidature, claiming that he was not properly qualified: the Senate ordered them to drop their objection and let the Roman People choose.[11] The tribunes complied; and it was safe to conclude that Flamininus' election would be welcomed by the Senate as a whole. He was duly elected, with Sex. Aelius Paetus as his colleague.[12] The lot—we are told by both Livy (32,8,4) and Plutarch (*Flam.* 2,3)—assigned him the Macedonian War as his province.

The outcome of that lot was a very happy one for the Roman People. The process merits speculation. In fact, most scholars writing about the incident have assumed without argument that Flamininus was *appointed* to his task, and some have even stated it as a fact; while those who have accepted the lot have gone on to write as though they had not.[13] I think they are basically right; but the assumption should at least be made explicit, and defended. Several facts may be adduced. We have seen that the Senate went so

[10] Plutarch's insistence on the support must be accepted: presumably it came from the veterans who hoped for land assignations, and from the families of the Venusia colonists plus any of the colonists themselves who had not yet taken up their colonial citizenship.

[11] Livy 32, 7, 8f.

[12] *MRR* 1, 330.

[13] Stier, *Roms Aufstieg* (1957), 121 states that Titus was appointed and bases his argument on this, without discussing the sources. Scullard, both in his discussion in *Roman Politics* and recently in *Scipio Africanus* (1970), 182f., implies appointment, as I myself did, *Foreign Clientelae* 70. Of older writers, Niebuhr (*Lectures on the History of Rome*, transl. Schmitz, 2³ (1853), 164) implies appointment; Mommsen (*Hist. of Rome*, tr. Dickson, 2 (1898), 428—similarly in earlier editions) speaks of the "choice" of Flamininus for the command. Gundel (*op. cit.* (n.2), col. 1052) admits the lot without discussion; but his discussion of Flamininus' election seems to imply that he was intended for the command.

far as to smooth the way for Flamininus' candidature and virtually to express its support; and that his career must have been favoured in high places. One would expect those responsible to have had some major purpose in mind. Moreover, his colleague Paetus, though (unlike Titus) he had held curule office,[14] had (again unlike Titus) no experience whatever of military command. In fact, he was destined never to acquire any that mattered, and to make his name as an eminent lawyer. On this occasion, having drawn "Italia," he went to Cisalpine Gaul, where he did "nothing noteworthy," the Gauls being "unexpectedly quiet."[15] A man who, at this time, found the Gauls quiet was surely a peaceable soul. One doubts whether he would have seriously wanted that difficult assignment in the East.

It was Flamininus who, with military experience, with support from Roman veterans, and with success at handling Greeks, had been groomed for the task. Nor is it technically difficult to believe that the lot might be an empty formality. Miss Taylor has recently demonstrated how it was done.[16] But the circumstances of those very years must make us suspect that it was done whenever it appeared necessary. In 200, the first year of the Second Macedonian War, the consuls had also drawn lots for the command. One of them was P. Sulpicius Galba, consul for the second time, who had fought in the East for many years in the First Macedonian War and was one of the leading Eastern experts. The other man, C. Aurelius Cotta, had no such qualifications. It was Galba who received the Macedonian *prouincia* "by lot."[17] Yet his election to a second consulship at this precise time, when war against Philip had just been decided on by the Senate, cannot be accidental: he must have been intended for the command. Indeed, Münzer[18] rightly describes the drawing of lots on that occasion as "an empty form." With that

[14] As aedile 200 (*MRR* i 323). See *RE*, s.v. 'Aelius,' no. 105. He is Ennius' "Catus Aelius Sextus."

[15] Livy 32,26,1f.: he merely made the colonists of Placentia and Cremona return to their colonies.

[16] *Roman Voting Assemblies* (1966), 73f., with notes (also collecting evidence for faked allotment). I was privileged to watch her demonstration of the technique with her specially constructed reproduction urn and lots in Rome.

[17] Livy 31,6,1.

[18] *RE*, s.v. 'Sulpicius,' no. 64, col. 805. As in the case of Titus, modern scholars are practically agreed on this. Compare, over a century later, Sulla's usual luck in gaining the Mithridatic command by lot (App. *b.c.* 1,55,241).

recent precedent to guide us, we may be sure that Flamininus' drawing the same *prouincia* was no more of an accident. One might speculate why the ceremony was performed, when *comparatio* between the consuls would have had the same effect. There can be no certain answer; but one might conjecture that the lot conferred an element of divine sanction, which, in a major war, might be important in raising morale. The favour of the gods was always important to a Roman general.[19]

There has been much discussion as to who Flamininus' supporters at this stage were. The view that there were major factional differences on the conduct of foreign policy is one that I cannot share. The Senate, in any crisis, showed remarkable unanimity in its objectives, even though methods might be debated. At this particular time, the guidance of the "eastern experts" was accepted for many years, and before long Flamininus was to be the chief of them. The average senator, even of high station, must have realised how little he knew about that strange world. As far as personal connections were concerned, Flamininus' were obviously good. His wife was either a Fabia or related to that powerful family. The point, though it cannot be decided, needs discussion. A Q. Fabius, whom Flamininus sent to Rome as an envoy in 198, is described by Polybius as his ἀδελφιδοῦς: a word that Livy translates as "uxoris sororis filius."[20] There is an even chance that Livy may be right. Münzer and Scullard conscientiously leave the matter open.[21] Balsdon, less conscientiously, misrepresents Scullard as making Titus' wife positively a Fabia, and, with his distinctive brand of intuitive *Quellenkritik*, adds: "As Livy has taken the trouble, *improving* on P. 18.10.8, to make Flamininus' relationship to Fabius absolutely clear, he had better be believed."[22] Alas, as less intuitive *Quellenforscher* have long known, the clarity—here and in many other places—is specious. In a classic of scientific source study, Nissen long ago showed[23] that Livy has no hesitation in

---

[19] On this aspect of the lot, see Taylor, l.c. (n. 16). The *locus classicus* for the *fortuna* of a Roman general is, of course, Cicero's *de imperio Cn. Pompeii*.

[20] Pol. 18,10,8; Livy 32,36,10.

[21] Münzer, *Röm. Adelsparteien* (1920), 117; Scullard, *Roman Politics* (1951), 98, n.1.

[22] *Phoenix* 21, 1967, 181, n. 19; my italics.

[23] *Kritische Untersuchungen über die Quellen der vierten und fünften Dekade*

mistranslating what he does not precisely understand, or in adding spurious specification to a Polybian term. And what reliable record did that great *Quellenforscher* Livy have at his disposal, and consult, before he penned his "correction?" His modern successor might be wise to ask.[24] We must regretfully be content with Polybius' term, on which we cannot obtain clarity. All that is certain is some *adfinitas* to the Fabii, and there is (as we saw) an even chance that Flamininus had a Fabia for his wife.[25]

M. Marcellus had been dead for some years and we cannot tell whether early service under him would still be of practical help.[26] As for others, we know that two Appii Claudii served under Flamininus, as envoy, as military tribune and as legate. Their appearances are hard to sort out and are probably misreported in the standard works.[27] But their presence is securely attested. So is that of another young officer, Q. Fulvius Flaccus.[28] The service of these young nobles—a Fabius, two Claudii and a Fulvius—surely gives us a good clue as to Flamininus' broad basis of support. Next, Scipio Africanus. Tenney Frank thought to establish philhellenism as a link between them.[29] That is unconvincing. Philhellenism—

---

des Livius (1863), 21f. This is one of the few source studies of the nineteenth century that has not been and cannot be superseded.

[24] That Livy did not himself consult documents need hardly be established by now. In this case, the easiest answer is that Livy was simply taking a translation of a difficult Greek term, which made sense, without worrying too much about the historical facts. See next note.

[25] An even chance simply because it is a toss-up whether Livy got the right translation. Polybius uses the term only of three men (though more than once of one). One case is ours; another is the relationship of Demochares to Demosthenes (in fact sister's son); the last (three times) that of Antipater to Antiochus III, which appears to be that of cousin on the father's side. (For the complex facts of this case, see Schmitt, *Untersuchungen zur Geschichte Antiochos' des Grossen* (1964), 29.) Mauersberger's treatment in the *Polybios-Lexikon* is wrong, as on some other occasions. Schmitt incidentally notes that Livy, twice translating ἀδελφιδοῦς where Polybius applies it to Antipater, renders it "fratris filius" (37,45,5; 55,3)—no doubt, Balsdon would maintain, "taking the trouble to make the relationship absolutely clear," and therefore to be believed. This parallel shows with all necessary clarity that Livy is simply guessing and not caring. F. Cassola (*Labeo* 6, 1960, 108) acutely points out that, in any case, these Fabii were Buteones, not Maximi. This cuts the ground from under much woolly prosopography; but my case here is not affected.

[26] Scullard, *Rom. Pol.* 98, despite his customary skill at tracing such relationships, finds no relevant facts.

[27] They will need separate discussion (n. 57 below, with text).

[28] *MRR* i 331.

[29] *CAH* 8, 368.

whatever the term means—was not an issue that can be shown to
have divided the Senate into parties. Scullard adduces a more
persuasive argument:[30] the fact that Scipio's veterans were willing
to enrol under Flamininus at a time when veterans in Epirus were
in mutiny suggests political co-operation—or at least absence of
opposition. Flamininus' activities in 201 and 200 had no doubt
helped him to acquire veteran support; but positive opposition
from their old commander would certainly have nullified it.

Another name springs to mind, more important to Flamininus
than any of those hitherto mentioned; and although we have, once
more, no direct account, strong arguments may be produced to link
the two men. P. Sulpicius Galba had fought in the East from some
time late in his second consulship (200 B.C.) until his successor P.
Villius arrived, late in the following year. It may be presumed that
he was back in time for the elections; and that his voice would be
listened to, where the prosecution of the war was concerned. There
can be little doubt that he was one of those who had pressed for
action against Philip in the first place; and by now he knew the
theatre as well as the whole area and the opponent. In addition, the
two men had remarkably similar careers. We have already seen that
Galba, like Flamininus later, was elected (it seems) in order to be
given the province that fell to him "by lot." But Galba, like
Flamininus later, had also gained his (first) consulship without
having held curule office before, and his *prouincia* had been the First
Macedonian War.[31] He obviously thought that such a deficiency
should not debar a suitable man from gaining the highest office and
taking charge of a war in the East. Relations between the two men
at a later stage are close and good.[32] The great man who had been
one of the chief sponsors of the new war and had been elected
consul in order to conduct it; and who, in the field, had seen how
difficult it was to consolidate territorial gains and had finally handed

[30] *Rom. Pol.* 99, n. 1. Accepted by Cassola, *op.cit.* (n. 25). Cassola denies opposition by Scipio even in 195-4 (*op.cit.* 123f.)—a little paradoxically, and forgetting his own point that personal ambition often disrupted friendship (*op.cit.*
113f.).

[31] Livy 25,41,11. On Galba's career, see *RE*, s.v. 'Sulpicius,' no. 64. We know
nothing about his early career; but some military distinction (like Titus') is likely.

[32] Aymard, *Premiers Rapports* (1938), 131, n. 61. Confirmed by Balsdon,
Phoenix 1967, 185f.

over to his successor an army in a state of mutiny[33]—the man who, over a decade earlier, as a much younger man, had been chosen consul in an extraordinary manner and sent to fight the same enemy in the East—that man was surely the most likely to think of the possibility of choosing a brilliant young noble (a Patrician like himself) in an unusual manner for an unusual task. We should bear in mind that Galba had been consul in 200, when Titus was elected to a colonial commission while still agrarian commissioner—a step of the utmost significance in the story of his rise to the consulship; and that Galba had been in Rome most of the time, that year, arriving in his province late in the season. He may well have had something to do with the young man's election to his useful post: it may be he who, as early as this or even earlier, had spotted Titus as a man of promise, akin (he might think) to himself.

Titus Flamininus' *amici* in Rome play an important part in the story later. It is clear that he must be well provided with them even at the start, and the names we have turned up help to explain the support of the Senate as a whole for his candidature.

2. *The Mission*

As we have noted in passing, Galba had been unsuccessful in his campaign. He had been ill for some time after arriving in his province,[34] yet had waged a strenuous and by no means ill-planned campaign.[35] He had won battles and gained territory, but he had found out the supply difficulties that beset any invasion of Macedonia by the most direct route. This was why he had withdrawn, to winter near the coast—obviously to the annoyance of his men, who saw that their marching and fighting had been wasted and that in the end no progress had been made, and who made their complaints heard in no uncertain terms. Galba was a tired man: probably, in the circumstances, not particularly eager for an extension of his command beyond the time that Villius' delay in any case allowed him; he did not make very much use of that time.

[33] The mutiny: Livy 32,3,2, with explicit blame for Galba, though he is not named. The campaign is illuminatingly discussed by N.G.L. Hammond, in one of his masterly studies of military history, *JRS* 56, 1966, 39f. (especially 42f.). (The maps, except for Map IV, are unfortunately inadequate.)

[34] Zon. 9,15,2.

[35] Hammond, *op.cit.* (n. 33).

Politically he had done little better. His two subordinates in charge of the fleet, had copied the tactics used by Galba himself in the First Macedonian War: plunder and destruction wherever they appeared.[36] To the Greeks, the time of that war had returned. If it was hoped that frightfulness would discourage resistance, that hope was mistaken. Resistance was firm, at times desperate. In any case, this was not the way to make friends, the way to implement what had seemed to be a new Roman approach announced before the outbreak of the War.

The First Macedonian War, begun by Philip's unprovoked attack upon the Romans when they seemed weak, had led to the alliance of Rome and the Aetolian League, in 212 or 211.[37] It was merely an agreement on how to divide the spoils. The Romans, uninterested in the war as such, had let their allies go down to defeat in 206, and had then themselves made the ignominious Peace of Phoenice with Philip: they were still uninterested in the East.

The next few years saw a revolution in Roman attitudes to that area. We need not enter into the old question of the causes of the Second Macedonian War.[38] It is the change in policy that interests us. For, after deciding that war must be risked, the Senate sent Philip the famous demand that he should stop attacking Greeks; and it had this demand read to assembled Greeks in several states.[39] In the First Macedonian War, Greeks had been merely objects of plunder. Now they were objects of concern. The conclusion must be that, for the first time, the Senate had decided not only to intervene in the East, but to keep up an interest there. Given the aim, the method followed. Philip had been unwise enough to turn Greek opinion decisively against himself by the cruelty and treachery of his attacks on cities in the Aegean: any proclaimed intention of

[36] Chalcis, Andros, Oreus: Livy 31,23; 45; 46, 9f.

[37] Cf. *Foreign Clientelae* 55f. The fragment of the treaty was first published by Klaffenbach, *SDAW*, no. 1. The most recent discussion I have seen is by G. A. Lehmann, *Untersuchungen zur hist. Glaubwürdigkeit d. Polybios* (1967): more than half this work is devoted to the treaty. See p. 25 above.

[38] I discussed the problem in *Foreign Clientelae* 62f., drawing attention to what had tended to be overlooked, even though it must have had a profound influence on the Senate: Philip's attested aggression in Illyria. This, of course, is not to deny other motives, such as general suspicion of Philip, due to his behaviour in the Hannibalic War.

[39] *Foreign Clientelae* 66.

stopping him would find a widespread welcome.[40] That the form
of the ultimatum by no means as yet implies the "freedom of the
Greeks" as later formulated[41] is obvious not only from the words
used, but from the way in which the war was in fact waged. To
stop attacks on Greeks was a worthy cause. But few men in Rome
seem to have adjusted themselves to what it implied: to the fact
that, if the claim was to be plausible, methods would have to be
changed, and attitudes to the Greeks as a whole. Of all the free
Greeks, only the Aetolian League seems to have been impressed by
Galba's conduct of operations; and they did not object to plunder-
ing Greeks. It was after the first Roman victory[42] that the League
decided to join in. Yet they were demoralised by their earlier
defeat. Many young men preferred the lure of mercenary service in
Egypt;[43] and though the League's accession was welcome, it was
not enough—any more than it had been in the earlier war, when
the League was stronger.

There is reason to think that Galba himself—an experienced
soldier of the old school and familiar with Greece from two wars—
realised that his methods had failed: there had been a singular
inability to take advantage of the new image of Rome apparently
fashioned in 201—no serious attempt to follow it up by diplomatic
action, or to adjust Roman practice so as to give it credibility. What
was needed was a man who could present a new image in a new
manner: who could get on with Greeks and reassure the dissatisfied
Roman soldiers. The man was Titus Quinctius Flamininus. We
have seen that there is reason to think Galba himself was his chief
supporter for the role. What is more, he seems to have suggested
that Titus take over as soon as possible. In view of the state in
which he himself had recently left the army and the war, that was
not surprising. We later find P. Villius, the consul of 199, not in the
least hostile to Flamininus, even though Titus hurried to relieve

[40] Philip's aggression is treated in the standard works, e.g., Walbank, *Philip V
of Macedon* (1940), ch. IV. Cf. Pol. 16,34,5.

[41] See *Foreign Clientelae*, ll.cc., for the development of Roman policy (accepted
by Walbank, *Historical Commentary on Polybius* 2 (1967), 537).

[42] At Ottolobus: Livy 31,40,7f. Previously they had refused (ib. 32).

[43] Livy 31,43,5f.: if we are to believe that account (from Polybius), there was
such a general exodus that the *strategus* had to intervene in order to retain some
troops at home for the war.

him, arriving much earlier than expected.[44] There is only one explanation: Titus could plead orders from the Senate.

3. The Campaign

There is no need to go once more into the details of Flamininus' military and diplomatic campaign in Greece in 198. I have little to add to what is in the standard works, and what I have to say I have put on record before.[45] After theatrically announcing the new policy —that Philip was now required to give up the *whole* of Greece, no matter how long established his family's claim to control—he drove Philip out of his prepared position, with the help of an Epirot chieftain with whom Villius had established contact. However, he did not pursue the enemy, but marched through Epirus, demonstratively treating it as friendly territory, even though the Epirots as a state had not officially joined him. At the same time, cities that resisted were still treated, both by him and by his brother Lucius (now in charge of the fleet), with the full rigour of war. On the diplomatic front, Rome's neglect was repaired and contact was established with the Achaean League, the most important of Philip's Greek allies, and quite probably with other states in whom our sources are less interested.[46] Finally, when the Greeks proved singularly lacking in enthusiasm for their new champions, the Achaean League was brought over to the Roman side by pressure and menace, with the help of a friendly *strategus*.[47]

Roman diplomacy could not dispense with force. But the interesting aspect in all this is the amount of time and care that Flamininus devoted to this kind of diplomatic activity, giving Philip time to recover his strength and muster his forces. After the Aous victory, there was no serious attempt to pursue; later, no real effort to invade Macedonia. In the military as in the political sphere, all energies were devoted to Greece. Of course, the purely military

---

[44] Livy 32,6,4. Livy implies that Villius heard at the same time of his successor's election and arrival. That is impossible and merely one of his dramatic devices. Balsdon (l.c. (n.32)) has demonstrated that Villius, no less than Galba, loyally co-operated with Flamininus.

[45] *Foreign Clientelae* 70f. (political). The fullest treatment is in Aymard, *op.cit.* (n. 32).

[46] See Aymard, *op.cit.* 76f.

[47] Most recent discussion in Errington, *Philopoemen* (1969), 87. Fuller discussion Aymard, *op.cit.*

problem—the problem of supplies, which Galba had encountered—
must not be ignored. On the other hand, it must not be exaggerated.
In fact, the road to Pella is much shorter from Epirus or Illyria
than from the Gulf of Corinth, and Galba had managed to advance
a fair distance along it. Roman armies, before and after this, were
not usually beaten by supply difficulties, and with the Macedonians
defeated and hence at least to some extent demoralised, any competent Roman commander should have been able to plan the
logistics of an invasion. Titus had an army much bigger and better
than Galba's had been: consisting largely of veteran volunteers,
superior in mobility—both on the march and on the battlefield—to
anything Philip could muster, and almost certainly superior in
numbers as well. It should be recognised that the decision not to
invade Macedonia by the shortest or the easiest route (the later
Via Egnatia), in a campaigning season that must have been several
months longer, ahead of the Romans, than what had been left after
Galba's delayed arrival—that decision was chiefly a political one, a
new phenomenon in Roman annals. What mattered was less the
quick defeat of Philip than the winning of Greece. And when
diplomatic progress in Greece proved slow, because of well-founded
old suspicions, which the first two years of the new war had done
nothing to dispel, the resort to military pressure against the
Achaeans can be seen as almost a measure of despair. Had the
Assembly at Sicyon held out—had one *demiurgus* not changed his
mind, permitting the motion on the Roman alliance to be put[48]—it
is difficult to see what Flamininus could have done. The threat of
Roman hostile action, which the complaisant Aristaenus, as presi-
dent, held over the Assembly—we do not know whether the Roman
speaker had mentioned it, but there is no reference to his doing
so—was a little unreal. The policy of frightfulness, amply tried
under Galba, had not helped. Where Titus had known better, he
had (to some extent) been successful—as in Epirus. But he in turn
was being diplomatically impeded by terrorist action against recalci-
trants (perhaps regarded as a military necessity, in difficult coun-

---

[48] Livy 32,22,4f.: he was persuaded to do so by his father's threatening to kill
him if he refused! For the threat developed by Aristaenus, ib. 21,34f.: if the
League does not join Rome, "praeda uictoris erimus"; and the grand conclusion
(s. 37): "sed aut socios aut hostes habeatis [*sc.* Romanos] oportet."

try): the destruction of Eretria and Carystus and the grim measures in Thessaly cannot but have discredited the new policy that Titus had proclaimed at the Aous and practised in Epirus. If Greece was to be destroyed, it would find little profit in being liberated from Philip. Had the Achaean League clung to neutrality—hostility was not in point, and not suggested—it is doubtful whether the Romans would have dared to attack it, at the risk of making diplomatic success (which their commander clearly thought important) totally impossible for the foreseeable future. Indeed, he would then have been left with no option but to acknowledge diplomatic defeat and return to a strictly military solution: to find Philip's army, bring it to battle and destroy it, in the hope that Greece would fall to the victor without resistance or enthusiasm. And that, by now, would have been difficult. The season was advanced, the road to Macedonia long and strenuous. And if Philip could elude him into the winter, Flamininus would have failed and could expect recall. But he had the luck that distinguished a good Roman commander. The League yielded and joined Rome. At last he had respectable Greek allies. Others soon followed.

4. Nicaea

We can now move to the end of 198: the negotiations between Philip and the Greek allies led by Flamininus. We have seen the much-debated question: was Titus willing to betray, not only the Greeks, but Roman interests? That is, if it turned out that he would not be continued in his command, in charge of the war.

Holleaux's answer was that this was precisely what he intended to do. Polybius, followed by Livy and Plutarch, is explicit: his friends had instructions to end the war if he were to be recalled, and to prevent its being ended if he were prorogued; and, of course, he asked them to ensure that things turned out the latter way. In other words, as far as he was concerned, the decision was to be taken, not on the grounds of the public interest, but on personal criteria. And in order to drag out negotiations until he could be sure what was to be, he held out hopes to Philip that the Senate might relax some of its conditions as proclaimed to him at the Aous. So far

Holleaux.[49] On these premises, he rightly concluded, it is obvious that someone would be cheated: the Greeks if Philip got his terms, or Philip himself if he did not; and in any case (we might say) Rome.

The three days of negotiations at Nicaea, and particularly the secret colloquy on the second, which was clearly crucial in producing the agreement that emerged,[50] certainly offer some puzzles. Flamininus' apologists are right in drawing attention to them; they are unjustified merely in using them as they do.

First, Polybius admits that what went on at the secret talks was never really known: he only knew what Titus announced when he came back (and, Polybius implies, this need not be regarded as the whole truth). That was that Philip was willing to turn over Pharsalus and Larisa to the Aetolians, but not Phthiotic Thebes; that he would give Corinth and Argos to the Achaeans, and the Peraea to Rhodes (but not the cities of Iasus and Bargylia); and that the Romans would get back their Illyrian protectorate. Obviously, this was well outside the Aous terms: that all of Greece should be free.

Now, on the next day of the negotiations (the last), all that happened was that Philip suggested that the whole matter should be referred to the Senate; and Flamininus imposed agreement to this on the unwilling allies. In return for a two months' truce—an extraordinarily short period, if embassies had to go to Rome and back: it is clear that prolonged negotiations in Rome were not expected—he received the surrender of the whole of Phocis and Locris. Not a bad bargain, in view of the difficulty of conquering those areas. It gives good reason to think that Philip, who was an experienced soldier, must have received some promises or reassurances. Holleaux concluded that Titus had seemed willing to let him keep "the greater part of his old Hellenic dependencies," i.e. to give up the Roman terms almost entirely. Further puzzlement is added. For once the talks adjourned to Rome, it soon became clear that Flamininus' prorogation was assured; and at this point the

[49] *Études d'Épigraphie et d'Histoire grecques* 5,2 (1957), 29f. The argument is also summarised in Balsdon's article (n. 22 above), most of which is intended as a reply to Holleaux.

[50] Pol. 18,8. (I give the main points of the reported agreement.)

envoys of the Greek states were encouraged to come forward and stress the importance of the three "fetters of Greece"—Demetrias, Chalcis and the Acrocorinth: if Philip were unwilling to surrender these, there would be no freedom for Greece. The Senate therefore asked Philip's envoys about these three specific places; and they replied that they had no instructions on them. Thereupon the talks were at once declared over.

How is it that they had no such instructions? We have seen what a high price Philip was willing to pay even for the right to take his case to Rome at all. How could he fail to provide instructions on this particular question? The only answer is that he can have had no idea that this question would be asked. It would have been easy enough to prepare a non-committal answer that would keep negotiations going without giving anything away: Hellenistic kings were no novices at diplomacy.[51] They knew, as we do, the technique of "negotiations without preconditions," at which each side, from the start, has a clear idea of the maximum that it is prepared to give away. Now, if Philip was not expecting to be asked about those three fortresses, it follows that Flamininus had given him some specific reassurances about the agenda.[52] This only confirms what we have already noted: that Philip would not easily have paid such a high price for the right to negotiate, unless he had specific expectations. Of course, we cannot know the details that not even Polybius knew. But the facts themselves force us to assume that Titus at least held out hope—Philip might regard it as a promise—that he would see to it that the agenda contained only the places specifically named in his report on the secret colloquy: Argos, Corinth and the rest. In other words, it follows from the facts as we know them that Philip can have expected, at most, to be pressed to give up the places that he had declared he would *not* give up (Phthiotic Thebes, Iasus, Bargylia) and that he was almost certainly prepared to surrender,

[51] Pol. 18,11f. Balsdon comments (*Phoenix* 1967, 184): "They gave the only answer which, in such circumstances, a diplomat could give. They said they had no instructions." Diplomatic lies and evasions are not usually employed for the purpose of precipitating an adverse decision. There can be no doubt that the answer was true; and the question is: why?

[52] This was suggested by Holleaux, though his actual guess at the reassurance— that Flamininus had promised Philip that he would be able to retain (i.a.) the "three fetters"—is rightly rejected by Balsdon. Who first thought of referring the whole question to the Senate is not worth debating.

if it were the price of peace: the diplomat must hold some concessions in reserve. The surrender of the "three fetters" had evidently
not been mentioned at the colloquy: Titus' report did not refer to
them. Of course, any such limitation of the agenda meant the
abandonment of the Roman demand for the evacuation of Greece:
he may well have hoped even to retain the Acrocorinth; for the
promise to give up "Corinth" is ambiguous.[53]

Was the abandonment of Rome's Aous conditions inconceivable?
By no means. In the history of diplomacy, ancient and modern,
sweeping claims have often been modified at the conference table,
in the light of experience and of the price to be paid. The war that
was undertaken to defend the freedom of Poland ended with total
victory, and Poland enslaved. Nearer the time, we all know how the
Senate sent a commission to Greece with a decree proclaiming the
freedom of all Greeks in Europe and Asia. That was meant as a
threat to Antiochus the Great. The freedom of the Greeks in Asia
turned out to be very negotiable: at a conference with Antiochus'
ambassadors in Rome, Flamininus offered to forget about it if
Antiochus agreed to withdraw from Europe;[54] and after total victory it was totally forgotten, and most of the Greeks of Asia became
subjects of the King of Pergamum. We need not be surprised that
Philip thought the freedom of the Greeks in Europe might be
equally negotiable. Arguing *ex post facto*, the trusting scholar regards the very suggestion as infamous. Working diplomats, and
students of diplomacy, cannot see anything unreasonable in such a
hope. Feyel suggested that Flamininus perhaps promised that he
would secure Thessaly for Philip in return for his giving up everything else.[55] As it stands, the suggestion will not do: it fails to
account for the lack of instructions on the "three fetters." But that
there must have been the sketch of some sort of bargain—possibly,
but not necessarily, in geopolitical terms, like the one that Titus
himself later proposed to Antiochus' envoys—is an inevitable conclusion from our evidence. In fact, as Holleaux said, Flamininus
was preparing to betray either Philip or the Greeks.

---

[53] As pointed out by Aymard, *op.cit.* (n. 32),: the citadel is sometimes excluded.
[54] See my *Studies in Greek and Roman History* (1964), 126f. (with notes).
Balsdon's comment on this (*Phoenix* 1967, 188f., with n.66) is a splendid mixture
of misunderstanding and misrepresentation. It needs no discussion.
[55] Discussed and rightly rejected by Balsdon, *op.cit.* 184.

Balsdon, in highly emotional language, has recently objected to this interpretation and tried to counter it. His first point is that no one knew what went on at the secret colloquy, except for what was announced after; hence Holleaux has no right to speak as if he knew. But this is absurd. Insistence on such a rule would almost bring historical enquiry to a standstill; and not only historical enquiry! One is perfectly entitled to deduce what one does not know, from the evidence (which, in history, includes later developments). Our newspapers and our courts of law rightly do it every day. It is to be noted that Balsdon has no explanation at all for the envoys' lack of instructions on the "three fetters": he has to pass it off with a facetious phrase.

Next, he objects that there was, after all, another person present at the colloquy: the military tribune Appius Claudius. Would he, when sent to Rome as an envoy, not tell the truth, thereby exposing Flamininus as a trickster and a traitor to his country?

The first point to be made in reply to this is that—through no fault of his, since he took his facts from reputable modern works—Balsdon is almost certainly mistaken in his basic fact: Ap. Claudius did not go to Rome as an envoy from Flamininus. Since Balsdon's use of the identification has made it important, the matter needs detailed discussion. In 18,8,6 Polybius says that Titus took the military tribune Ap. Claudius with him to the colloquy: the only other person present on his side. In 18,10,8 he says that Titus sent to Rome "Quintus Fabius . . . and Quintus Fulvius, and with them Appius Claudius who was surnamed Nero." Note that no *cognomina* are given for the first two envoys, nor for the Appius Claudius who was present at the colloquy.[56] It is only the Appius Claudius who goes to Rome, two chapters later, who is described with laborious precision—for what other reason than to distinguish him from the homonymous man recently named? Surely Polybius could hardly have made his point clearer. There were indeed two Appii Claudii with Flamininus—this has long been known; the question is how to distribute their roles. And in this Polybius' attempt at distinction

---

[56] Identification of the first two has therefore been difficult. See Walbank, *Hist. Comm.* 2, 561. Unfortunately he regards the two Appii as "almost certainly" identical (558), without discussion.

is a vital clue.[57] We are not entitled to "improve" on his evidence.[58] In other words: Balsdon's point can, if anything, be used only *against* his thesis: Titus was obviously taking no chances about immediate revelations in Rome! If the facts were found out later, success—as was usual in Rome—would justify the means, and all would be forgiven, if there was anything to forgive.

But *was* there anything to forgive? This is not as certain as anachronistic modern judgment considers it. The Senate, a little later, would almost certainly have had no objection to the bargain with Antiochus, if Antiochus had accepted it; just as, later still, it had no objection to the bargain with Eumenes that gave up the freedom of the Greeks in Asia. There is no real reason to think that the majority (at any rate) would have objected to an attempt to deceive either Philip or the Greek allies, if it held out promise of advantage and could be done without paying a penalty in terms of *Realpolitik*. Still: this is speculative judgment. The fact is that Titus took no chances.

As for his instructions to his friends in Rome, Balsdon can do no more than flatly refuse to believe Polybius. The master of intuitive *Quellenforschung* again has an answer: "We are confronted by the invention of someone who, as the prominence of 'the Friends' in the story suggests, pictured Roman politics (about which he was not well informed) in the image of a Hellenistic court."[59] Now, we do not know whether anyone "invented" the story—that, of course, is precisely what ought to be proved; but we do know who transmits and unhesitatingly believes it: the historian Polybius, who lived in Rome for a generation and moved in

---

[57] An Ap. Claudius appears as commander under Flamininus in 196-194 (when Livy calls him *legatus*); he cannot be identical with Flamininus' envoy Ap. Claudius Nero, who was praetor in 195. (See *RE*, s.v. 'Claudius,' nos. 245; 294 (confused); *MRR* i 331 (confused); 332, n. 4; 337 (described as military tribune, without evidence); 341, 344 (correctly listed as legate both times). In view of Polybius' care in distinguishing the two men, the later legate (Pulcher) must be the tribune who accompanied Titus to the colloquy. We cannot tell in what capacity Nero had served in 198; since he was praetor three years later, we may presume he had been a legate.

[58] As Balsdon light-heartedly does, after the manner of Livy: the man at the colloquy is "not military tribune, *as P[olybius] wrongly states*" (*op.cit.* 180, n. 15; my italics). Like Livy, he vouchsafes no evidence for the "correction."

[59] Balsdon, *op.cit.* 181.

senatorial circles, while he had never lived at a Hellenistic court. It is strange that the modern scholar, with his patchy evidence, should presume to correct his picture of Roman politics and charge him with being taken in by such childish confusion with an environment that he (Polybius) did not even know by experience![60]

He has one more shot in his locker. If the "friends" failed to bring about prorogation, how could they hope to bring about peace with Philip after that failure? "How was a minority vote to change into a majority vote overnight?"[61] This unfortunate "difficulty" was made up by Holleaux, as Balsdon notes; and it is poetic justice that it should now be used against him. But it is nonetheless imaginary. First, the argument assumes that a major effort was needed to induce the Senate to make peace. But perhaps it was the other way round: perhaps Flamininus knew that there was a strong sentiment in favour of ending the futile war, which the People (at any rate) had not much wanted? How can we know what information Flamininus had on Senate sentiment? But there is a more general and more important refutation. The view expressed by Holleaux and taken up by Balsdon reveals a misunderstanding of the way in which the Senate worked. It is anachronistic to see it in terms of the House of Commons or the Chamber of Deputies.[62] Roman government proceeded by *auctoritas* and consensus. Actual voting was rare, and might be ineffective.[63] Terms like "majority" and "minority" are almost meaningless: the important thing was to *persuade*. If the Eastern experts (who, as we have seen, were Flamininus' friends) suggested peace, there was no reason to think that the Senate would

---

[60] On political "friends" in Rome and their importance, see the classic discussion in Gelzer, *Die Nobilität der römischen Republik* (1912; reprinted in *Kleine Schriften* i (1962)). It is now available in English: *The Roman Nobility*, transl. Seager (1969). That this political use of the term "amicus" does not exclude its personal and philosophic use has been shown by Brunt, *PCPhS* 11, 1965, 1-20. But no one ever doubted that Romans could have friends in the ordinary sense, and this is no argument against the existence of political *amicitia* as discovered by Gelzer. For a just appreciation, see Seager, *The Crisis of the Roman Republic* (1969), p. xii. (That work contains a reprint of Brunt's article: pp. 199-218.)

[61] Balsdon, *op.cit.* 181.

[62] Though in the Third Republic (when Holleaux lived) quick changes of parliamentary opinion were not unknown.

[63] The best-known example is the massive vote in favour of Curio's proposal that both Caesar and Pompey should disband their armies: it went 370 against 22 (App. *b.c.* 2,30,119), but the only result was that the presiding consul refused to accept it.

reject their advice. On the other hand, personal appointments were quite a different matter. As has often been shown, each man essentially stood for himself, and bonds of long friendship might be torn by opportunist ambition. It is interesting to note that, in the following year, the man who fought hardest against Titus' prorogation—simply because he was consul for 196 and wanted to fight Philip—was none other than M. Marcellus, son of Titus' old commander and (therefore) old patron.[64] The issue of prorogation was a different *kind* of issue from that of peace, and there is no *a priori* reason to think that the House would divide (if it did divide) the same way on the two. Flamininus knew the Senate better than his modern defenders.

Finally: would "the friends" co-operate in treason against Rome? Here, as we had occasion to note in the first lecture,[65] one can again easily ask anachronistic questions and get anachronistic answers. Indeed, the subject we are discussing is a perfect example of this danger. "In Dante's eyes, Virgil was a Lombard," as B. G. Niebuhr put it.[66] To many of us, just as the Senate is a modern Parliament, a Roman leader is a Christian gentleman.

The fact is that there was nothing shocking, to Romans, in seeing a noble politician work for war or peace in accordance with his personal interests: we have just seen the example of M. Marcellus; and it was typical rather than exceptional. At the end of the Hannibalic War, Scipio had to face much the same kind of opposition.[67] Polybius—thoroughly familiar with his Roman environment—tells the story, with admiration for Flamininus' shrewdness (*anchinoia*). Plutarch tells it without comment. The fact that we do not admire such conduct gives us no justification for assuming, as self-evident, that Flamininus and his friends would be ashamed of it. Each society accepts the risks inherent in its system as the price to pay for the preservation of the system, and it learns to live with those risks. This particular convention of aristocratic Roman government was, of course, sometimes harmful to Rome, but not fatal for a very long time. What would Roman senators have thought of

---

[64] Livy 33,25.
[65] See p. 25f above.
[66] Niebuhr, *History of Rome*, transl. Hare and Thirlwall 1 (1831), p. xxi.
[67] Livy 30,40,7f.; 43,1f.

present-day opposition, within this country, to a major war fought by the armed forces of the state, and of the form that this opposition is allowed to take? They would surely have judged it as treasonable as Balsdon, looking through modern spectacles, considers the behaviour attested for Flamininus and men like him; and, had they been filled with sincere admiration—though an admiration not always based on profound understanding—for the institutions of this country, they might well have been tempted to explain away reports of such behaviour as the implausible invention of hostile propaganda.

As a footnote to this discussion, we may observe that, when proroguing Flamininus for 197, the Senate decided to appoint P. Galba and P. Villius as his legates. Much debate has been devoted to finding out what supposed alignment of Senate factions was placated thereby. But there is no reason to think that faction enters into it. Galba, as we saw, must have been one of Titus' original sponsors; and both men always got on well with him. If one must suggest an answer, it might well be that the Senate did not like Flamininus' practice of secret colloquies and would make sure that it would not happen again. They had confidence in his military and diplomatic ability; but they were determined that henceforth two experienced senators—known not to be hostile to him, but men of independent status and *auctoritas*—would be there to watch over what he did. He had not done the State any harm; but an oligarchy cannot leave too much to an individual.

5. *The Aetolians*

That Titus' *anchinoia* was what we should regard as cunning (or perhaps trickery) may now be regarded as established in one instance, despite modern whitewash. It is in fact made clear by another incident, which Balsdon does not notice in his apologia: the way in which Flamininus got his forces into Thebes, while pretending friendship for the inhabitants.[68] However, the general point must be carefully made, as it helps us to assess cases where we merely have his word against that of an opponent. The politician who possesses this kind of *anchinoia*—and we have seen his like—is not usually believed when we have only his unsupported word against

[68] Livy 33,1; Plut. *Flam.* 6.

another's. This elementary criterion of daily life is one that the historian will do well to bear in mind.

We are now prepared to approach the incident of Flamininus' dispute with the Aetolians after Cynoscephalae. Let us recall the outline of the story. After the battle, in which the Aetolians had played a brave and probably decisive part, their leaders demanded to have four cities restored to them.[69] Philip was willing to restore them: he no longer physically controlled them anyhow. But Flamininus suddenly intervened and said they could have only one (Phthiotic Thebes): the other three had surrendered into the *fides* of Rome and could not be handed over. The Aetolians were indignant, claiming that they had a right to the cities, not only in equity (as allies of Rome in the present war), but under the terms of the treaty of 212/1, according to which all cities conquered by the League or by the Romans would go to the League (the Romans keeping only the booty they had taken). Flamininus said they were mistaken: first, they had abrogated the treaty when they made a separate peace in 206; next, even if the treaty was still in force, they would be entitled only to cities actually conquered, not to cities surrendered *in fidem*. It was here that the fragment of the actual treaty published by Klaffenbach turned out to be vital: it makes it clear that there is no distinction between the cities taken by force or otherwise, except that the latter—for what that was worth—were to receive autonomy.[70] It was for this reason that Klaffenbach felt sure that the new fragment condemned Titus beyond hope of whitewashing.

Nearly half of a recent book by G. A. Lehmann is nevertheless devoted to the most serious and most scholarly attempt to do just this which we have yet seen.[71] But I think he fails to clear his hero of this charge: we must accept the fact that on the basis of the treaty the League was entitled to the cities. Balsdon, on this point, is brief and wary: Titus "need not have been a deliberate liar; he may well have been genuinely mistaken. In any case the point at issue was purely academic, since the Romans had informed the Aetolians over

---

[69] Pol. 18,38; Livy 33,13.

[70] See my review of Lehmann (n. 37 above). Since there was no claim that the autonomy clause had been broken, this small point does not need discussion.

[71] See n. 37 above, with my review there cited.

and over again . . . that they did not consider the . . . alliance to be in operation any longer."[72]

Let us ignore the picture of the politician who, on a major point of international law, is not lying, but genuinely mistaken—to his country's advantage, as it happens. Flamininus did not offer to let the Aetolians refresh his memory; so that point *was* "purely academic." But "over and over again"? As far as I can discover, there is only a single occasion when the Aetolians are supposed to have been informed that the Romans considered the old treaty at an end. At some time between 205 and 200 the League is supposed to have sent an embassy to Rome to ask for help against Philip; which the Senate curtly refused, advising them that their separate peace had abrogated the alliance. I have argued at length that this report— conveniently absolving the Romans of a charge of trickery in 197/6 —is an annalistic fabrication, like so many stories advanced solely with a view to defending Roman *fides*.[73] There are two good reasons for such a view: first, the story appears in Appian's *Macedonica* at a time when the Senate had already decided to start another war against Philip. By then it is hard to believe that they would have disdained Aetolian support—which, indeed, P. Galba sought in the following year. Hence we are told: Appian merely put the incident in the wrong place. But why? Was he combining two sources? Hardly anyone would give Appian credit for so much scholarship. No, he found it, obviously, just where he put it; and it can have been put there only by a late annalist, out to justify Roman actions, but with no clear knowledge of the history of those years. Secondly, we have only one reference in Livy (in a highly rhetorical speech) to this rejection: it is put in the mouth of a Macedonian trying to dissuade the League from again joining Rome. The reference is ignored in the Roman reply, and there is no reason to think it Polybian: Nissen long ago showed[74] that Livy freely incorporates reminiscences of annalistic material in basically Polybian speeches, and I gave an undeniable example from this very speech.[75] The case against the authenticity of the supposed rebuff to the Aetolian

[72] *Phoenix* 1967, 185.
[73] *Latomus* 17, 1958, 208f. (with all source references and discussion).
[74] *Krit. Unt.* 24f.
[75] *Op.cit.* (n. 73), 209f. Cf. Holleaux, *Études* (n. 49 above) 5,2, ch. 4, showing how Livy will adapt and change even plain narrative.

embassy seems to me unshaken.[76] Now, *if* this embassy was made up by an unskilful annalist, it was (as we saw) for the sole purpose of showing that the Aetolians knew that the treaty with Rome was no longer in force. There is literally no other evidence to show that they knew it, or indeed that this was the situation. They can hardly have gathered it from the various Roman negotiators who, after 200, tried to attract them into renewed alliance;[77] certainly not from Titus Quinctius Flamininus, who, after the colloquy at Nicaea, reported Philip's willingness to give up Larisa and Pharsalus to the Aetolians—with not a word to the effect that he would not permit them to have the cities. Moreover, it is clear that at least Philip, when he said that the Aetolians could have those cities, had no idea that Titus had decided they should not, or that there were legal obstacles against their doing so. Then there is the Aetolians' own behaviour: as various towns surrendered to the *fides* of Rome, we never hear of their voicing the slightest complaint or suspicion; yet they were not people who would suffer injury in silence. If indeed it was a fact that the treaty of 212/1 was no longer in force, there is not only no evidence that the Romans had ever informed the Aetolians of this fact—there is good evidence that the Aetolians and Philip were not aware of it; and that Titus himself, at one stage, showed no awareness of it either.

But *was* it a fact—whether or not the Aetolians, or Philip, or even Titus, knew of it? It could be argued that the Roman failure to support the League for two campaigning seasons in the first war[78] amounted to a *Roman* abrogation; but the Romans clearly did not take this view, since in 205 they sent an expeditionary force across and expected the Aetolians to fight by their side. Was the treaty abrogated when the League made a separate peace in 206? It depends, in strict law, on whether the peace contained an *adscriptio*

---

[76] Only one objection has been raised: Dorey (*CR* 10, 1960, 9) thought he found a reference to the embassy in a fragmentary passage of Polybius (16,24,3)—which would prove that the embassy was reported by Polybius and is therefore historical. Walbank (*Hist. Comm.* 2, 530f.) recognises that the Polybian passage cannot refer to any such embassy; but he nevertheless chooses to believe that the embassy was reported by Polybius. Dorey was anticipated by Holleaux, who spotted the passage (Pol. 16,24,3) and at once realised that it had nothing to do with the case!

[77] Livy 31,31; 46,1f. (Note s. 5: "Romanis omnia pollicentibus.")

[78] Livy 29,12,1: probably not two whole years.

securing peace for Rome.[79] If it did—as it seems to have done for the three Peloponnesian allies of the League—then the League was no more breaking its treaty obligations to Rome than it was to its Greek allies.

Now, we cannot be sure whether or not it did. The Romans, of course, chose to start up the war again in 205 and then make a separate peace. That, in any case, would be their right: *adscriptio* could only protect the *adscriptus*, not bind him. It was, in fact, a category that had obviously been evolved for the very purpose of allowing a partner to an alliance to make a separate peace without either deserting the others or having to depend on their approval. There is no doubt that Philip, for his part, was eager for peace with Rome in 206: he would have supported—even urged—such a clause, in the hope that the Romans might abide by it.[80] Even when the Romans crossed to Illyria with a large force in 205, Philip—hoping for peace or at least a truce, we are told—refrained from offensive action.[81]

We do not in fact *know* whether the Romans were *adscripti* to the peace of 206, i.e. whether the Aetolian League had fulfilled its minimum obligations to keep the treaty with Rome in force. The situation both in 206 and in 205 suggests, as we have seen, that it may have; and the fact that it had scrupulously protected its Greek allies makes it very likely that it did the same for Rome—particularly since Philip would be positively delighted at this. If we had good reason to take Flamininus' word for statements we cannot check, we might do so here and believe that, in spite of all these considerations, the Aetolians had broken their treaty and abandoned Rome; and that they ought to have been—even if in fact they

---

[79] *Adscriptio* has been much discussed, especially in connection with the Peace of Phoenice (see Walbank, *Hist. Comm.* 2,516f.; 551f.). It means, roughly, that the *adscriptus*, without any positive action on his part, is secured against hostilities. It is difficult to avoid the conclusion (*For. Client.* 59; accepted by Walbank, *op.cit.* 516f.) that the Aetolians' Greek allies—Elis, Messene and Sparta—were *adscripti* to the peace between Philip and the Aetolians in 206. (Walbank is needlessly puzzled at their allowing themselves to be *adscripti*, since this might involve breaking their obligations to Rome: no action on the part of an *adscriptus* appears to be called for, and their permission need not have been asked.) Of course, *adscriptio* would not have to be accepted: if the Romans were *adscripti* to the peace, they certainly refused to accept this.

[80] See Dio, fr. 57,58-9; Zon. 9,11,4.

[81] Livy 29,12,6f.

demonstrably were not—aware of it. But it is merely a case of having to take his word against the Aetolians' (who had no idea that the treaty was abrogated). It would be foolish to assert the total veracity of the Aetolians, to the point of thinking them incapable of diplomatic fraud or pretence. But Titus Flamininus is too obviously and unashamedly guilty of what we must regard as sharp practice and deceit in his diplomacy, for anyone to accept his word against an opponent's. Those who talk most insistently about *fides*, like those who talk most insistently about freedom, are not always its most conscientious practitioners.

The Aetolians' whole behaviour—before the negotiations and at them—demonstrates their firm conviction that the old treaty was still in force.[82] It is unlikely that they would have entered the War without a specific guarantee of some sort; it is certain that they would not have entered it, and behaved as they did in it, had they known that the treaty was regarded by their "allies" as no longer in effect, so that they had no formal claims whatever. What is more: not all Romans were apparently as certain as Flamininus claimed to be. When the ten commissioners came to make their final dispositions, they felt sufficient doubt to send some of the League's claims to the Senate for arbitration. The Senate sent them back to Flamininus, and we hear no more about the matter.[83] We can guess the outcome. This, however, throws no new light on the legal question, which we must regard as (strictly) insoluble, with a slight preference for the Aetolian view.

6. Philhellenism and Policy

For a complete study of Flamininus much more would be needed than can be provided here; it is a pity that the restrictions imposed on me do not allow me to attempt it. It would be necessary to trace his treatment of the Greeks after the Isthmian declaration in detail; and it would be necessary to follow his diplomacy in the negotia-

---

[82] The phrase "the original treaty," which they use at various times (as reported both in our text of Polybius and in Livy), may even imply a new one for the Second Macedonian War, confirming the first. If so, it would be what Täubler called a *Feldherrnvertrag*, which, in strict Roman law (but who was to know that?), would not be binding on the Senate and People. Such an agreement is not impossible (e.g. at Livy 31,46,5), though not attested. One would not expect attestation.

[83] Pol. 18,47,8f.; Livy 33,49,8.

tions, and later in the war, with Antiochus the Great. Some of this I have done before; and it is clear that the general picture that would emerge would not be so very different from the one that emerges from this present discussion. What we must finally ask, however, is: to what extent was he a philhellene? Now that we have seen the absurdity of the "sentimental" interpretation of his policy, the interpretation of Mommsen and Frank, we must ask whether the term is altogether a misnomer. Balsdon has no doubts: we are assured that Titus was "a person of deep and evident culture."[84] The belief, as we saw, goes back a long way, to eminent scholars of the nineteenth century; and in this case it is a great tribute, from a contemporary scholar who is himself an obvious example of such a person. But how much do we know?

We are told that he was good at small talk, to the extent of being thought κοῦφος (the Latin levis, a term of disapprobation); that he had a flair for humour and anecdote, of rather a grimly Roman sort, if Plutarch's examples are typical; and that he had epigrams in verse engraved on his gifts at Delphi.[85] Perhaps he would have been welcome in an Oxford common-room. But there is no hint of an interest in literature or philosophy, about patronage of poets and artists—points in which Plutarch regularly shows an interest, and which not only Hellenistic kings, but even some contemporary Roman aristocrats, regarded as essential. Titus was no Scipio Aemilianus; for that matter, no Alexander the Great, who, though he unhesitatingly used the Greeks and philhellenism for his political purposes, did sleep with a copy of Homer under his pillow. Titus' epigrams at Delphi are nowhere ascribed to his own composition. When the poet Alcaeus of Messene angered both Philip and Flamininus, Philip (for all his faults a Hellenistic king) replied with an epigram; the Roman (according to Plutarch) merely grew angry.[86] What we know of his Greek prose style shows some acquaintance with koine usage, but a harsh and unidiomatic use of the language, which will not have impressed an educated Greek.[87]

---

[84] *Phoenix* 1967, 179.

[85] Plut. *Flam.* 12; 17.

[86] Plut. *Flam.* 9,4f.: the matter οὐ μετρίως παρώξυνε.

[87] See the letter to Chyretiae, Sherk, *Roman Documents from the Greek East* (1969), 199, with Sherk's discussion of the style. (Though I do not subscribe to all of his strictures.)

It is difficult to see how the myth of his being an educated Greek by nature and inclination ever got into the modern tradition. There are simply no facts to give it the slightest support. It would be fairer to say that he was a traditional Roman aristocrat, in that he enjoyed ruling over those who possessed culture—he preferred it to having culture himself, just as his ancestors, in a fine moral tale, had preferred ruling those who had wealth to having it themselves.[88] This does show a certain respect for Greek culture, which we must grant him, but not exaggerate or misunderstand. His bronze statue in Rome, which Plutarch still saw, had a Greek inscription;[89] it was no doubt the first instance of this in the city, and it was clearly done to advertise not his learning, but his *clientelae*. One can be a culture snob without being cultured, and the statue, in its way, is symbolical.

But his real achievement as a philhellene is political. We have seen that as recently as the First Macedonian War the Romans had still regarded Greeks as mere objects of plunder. Events had changed this approach, making a formula for permanent interest necessary by 200. The Senate had responded by forging the policy of protecting the Greeks against Macedon; but P. Galba at once showed that there was no consciousness of a new attitude to the Greeks. Out of this ambiguous beginning, it was clearly Titus Flamininus who developed the principle of the "freedom of Greece" in the form in which it was proclaimed at the Isthmian Games and carried out after—that principle of which he was later so proud and for which he demanded, and received, exuberant gratitude. When the Senate—largely at his prompting, we may be sure —framed its decree after Cynoscephalae, laying down the principle of this freedom, many eminent members, no doubt, like some of the ten commissioners, still thought in terms of retaining possession of the "three fetters." There is no reason to think, as some have done, that they would have been evacuated after the danger from Antiochus was past: to those who think in purely military terms— as much of Roman history proves—one danger is followed by another, and what has been won is not lightly abandoned. It was

---

[88] See Val. Max. 4,3,5 (M' Curius Dentatus). The story is widely told, and even transferred to Fabricius (*RE*, s.v. 'Curius,' no. 9, col. 1844).

[89] Plut. *Flam., init.*

surely Titus who laid down the principle that Greeks should not be treated like (e.g.) Iberians. And by speaking to them—however imperfectly—in their own language, he showed himself in advance of that later philhellene and mass enslaver of Greeks L. Aemilius Paullus, who thought this too much of a sacrifice of Roman *dignitas*.[90] In this way, as Plutarch well understood and makes clear without the exaggeration of modern myth, he made Roman control psychologically acceptable to many of the Greeks: but for him, the future of Greeks and Romans and their mutual relations might have been very different. As I have shown at length elsewhere,[91] he took traditional Roman diplomatic categories and weapons—the free ally regarded as a client; the control over an ally's policy without administrative commitment or the odium of a conqueror's presence—and put them, both literally and in an extended sense, into Greek: the Isthmian proclamation shows how carefully it was done. One might see him in terms of McLuhan, as recognising the demands and the possibilities of a new medium: Greek public opinion in the East.

He always remained, in essence, a Roman noble. We have seen this in his attitude to Greek culture, and I have pointed it out in his attitude to diplomacy. He drew back before the ultimate implications of his own diplomatic efforts, still not venturing too far ahead of the supporting show of force, which many of his colleagues regarded as the only safe way, if not of making friends, yet at least of influencing people. But in the circumstances he deserves credit for venturing as far as he did. In the process, he introduced greater flexibility into Roman diplomacy, moving away from the crude reliance on positions of strength that had been characteristic of the conquest of Italy, had gradually loosened up after it, but—perhaps as a result of twenty years of war—now threatened to become hard official policy once more. He thus contributed to making the further

---

[90] Livy 45,29,3. There is no question that he knew Greek; see, e.g., Livy 45,8,6. For the notorious enslavement of the Epirots, carried out with treacherous efficiency, see Livy 45,34; Plut. *Paul.* 29; Plin.*n.h.* 4,39; Strabo 7,7,3 (322C); cf. also his approval of a massacre in Aetolia (45,28,6f.; 31,1f.). Flamininus appears resplendent by comparison.

[91] *For. Client.*, ch. III; *Studies* (n. 54 above), 123. Cassola (*Labeo* 6, 117) totally misunderstands my arguments *For. Client.* 81f.: in fact, my views agree closely with his own.

expansion of Roman power technically much easier, as well as more acceptable to those who became subject to it.

It is strange that historians tend to admire great men indiscriminately, more often than not precisely for the wrong reason. Titus Quinctius Flamininus as the sentimental philhellene, or as the example of deep and sincerely felt Hellenic culture, is about as real as Alexander the humanitarian philosopher. But his petty vanity and his personal shiftiness and trickery (which have had to be stressed, perhaps to excess, after the recent coats of lavish whitewash) and his inability to rise as far as we should have liked above his environment—all these faults, though they must be recognised, should not blind us to his real importance in Greek and Roman history.[92]

[92] I should like to thank Professor Harry Rutledge for helping to make these lectures less unreadable than they might otherwise have been. I owe a particular debt of gratitude to the Department of Classics of the University of Cincinnati for coming to my rescue when my own University had disintegrated into anarchy, and offering me its friendly hospitality and a congenial atmosphere for working on the lectures. One or two of the ideas here propounded regarding the Aetolian treaty were first presented to a seminar at Heidelberg. I should like to thank my friends there (Professors Habicht and Gschnitzer and their staff), and what is probably the best doctoral class I have ever addressed, for long and stimulating discussion of those points.

8

Prologue to Greek Literacy

BY ERIC A. HAVELOCK

Delivered November 11 and 12, 1970

PROLOGUE TO GREEK LITERACY

1. THE TRANSCRIPTION OF THE CODE OF A NON-LITERATE CULTURE

A GENERATION AGO, there existed a consensus among scholars in the field of antiquity[1] that the Greek alphabet must have come into use by the Greeks not later than the tenth century and perhaps earlier. This dating could not be supported by any evidence from epigraphy; the inscriptions which could reasonably have been expected to survive from such a period are nonexistent. Nor does Homer's text supply any references to alphabetic writing.[2] If such a date seemed reasonable, the evidential grounds for accepting it lay in the history not of the Greeks but the Phoenicians. A majority of the Greek letter-shapes and their names were borrowed from the script used by this people, a script which was certainly in use in Mediterranean lands by that date. A variant of it must have been borrowed for example by the Hebrews[3] to transcribe the content of the earliest documents of the Old Testament in the eleventh or tenth century.[4] More recently, archaeology has demonstrated that it was in use in Palestine much earlier.[5] It therefore seemed plausible to conclude that the Greek adaptation[6] should have occurred in the same period or a little later.

The Phoenicians were not the only people living on the littoral

---

[1] Earlier opinions on this question are reviewed by H. J. Lorimer, "Homer and the Art of Writing," *AJA* 52 (1948), pp. 11-19: vid. also Rhys Carpenter (below n. 12).

[2] The two possible allusions are *Il.* 6.155ff. and 7.175, 187, 189, both dismissed by Lilian Jeffery in *A Companion to Homer*, ed. Wace and Stubbings, London 1962, p. 555.

[3] David Diringer, *Writing*, N.Y. 1962, observes (p. 125) that both the Phoenician and the Early Hebrew scripts are branches of the North Semitic alphabet.

[4] Authorship of the original "Biography of David" has been ascribed to a younger contemporary of the king, i.e., to the tenth century: vid. R. Pfeiffer, *An Introduction to the Old Testament*, N.Y. 1948, p. 342ff., who asserts (p. 357) that the author is "the father of history in a much truer sense that Herodotus half a millennium later." The "Song of Deborah" (Judges 5), originally an oral composition, describes an event of the eleventh century.

[5] Pfeiffer, *op.cit.*, p. 73, deduces that Phoenician script was invented c. 1500 B.C.; vid. also Diringer, *op.cit.*, p. 131 and Carpenter (below n. 12).

[6] Adaptation of Phoenician letter-shapes in the formation of the Greek alphabet is discussed by Nilsson, "Die Uebernahme und Entwicklung des Alphabet durch die Griechen": *Opuscula Selecta*, Lund 1952, vol. 2, pp. 1029-1056: but vid. also Carpenter (below n. 12).

of the Mediterranean who in the pre-Homeric period used script. For a generation now, it has been known that the Mycenaeans used a writing system identified by scholars as Linear B, apparently adapted from a Cretan prototype. Its decipherment though only partially successful was achieved on the hypothesis that the Mycenaeans spoke an early form of Greek.[7] The system, judging from the content of the records that have been deciphered, was used for very limited purposes, but its existence has supplied a second excuse for believing that the Greeks between the eleventh and eighth centuries B.C. used writing. If Linear B, so this assumption runs, was in use before 1150, it must have continued in use after 1100. Was it credible that a people who had used such a tool of commerce and civilisation would ever forget it?[8] But alas! the epigraphical evidence for the survival of Linear B is equally non-existent.[9] In dealing with the question of Greek literacy, the supposed "literacy" of the Mycenaeans has proved to be a red herring drawn across a problem which is not soluble on these lines.

The fact that the problem exists is a reflection in part of that state of mind in which we as members of a literate culture approach the study of the civilisation of the Greeks. Behind the reluctance to trust the negative influence of epigraphy it is possible to discern the influence of an assumption, or set of assumptions, working in the unconscious mind of scholars and historians, which run something like this: Any civilised culture worth the name has to be a literate culture, and while we recognise such a culture by many hall-marks, the chief one is the production of a sophisticated literature, and this is particularly true of the Greeks. In the field of literature, composition takes place most readily in prose, even though much of the prose does not aim at high literary pretension and is consequently ephemeral. Superimposed, so to speak, upon the prosaic

[7] John Chadwick, *The Decipherment of Linear B*, London 1967, describes the procedure followed. Cautionary qualifications are set forth in G. S. Kirk, *Songs of Homer*, Cambridge 1962, pp. 24-28.

[8] This is the argument put forward by G. Kahl-Furthmann, in *Wann lebte Homer?*, Meisenheim am Glan 1967, who proposes that the Homeric poems were originally written in a refined Linear B script, but much later transcribed in the Greek alphabet in the eighth century.

[9] "There is no evidence available that knowledge of the script survived the 'dark age' which followed the end of the Mycenaean period"—so J. A. Davison in *A Companion to Homer* (above n. 2), p. 217.

sub-structure of the culture are the works of poetry. They represent a form of composition of an exceptional sophistication and refinement, a supplement to the prose literature. A civilisation in short includes as part of its equipment both a literature of prose and a literature of poetry, but the prose has priority and is more extensive. The Greek literature that has been preserved begins with Homer and Hesiod, followed by the lyricists, Pindar, and the Greek dramatists. Here is a poetic literature as sophisticated as any the world has seen. It must therefore represent the refined product of a culture which had begun its ascent to supremacy a considerable time before these works appeared, one which indeed must have rested on a foundation of discourse written in prose, even if most of it has been lost. Such poetic refinement presupposes a long previous period of development in the art of the written word. It is therefore incredible that the Greeks who either preceded Homer or were contemporary with him were completely non-literate.

This argument so far as I know has not been explicitly formulated by scholars. In stating it as I have done,[10] I have tried to make explicit what was there by implication in the way in which they have viewed the history of Greek literature and have written about it. The argument of the following pages, as it step by step unfolds, may lead to the conclusion that such premises are mistaken; that in fact, given the conditions under which Greek civilisation developed, the order of priorities should be reversed.

Between the years 1928 and 1938 there came to light the results of two investigations in the field of classical antiquity, which in retrospect can be seen to have intimate connection, but which at the time were pursued in separate areas of scholarship and in independence of each other. It is perhaps noteworthy that the authors of both were Americans. In 1928 Milman Parry published, initially in a French thesis, his analysis of the metrical and verbal structure of the Homeric poems, drawing the conclusion that the *Iliad* and *Odyssey* were examples of a strictly oral composition which employed a formulaic and highly traditional language. The 'author' or 'authors', terms henceforth to be placed within quotation-marks, were therefore bards who were non-literate, who composed from

---

[10] Vid. also Havelock, "Pre-Literacy and the Pre-Socratics," in *Institute of Classical Studies*, Univ. London Bulletin no. 13, 1966, pp. 44-45.

memory in their heads, for audiences who listened but presumably did not read.[11]

In 1933 and again in 1938 Rhys Carpenter published his demonstrations that the Greek alphabet could not have been invented earlier than the last half of the eighth century.[12] I have adverted elsewhere[13] to the reluctance with which this conclusion, reached on epigraphical grounds, has been accepted by students of language and literature.[14] Clearly the presupposition that Greek literature presented the full flowering of a literate culture which had already been incubating for some centuries was put in jeopardy. Carpenter's date meant that prior to the last half of the 8th century, and very probably during the last half itself, any composition in Greek that we would style "literary" had to be oral anyway. This would still leave a choice of dates for "Homer," using his name as a convenient shorthand for that process of composition, whatever it was, of which the *Iliad* and *Odyssey*, much as we have them, were the end products. Either "he" composed earlier, perhaps much earlier, than the last half of the eighth century, and the poems were then memorised and so preserved more or less intact until they could be written down at the close of the century: or else "he" composed very near the time that the alphabet was introduced, so that "his" composition could be given documentary form either in "his" life time or soon after "his" death.

At this point the oral theory, supplemented by previous research into the language and content of the Homeric poems, determined the choice that should be made. The formulaic technique, carried only in the living memories of bards, was shared and transmitted between the generations. Since it was never frozen in documented form, its language could slowly respond to dialectical changes over periods of time, and the content of what was sung could reflect not only memory of the remoter past but experience contemporary

---

[11] See now *The Making of Homeric Verse*: The Collected Papers of Milman Parry, edited with introduction by Adam Parry, Oxford (Clarendon) 1971.

[12] Rhys Carpenter, "The Antiquity of the Greek Alphabet," *A.J.A.* 37 (1933), pp. 8-29, and "The Greek Alphabet Again," *A.J.A.* 42 (1938), pp. 58-69.

[13] Havelock, *Preface to Plato*, Cambridge, Mass. 1963, p. 49 n. 4.

[14] Vid. most recently Kirk, *op.cit.*, pp. 69-71, who is willing to assign the transmission of the Greek alphabet from the Phoenicians to the early eighth century, while noting that none of the inscriptions can be dated before the last decade of the eighth.

with the time of the singer. Homer's dialectical forms, and the report which his poems give of historical and social conditions, are demonstrably an amalgam which ranges forward from Mycenae as far down as the conditions in which the Ionian Greeks spoke and lived in the eighth century. Previous efforts to separate these chronologically disparate elements and allot them to different portions of Homer's text had failed. The Homeric mixture is so to speak chemical not mechanical.[15] Recognition of the flexibility of response inherent in the oral technique had now solved Homeric problems which had previously seemed insoluble. Equally, it was now demonstrated that the creative process, which produced Homer, had ended only at that point, or shortly before it, when the Greek alphabet was invented.[16]

There were some peculiar merits enjoyed by the Greek alphabetic invention, when it is compared with all previous writing systems.[17] The issue here does not lie between ideographic and phonetic systems. All the nearest competitors of the Greek system were already phonetic, though it is indicative of the comparative "backwardness" of Linear B that it still employed some ideograms.[18] But at the level of phonetic invention, the issue still lay between systems which were content to symbolise actual sounds which any mouth makes when it speaks, and a system like the Greek which analysed such sound into abstract components. An actual linguistic sound is produced either by the vibration of a column of air in the larynx, or by this vibration as it is variously restricted, controlled and released by the tongue, teeth and lips. The former

---

[15] M. P. Nilsson, *Homer and Mycenae*, London 1933, found elements in the poems ranging from the Mycenaean to the beginning of the Orientalising period (and especially pp. 158-59): these are "inextricably mixed." Kirk, *op.cit.*, pp. 179ff., reviews the "cultural and linguistic amalgam," containing dialectical forms and reports of customs and objects from widely divergent periods, fused to a degree which allows "the identification of only a few elements in the amalgam." (p. 181).

[16] Kirk, *op.cit.*, p. 180, notes that in the case of certain elements incorporated by oral tradition there is a *terminus post quem* of about 750 B.C.

[17] For general discussion of the alphabet and particularly of the Near Eastern scripts from which the Greek alphabet was adapted, see D. Diringer, *The Alphabet*, London 1948, and *Writing* (above n. 3) (esp. pp. 123ff.), as well as C. F. and F. M. Voegelin, "Typological Classification of Systems with Included, Excluded and Self-sufficient Alphabets," in *Anthropological Linguistics* III (1961).

[18] Vid. Ventris and Chadwick, *Documents in Mycenaean Greek*, Cambridge 1956, pp. 48ff.

in simple terms is equivalent to a vowel, the latter to a combination of a vowel with consonants either preceding, following, or enclosing. We can think of all these sounds actually made as syllables, whether they consist of vowels alone or vowel-consonant combinations.

The systems of writing including the Phoenician which had been in use in the Near East in the period preceding the Greek invention were themselves all syllabic. That is, they sought to represent the sounds actually made by the mouth as these are put together in words. Mostly these were vowel-consonant types, but also vowels alone, as we can see for example from the practice of Linear B[19] (if the decipherment be accepted). Their achievement therefore was empirical. They took the language so to speak as they found it and sought to objectify the actual sound-units as these existed in pronunciation.

But this effort to create a one-to-one correspondence between signs and speech-sounds produced an inherent difficulty. The distinct syllables into which any given language can be divided might theoretically run into the hundreds, especially if the language uses vowel-consonant combinations not only in pairs but in triplets. A spoken tongue is probably always looser, richer, and more idiosyncratic than the rules of its transcription would imply, however perfect a copy they be, but in the case of the syllabaries, the gap between what the system might indicate was being said and what actually had been said could be very considerable.[20] To symbolise what might actually be said with approximate fidelity might mean multiplying the number of different signs to an unmanageable extent. Or else, the number could be cut down to manageable size, with the result that a single sign had to serve double or triple duty. Ambiguity in decipherment became inevitable, in varying degree. All these sign systems were placed in a theoretic dilemma: either to increase the register of symbols to achieve a one-to-one correspondence with possible syllables, and so achieve relative acoustic accuracy, or to cut down the register to a manageable number, at the cost of increasing ambiguity. The Phoenician system alone

---

[19] Ventris and Chadwick, op.cit., pp. 76ff.

[20] By way of example, in Documents, p. 170, a word deciphered as e-so-to is interpreted as either esto ("let there be") or essontoi ("there shall be").

achieved maximum economy, which is why it is sometimes falsely likened to an alphabet, but in fact it provided what has been correctly described as an "unvocalised syllabary,"[21] which still left the reader to make the correct choice of possible vocalic combinations.

These inherent difficulties would seem to have placed some important limitations upon the actual use of such systems. Their management called for a degree of professional skill restricted to a class of specialists who had the ability and leisure to master it. In cases where the signs had accumulated in the interest of acoustic fidelity, the skill called for special training in the memorisation of the system. So far on the other hand as the system practised economy, the skill needed was one of interpretation. The "scribe" of the time of Christ was still the required and recognised interpreter of scripture, in the first place because he was prepared to say what a given transcription "meant," that is, in practice, what choices to make of key syllables where choice was possible.[22] To read such a script required a series of decisions basically acoustic in their nature. This should call our attention to the fact, usually neglected, that in the history of writing systems the relative degree of success obtained is tested not in the act of writing, but in the act of reading.

It follows that pre-Greek systems of writing in their application could not be democratised. Their management remained in the hands of experts, lay or priestly. It is a question whether, if we apply the term literacy to such cultures as employed them, we are not mis-using the term.[22a]

But while reflection on these technological difficulties makes it easy for us to realise how restricted the expertise might be, it is not at first so easy to recognise that similar restriction would apply

---

[21] By F. Householder in review of Emmett Bennett and Others, *C.J.*, 54 (1959), 379-83. For further discussion of this question, see Havelock, *op.cit.* (note 13), p. 129, n. 6.

[22] Pfeiffer, *op.cit.*, pp. 73ff., notes how, in the period of stabilisation and canonisation of the text, there was room for scribes to interpret the unvocalised script in different ways according to their theological inclinations.

[22a] A small flat rectangular piece of stone found at Thera has been interpreted by Prof. Marinatos (in his catalogue of the Thera exhibit in the National Museum at Athens) as "the earliest example of the present day slate used by school children on which they scratched designs and learnt their first letters." My own recent inspection of this object (in show case No. 7) reveals with clarity, as he himself notes, only a drawing of a lily-flower.

not only to the people who could use the system, but also to the kind of material they were likely to put into it. If the number of those who could read and write remained limited, so also did the content of what was transcribed. When used to record catalogues and numerical quantities, such systems functioned without much ambiguity. But when it came to transcribing discursive speech, difficulties of interpretation would discourage the practice of using the script for novel or freely-invented discourse. The practice that would be encouraged would be to use the system as a reminder of something already familiar, so that recollection of its familiarity would aid the reader in getting the right interpretation. And to be familiar, this something would resemble material already on the lips of people, independently of any existence in writing, and so independently "known." It would in short tend to be something— tale, proverb, parable, fable and the like—which already existed in oral form and had been composed according to oral rules. The syllabic system in short provided techniques for recall of what was already familiar, not instruments for formulating novel statements which could further the exploration of new experience.

The rules of oral composition themselves laid strict limitations on the kind of statement which could be made, if it was to be preserved. Precisely what these were will be examined later. It is sufficient for the moment to recognise that they existed in order to recognise a further restriction which was placed upon the range and scope of oral statement when it came to be encased in the syllabaries. Ambiguities of the script would be bound to encourage a selectivity practised at the expense of the oral originals, a selectivity which concentrated upon central facts and sentiments, at the expense of the more unique, eccentric, and we might say, the more personal element in the oral repertoire. The former were more easily accommodated to or matched with the script, the latter more difficult to document adequately and more difficult to recognise when documented. Syllabic scripts would tend to produce paraphrases of oral originals rather than the originals themselves, and even to simplify somewhat their syntax and vocabulary.

A glance at the literatures so called preserved in hieroglyph, cuneiform or Phoenician will confirm that these characteristics of content do exist, characteristics for which I have sought explanation in the technological difficulties created by the writing systems in use. We gain an overall impression, as these documents are translated for us,[23] that we are being asked to read a rather formalised version of what went on, what people actually said and did and believed. A few central stories or myths recur, usually focussed upon the careers of a limited number of persons. Story and person are alike familiar. Rituals in regular use are described, parables and proverbs abound. But when all allowance is made for simple grandeur of conception or refinement of design, the basic complexity of human experience is not there. The full report of oral utterance is missing. We are being treated to an authorised version. The common reader can test this statement for himself, by taking up the Old Testament. The older parts of this compendium were inscribed and so preserved in a version of the Phoenician Syllabary.[24] To be sure, some theological rewriting of these records occurred in the period after the Second Temple was founded.[25] But it remains true that the original narratives and the surrounding sentiments are syntactically repetitive, that typical situations recur, that the relationships between the characters are relatively simple, and their acts take an almost ritual quality. We feel the simple rhythm of the record as it unfolds.

It is precisely these limitations imposed upon the possible coverage of human experience that give to the Old Testament its power of appeal, as we say, to simple people. The record of a culture which is composed under these restrictions is likely to center upon religion and myth, for these tend to codify and standardise the variety of human experience so that the reader of such scripts is more likely to recognise what the writer is talking about. It is therefore no accident that the cultures of the Near East which precede the Greek and are recorded in hieroglyph, cuneiform or Phoenician seem on the basis of the record to be peculiarly occupied with such matters. We normally take it for granted that such pre-

[23] As for example, in the case of that kind of material assembled in *Ancient Near Eastern Texts Relating to the Old Testament,* ed. J. B. Pritchard (2nd ed., Princeton 1955).

[24] Above, notes 2 and 3. Pfeiffer, *op.cit.,* pp. 72ff., observes that the Samaritan Pentateuch was written in an ornate form of the Phoenician letters and preserved in that form, while in the case of the Masoretic Pentateuch a different and more developed script was used.

[25] Pfeiffer, *op.cit.,* p. 56.

occupation was an inherent characteristic of such cultures, and it is often put down to the fact that they were at a more primitive stage of cultural development. The reason, I am suggesting, is rather to be sought in a fact of technology. If it is easy for modern research to discover archetypal myths in these so-called literatures, may this not reflect the fact that the original transcribers, given the limitations of the medium they were using, found it equally easy to write down the archetypes with some assurance that they would be read easily and correctly?[26]

To enter the world of what we call Greek literature, from Homer on, is to encounter a larger dimension of human experience, so much wider, more diverse, personal, critical, subtle, humorous, passionate, ironic and reflective. This remains true even when all allowance is made for the limitations imposed by the poetic form in which so much of this literature is cast. If we ask ourselves the reason why this may be so, we usually find the answer in what is assumed perhaps unconsciously to be a racial superiority. The Greek genes conferred upon adults a better equipment with which to achieve creative effort in art and intellect. But I doubt whether such a racial hypothesis has any more scientific foundation when applied to the Greeks than it has when applied to the Germans. If the clue to the selectivity of content found in Near Eastern texts resides in the nature of their orthography, may it be true that the comparative richness of content of Greek texts is correspondingly due to the superior technical resources of Greek orthography?

Pre-Greek systems, we recall, sought to symbolise the actual sounds which a mouth makes when it adds sound to sound to produce speech. They therefore were empirical inventions which sought to copy linguistic sounds on a one-to-one basis. Although they analysed words into their syllabic components, they still provided as it were visual reproductions of language rather than analytic definitions of the elements of linguistic noise. The Greek invention, which perhaps betrays the application to language of a mathematical type of reasoning, consisted in pursuing the analysis of linguistic sound to the level of complete abstraction. It is commonly said that the Greeks accomplished this by inventing signs

---

[26] Possible implications, as they bear on the structuralist theories of Lévi-Strauss and his followers, cannot be pursued here.

for vowels.[27] This is not a true statement of what actually happened. The trick of symbolising vowels, as previously noted, had already been tried and achieved, for example, in Linear B.[28] What the Greeks did was to invent the idea that a sign could represent a mere consonant, a sound so to speak which does not exist in nature but only in thought. It requires an effort of reflective analysis to realise and recognise that the movements of teeth, tongue, palate, and lips are ineffective, considered as linguistic sound, except when accompanied by vocalic breath of varying compression. Strictly speaking, a consonant is a non-sound. When we memorise our consonants by repeating our ABC we have to add vocalic values to them to make them pronounceable, which is another way of saying that alphabets taught orally by rote to children still have to be taught as syllabaries. The Greek alphabet, when it took over the Phoenician signs, made the crucial decision of restricting the function of most of them to the symbolisation of non-sounds. The syllables actually pronounced in any language were broken down and dissolved into abstract components. These, so far as they were what we call consonants, were objects of intelligence, not units of actual speech. At a stroke, by this analysis, the Greeks provided a table of elements of linguistic sound not only manageable because of its economy but, for the first time in the history of homo sapiens sapiens, also accurate.

The term accurate must not be pressed to an absolute degree. It may be doubted whether any given sign system inventible by man could accommodate without ambiguity all the possible noises made in the course of speaking a given language. All systems depend for effective functioning upon the principle that agreed acoustic values are attached to given inscribed shapes. We can posit that the Greek alphabet embodied the first system in which in all cases one and only one acoustic value was theoretically attachable to one given shape. From this fixed rule there followed a second: any actual sound could be achieved only in combinations of two or more shapes. It is theoretically possible that this principle of uniform orthography as it is pursued in literate cultures has encouraged some reduction in what might be called erratic language sounds.

[27] Thus Kirk, *Songs*, p. 70 and Diringer, *Writing*, p. 152.
[28] Above note 19.

Modern French, to a foreigner at least, seems to be a tongue which in the course of centuries has submitted to some acoustic rationalisation induced by the fact that a given spelling may have a tendency to mould a pronunciation to correspond. This, if true, reverses the rationale which guides the science of linguistics, which as a science has to presume that acoustic usage in a given language is logical and invariable and which may even enlarge the presumption into a belief that a common rationale is discoverable behind all languages. Such conceptions are assisted to become pervasive to the degree that we are compelled to study languages in written versions of what was once spoken. I offer this as a speculative aside. The sometimes erratic orthography of Greek inscriptions and graffiti[29] should at least alert us to the possibility, not that the writers were unskilled, but rather that the linguistic sounds they were transcribing did not always fit neatly and unambiguously into the agreed values of the marks they were obliged to use.

Subject to these qualifications, we can still say that the sign-system used in the Greek alphabet, thanks to its ability to identify the abstract components of syllables, provided in theory an instrument of unique efficiency for transcribing any language, and in practice one of peculiar efficiency for transcribing the Greek language, a tongue in which the vocalic component of a syllable was enlarged in comparison with the usage of Semitic tongues, and which therefore encouraged a more ready identification of the difference between a vowel and its consonantal accompaniment. While the practical effect was to insist that a consonantal syllable required at least two signs for its transcription, the signs employed, because of the level of analysis now applied were not only economical in number but by permutation and combination could provide exhaustive coverage. Thus was revealed the fact that the complexity and variety of linguistic noise is achieved by combinations and permutations of a few theoretically fixed elements.

When therefore it came to transcribing a given oral statement, the signs employed, through the abstract values attached to them, produced a relatively clear, unambiguous and economical register of the exact sounds of what had been said. The reader therefore—

[29] Vid. below note 32.

and it is in the act of reading rather than writing that the secret of the alphabet subsists—the reader of any transcription who had previously memorised the proper values could acquire automatic and rapid "recognition"—the Greek word for the act of reading— of what was being said.

The invention therefore brought within the reach of any people using it a degree of fluency and ease in reading which had hitherto been unknown. A sign-series which numbered thirty or less placed the act of memorisation of the system within the competence of a majority of men, and for the first time made it possible to democratise its use. Whole populations could theoretically become literate, if by the term literacy we mean to identify a situation of socialised readership. And if we do, it is proper to apply the adjective literate only to those cultures which used or adapted the Greek invention.[30]

This kind of literacy depended not merely upon the invention, but upon its application in a system of programmed instruction for children. This in turn depended upon the accumulation and availability of alphabetic documentation in sufficient quantity to make it worth while for children to be taught to read. As they were taught, the alphabetic skills would be convertible into an automatic reflex, not something laboriously mastered in maturity. These developments towards literacy in a meaningful sense involved social and institutional changes covering the manufacture and distribution of script and the introduction of a reading curriculum at the school level with an adequate instructional base. No doubt informal starts were made in this direction on the model of the village dame-schools of England a century ago. But these would take a great deal of time. The Greeks were unlikely to organise programmed instruction in reading in order to facilitate the decipherment of a few inscriptions. Even the political device of ostracism initiated in the first quarter of the fifth century called for nothing more than the ability to inscribe and therefore to spell a personal name which had perhaps already been announced in

---

[30] For a discussion of what degree or diffusion of readership constitutes literacy, vid. Jack Goody and Ian Watt, "The Consequences of Literacy," in *Literacy in Traditional Societies*, Cambridge 1968, pp. 27-68.

previous voting.[31] Many groups of voters found it more feasible to have even this office performed for them by someone else.[32]

In 700 B.C., at the time when the alphabet first came into use, the conditions of socialised literacy lay far in the future. But something can be said immediately about the unique role which at its inception this invention was called upon to play in the documentation of Greek culture. During the centuries immediately preceding, this culture had been totally non-literate. Yet it was a culture, a civilisation; I shall later defend the use of this term as applied to the period in question. It must therefore have devised and relied upon its own forms of linguistic record. These must have been oral, and relied on oral rules for their preservation and transmission. These again are matters to be explored later. The Near Eastern cultures were equipped to inscribe their own oral records, but at the cost of selectivity and simplification.

The alphabet's intrusion at this point into the history of homo sapiens sapiens introduced not literacy, but a permanently en-

---

[31] This is A. W. Gomme's suggestion, *O.C.D.* s.v. "Ostracism," but it is omitted in Vanderpool's account (next note).

[32] See now Eugene Vanderpool, *Ostracism at Athens*, Semple Lectures (1969), University of Cincinnati. His statement (p. 15) that "obviously the very existence of a law such as the law on ostracism presupposes that the electorate was largely literate" reflects what has been *communis opinio*. He supports it by appeal to a sentence in Plutarch (Aristeides VII.5) who, however, could only interpret the institution in the light of the literate expectations of his own day, as do we. The tabulations and descriptions of actual *ostraka* in this admirable monograph would seem to point to an opposite conclusion. (a) Uncertain orthography and spelling is fairly frequent. Was this commoner in the earlier samples? (b) evidence that some of the graffiti were "prefabricated," Vanderpool suggests by scribes, for voters presumably non-literate. This presumption, now necessary to cover some of the finds in the Kerameikos (Vanderpool, p. 11), would seem to be extendible to the case of the "Themistocles" collection (Vanderpool, pp. 11-12 and fig. 30) whether or not the common hands there discernible represent an attempt at "ballot-stuffing." There are three general considerations usually ignored in this question which should have some weight in favour of at best a "semi-literate" condition when the institution was first used: (i) The choice of sherds presupposes absence of any ready supply of appropriate writing materials, and *a fortiori* of a reading and writing public. Vanderpool (p. 12) notes the tediousness of the operation; (ii) In semi-literate societies, the first and often only thing you learn to write is personal names, your own and those of others, needed for legal signature; (iii) the writing down of a man's name recalled magical practice. You could put a curse on him by naming his name and putting the curse on the name, or by drawing his picture or his "sign" and cursing it.

The institution may indeed have been inspired by this ancient practice. The little drawings noted by Vanderpool are therefore not "doodlings" (p. 29) and the curses (some metrical) are not an indulgence but a "making sure."

graved and complete record of the ways of non-literacy. That is the paradox. Because of its phonetic superiority, it provided an instrument in which for the first time the full complexities of an oral tradition could be adequately revealed, for in theory any linguistic noise could now be automatically recognised in transcription. Previous writing systems had reported a muffled version of what went on in pre-Homeric cultures. Where on the one hand oral composition still survives into modern times, and has been recorded, as in the Balkans and elsewhere, it can give us only what lingers on as entertainment on the margins of cultures which administer their affairs by literate methods. As for the true oral cultures which have enjoyed isolated survival in Polynesia and elsewhere, these can be transcribed only in anthropological reports which are compelled to use the vocabulary and thought forms of that literate culture in which the anthropologist was trained.

On the other hand, the documentation furnished by the Greek alphabet, juxtaposed as it was, by the accident of technological invention, against the immediately preceding oral culture, constituted as it were an act of precipitation in which the identity of that culture could crystallise and preserve itself to an unusual degree in unusual purity. It made visible the rules by which personal intercourse was regulated, how its members thought and felt, the consciousness in short of the people concerned. Such documentation, as I shall later seek to demonstrate, should not be understood as completing itself with the appearance of the Homeric poems.

What was the character of this culture of pre-literate Greece? Before an answer is attempted, it is well to recognise that it could not have automatically terminated itself at the date of the introduction of the alphabet. Greece must have remained largely non-literate till at least 650 B.C. "The alphabet," says Denys Page, summarising the epigraphical evidence, "was not in common use anywhere until the life time of Archilochus, and indeed we have no right whatever to believe that the use was common even then."[33] My own more radical view would urge that there are serious reasons for postponing its common use to a date much later

[33] Fondation Hart Entretiens X: "Archiloque" Vandoeuvres-Genève 1963, p. 121.

than this. But on a conservative showing, the Greeks between 1100 and 650 achieved what they did without the help of any script whatever.

Perhaps from about 1100 to 900 this achievement did not amount to much. Archaeology has made evident the physical ruin of the Mycenaean palace-complexes and it is usually deduced that with this went also the destruction of those political and social arrangements which had previously rendered commerce, art and a settled way of life possible.[34] Even this hypothesis of a totally dark age supervening upon the Mycenaean period has been lately questioned. Whatever the truth of it, there is no reason to doubt that, as Professor Geoffrey Kirk has recently emphasised, the centuries after 900 were "Dark" only in the sense that so much about them is unknown. If we consider the period from 900 to 650 as a chronological unit, it is obvious that we view in this period, however obscurely, the genesis of that classical culture which becomes evident to documentary inspection only in the 6th and 5th centuries. In what forms had this genesis appeared? The primary one was institutional, embodied in the formation of those corporate identities known as *poleis*, the Greek city states. All the essential features of this Greek way of life seem to have been organised and functioning by the 10th century. Professor Kirk remarks on the settlements of the Anatolian sea-board which followed the early migrations: "This (viz. some social stability) the Ionian towns with their aristocratic form of government and their federal system had probably achieved to a high degree by the ninth century and to a moderate degree before that." Ionia, it is now agreed, did not become wealthy, in comparison with the mainland, before the seventh century. A fortiori, the towns of mainland Greece must be deemed already capable by the tenth century of supporting forms of social life which went well beyond the limits of village existence. At the level of technology, these communities were capable of forging iron, and presumably of smelting it, a feat beyond the competence of the Mycenaeans.[35]

---

[34] Thus, for instance, A. W. Lawrence writes, in *Greek Architecture*, London 1957, p. 83: "The Bronze Age ended in wholesale destruction, about 1100 B.C., after which four centuries of poverty ensued." The "Hellenic" civilisation, he assumes, begins only when they terminate.

[35] Vid. Kirk, *Songs*, p. 130.

Their activities in commerce and navigation may not have exceeded Mycenaean standards. Their temple architecture not later than the end of the eighth century can be shown to have anticipated in wood the conceptions and refinements of the archaic age now partially preserved for us in stone.[36] In the realm of the arts, this period saw at its inception the invention and perfection of the geometric style of decoration, followed by the introduction of naturalistic motifs in the so-called orientalising period which began, appropriately enough, about the time that the Phoenician letters were put to Greek use.[37]

In the face of these facts, a conception which identifies cultural sophistication with a degree of literacy must be discarded. A culture can somehow rely totally on oral communication and still be a culture. The contrary presumption, as I said earlier, was originally responsible for reluctance among scholars to accept a late date for the alphabet. But this kind of thinking is not confined to the learned. Parenthetically, its effect may be noted in our own discussions of modern problems, educational, social, and political, as these arise in the world at large today. Consider, for example, the following quotation from a recent editorial by a vice-president of the *New York Times*:

"Between a third and a half of the world's people suffer from hunger or malnutrition. The people of the undeveloped world are the majority of the human race, and are breeding faster than the people of the Soviet Union, the United States, or Western Europe. There are one hundred million more illiterates in the world today than there were twenty years ago, bringing the total to about eight hundred millions."[38]

It will be noted in these words that hunger, malnutrition, and backwardness, on the one hand, are automatically linked with a

---

[36] Admittedly the surviving evidence for public or religious architecture before 700 remains meager. For a list of nine structures identified as "early," vid. G. Becatti, *The Art of Ancient Greece and Rome*, London 1968, p. 56. Of these the Heraeum at Samos and the temple of Artemis Orthia at Sparta are dated to the eighth century by Lawrence, *op.cit.* (above n. 34), pp. 88ff. On wooden structure, metopes, entablature, etc. in the seventh century yielding to stone vid. Becatti, *op.cit.*, p. 57.

[37] For a convenient review of these developments vid. Becatti, *op.cit.*, pp. 14, 27-28.

[38] James Reston, *New York Times*, October 16, 1970.

condition of non-literacy on the other. It has in fact become a fashion in the Western industrialised countries to regard all non-literate cultures as non-cultures. This, in spite of the fact that a segment of our own population never learns to read, and a significant segment never learns to read fluently. Yet somehow we manage. In considering the Greeks, we had better come to terms at once with the fact that their civilisation began in non-literacy. An oral culture deserves to be considered and studied in its own terms, so far as these can be recaptured.

Technology at varying levels supplies the necessary basis for all cultures modern and ancient. We have detected its presence in the non-literate period of Greek culture as applied to architecture, metallurgy and navigation. The ability to document a spoken language is itself a technological feat, one on which the cultures which preceded the Greek placed some reliance, and which has become essential in post-Greek cultures. This brings us to ask an important question in the following terms: Failing a technology of the written word, did non-literate Greece rely on any technology of the spoken word? Was oral communication formulated in any contrived fashion to assist that preservation of record which is more obviously achievable by the use of writing? Were any methods available for managing ephemeral speech in such a way as to render it less ephemeral?

The answer to such a question is more easily perceived when it is placed within a larger context supplied by the science of anthropology. The non-literate character of Greek culture before 650 B.C. reproduced conditions of immense antiquity. These bore some resemblance to those which had obtained in the pre-Greek cultures of the Middle East, so far as these had remained unaffected by the limited use of inadequate writing systems. Non-literacy had been the rule for tens, nay hundreds of thousands of years during which homo sapiens became homo sapiens sapiens. This creature—the prototype of ourselves—achieved that condition of culture which we can identify as societal and humane only after his achievement and mastery of language. The emergence of human culture is often identified, in the popular mind at least, with the invention and manipulation of tools. It does not appear however that this capacity in itself is the hall-mark of our particular species among the animals. The more correct view can be illustrated by quotation from that classic work by Ernst Mayr, *Animal Species and Evolution*:

"It has been claimed that the skillful use of tools set up a strong selective pressure for increased brain size until the brain was large enough to enable its owner to manufacture his implements himself. The discovery of stone cultures among rather small-brained hominids forces us to modify our ideas. It now seems probable that the use of tools is an ancient hominid trait, an assumption supported by the readiness with which, for instance, chimpanzees adopt implements." Mayr also points out that many anthropologists are unaware of the widespread use of tools in the animal kingdom, of which he cites many examples, and he then continues:

"The assumption that rather small-brained hominids were experienced tool users and manufacturers raises at once the question of the nature of that (tremendous) selection pressure which caused an increase of brain size during the mid-Pleistocene at an unprecedented rate. Average cranial capacity rose from a thousand to 1,400 cubic centimeters in less than one million years. . . . It seems likely that the ability to make tools contributed far less to this selection pressure than did the need for an efficient system of communication, that is, speech. Foresight and capacity for leadership would be greatly enhanced by an ability for articulate communication. Many aspects of intelligence and planning would have little survival value without a medium of communication far more efficient than that of the anthropoid apes."[39]

To achieve a capacity for enunciating that complex register of sounds which are represented in a language required the evolution of a physical apparatus suitable for making them. If we may amend a statement attributed to the Greek philosopher Anaxagoras,[40] "Man is intelligent not because he has hands but because he has a mouth." In modern scientific language, which I again borrow from Ernst Mayr, we read this lesson as follows:

"The hominid line was well preadapted for the development

---

[39] Ernst Mayr, *Animal Species and Evolution*, Cambridge, Mass. 1963, pp. 634-35.
[40] D.-K. 59 A 102.

of speech, owing to the low position of the larynx, the oval shape of the teeth row, the absence of diastemas between the teeth, the separation of the hyoid from the cartilage of the larynx, the general mobility of the tongue and the vaulting of the palate. . . . The transfer of the food-uptake function from the snout to the hands further facilitated the specialization of the mouth as an organ of speech. Speech does not fossilize, and all we can say about the origin of language is pure conjecture. Yet it is evident that a superior ability for communication and the possession of associated brain functions to make such communication optimally effective would add enormously to fitness. The hominid evolution is an impressive example of the chain reaction of evolutionary change that results from key innovations such as bipedalism and speech."[41]

An animal can bark, bellow, grunt, and whine, and a bird can warble. Man's mouth represents an apparatus which, by using tongue, palate, teeth and lips to impose closure upon various pitches of vocalic vibration, can produce an enormous supply of diverse sounds suitable for organisation in human language. This instrument of communication was perfected over a long span of time—was it 30,000 years or 3 million years? A satisfying answer to this particular chronometric problem does not seem to be forthcoming, so far as I can discover. But its perfection came about— and this is the point crucial to our present investigation—before it ever occurred to our species to enlist the hand and eye in the service of the mouth and ear so as to inscribe a code of visible signs which should correspond to the sounds of any language in use. The non-literate condition of Greek culture between 1100 and 650 B.C. was one which responded to immemorial habits and needs, compared with which the history of literate habits, even if we include the Egyptian and Near Eastern civilisations, is a mere moment in time.

Language is an act of management of sound, not an arrangement of letters. But it does not consist in the mere enunciation of sounds by the mouth, however extensive these may be. It comes into existence only as these sounds are arranged in patterns with corresponding signification. But signification cannot take place

[41] Mayr, *loc.cit.*

unless the patterns are shared between members of a group, and to be shared they must be standardised. So they become a code, of fantastic complexity. But this code can function as a code only as it is embedded in the memories of all the individuals using it. It is there stored up for continual re-use, and memorised with that complete accuracy which will alone make it an effective means of shared and instant communication. Men do not gather grapes from thorns and figs from thistles. More correctly, they do not allow themselves to speak that way. To do so is to break the code. This requirement of memorisation, I suggest, lay behind those selective pressures which accelerated the growth of the brain, at such a fantastic rate, as noticed in a previous quotation from Mayr. Without the memory, communication was impossible. The human brain is a computer which far outdoes any imaginable artifact turned out by IBM.

The central role played by memory in the achievement of culture by man should alert us to the fact that the significance of language as a historical phenomenon does not lie primarily in its function as communicator: or rather, that communication is only half the story. It does not in itself define the peculiar resources which are made available.

Every species of animal has its own intra-specific method of communication, for mating, food gathering, migration, defense and the like.[42] Some of the sensory apparatuses are superior to anything human, as I can note by walking out of my house quietly to observe a woodchuck a hundred yards away. My appearance will be an intrusion to him because he can sense it, but if our roles were reversed, I would not recognise his presence with the same automatic response. Aside however from the advantage which animals have over man in scent, hearing, and sensitivity to light, air pressure, and so forth, the plain fact is that man, considered as a single species, has in the invention of language developed one intensive type of communication at the price of destroying another more general type. The best that language can do is to function within separate groups within the species. We live in a tower of Babel. Language in the singular has become languages in the plural, and these, so far from improving communication within

[42] Vid. N. Tinbergen, *Social Behaviour in Animals*, London 1953.

the species, taken as a whole, have disrupted it. This violation of what seems to be one of the rules of effective speciation may help to explain those aspects of human culture which seem self-defeating, especially its tendency to self-destruction by war. A given animal species is protected against self-destruction by the fact that its individual members recognise each other by using a common communication system. In man, the fragmentation of the communication system has the effect of splitting the single species into apparent sub-species which can become alien to each other.

A common language is the first prerequisite for a given human culture, and a common language is built on a common memory. This memory finds its existence not in some vague tribal consciousness but in the living brains of all individual members of a species. Its function is to codify a pattern of behaviour on the part of the mouth. The code thus programmed in the memory can be regarded as a body of information hoarded up and stored for continual re-use. The primary purpose of speech however as it is produced by the mouth is to direct action and effect response between two or more individuals of the species. To speak of talking to myself is to use a metaphor. Talk is sponsored by the need to programme some mutual activity, which is the essence of communication. The information stored in language thus becomes a means of programming a continual series of acts. The purpose is not merely informational but directive.

The validity of the concept of linguistic storage when it is used to explain the initial phenomena of human civilisation lies in the fact that it supplies continuity with man's pre-civilised history, that is, his physical evolution. Biological information is stored in the genes, where it is programmed to produce the biological behaviour of all individuals of a given species. This procedure has recently been opened to scientific inspection.[43] It determines not only the colour of our eyes and skin, but how we are born, grow, eat, sleep, and die.

With the achievement of language, our species was placed in a position to invent a supplement to the genetically imprinted code. A second form of informational storage became available for man

---

[43] The spectacular discovery of the structure of D.N.A. is recounted autobiographically by James Watson in *The Double Helix*, New York 1968.

to use, and this enabled him to some extent to take charge of his own further evolution. Instead of adapting to his environment, he acquired the ability to change it, and also to change himself. The first initial use to which this ability was put was to devise the primary structures of human society. These grew up as they were incorporated in the language of a linguistic group, the individuals of which were required to memorise behaviour patterns shared by all members of the group. By the act of communicating in accordance with these memorised codes, mere herds and tribes gave way to societies with socially conditioned habits, customs, laws, history. All of this information had to be transmissible between the generations to ensure continuity. The biologist's description of this procedure reads as follows:

"Through the higher mammals, and most strikingly in man, there has been a trend towards replacing rigidly genetically determined behaviour patterns by behaviour that is subject to learning and conditioning. The closed programme of genetic information is increasingly replaced in the course of its evolution by an open programme, a programme that is so set up that it can incorporate new information. In other words, the behaviour phenotype is no longer absolutely determined genetically, but to a greater or lesser extent it is the result of learning and of education.

This involves not only a capacity for learning but also a readiness to accept authority. 'The newborn infant has to be ready to believe what he is told.' It is this system of non-genetic determination of the behavioral phenotype that permits the development of religious dogmas (based on revelation), and of ethical codes. The capacity to accept concepts, dogmas, and codes of behavior is one of the many forms of imprinting. The greater the amount of parental care and education, and the more highly developed the means of communication, the more important becomes "conceptual imprinting." The acceptance of ethical systems and religions is as much testimony to this as is the success of demagogues and of the mass media."[44]

Some rather crude illustrations may suffice to illustrate the difference between genetic encoding and cultural encoding. A child

[44] Mayr, *op.cit.*, pp. 636-37.

is genetically equipped to stoop and pick up a pebble and throw it at a target which attracts his vision, say, a glass window reflecting the light. The cultural code, transmitted in language, will direct him however not to destroy property, and so inhibits the action that might otherwise be taken. Common sense recognises the difference when we say that stone-throwing is a habit we grow out of. Genetically coded behaviour at first predominates in children, until it is by degrees overlaid by the cultural code imprinted through language and teaching. After puberty, the genetic code will propel us at physically appropriate times to attempt to reproduce ourselves by sexual union. The culturally transmitted code will surround this procedure with a whole set of social regulations, the pattern of which will vary from culture to culture, depending on the family structure. This example indeed furnishes a case where under our eyes a further addition to the cultural code is slowly being formulated, when we recognise something we call today the Population Explosion and formulate a need to control it. The very phrase as it stands carries directive force suggesting further conditions which should surround the act of reproduction. We call these artificial, these proposed regulations, but from a strictly scientific point of view, and considered in relation to the genetic codes of behaviour, they are neither more nor less "artificial" than familial and social regulations which have governed in this area for millennia. They remind us that the storage of information which man now carries out for himself in language is carried out according to an open programme, not the closed one which is characteristic of genetic encoding.

So far, the terminology I have used, and which professionals in the field of anthropology also use, to describe the function of language as a builder of culture has assumed that language takes documentary form. Words like code and programme, information and storage, imply a visible or physical existence. When applied, however, to an oral culture they become only metaphors which disguise from us the interesting question, rarely if ever asked: How does cultural storage take place in a non-literate culture? How is it built up in language as ephemeral as the spoken word?

An initial answer seems to lie in the mere fact that a given language exists. I mean that by existing it maintains a usage of vocabulary which incorporates, at an unconscious level, a good deal of information and direction which covers the behaviour of the group that uses the language. The words employed identify not merely objects but fields of meaning surrounding the objects. They carry associations, as we say, and are customarily arranged in syntactical situations which express these associations. This quite fundamental aspect of language as itself a conserver of culture-pattern lies beyond my present limits. I can give it only cursory attention as a preparation for the next step in our analysis. Once more, illustration crudely chosen will have to suffice.

In the vocabulary of monogamous culture, polygamy and promiscuity are dirty words, fidelity and faithfulness are approval words. These latter, though borrowed from the terminology of contractual relationships, become synonymous with the maintenance of monogamy. You do not need to be told what to do and what to avoid doing. The tonal inflexion of the words as they are pronounced and used carry the directive message. To give a more sophisticated example: any given culture group will codify the procedures of marriage, child-rearing, and property holding within a given family structure. The words for cognates and relatives within this patterned structure come into existence in obedience to the kind of pattern of relations that is set and assumed. They will themselves carry associations which automatically denote appropriate status and prescribe mutual behaviour. An unusually striking example of the way this works can be supplied from Homer's own text. It is found in that moving lament for Hector which on the lips of. Helen brings the *Iliad* towards its close. The modern translator renders the relevant terms that she uses as follows:

Hector, of all my lord's brothers dearest by far . . .
I have never heard a harsh saying from you, nor an insult.
No, but when another, one of my lord's brothers or sisters, a fair-
    robed
wife of some brother, would say a harsh word to me in the palace,
Or my lord's mother—but his father was gentle always, a father
indeed—then you would speak and put them off and restrain them
by your own gentleness of heart and your gentle words.[45]

[45] *Iliad* 24.762, 767-773, translated by Richmond Lattimore, Chicago 1951.

The English formulas, my lord's brothers, lord's sisters, wife of some brother, my lord's mother, his father, are renderings of five single Greek words, each distinct from the others and all specific, denoting definite relationships in which these people stood to Helen, and she to them. In the English version they have all been translated into appendages of her husband. The Greek vocabulary denotes that Helen, by marrying Paris, became a member of a complex family group system with which she would normally enjoy complex relations and from which she could normally expect support, for they all have specific roles to play vis-à-vis her, and the roles are indicated by the words. The pathos of her isolation is that she has been rendered a woman without a family. The marriage therefore has not worked, but its failure is not one we would understand in modern terms. It does not concern herself and Paris alone. This kind of vocabulary implies a set of proprieties quite unfamiliar to Western or English manners and mores, and as it implies them, it also recommends, as it were, the maintenance of such relationships and of the behaviour that goes with them, which, as they become incorporated into the language structure, are also incorporated into the tradition of the culture. We realise this when we come up against our failure to translate. We cannot do it because the vocabulary of our language is programmed to express a set of directives, legal and social, covering the family which are quite different from the Greek directives.

A non-literate culture, then, could maintain some basic identity for itself simply by maintaining the stability of its vocabulary and syntax. The vernacular can do this. Using such a vocabulary you acquire from childhood the information whom to marry and whom not, whom to consort with and whom not, whom to love, whom to hate, what to eat, what to wear; you learn automatic responses to given situations; your cultural expectations are supplied to you. In using the term 'stored information' we include both description and prescription. The two modalities overlap. To describe the done thing is also to prescribe it. The necessary information, at this level, to repeat, is storable in any brain which is equipped to memorise a linguistic convention of the necessary complexity.

But will this be enough to supply a culture with that degree

of self-consciousness, of awareness of identity, which entitles it to
be called anything except primitive? How does a culture become
a civilisation? Admittedly, to put a question of this sort in this
form involves the use of terminology which is imprecise. What
are the meanings of primitivism versus self-consciousness when
applied to a total culture? I suggest that the operative meaning
appears at that theoretical point when a linguistic group ceases to
be satisfied with the encoding of its folkways at the unconscious
level, and instead seeks to devise a special statement of what these
are in order to identify them. If such a statement is to be special,
it must lie outside the casual usage of the vernacular, for at the
conversational level language is ephemeral.[46] To be effective as a
statement, however, it must be preservable, and to be preservable
it must rely, like the language itself, on the resources of memory.
But whereas the ability to memorise a language has been genetically encoded in our species by a million years of selective evolutionary pressures, the unconscious resources of the brain stop there.
To what extent we are programmed biologically to memorise
special statements without conscious effort seems uncertain and
ambiguous. What is certain is that to formulate, hoard, and transmit such statements will require extra efforts of memory, and for
this some assistance will be required. These statements when
formulated, and however they are formulated, will express the
cultural code of the group. Today we can see this code in all its
increasing complexity as it is accumulated in documentary form,
in literature, philosophy, theology, law, science. But how is it to
be documented, so to speak, in an oral culture?

The essential fact in the preservation of record which is carried
out by documentation is that a given statement remains unchanged,
and this means that the syntax or order of words in the statement
remains unchanged. This is automatic in the case of any inscribed
statement. We can change it only by an act of physical destruction
which substitutes another piece of documentation in its place. If
then we ask how, in an oral culture, can statements be preserved,
we are asking what device is available to guarantee the preservation of a fixed syntax and word order. There is only one way of

[46] Historically this has been true, prior to the invention of recording devices.

doing this, by the arranging of words in a rhythmic sequence which is independent of the words, but to which they have to respond acoustically. Even the word "arrange" suggests a literate metaphor, as though language were something we could touch and move on a chessboard. More accurately, the mouth, which has learnt to arrange speech sounds to conform to the grammar of a linguistic code, must now learn the further trick of so selecting these sounds that they not only make sense, but set up a kind of music in the ear—both of speaker and listener—which is governed by rhythmic periods which repeat themselves.

It will be realised now that I am pointing to what we call poetry —I prefer to call it poetised speech—as a device contrived to produce what might be called paradoxically the oral documentation of a non-literate culture. It is not in genesis a sporadic activity of inspired persons who did it for fun, but a serious instrument—the only one available—for storing, preserving, and transmitting that cultural information which was felt to be important enough to require separation from the vernacular. Poetic composition therefore formed an enclave, so to speak, constructed within the vernacular of a given non-literate culture, and provided the culture with its cultural memory.

Rhythm as a principle of composition is more extensive than meter. It is the genus of which meter is a species. At the acoustic level it can be set up by assonance, alliteration and the like, and at the level of meaning it can be generated by parallelism, antithesis and the simpler figures of speech like chiasmus. These principles are all evident in the construction of what we call, quite correctly, a "saying," whether this takes the form of proverb, aphorism, maxim, adage, epigram. Parenthetically it will be noted that here too our terminology while seeking to describe phenomena of oral communication is often induced to borrow metaphor from the practice of inscribed speech.

I select the saying as being for theoretical purposes the primary form of preserved oral speech because of its obvious role as the container of directive information which is placed in linguistic storage for repetition, that is, for re-use. An appropriate illustration can be cited from the saying which happens to head the collection known as the Book of Proverbs in the Old Testament:

My son hear the instruction of thy father
and forsake not the law of thy mother
for they shall be a chaplet of grace unto thy head
and chains about thy neck.

The rhythmic devices which at the acoustic level contribute to
the memorisation of this statement, and hence to its survival value,
can be properly observed only in the original. But even the English translation brings out the system of balances, parallelisms and
contrasts which at the thematic level contribute to the total rhythm
of the saying. The sentiments are arranged in pairs: the first couplet
lists two directives referring to two parallel figures, father and
mother, while at the same time exploiting the antithesis between
father and son, and the correspondence between instruction and
law. The second couplet lists two parallel statements which are
linked to the two preceding directives as a commentary upon them
and are put together with the aid of similar parallelism and antithesis. (Once more it will be noted that our attempt to analyse a
strictly oral-acoustic procedure is forced to borrow its metaphors
from the conditions of inscription.) This saying provides an example of particular appropriateness in the context of my present
argument, for it happens to identify that cultural procedure which
guarantees the life of the saying itself. It is indeed like a chain
placed round the neck, for the child, in order to acquire the cultural tradition, has to respond to adult instruction. The convenient
adult, chosen by most if not all cultures for this purpose, is the
parent. There is no other way in which the identity of the tradition can be preserved, for being wholly oral it is carried solely
in the personal memories of individuals in the succeeding generations as they memorise it.

It is unlikely that extensive collections of sayings like the Book
of Proverbs would come into existence without the aid of inscription, even though the component parts are formed according to
oral rules. It is essential to the rhythm set up in a saying that it is
complete in itself and does not allow of extension. It does have
relatives, so to speak, in the oral repertoire which are somewhat
longer, like the parable, the fable, and the ritual incantation. Very
often, as in the case particularly of the fable, the versions now in

circulation in literate cultures are themselves the product of literate paraphrase in which some of the original rhythmic elements have been suppressed. This was very likely true for instance of the fables of Aesop as they were available for literate Greece, though if their models were Egyptian, these would have been inscribed at a time when Greece was still non-literate, and so attained the form of prose paraphrase at an early date.[47] But even in prose versions, the thematic rhythm of parable and fable persists, reminding us of their genesis and function in an oral culture. Nor must the humble nursery rhyme be forgotten, which can sustain a single memorised narrative statement, but within its own unique metric. The readiness of children to memorise this form of speech suggests that it may have served from time immemorial as a training in the handling of rhythm. The child thus becomes accustomed to managing the acoustic aids to memorisation. They are the oral equivalent of instruction in reading. Hence the proclivity observable in children to indulge in nonsense-language chosen for its sound values as a mnemonic. The nursery rhyme has proved ephemeral so far as the cultural record is concerned, though indications of its wide use can be found in some corners of surviving Greek literature. Considered in terms of its length and self-containment, it resembles an extended saying. It can be regarded as a preparation for more meaningful and lengthy efforts of memorisation which are to come later as the capacity of the brain is more effectively mobilised.

The rhythms of all these forms of preservable speech whether acoustic or thematic are governed by an important limitation. They are self-contained and complete in themselves. The parable or fable comes to a stop. If it did not, its unique rhythm would be destroyed. The meter of a nursery rhyme is unique to itself. None of them admit of extended statement; none of them are open-ended.

Yet a culture which had reached the stage of seeking to incorporate its traditions in memorisable speech would surely wish them to take the form of an extended statement, a connected report, we might say, which would command attention and provide a verbal

---

[47] An examination of the relationship between the Greek fables attributed to Aesop and the fable-tradition of the Near East is promised by B. Perry in the "Preface" (p. VII) to Vol. 1 of his *Aesopica*, Urbana 1952.

nexus round which the consciousness of the culture could rally. The saying or the parable can furnish clues to the consciousness of a people, but not the key to that consciousness. To achieve extension of statement required the invention of an extendible rhythm. This could be achieved by simplifying and formalising rhythm, converting it into a repetitive meter, which produced, we might say, a series of sayings of roughly equal acoustic lengths, which could follow one another like a series of waves in extended duration. The oral memory could then be led on to recall the sequences, and so retain a coherent and extended statement, a program of instruction, so to speak, in the accumulated cultural information. Such, I suggest, was the genesis of the epic as it has subsisted in all oral cultures. It arose in response not to artistic impulse but functional need. It constituted a massive attempt at oral storage of cultural information for re-use.

The time has come to draw together the two threads of my argument: on the one hand the peculiar powers possessed by the Greek alphabet for the accurate and fluent transcription of oral speech; on the other hand, the measures taken by a non-literate culture to preserve its corporate tradition in an enclave of language existing apart from the vernacular, metrically contrived to preserve an extensive statement in the memories of the members of the culture. To transcribe this enclave became the first business to which the alphabet was put. And so we reach in the first instance the poems that pass under the name of Homer. The notion that they represent survivals of a form of entertainment marginal to the day's work must be abandoned. They require to be estimated in the first instance as a report on the day's work, and to be understood in terms of their function rather than their contribution to the aesthetics of literature. Such a revaluation is bound to meet with considerable resistance from the advocates of a purely literary and aesthetic approach to these poems, and may take a long time to achieve.

But Homer constitutes only the first installment, albeit the purest, of that act of precipitation as I have called it which brought the oral tradition of Greece into corporate documentary form. He is followed by Hesiod, the lyricists, Pindar and Attic drama. Should we not in these works also be prepared to view the presence of a continuous transcription of that enclave of contrived language which had nourished the previous oral culture? This is not to say that new facilities of composition opened up by the written word remained uncultivated. Authorship in the literate sense was becoming possible, for the novel statement, poetic or prosaic, could now be assured of adequate transcription, and also of recognition once a reading public had been supplied. But it was not supplied at once, and in any case cultural habits survive their technical obsolescence.

Given the fact that the composition of verse to serve functional ends was a skilled procedure of great antiquity, universal among non-literate cultures, is it credible that with the arrival of the alphabet, the procedure would be quickly abandoned? Is it not much more likely that for a long time after the resources of transcription became available, they would be used still to transcribe what had previously been orally composed, that the transcription would be made in the first instance for the benefit of the composers themselves rather than their public, and that the products of the Greek poets who followed Homer would be devised for memorisation by listening audiences, not for readership by literates? And is it not therefore also likely that the didactic and public purpose of such oral composition would not be lost sight of, that the poetry of Greece even as late as the death of Euripides can still recall in varying degree the stylised storage of cultural information which had been poetry's immemorial function? This, I feel convinced, is a clue to that peculiar quality which we identify as classic in the antique sense of the word.

Homer's documentation however was the alphabet's first gift to the Greeks as to ourselves. His orality need not now be defended. Scholarship with the aid of comparative studies has established it on linguistic and metrical grounds. The distance between his contrived dialect and the vernaculars of Greece, no less than the Mycenaean memories in his tales, attest his ultimate attachment to pre-literate Greece. His survival on the other hand, carefully guarded in the memories of the citizens of the Greek states, ensured that the paradox of complete preservation of orality by a non-oral device persisted into the classical age. Side by side with the new forms of prosaic expression slowly made possible by grow-

ing literacy, there existed in Homer through Greek history a completely articulated transcription of the old pre-literate ways of
speaking. This transcription was read and recited for centuries,
becoming a partly foreign language in competition with the forms
and idioms of current speech. It is scarcely to be doubted that the
tension thus built up between oral and written proved fruitful in
helping to release those post-Homeric energies, mysteriously creative, which remain the secret of Greece in the archaic and high
classical epochs.

2. THE CHARACTER AND CONTENT
OF THE CODE

I F THE ORIGINAL use to which the Greek alphabet was put
had to be the transcription of that tradition which had previously enshrined the code of a non-literate culture, then the
first documents of what we call Greek "literature" could not be
compositions freely invented by individual artists. They would
rather be in the nature of what I have elsewhere described as
"tribal encyclopaedias."[48] This view of them is a good deal easier
to accept in the case of Hesiod than in that of Homer. If the *Iliad*
and the *Odyssey* are transcriptions of oral information framed and
stored for cultural re-use, why do they insist on disguising this central fact by telling stories of the *Wrath of Achilles* and the *Home-
coming of Odysseus*? This is the crucial problem with which we
are now confronted, and which demands urgent solution. The
Homeric poems have invited decades of critical admiration and
dissection, guided by the assumption that the tale was the thing,
and that the poet's primary intention was to entertain rather than
instruct. Any attempt to reverse this priority will invite disbelief.

As a preface to any explanation of why the tale is to be treated
as a disguise for something else, I will ask the reader temporarily
to suspend his disbelief, in order to consider that view of the matter which was taken by the Greeks themselves. The earliest stated
opinions concerning character or function of the Greek epics are
found in the philosophers Xenophanes and Heraclitus in the archaic period, and in Herodotus, Aristophanes and Plato during the
classical period. When the quotations are tabulated, certain features recur with surprising consistency:

Xenophanes contributes two statements as follows:

> (i) Since from the beginning according to Homer all men
> have been instructed that . . .
> (ii) All things to the gods did Homer and Hesiod assign
> which among human beings are a reproach and shame
> thieving, adultery and telling lies

Heraclitus likewise contributes two statements:

[48] Havelock, *op.cit.*, p. 66 and *passim*.

364

(iii) Of the most is Hesiod instructor
Him they conceive to know most
who did not recognise day and night.
They are one.

(iv) . . . what Homer deserves is to be flung out of the
assemblies and beaten up (and Archilochus too).[49]

Cross comparison of these sayings, brief as they are, reveals an estimate which agrees in the following features: Homer and Hesiod are epic partners between whom no distinction is drawn; they are partners in an enterprise which is viewed as the instruction of Greece; this instruction deserves severe criticism.

Between fifty and seventy years later, Herodotus committed himself to the following:

(v) As to whence the gods severally sprang, and whether all of them were eternal, and the several shapes of some of them—it was a manner of speaking only yesterday that the Greeks formed a clear idea about these matters. For in my opinion, the generation of Hesiod and Homer preceded me by not more than four hundred years, and it was they who composed divine genealogies and assigned the titles and distributed the privileges and skills over which the gods preside, and indicated their respective shapes.[50]

This opinion seems unequivocal: it agrees with those previously considered in treating Hesiod and Homer as partners in a didactic enterprise undertaken for the benefit of Greece as a whole, and agrees with Xenophanes in identifying one element of this enterprise as theological instruction: they were the first to document the Greek pantheon.

The judgment voiced by Aristophanes, as the fifth century drew to its close, still insists that they are teachers, and enlarges the dimension of what they taught:

(vi)   Consider from the beginning
How the master-poets have been the poets of utility:
Orpheus published our rituals and the prohibition against homicide
Musaeus published medical cures and oracles, Hesiod
Works of tillage, seasons of harvest and ploughing; as for
                    divine Homer

---

[49] See Havelock "Pre-Literacy" (above note 10) from which these translations are taken. They pertain to D.-K. 21 B 10, 11; 22 B 57, 42.

[50] Herodotus II 53. The criticisms elsewhere directed against Homer as a historian, as also by Thucydides, underscore the didactic view of his function.

Surely his honour and glory accrued simply from this, that he
gave needful instruction
In matters of battle order, valorous deeds, arms and men.[51]

Homer and Hesiod are again paired together, but their spheres of instruction are now distinguished, as pertaining to agriculture and warfare respectively, in company with religious ritual, oracular wisdom, moral guidance and medical lore, which are parcelled out among two other traditional authorities. Taken together, these items bear some resemblance to a summary of that kind of information which an oral culture required to be placed in storage for re-use. This fact seems to be half-acknowledged in the emphasis which is placed upon the utilitarian function performed by such poetry.

The overall debate between Aeschylus and Euripides of which this passage forms a part extends itself to the larger and still more surprising assumption that all poetry is didactic and utilitarian, and that its success as poetry is to be judged by this criterion. Such a perspective extending from oral epic into post-Homeric literature offers a prospect which must here be postponed for later examination. But precisely this assumption, some twenty years later, provides the starting point for Plato's proposals to reform the Greek educational system.

(vii) What is to be this education? It is difficult to devise one any better than that which tradition has discovered for us. This of course means "gymnastic" for the body and "music" for the soul. . . . The content of music is discourse . . . factual and fictional . . . you realise of course that initially we start children with tales, mostly fictional, in part factual. . . . Looking at the greater tales, we shall see the models for minor ones. . . . The greater ones are those told by Hesiod and Homer, as well as other poets. They were the composers of fictions related by them to mankind, and which continue to be related.[52]

The fact that the philosopher proceeds to recommend censorship of these two epic composers, far from denying them the role assigned by tradition, only places them ever more firmly in the category of didactic poetry, a category which Homer once more shares with Hesiod in a partnership affirmed even to the extent of using the verb of which they are joint subjects in the dual number. And

[51] Aristoph. *Frogs* 1030-1036.   [52] *Republic* 2. 376e2.

it is now on the epic tale itself rather than on incidental material contained in the tale, that the philosopher confers the didactic function.

At a later stage of the same treatise, Plato's position hardens: censorship is no longer enough; the poets must be banned altogether. Plato is now legislating not for schoolboys but for the prototype of a university. Once more, his hostility to the role of epic in Greek society only serves to make plain what that role in fact was.

> (viii) It is now time to consider tragedy and its master Homer, because we are sometimes told that "they" are masters on the one hand of all technology and on the other of all humane matters pertaining to virtue and vice, not to mention divine matters. . . . There are matters of supreme importance on which Homer proposes to speak, warfare, military command, civic management and a person's education. . . . If Homer were really competent to educate persons and render them better . . . would he not have acquired a company of disciples, just like Protagoras or Prodicus. . . . If Homer were of utility to men in gaining virtue, would his contemporaries have been content to let him, and Hesiod too, make their rounds as reciters, rather than attaching themselves to them as precious objects, to be retained in their households, or failing that, to be followed around by themselves as their pupils until sufficiently educated?[53]

These eight notices extend over a period of perhaps a hundred and fifty years. If the earlier ones are brief, they are not ambiguous, and their full effect is spelled out in the pages of Plato. For those who lived within three hundred years of the invention of the alphabet, Homer stood with Hesiod as the original teacher of Greece. The instruction for which he is given credit is not literary or aesthetic, but sociological and utilitarian. It covers technology, including both military skills and (in the case of Hesiod) agricultural, and also civic conduct, morals, and religion. He is viewed in short in those terms which I have already indicated to be appropriate to the documentation of an oral tradition, in which the epic has served as an exercise in the storage of cultural information for re-use.

Is it possible to formulate more precisely what kinds and types of information an oral culture was required to preserve? The indications given in the Greek notices are not systematic or exhaustive,

---

[53] *Republic* 10. 598d-600d.

nor intended as such. To attempt a more formal classification would appear useful as a preface to further examination of the epic structure and content, if indeed the epic is to be estimated as an encyclopaedia. The easy and tempting path of investigation would seem to direct itself in the first instance towards Hesiod, viewed as Homer's partner, for in him the didactic function is perfectly evident. Information covering the gods on the one hand, as noted by Herodotus, and agricultural procedures on the other, as noted by Aristophanes, is presented in catalogue format. Nevertheless, to read backwards towards Homer from the example of Hesiod is to distort the priorities. There are serious reasons for thinking that direct didacticism is a reflection of post-oral development, that is, it exhibits some of the new possibilities inherent in the use of visible script; that the indirect or disguised didacticism of Homer himself provides a more reliable model of the mode in which a strictly oral culture preserved its traditional lore.

Technological procedures, though they would seem to be those items of information most easily identifiable, need not in fact be stored as such, orally that is, with any precision or detail. The reason lies in the material and visible character of their products. An artifact, say a house, a ship, or a pot, once constructed constitutes a model for the artist to reproduce or to modify, and it remains a visible example for the apprentice to follow. The transmission of skills in such a culture can therefore proceed by copying, to which the necessary detailed verbal instructions form an adjunct. These have no need of incorporation in that enclave of memorized and poetic speech. They can rely on the use of the vernacular because the formula, so to speak, is there visible before the eye and has no need of verbal incorporation. Yet even so, the epic is not innocent of technological formulae. For example, heroic confrontations are often preceded by "arming scenes"[54] which provide samples of military instruction covering the warrior's equipment; or again, that embassy by sea which restores Chryseis to her father in the first book of the *Iliad* provides occasion for four passages describing the voyage which "preserve a complete and formulaic report on loading, embarking, disembarking and un-

---

[54] J. I. Armstrong, "The Arming Motif in the *Iliad*," *AJP* 79 (1958), pp. 337-54.

loading."[55] And yet these, and similar reports, do not go into detail. They fail to incorporate the dozens of minutiae which an experienced warrior or a skilled navigator would observe in the course of such operations. Rather do they set up the general order of procedure; they describe what we might call the proprieties of the operation. This applies to all technological information formulaically stored in the epic, not least in those many Homeric similes drawn from contemporary life. Overall, this kind of information forms an exercise in general education, not in the specifics of skilled performance. Some specifics occasionally get into the formulae but seem to linger there by accident. Their presence is not functionally necessary.

But while in the case of the manufacture and management of artifacts the material model serves as embodiment of the tradition, it is otherwise in that area of information which covers human relations, opinion, and belief. To be sure, even here, if artifacts are employed, for example in the service of cult, the appropriate behaviour is supported by the existence of the priestly equipment or even the shape of the temple architecture which may suggest, and help to conserve, appropriate processional formalities or sacrificial operations. Nevertheless, the religion, law, and custom, the ethical and historical consciousness of an oral culture are not in themselves capable of incorporation in visible models. Their close conservation depends upon strictly verbal description handed down between the generations. Description here passes into prescription. What is done becomes what ought to be done. It is the storage of such social directives *par excellence* which is entrusted to the enclave of contrived and memorised speech, and in particular to the epic.

In outline, these constitute the affairs of men, their doings and dealings.[56] Primary among such is the role of the familial structure of any given culture, comprising in the first instance relationships between children and parents, and also those of the mature but younger generation towards the elders. Both sets of relationships require the management of an educational process whereby tradition is transmitted by indoctrination, and the epic is likely to memorialise with some emphasis the respective deportments and

[55] Havelock, *Preface*, p. 84.   [56] Cf. Plato, *Republic* 10.603c4-7.

attitudes which guarantee this: the choice of a wife, the status of the concubine, the acknowledgement of legitimacy, and the inheritance of property—all these are matters which cannot be left to the vernacular for conservation. They require embodiment in contrived speech. This is particularly true of the procedures to be followed at death, covering the choice of mourners, and content of the lament, and type of offerings at the tomb, which indirectly acknowledge the heir or heirs and guarantee orderly succession of authority.

Outside the family, there is the larger political structure of a people, less deeply rooted in tradition, looser and less formulaically determined. Nevertheless, it will comprise, and so sanctify, some description of the status of the ruler and the subject, the procedures for reaching and implementing decisions for war or for peace or for legal arbitration. It will perhaps include indication of some hierarchy of rank and privilege governing communal relations within and beyond the village precinct.

As for the economic support of the society, so far as it is pastoral its procedures will be described in terms of the rearing and protection, the breeding and the use of flocks and herds. So far as it is agricultural, it will require some kind of annual calendar governed by motions of the stars and sun, and a general account of the basic operations of raising crops, the management of the vintage, and the like. It is less the technical details of such that is called for in memorised and verbal form, but rather the social management and distribution of such resources.

Finally, there is what we might term the historical consciousness of the group embodied in the first instance in its cult and religious practices. The gods are its ultimate ancestors and arbiters of its destinies; they set the geographic and temporal borders within which the group discovers itself and finds its identity. Cult hovers over that entire body of custom law previously described, regulating and regularising everything from family relationships to harvesting the grapes. The role of religious practice is to protect and conserve the culture pattern as well as to give it a historical and perhaps cosmic dimension.

The burden of instruction thus entrusted to the muses of oral verse was summed up in the post-Homeric generation by Hesiod who described the content of their song as "the custom-laws of all, and folkways of the immortals."[57] Both terms employed in this quotation signify usage as predetermined by a given culture pattern to which the members are bound to conform. But whereas *nomos* indicates usage in its aspect of what we would call public law, *ethos* focusses more on private practice and personal habit. In an orally preserved tradition, it is difficult for a split to develop between these two. They remain separable aspects of a single custom-law-and-ethic.

In the Socratic period there developed an intellectual movement which sought to rationalise these patterns to discover uniform principles which might lie concealed within them. It is therefore not surprising that the dialogues of Plato are preoccupied with the centrality of *nomos* in the structure of any society and the way that it sanctions in particular the family structure and civic identity.[58] On the other hand, the earlier dialogues, as they seek to focus on the *ethos* of men, attempt to reach precise definition of the demands made on the members of a *polis* by, respectively, piety (the proper practice of cult), by courage (the military posture required for defense of the society), by temperance (the proper relationship between the generations, and particularly between parents and children), by intelligence (the proper direction of skillful management and the methods of reaching correct decision), by justice (the proper determination of reciprocal responsibilities to preserve social cohesion), and in general by education itself viewed overall as that enterprise which maintains a culture pattern by watching over its transmission, either within the family or as an undertaking of professionals.[59] From the matrix of traditional *ethe*, these are now emerging as "ethical norms," constituting separate objects of knowledge, at a level of consciousness of which the oral culture itself was innocent.

The oral enclave of contrived speech therefore constituted a body of general education conserved and transmitted between the generations. In addition, any organized society, and the Homeric

[57] *Theog.* 66.
[58] This is a constant Platonic preoccupation, from *Crito* through *Republic* to *Laws*.
[59] *Euthyphro* (piety), *Laches* (courage), *Charmides* (temperance), *Meno* and passim (intelligence), *Republic* (justice), *Protagoras* and passim (education).

one was no exception, stood in constant need of "short term directives and legal formulas which, though designed to suit specific occasions, were nevertheless required to have a life of their own in the memories of the parties concerned for varying periods of time, or else the directive failed through lack of fixity in transmission, or the legal formula became unenforceable because the parties concerned had forgotten what it was or were in dispute because of variant versions. Such directives could therefore remain effective only as they were themselves framed in rhythmic speech of which the metrical shape and formulaic style gave some guarantee that the words would be both transmitted and remembered without distortion. The colloquial word of mouth which in our own culture is able to serve the uses of even important human transactions remains effective only because there exists in the background, often unacknowledged, some written frame of reference or court of appeal, a memorandum, or document, or book. The memoranda of a culture of wholly oral communication are inscribed in the rhythms and formulas imprinted on the living memory."[60]

These short term directives combined precedent with current application, or more precisely tended to frame a judgment or order addressed to an immediate occasion within the confines of formulas sanctified by tradition. In both legal and governmental spheres such oral pronouncements were styled *themistes* and *dikai*, and those with social authority to pronounce them had their corresponding titles. They might require promulgation by herald as the agent whose task it was publicly to repeat a directive for retention in the popular memory. In post-Homeric times such oral directives were often styled *kerugmata*, that is "heraldings." An illustrative example of the practice as it survived into the post-Homeric period can be drawn from Sophocles' *Antigone*. There one of the dead brothers has received burial, rightfully, says Antigone, which in the context means with propriety. This does not require any special rescript and none is mentioned; the act of burial responds to the unwritten *nomos* of the society. But in the case of the other brother, if his corpse, and therefore his name, are to be dishonoured, normal social procedure must be interrupted.

[60] Havelock, *Preface*, pp. 106-7.

This requires a special instruction promulgated by herald, a *kerugma* which has already been issued as the play opens. To be effective, it must be remembered and repeated by the citizens. So it is reported as what "they say," not what the herald has said.[61] Its content is naturally framed in metrical terms to conform to the diction of drama. But the verbal arrangement of the proclamation in Sophocles' text employs repetition, parallelism, consonance and assonance, in a manner which recalls precisely those formulaic peculiarities which in a society of oral communication would help to guarantee memorisation and so fidelity. Moreover, the instruction is clinched, or sealed as it were, by an embellished version of the fourth and fifth lines of the *Iliad* itself:

> They say that to the citizens has proclamation been made;
> Cover not up in tomb the corpse nor cry lament for it
> Leave it unwept, untombed, for the observing birds
> A treasury delicious to gratify their forage.[62]

When we turn to Homer's epics, all these things are there embedded in the narrative sweep as it proceeds, and they are there over and over again. Agamemnon demanding that he retain his prize-woman memorialises the accepted role of the concubine, and in the same breath itemises the requirements which are to be met in choosing a wife. The disputants mirrored on the sculptured scenes on Achilles' shield perform the proper ritual of debate and decision before the judges which will settle a blood feud. Penelope and her son confront the suitors to protect the inheritance of the missing husband and father. The gods rise up as Zeus enters for dinner, to give an example of table manners. Achilles' repeated memories of Peleus and his interview with Priam furnish the archetypal pattern which governs the relationship of father and son, as does the return of Telemachus to his father's side. The obsequies of Patroclus or Hector are carefully itemised and identify the chief mourners as heirs to the memory and fortunes of the dead. The lament, the offering, the encomium, the burial procedure are all there. The counsels of Nestor enshrine the authority of the elders to direct policy and provide advice and precedent. The demeanor and courage of the warrior are presented in a

---

[61] Soph. *Antig.* lines 23, 8, 27.   [62] *Ibid.* lines 28-30.

hundred episodes as examples, while on the other hand, Penelope and her staff furnish the paradigm of the proper management of a household economy. Even when the tales, in order to heighten dramatic interest, describe situations which violate these norms—the reflections of Achilles as he withdraws from war in Book 9, or the illegal rapacity of the suitors in the *Odyssey* are conspicuous examples—the listener is still reminded all the more forcefully of what the basic paradigms are. As for cult and sacrifice and ritual hymn, their presence and procedures pervade the narrative with repetitive, and one might say, affectionate familiarity. In a hundred similes we are told how to fish and hunt, to protect cattle, to snare birds, to weave and to plant and to reap.

And yet the tale remains the thing. This great accumulation of precedent, custom, and propriety is memorialised by indirection in the things that men and women are saying and doing, in those recurrent narrative situations in which the poet chooses to place them, and which call for them to say and to do. It is not spelled out in treatise form. It is not even catalogued. Why did it have to be this way? Why was it essential for this contrived enclave of oral speech that it should achieve its task of storage of information for re-use only by disguising essentially what it was doing? To this last question I now address myself.

A first step towards an answer is to consider the formidable effort on the part of the human brain which is required to memorise extensive portions of discourse. We are aware, are we not, that over two thousand years of literate habit has robbed us—or robbed the average man—of this capacity. The psychology which is required to explain this loss I do not intend to explore in this place. I would suggest however that if those conditions of social pressure, exerted on the unconscious, were ever revived, in which the act of memorisation as a means of cultural storage was again required, then the capacity for the act would revive also, and the act itself once more be performed. I have earlier pointed out that the retention of discourse in a fixed word order could be achieved only by placing discourse in rhythmic shape, of which the epic supplies the most regular and continuous example, suitable for framing a content which shall be lengthy yet coherent. But is an epic any easier to memorise than a book of Thucydides? If it is, what are the psychological reasons for this?

We take a second step towards a solution to our question when we recognise that human energy becomes available for performance of necessary functions as it is accompanied by a feeling of pleasure. This linkage between function and pleasure received an analysis in Aristotle's *Ethics* twenty three hundred years ago which still seems adequate. However, the argument can be made directly pertinent to our present context, without benefit of classical authority, if I revert once more to a consideration of the genetic and precultural level of behaviour.

The human organism, in order to develop, live, and perpetuate itself, is called upon to perform elementary but necessary biological functions; to ensure their performance, a pleasurable feeling is genetically encoded to accompany the performance; eating, drinking, excretion, and copulation are obvious examples. We indeed automatically link these experiences with appetite which requires "gratification," as we say. The infant, as he sucks, enjoys sucking. The operation requires some output of energy which the organism has to supply. Pleasure expected and savoured guarantees the response.

The management of a language, the ability, that is, to store and speak a language system even at the vernacular level, makes a severe call upon the energies of the enlarged brain. We would therefore expect that the performance of a language, an ability which is genetically encoded, would be assisted by an accompanying pleasure so that the effort of recollection involved in using the vocabulary and syntax would be encouraged by response to pleasurable stimuli of the same automatic character as accompanies biological functions. The behaviour of children indicates that this is so. The child indulges in linguistic noises before he can properly speak as well as after, and often converses with himself in private manipulations of linguistic sounds. Children chatter to children to a point which wearies an adult and they enjoy the repetition of words, questions and answers which to an adult seem mechanical and unnecessary.

The same principle would surely have to apply to the mastery of contrived speech above the vernacular level, that is, to the retention of words in a fixed order to achieve perpetuation of fixed meaning. But at this level the effort of memory is no longer automatically assisted; that is, we can distinguish between the use of the mouth to speak a vernacular, an ability which is genetically encoded, and so has its encoded pleasure, and the ability to speak a poetised tongue of artificially contrived speech for which it would appear genetic coding is not available, or is minimal. The art of the contrived metrical word will require the invention of further pleasures to supplement those that already accompany the use of language *per se*. For the degree of memorisation now required to hold words in fixed succession requires a new order of mental effort.

The necessary concomitant pleasure is discerned in the operation of rhythm itself. Rhythmic speech involves a repetitive modulation of the motions of the mouth. This dance, so to speak, performed in fractions of seconds by the combined manipulation of larynx, tongue, teeth and palate can be further accentuated by a parallel movement of the body, often imperceptible, but capable of further mobilisation by being incorporated in gesture and dance in which arms and legs become fully involved with torso in the performance of motions which are accompaniments to the rhythm of the mouth and proceed in parallel with it. Finally, it became possible to devise instruments, the drum, the strings, the pipe, which if manipulated either by the reciter or an acolyte would still further reinforce the rhythms already described.

I do not have to argue for the instinctive pleasure felt in rhythm. It is a matter of common observation, and indeed the possibility of rhythmic ecstasy may suggest that the rhythmic pleasures, of all available gratifications, are the most complete. At any rate, while we have hitherto viewed metre as a functional device to hold the words in a fixed order, so as to freeze, as it were, a given statement and therefore a given meaning, the users of metre in the oral culture were much more aware of the ecstatic emotions which accompanied this function. And rightly so, we may say, for while the informative function was socially useful, the emotions aroused to assist memorisation were immediately sensible to the individual who listened and to the poet who manipulated them. So far as dance and melody were added to the performance, the awareness of pleasure was reinforced. It therefore need not surprise us if Homer, in the incidental notices of the bard's activity which occur in his poems, pays more attention to his power to evoke emotion than to his didactic authority. Hesiod as we have seen does attempt some rationalisation of the instruction which the Muses make available, but he too emphasises over and over again the pleasure that they give.

"One of the Muses, indeed is called The Enjoyable. Metaphors like 'sweet dew' and 'honeyed utterance' which 'pour' or 'gush' or 'are spread' suggest the sheer sensuality of those responses which the technique could evoke from its audience. Both the dance and the chant are labelled 'desireful' (*himeroeis*) and Desire, as well as the Graces, has her dwelling near the Muses. The beat of the feet and the voices speaking or singing are likewise linked by epithets with *eros*, and another of the Muses is named Erato—the 'Passionate' . . . The language . . . is highly emotive and suggestive. It allows us, as it were, to hear the actual performance, the effects of which are all-pervasive, for they not only . . . 'rejoice the *noos* of Zeus', but also . . . seem to constitute the atmosphere in which we live, as when 'the halls of the gods laugh' and 'the surrounding earth rings aloud' . . . In one of his most melodious lines the poet signalises oral poetry's hypnotic and curative powers:

A forgetting of what is bad and a respite from anxieties.

The listener may have

Grief in a spirit newly wounded
And endure drought in his heart's anguish

but once he listens to the minstrel

Straightway he does forget his dark thoughts nor are his cares Remembered any more."[63]

Oral poetry therefore constituted a didactic entertainment, and if it ceased to entertain, it ceased to be effectively didactic. The paradox is well exposed and expressed in the usage of the Greek word *mousike*, evocative at once of the charms of the poet's art

[63] Havelock, *op.cit.* (n. 55), pp. 154-55.

and the sterner requirements of educational discipline. It blends the aesthetic with the didactic, but keeps the aesthetic subordinate. Music in the melodic sense is only one part of *mousike*, and the lesser part, for melody remained the servant of the words, and its rhythms were framed to obey the quantitative pronunciation of speech, and this meant it also obeyed the syntax of speech. Its function so far as it was employed to assist the preservation of the metrical enclave contrived within the vernacular was to assist in imprinting that syntax on the memory by maximising the pleasure in reciting it.

Today, after music in a narrower and more technical sense has been separated off from the verbal art and identified in its own right as a separate discipline, we reverse the relationship and lay words on the rack to suit the rhythms of the melody, as any opera or church service will demonstrate. It is entirely possible that the ability of melodic music to disentangle itself from verbal control, to emerge in its own right, and so undergo those formal developments which give it its present character, depended on the achievement of literate storage of information, in which the functional aspect of melody as a preservative was no longer required. Correspondingly, it was in that era which saw the beginning of literate storage of information that Aristophanes and Plato were able to realise with sharp clarity the informative role which traditional poetry had served hitherto.

So far, I have analysed the concomitant pleasure as restricted to the enjoyment of sound, verbal or melodic, and bodily motion. Can the same type of pleasure become attached also, by some act of transference, to the verbal content of sound, the meaning? To ask this question in this form and after this preparation is to approach at last the crucial puzzle: Why does *epic* oral storage of cultural information have to take narrative form? Why is the storage carried out by indirection?

The pleasures of rhythm are motor responses, they accompany actual motions of the body and mouth. This means that the process of recitation and of remembrance is itself a performance, a doing, a series of rhythmically co-ordinated actions. In choosing the statement which is to be recorded in this way the composer-reciter—no functional distinction should be drawn between them—would insensibly prefer that type of statement which lends itself to a parallel enactment so that he can act it out in imagination, and even in gesture. This means that the preferred form of statement for memorisation will be one which describes "action." But acts can be performed only by "actors"; that is, by living agents who are "doing things." This can only mean that the preferred format for verbal storage in an oral culture will be the narrative of persons in action, and the syntax of the narrative will predominate.

The actions of any actor in narrative can also comprehend his utterances. These are, in fact, acts of speech, part of his continual, flexible, dynamic response to the actions or speech of others. The more rhetorical the form in which these are cast, the more they will tend, as it were, to express argument in action. Not a sequence of propositions, couched in the syntax of the verb to be, logically employed, but a stream of simile, metaphor, instance, and example, angry defiance, fear, despair, sorrow—these are what issue forth in the mouths of Homeric orators, and as they issue they become themselves part of the narrative, in which the speaker remains an actor in action even as he speaks. Such epic utterances, filled as they are with incidental instruction, will therefore be as congenial to the memoriser as the narrative of action itself. Moreover, what a speaker says will not be reported in the syntax of *oratio obliqua*, but kept vividly before the memory as actual utterance. The syntax of Caesar's *Gallic Wars*, with its elaborate resort to the reportage of the gist of a speaker's words or thoughts, reflects the wholly different modalities of speech which become possible as it is written down and stored for literate readers. Homer's rhetoric is a recitation: Caesar's reports are for visual reference and consultation.

Contemporary experience can still supply evidence to support this view of the matter, if we turn to a homely illustration. The gossip which provides all classes of a community with a recurrent pleasure, which as we say is "all too human," reveals that type of discourse in which narrative of event and act and of actual quotation predominates over more sophisticated forms of reporting. "He says to me, he says, and do you know what she did? Of course I can't repeat everything that went on, but I know he was seen going into the house . . ." and so forth.

Gossip, by definition, dealing as it does with the current, and familiar, also deals with the insignificant and the ephemeral, and is not for the record. The personalities who are talked about are liable to be contiguous to the speaker, that is, his neighbours or relatives. When we consider the mnemonic necessities which govern the choice of a medium for speech preserved for the record, it is possible to see that the pleasure principle, as I may call it, is extendible to the choice of special personalities who perform the acts in the narrative. They are not the ordinary topics of gossip. The spectacle of personal importance, status, power, evokes a wonder from *homo sapiens* which seems to be instinctive. If we feel we like the person, we feel admiration; if we are repelled by him, or are frightened by him, we feel awe. But the verbal report of either is pleasurable. Do I need to cite once more, from the area of common-sense observation, the universal habit of turning to illustrations of people in a newspaper, or our preference for descriptions of even the trivial acts of important persons, or persons who have been rendered important by involvement in bizarre or catastrophic action. If such types are pleasurable to the imagination to contemplate, rather more than the actions of my next-door neighbour, then the effort to retain in the memory a tale of action will be further assisted if the actors are such as to excite awe or admiration, envy or fear, and occasionally, affection, though it should be noted that this latter emotion, which presumes some equality between audience and actor, is less likely to produce memorable narrative if indulged in too freely.

This psychological principle, when applied to the construction of memorisable narrative, will favour the choice as actors of gods, demigods and heroes, persons of some exotic status, whose acts and utterances will excite awe because of this special status, or importance, or power, or vigour. So that the contemplation of the status adds to the pleasure of memorisation.

The hedonistic advantage possessed by gods and heroes reacts in turn upon the function of the narrative as a vehicle for cultural information. So far as the stored information of what is done is also a prescription for what should be done, its embodiment in narrative in the acts of status-personalities encourages the listener to regard the tradition with reverence. The actors in the narrative become paradigms round which the tradition clusters.[64] This does not mean they become copybook exemplars of the proper way to behave. Narratives of ideal types would fall far short of stimulating the necessary pleasure in memorisation. A hero can memorialise the correct procedures and attitudes by what he rejects or refuses just as much as by what he performs. What he does is to shed a lustre on the overall context of hoarded information within which he is described as operating.

The syntax of memorised rhythmic speech is therefore not friendly to that type of statement which says "The angles of a triangle are equal to two right angles" or "Courage consists in a rational understanding of what is to be feared or not feared." It is not friendly precisely to that kind of statement which the Socratic dialectic was later to demand, a statement which prefers its subject to be a concept rather than a person, and its verb to be an "is" verb rather than a "doing" verb. Neither principles nor laws nor formulas are amenable to a syntax which is orally memorisable. But persons and events that act or happen are amenable. If a thing always is so, or is meant to be so (or not so), it is not a living (or dead) man or woman, and it is not to be discovered in action or situation. It is not a "happening." Orally memorised verse is couched in the contingent: it deals in a panorama of happenings, not a programme of principles. Parenthetically, it can be noted that the hostility to motion expressed in early philosophy as it became a separate discipline was based not on physical but syntactical grounds. Once you tried to talk about reality in an abstract sense, a form of speech was required which discussed properties and relationships, not the areas of activity in which these were implicit, and the statements about these had to be made to "stand still," as the Platonic Socrates graphically puts it.[65] Whereas information stored purely in the oral memory subsisted there as a series of actions and movements. It followed that the didactic function of oral storage was carried on through the use of concrete examples furnished in the actions and reactions of specific men and women. To be sure, Homer's syntax can accommodate aphorism and proverb, and occasionally includes programmed statements which have the appearance of "truths." But the saying itself is usually cast in narrative

<hr />

[64] Cf. Aristoph. *Frogs* 1040-1042.   [65] *Euthyphro* 15b.

terms: its subjects are specific, rarely abstract, and if abstract, they still "behave" rather than just "are."

The memory then requires that it be confronted with acts and events for its accommodation, so that all remembered statements be cast as far as possible in this form. This ensures a narrative format for the encyclopaedic epic as a natural consequence, and a grammar of connection which is correspondingly paratactic, rather than syntactic. Action succeeds action in running sequence, and subordination of cause to effect, of condition to consequence, in periodic sentences, is discouraged. But memorisable epic narrative is not simply paratactic;[66] that is, it does not proceed in linear fashion to add item to item in a theoretically endless sequence. Herodotus is much more paratactic in this sense, because he is a writer who is able to compose for the eye as well as the ear: his composition does not rely for its preservation solely upon the resources of individual memory.

The Homeric epic reveals the fact that it does so rely not merely by the use of those formulae, which have recently received extended study from scholars, nor merely by those verbal and physical rhythms on which I have laid such stress. To assist the retention of the material in the memory, the principle of rhythm may be said to have extended itself to content, producing patterns of reverse correspondence as the tale unfolds, mainly of the prototypes ABA or ABBA and extensions of these. Like the formulaic structure of the Homeric line, these have recently received the attention and study they deserve.[67] If I mention them here, it is because I think their cause and character have been misunderstood. Scholars who have otherwise given allegiance to the doctrine of the oral character of Homeric verse have sought explanation for thematic symmetries not in oral but visual terms. They have been explained as exhibiting a geometric design corresponding to that of the visual art of the period. But if the psychology of the poet is oral, this connection is impossible. The correspondences in Homeric narrative must be explained not on visual but acoustic principles. They are not patterns, in short, but echoes.

---

[66] Vid. J. A. Notopoulos, "Parataxis in Homer," *TAPA* 80 (1949), 1-23.

[67] C. H. Whitman, *Homer and the Heroic Tradition*, Cambridge, Mass. 1958, pp. 259f. Vid. also the critique by Kirk, *Songs*, p. 261-64.

This is not the place for an exhaustive examination of this aspect of epic technique. But enough must be said to demonstrate that, as an epic habit, its source lies in mnemonic necessity, in order to complete the analysis here offered of the epic format as built up out of a series of devices to ensure oral preservation of the cultural encyclopaedia.

The psychological reason for correspondences and symmetries lies in the difficulty of remembering an adequate connection between statements which are novel and which therefore have minimal connection with each other. The problem confronting memory is to remember a host of what we would call "facts" or "data" which in separation cannot be remembered. Therefore one fact must be connected with its predecessor; therefore it must be framed in such a way as to recall its predecessor; therefore, while itself a "new" fact, it must nevertheless resemble its predecessor, as an echo resembles its original.

This is putting it retrospectively. As the metaphor of "retrospect" implies, we are once more using visual terms to try and understand an operation which is responding to acoustic laws. The eye can review, that is, retrospect: the ear and mouth cannot. The composer-reciter works steadily forward, and only forward, and the memory that repeats the composition works forward also. This means that what we are tempted to call correspondence or symmetry is really a process of continual anticipation. The composer has to hint or to warn or to predict what the next thing he says is going to be like, or the next after that, even in the moment when he is saying the thing in front of it. So that the memory as it absorbs statement A is half-prepared to move on to statement B. This produces an effect of continuous recall in the narrative, as names, and adjectives and verbs repeat themselves, evoking situations in series which are partly novel, partly duplicates of each other. Surprise, in short, is anathema to the oral composer, because it is anathema to the oral memory.

Consequently the epic is not only permeated by prophecies which continually but gradually expand the disclosure of forthcoming narrative; it not only arranges sequences of episodes which seem to resemble each other thematically. It also introduces anticipation and therefore echo into the warp and woof of the detailed narrative itself. We can call this method if we choose thematic rhythm: supplementing and extending the mnemonic principles already present in metrical rhythm. Meter leads on the memory by the sheer force of repetition, while admitting the inclusion, within the pattern of sound as it is repeated line by line, of a new set of sounds which as words constitute partly novel statement. The novel is thus remembered as it is contained within the frame of the familiar, working from line to line. The repetition of names, phrases and syntactical situations can achieve a similar result in working from episode to episode.

It is easy to expose this mnemonic technique as for example it operates to open up the story of the *Iliad*. To the listener the Homeric verse introduces the theme of quarrel (*eris*) between a pair of persons and then verbally repeats it (lines 8 and 10). So he waits for it to erupt. He has been alerted as to what to expect in the verses that follow, and will the more easily remember the progress of the sequence. Between lines 11 and 14 he is made aware of the presence of Apollo, and Apollo's priest, and of the fact of insult, of the intention to release a daughter, and of the offer of ransom. Thus alerted he is prepared to anticipate as possibilities in the story the refusal of ransom, the acceptance of ransom, the renewal of insult, the withdrawal of insult, the retention of the girl, the release of the girl. All these are subsequently acted out, to the completion of this portion of the narrative at line 457. The thematic names and words Apollo (and his variant titles), Chryses, Chryse, Chryseis, honour, release, ransom, are either repeated, or echoed in their opposites, over and over again. The prayer of *damnatio* when the girl is retained leads into the prayer of *expiatio* when she is returned, and in the repetition the memory gratefully accepts a verbal duplicate.

Agamemnon confronting the priest had added insult to injury by dismissing him in anger. As the Greeks assemble, Achilles proposes the presence of another priest to solve the problem of the plague. So the first priest, a foreigner, provides the cue for the second, a Greek, who is first offered anonymously, merely as a proposal in the mouth of Achilles, a cue to which Chalcas then responds by getting up. "Yes, here is the priest," but he does not abruptly propose the solution. Instead, he recalls the fact that a

powerful but angry man is present, an object of fear. Is it Agamemnon? Yes it is, and so the listener is led on by this connection
towards a solution to the problem, but only by way of a recapitula-
tion, in the mouth of the priest, of the angry scene already
described.

There is one break in the narrative where the scene and the
action shift, and where the rule of anticipation might seem difficult to apply. This is where Achilles resorts to an interview with
his mother, who is not part of the mis-en-scène. But as he goes to
her, a goddess, alone and prays to her on the sea shore, the listener
is ready for the scene. He has been prepared for it for he has
already listened to the verses which describe the priest alone on
the sea shore praying to his god. The cue has been given, and the
device allows a new character, Thetis, that is a novel "datum," to
be introduced to the memory within the framework of a datum
already present there.

In this way, the psychology of oral memorisation enters into
the warp and woof of the epics, no matter which epic or what book
is considered. It explains for example their remarkable consistency of characterisation, which has invited aesthetic appreciation
from literary critics but is not motivated by aesthetic reasons. The
naming of a given name, directly or by title, whether god or hero,
Zeus, Apollo, Patroclus, Achilles, Helen, acts as a kind of prompter.
It requires that in the memory there be provoked recollection of
sets of actions and sentiments previously attached to this name.
They will vary as the situation varies, yet stay within the type,
which has been standardised sufficiently so that when the poem is
rehearsed, the lines of speech or description which accompany a
given name can to some extent be anticipated and so more easily
recalled in recitation.

The review undertaken in these pages of the cultural context
in which the Homeric poems are to be placed is now complete.
They help to answer the question: How does a human culture
maintain an identity when its means of communication are pre-
literate? This is achieved in all cultures as information is stored
for re-use. Only this procedure makes possible the accumulation
of technologies, of arts, of social structures, and of codes of behaviour. But in a pre-literate society, the conditions of which are

very difficult for a literate person to imagine, this storage, apart from its presence in the shapes of artifacts, can occur only in the living memories of individuals, and for this purpose it is expressed in a specially contrived language which I have described as an enclave subsisting within vernacular usage.

The classic civilisation of Greece began its career under these conditions, and we are able to grasp the way in which they operated, through the intrusion of what may be viewed as a fortunate historical accident. In the last half of the eighth century, and possibly at the end of that century, a writing system was invented, superior to any of its predecessors, capable of transcribing linguistic sound with economy and accuracy, so that the full complexity of this enclave of contrived language could be exhibited in documentation. In the orally composed verse thus made available for inspection can be traced the operation of certain laws of composition which are mnemonic. They are at first sight unexpected, but they do explain an equally surprising fact, that under oral conditions of communication that body of cultural information necessary to the culture comes to be stored in narrative epic. Memory, as the Greeks themselves said, was indeed the Mother of the Muses.

In making transition from Homer to the Greek authors who succeeded him, one is tempted to turn over a new page of Greek history in order to view that first chapter which begins after the invention of the alphabet. For historians, themselves literate, it is a relief to get into a period which is documented adequately, as it is supposed, by writers, rather than one which is open only to inspection by what I may call the informed imagination. Were not the necessities surrounding oral storage of information, the preliterate conditions which required that society codify its traditions in an enclave of contrived language—was not all this swept away after 700? When we reach authors after Homer, cannot we deal with them as authors in our sense, rather than in the Homeric sense?

Yet our impatience may be premature. The utilisation of the rhythmic and contrived word as a mnemonic to accumulate directive information in personal memory was a habit that had been cultivated and applied for tens of thousands of years, and had been shared by total populations in varying degree. It controlled the ordinary expectancy of "authorship," if the term may be used to describe the compositional activity of a singer and reciter. If I may repeat a question which in an earlier context of this essay I have already asked: Is it likely that this expectancy would collapse at once before the onset of a new technology? The impact to be sure was formidable. A collision between old and new was inescapable. Precisely what form it took, cannot be considered in these pages. It is sufficient for the moment to note that the contrast between a technique of acoustic storage which depended on personal memory and one which depended on visual recognition of a script which could be stored outside the memory and could be re-used without any consumption or wear and tear, theoretically forever—this contrast was fundamental. The new technique still depended on that ability to encode a language which is basic to our species, but at a stroke the need for a further stimulus of memorisation achieved within the confines of a contrived linguistic rhythm was abolished.

Or rather, we should say that this was true in theory. The historian, looking back from an experience of over 2,000 years of literacy, has the advantage of retrospect. He can afford to be logical and clear sighted. Is it likely, in the known ways of things, the human ways, that men of the centuries that immediately followed the alphabetic invention would be equally logical? Is it not more likely that habits of oral conservation which had proved viable from time immemorial would seem to retain their viability with some persistence, that the possibilities of the new technique would meet with resistance from the users of the old? Was the professional skill of the rhythmic composer likely to yield with grace to the activity of the scribe? Had not the magisterial status of the composers of rhythmic speech been long acknowledged and entrenched? Were these same people likely to turn their energies to literate composition, or if they did, were they in a position to expect a public which would read their written compositions rather than listen to their recital?

Literacy, when finally achieved, presented a profound change in methods of communication. But the technology of the change was unusually complex. Many revolutionary inventions, perhaps most, supply a new tool or source of energy which has no organic connection with the means of production that has been displaced.

Horse-power, on the one hand, and the steam engine on the other, are quite disparate sources of energy. But in the present case, both old and new depended still on a manipulation of language, and the encoded ability to remember a language remained basic to both. The issue arose not over creating a new language, that is, over a new system of communication as such, but only over the best method of achieving storage and re-use of existing communication. The result was that the usage of the old and the usage of the new in the three following centuries continued to overlap. Composers of the contrived word originally, it is to be guessed, allowed their compositions to be taken down by a listener. Later they took to writing them down themselves at dates which cannot easily be settled. But whichever they did, their initial proclivity would be to use the script now available only to record what was already previously composed according to oral principles. That is, the oral habit would persist and would remain effective to a varying degree, even in the case of composers whom we would style writers. This habit, after all, had not been personally chosen by themselves; it was a conditioned response to the needs of an audience who still demanded of the compositions offered that they be memorisable.

This auditory expectation was not going to change overnight. Indeed, the problems surrounding the creation of a reading public to replace the previous listening public would be formidable. Their exploration, again, lies beyond the limits of the present essay. Consequently, it is likely that for a long time a classical author, aside from his personal proclivity to retain the Homeric habit of composing wholly in his head, would compose under audience control. He would perhaps be able to write, and so document his activity, and he was no doubt quickly aware of the advantage of this kind of permanence to assist his fame, if nothing else. But would he not continue to expect that his fame would mainly depend on the memories of audiences who would transmit his compositions by word of mouth, so that only slowly would he come to recognise the possibility of composing that kind of statement which need not be memorised?

To demonstrate that these probabilities were indeed fulfilled in the history of what we call Greek literature, one need only turn to a survey of its general course and character. Under non-literate conditions, poetic speech was the only preservable speech, that is, it constituted the oral "literature" of the time. Vernacular prose was by definition ephemeral. It lived only a temporary life in the memory of either speaker or listener. The literature of Greece which is documented after 700, down to the lifetime of Euripides, remains peculiarly poetic. The earliest prose attested by extant quotation is Ionic, dating from perhaps 500 or a little earlier.[68] The earliest work of prose literature that has survived in its own right is that of Herodotus. It also is in Ionic and dates from after 450 B.C. In the last third of the fifth century there possibly appeared a very few of the treatises in the Hippocratic corpus, a very few philosophical treatises, all short, and a very few sophistic essays, equally short. These again were composed in Ionic. The first surviving prose composition in the Attic dialect is a short anonymous and ill-written essay on the politics of the Periclean democracy. The first magisterial composition in Attic, equalling in length the achievements of epic poetry, was the history of Thucydides. Thus, while the last half of the fifth century begins to see the acceptance of prose as a viable means of publication, acceptance does not become complete until the fourth. This is three hundred years after the invention of the alphabet had rendered the monopoly exercised by poetry over the contrived word theoretically obsolete.

The arrival of prose composition, as it marked the growing expectation of readership, also signalised a growing distance between the composer and his public, a distance which the writer seeks to bridge by adding a signature like an inscription to his work. The two signatures of Herodotus and Thucydides in their respective differences cast some light upon the mode of the literate revolution now underway.

"Here is information acquired by Herodotus of Halicarnassus, now published to prevent what has happened from departing in the course of time from memory among men, and the mighty and marvellous deeds recorded of Greeks and barbarians from being deprived of their fame."[69]

---

[68] I exclude the Milesian philosophers whose *ipsissima verba* are beyond recall. Cf. Havelock, "Pre-Literacy," p. 51.

[69] Herod. *Proem.*

We observe in these words both his proximity to the epic role of storage, guarding the cultural memory, and yet the essential difference that separates him from Homer. The Greek term which I have paraphrased by the word "published" really indicates an oral performance for an audience, but the performance so indicated would now consist of reading aloud from a manuscript, not intoning an oral address. In terms of the technology of the communication, Herodotus occupies a position poised midway between complete non-literacy and complete literacy. But Thucydides, the historian of the Peloponnesian War, while still a bard in the sense that he is a celebrant of the great deeds of heroes, is himself modernised and literate, a singer no more but now a self-styled writer. As a writer he is able to insist on a new version of the bard's role, and on a revised conception of the bard's methods. The famous promise that his work will constitute an eternal possession, rather than a transient entertainment,[70] still asserts the traditional bardic claim upon the memory of posterity, and reinforces it by competitive disparagement of rivals in terms reminiscent of Pindar. The methods by which the claim is to be executed are different; the work in question is conceived as a written volume which can become a piece of property on a shelf, what he calls a *ktema*, rather than a performance offered in oral competition, the meaning of the word *agonisma* with which he points up the contrast. The effect of oral performance is ephemeral, but a document continues to exist in time, a second contrast to which he also gives expression.

And so, as the fifth century passes into the fourth, the full effect upon Greece of the alphabetic revolution begins to assert itself. The governing word ceases to be a vibration heard by the ear and nourished in the memory. It becomes a visible artifact. Storage of information for re-use, as a formula designed to explain the dynamics of western culture, ceases to be a metaphor. The documented statement, persisting through time unchanged, is to release the human brain from certain formidable burdens of memorisation while increasing the energies available for conceptual thought. The results as they are to be observed in the intellectual history of Greece and of Europe were profound. Their examination lies beyond the compass of my present inquiry, and indeed would be

[70] Thuc. I. 22. 4.

premature until the poetic literature of Greece between Homer and the death of Euripides has itself been re-evaluated. The paradox of the conditions of its composition, poised as it was between two cultures, the oral and the literate, and forming a bridge between them, was in the nature of things unique and can never recur. It was probably this, even more than the genius of the race, which called into existence those peculiar qualities in Greek literature, at once responsive to us and yet remote from us, which we identify as "classical." But this too must remain a vista for further exploration.